大跨拱桥建造关键技术创新与实践

——第二届世界大跨拱桥建造技术大会论文集

第二届世界大跨拱桥建造技术大会组委会　组织编写

人民交通出版社股份有限公司

北　京

图书在版编目(CIP)数据

大跨拱桥建造关键技术创新与实践：第二届世界大跨拱桥建造技术大会论文集/第二届世界大跨拱桥建造技术大会组委会组织编写.—北京：人民交通出版社股份有限公司,2023.2

ISBN 978-7-114-18350-8

Ⅰ.①大… Ⅱ.①第… Ⅲ.①大跨度结构—肋拱桥—桥梁工程—学术会议—文集 Ⅳ.①U448.22-53

中国版本图书馆 CIP 数据核字(2022)第 219679 号

Dakua Gongqiao Jianzao Guanjian Jishu Chuangxin yu Shijian——Di-er Jie Shijie Dakua Gongqiao Jianzao Jishu Dahui Lunwenji

书　　名：	**大跨拱桥建造关键技术创新与实践——第二届世界大跨拱桥建造技术大会论文集**
著　作　者：	第二届世界大跨拱桥建造技术大会组委会
责任编辑：	崔　建
责任校对：	孙国靖　宋佳时
责任印制：	张　凯
出版发行：	人民交通出版社股份有限公司
地　　址：	(100011)北京市朝阳区安定门外外馆斜街 3 号
网　　址：	http://www.ccpcl.com.cn
销售电话：	(010)59757973
总　经　销：	人民交通出版社股份有限公司发行部
经　　销：	各地新华书店
印　　刷：	北京印匠彩色印刷有限公司
开　　本：	787×1092　1/16
印　　张：	24.5
字　　数：	585 千
版　　次：	2023 年 2 月　第 1 版
印　　次：	2023 年 2 月　第 1 次印刷
书　　号：	ISBN 978-7-114-18350-8
定　　价：	168.00 元

(有印刷、装订质量问题的图书,由本公司负责调换)

目 录

大会报告

续写千年建桥传奇 打造当代工程经典 让中华拱桥技术更好造福世界 ………… 郑皆连(3)

Feasibility Study and Preliminary Design of Bataan-Cavite Interlink Bridge, Philippines
………………………………………………………… Naeem Hussain　Sammy Yip(8)

管内混凝土钙镁复合膨胀技术研究与应用 ………… 徐　文　李　华　王　毅　刘加平(21)

Sustainable Design of CFST Arch Bridges
………………………………… Bruno Briseghella　XUE Junqing　Alessandro Contento(27)

Spatial Arch Bridges: The Conquest of Space ………… Juan José Jorquera-Lucerga(33)

大跨度拱桥静动力风荷载稳定性 …………………………………………… 葛耀君(51)

钢管混凝土结构分析理论、标志性工程应用与国家技术标准 ………………… 韩林海(69)

大跨度系杆-撑杆协作抗推拱桥结构体系研究 ………… 徐升桥　杨喜文　李　辉(71)

设计与结构分析

钢管混凝土栓焊节点偏压力学性能研究 ………… 于　鹏　云惟经　郑皆连(83)

大跨度拱桥桩基承台加超长锚索组合地锚系统研究
……… 马少坤　李旭锋　李卓峰　侯凯文　黄　震　刘　莹　付晓茜　高　峰　曹　琛(88)

笛卡儿坐标系下拱结构面内非线性应变
……………………………… 胡常福　胡　星　罗文俊　李诚斌　韩春光(94)

600m级劲性骨架混凝土拱桥足尺模型试验 ……… 黄　酉　罗小斌　沈　耀　匡志强(103)

核心混凝土初始缺陷下钢管混凝土栓焊节点偏压力学性能研究
………………………………………………………………………… 云惟经　于　鹏(108)

1

A Study on the Strength and Fatigue Properties of Seven-Wire Strands in Hangers under Lateral Bending …………………………………… ZHOU Yiming　DENG Nianchun　YANG Tao(114)

特大跨拱桥拱肋子结构长期荷载作用下的变形分析
………………………………………………… 李松林　安永辉　马丹阳　钟锦祥(122)

Flexural Behaviour of Pultruded Circular Tubular GFRP Composite Truss Bridges with Novel Non-corrosive Connections
………………… Thumitha Mandula Higgoda　Mohamed Elchalakani　Mehrdad Kimiaei
Adam Wittek　YANG Bo(129)

GFRP 管约束钢管混凝土加劲混合柱轴压与偏压力学性能试验研究
……………………………………… 李双蓓　苏全福　曾钧柯　潘星年　梁睿(136)

超大跨度劲性骨架混凝土拱桥主拱圈构造参数优化分析
………………………………………………… 李芳园　刘梦麟　张晓宇(153)

超大跨径劲性骨架混凝土拱桥抗震性能研究分析 ……… 刘丽芳　陈鑫　张晓宇(160)

大跨度劲性骨架混凝土拱桥非线性稳定性分析 ……… 凌塑奇　张晓宇　黎栋家(165)

大跨度下承式拱桥面内自由振动的传递矩阵法 ……… 康厚军　邓力铭　丛云跃(170)

大跨拱桥施工阶段动力学建模与自振特性研究
……………………………………………… 丁文　康厚军　丛云跃　苏潇阳(174)

钢纤维对 UHPC 单轴受压损伤本构关系的影响
……………………………… 杨简　李洋　徐港　邓金岚　包逍逍　李聪　田秀娟(179)

不同循环加载路径下焊钉连接件抗剪性能退化规律
……………………………………………… 何东洋　刘玉擎　杨涛　徐骁青(189)

基于 IDA 方法的上承式钢管混凝土拱桥地震易损性分析
……………………………………………… 孙宝印　张达　申伟　孙天舒(191)

基于纤维模型的特大跨拱桥受力分析 ……… 钟锦祥　安永辉　马丹阳　李松林(198)

采用单边螺栓连接的可拆装式钢管混凝土 K 形节点力学性能研究
………………………………………………………………… 虞振波　侯超(203)

分环浇筑的劲性骨架拱圈混凝土环间界面受力试验研究
……………………………… 林春姣　朱剑宇　肖周强　罗转　卢章彦　秦昌宇　谭善晟(208)

一种拱桥用外置法兰连接构造研究 …………… 罗小斌　张晓宇　陆滨　马瑞艺(215)

大跨度钢管混凝土拱桥温度参数取值研究 …………… 石拓　郭晓　于孟生(217)

大跨度拱桥弯矩增大系数的计算分析及探讨 ………… 黄庆钧　黄君　滕晓丹(221)

钢筋混凝土拱桥强劲骨架成拱法的主拱结构设计技术
……………………………………………… 肖雨　牟廷敏　梁健　康玲(230)

施工与监测

连续拱桥施工方案优化方法 ………… 安永辉　陈晓煌　李连冉　郑皆连　欧阳效勇(241)

桁式组合拱桥拆除重建综合解决方案研究与应用 ……………………………… 张胜林(245)

大跨劲性骨架拱桥制造关键技术研究	罗小斌 马瑞艺 侯凯文	(251)
天峨龙滩特大桥斜拉扣挂系统关键技术研究	罗小斌 沈耀 唐雁云 侯凯文	(256)
组合式扣地锚施工关键技术及其应用研究	侯凯文 罗小斌 蒋鹏 黄酉	(258)
天峨龙滩特大桥钢管混凝土灌注技术研究	沈耀 侯凯文 罗小斌 匡志强	(260)
超大跨钢管混凝土劲性骨架拱桥外包混凝土施工方案研究	赵玉峰 罗小斌 沈耀 匡志强	(262)
大跨度劲性骨架拱桥外包混凝土快速施工关键技术	叶增鑫 罗小斌 沈耀 匡志强	(264)
特大跨中承式钢箱拱桥主拱空间复合转体合龙成拱关键技术	李畅 牟廷敏 梁健 王戈 范碧琨	(266)
基于多源感知的大跨径钢管拱桥整体提升智能化施工控制关键技术研究	张坤球 石拓 谢开仲 陈家海	(278)
基于改进PSO优化算法的CFST拱桥斜拉扣挂索力计算	谢开仲 傅灏 姚宏欣 陈齐威	(282)
劲性骨架混凝土拱桥钢管拱肋外法兰连接构造优化研究	杨盼杰 黎栋家 凌塑奇	(294)
缆扣塔合一的钢箱提篮拱桥施工技术研究	裴必达 姚浩真 李传习 冯浩轩 董创文	(301)
连续拱桥拉扣挂施工新型扣锚梁设计与分析	申伟 田曦 李鹏 安永辉 欧阳效勇	(317)
深山峡谷区隧间桥梁快速建造技术	许诺 牟廷敏 李畅 康玲	(322)
特大跨中承式钢筋混凝土肋拱桥成拱技术	康玲 牟廷敏 范碧琨 王戈	(329)
天峨龙滩特大桥缆索吊机设计与试验研究	匡志强 罗小斌 侯凯文 唐雁云 叶增鑫	(338)
600m级劲性骨架混凝土拱桥外包混凝土模板体系设计与施工	唐雁云 罗小斌 沈耀 匡志强	(340)
基于叩击声信号和决策树的钢管混凝土结构近壁脱空深度检测	陈冬冬 沈周辉 汪莹	(345)
FRP-钢管约束混凝土桥墩损伤声发射监测研究	都方竹 杨栋	(350)
基于光纤传感技术的钢结构腐蚀监测	樊亮 郭川睿 申伟	(354)
CE-CFST柱推出试验声发射特征分析	申伟 温宇嘉 王非 李聪	(358)
基于声发射的轴压荷载下CE-CFST柱损伤分析	李聪 白皓 王非 申伟	(362)
考虑多因素耦合的拱桥吊杆服役寿命预测	喻志刚 李启轩 邓年春 周筱航	(366)
基于实测数据的高铁大跨混凝土拱桥桥面线形分析与控制技术	杨国静 陈克坚 颜永逸	(372)
天峨龙滩特大桥外包混凝土设计及施工控制	陈正 陈犇 吴昌杰 郑皆连 罗小斌 徐文 杨阳 赵国欣	(383)

大会报告

续写千年建桥传奇　打造当代工程经典
让中华拱桥技术更好造福世界

郑皆连

（广西大学土木建筑工程学院）

桥梁历来是人类跨越江河湖海、高山峡谷的最主要方式。自上世纪 50 年代，现代桥梁形成了四种基本桥型即梁桥、拱桥、悬索桥、斜拉桥。它们的结构不同，跨越能力和工程造价、施工方式相异。每一座桥梁建设时选择什么样的桥型，必须根据跨越功能的需要、桥位和周边环境的特点而定。

在四种桥型中，拱桥的历史源远流长，受力最为合理，承受的垂直力自动转化为拱圈轴向压力，承载能力强、刚度大、耐久性好。中国古代对世界拱桥建造技术贡献最大，1400 年前建成的跨径 37 米的赵州桥是已知世界第一座敞肩石拱桥，比欧洲出现类似桥型早 500 多年，至今还屹立在河北省赵县的洨河上，被誉为"世界土木工程里程碑"。

令人遗憾的是，近 100 年来，中国除在石拱桥方面继续保持世界领先地位外，在混凝土拱桥、钢拱桥方面均落后于西方。1898 年，奥地利工程师约瑟夫·米兰发明了劲性骨架混凝土拱桥。1964 年，澳大利亚用支架法建成跨径 304.8 米的混凝土拱桥-格莱兹维尔大桥。1977 年，美国建成跨径 518 米钢桁拱桥-新河谷桥。1980 年，南斯拉夫用悬拼法建成跨径 390 米的钢筋混凝土拱桥-KRK 桥。直到 1982 年，中国才建成跨径 156 米的丹东沙河口钢筋混凝土拱桥，跨径与世界纪录相距甚远。

中国工程师奋起直追。1968 年，笔者提出了斜拉扣挂松索合拢架设拱肋的方法，解决了建拱桥不搭支架的难题，适合跨径 100 米左右拱肋悬拼。使用该方法可以大大降低建桥施工费用。据测算，跨径 100 米左右的拱桥单位造价可以降到与跨径 30 米的简支梁桥的造价持平。1994 年，笔者提出了斜拉扣挂合拢松索法，在静态中完成悬臂梁向拱的转化，使悬拼拱桥跨径大幅提高到 500 米成为可能。1977 年，中国工程师张联燕提出了拱桥转体施工工法，为

作者简介：

郑皆连，中国工程院院士，广西大学土木建筑工程学院教授，首创多项拱桥施工工艺，主持建造了多项创世界纪录的拱桥工程。

本文摘自《人民日报》（海外版）2022 年 1 月 17 日 09 版。

拱桥无支架施工又提供了新途径。在笔者看来,无支架施工是传统拱桥和现代拱桥的分水岭,上述施工方法和工法的创新使中国拱桥建设完成了从传统向现代的跨越,在中国拱桥建设史上具有划时代意义。

得益于施工技术、材料技术、计算技术的进步,拱桥建造风险降低、质量提高,竞争力增强,中国拱桥建造数量迅速增加,跨径获得重大突破。近30年来,中国建成了一系列世界最大跨径拱桥,其中有跨径146米的山西丹河石拱桥,跨径550米的上海卢浦钢箱拱桥,跨径552米的重庆朝天门钢桁拱桥,跨径445米的沪昆高铁北盘江混凝土拱桥,跨径430米的拉林铁路藏木钢管混凝土拱桥,跨径560米的广西平南钢管混凝土拱桥。它们的建成表明,中国在石拱桥、钢拱桥、钢管混凝土拱桥、混凝土拱桥、公路拱桥、铁路拱桥跨径均列世界第一,建造技术已挺进到世界前列。

最近30年,中国拱桥发展最快的分枝有两个:钢管混凝土拱桥和劲性骨架混凝土拱桥。

钢管混凝土拱桥的拱桁弦杆采用钢管混凝土截面,是优良的钢、混凝土组合结构,其中,管内混凝土提高了钢管壁的局部稳定性,而钢管的套箍作用则增强了管内混凝土的韧性和承载能力,也可认为,钢管混凝土拱桥是从钢拱桥发展而来,在受压的拱圈中,用廉价的混凝土取代了部分钢,降低了造价,加快了拱圈形成速度,因此多数情况下,钢管混凝土拱桥必然会替代钢拱桥。

钢管混凝土拱桥源于苏联,该国于1937年和1939年各建成一座该类拱桥。其施工方法是在预制场将钢管分段灌注混凝土,在满堂支架上拼装成拱,未能使钢管混凝土拱桥的结构优势、施工优势、经济优势发挥出来,以致在此后约80年间,苏联和之后的俄罗斯再也没有建设新的该类拱桥。

钢管混凝土拱桥在中国大放异彩,本土工程师利用自己开发的斜拉扣挂技术、转体技术架设钢管拱桁,真空辅助压力连续灌注管内混凝土,提高钢管混凝土拱桥质量,降低了造价,缩短了工期,增强了竞争力。30年来,各地建成了钢管混凝土拱桥近500座,最大跨径达到560米,创世界各门类拱桥跨径纪录且拥有自主知识产权。在中国,钢管混凝土拱桥建造之多,跨径发展之快在世界拱桥史上都是罕见的。所以我们有充足理由说,具有工程价值的钢管混凝土拱桥是中国工程师开发的。

2013年建成通车的合江长江一桥,是四川泸渝高速公路上的一座钢管混凝土拱桥,跨径530米,为当时国内外各类拱桥跨径之最,也是第一座跨径超过500米的钢管混凝土拱桥。该桥在拱桁、桥道梁施工中开展大型化、装配化、工厂化建造试点,拱桁采用缆索吊运,斜拉扣挂悬拼,合拢后松索工法安装,开发了真空辅助压力多级连续灌注管内混凝土工艺及设备,历时三年成功建成,竣工造价2.6亿元人民币,获第36届国际桥梁大会乔治·理查德森奖、国家科技进步二等奖、中国土木工程詹天佑奖、中国建设工程鲁班奖。图1为郑皆连院士在合江长江一桥(波司登大桥)照片。

2021年建成通车的合江长江三桥,是一座城市钢管混凝土系杆拱桥,跨径507米,为同类桥跨径世界之最。该型拱桥比钢拱桥拱圈重,系杆用量增大,但是拱圈用钢量减少一半,其经济优势依然存在。经多方案比较,合江长江三桥最终采用了钢管混凝土系杆拱桥方案。

2020年建成的广西平南三桥,是一座跨越浔江的钢管混凝土拱桥,计算跨径560米,为全球拱桥跨径之最。其建设不仅要成功解决超大跨径难题,而且还必须克服北岸桥台建在卵石层上、南岸桥台建在基岩导致的巨大困难。为此,笔者带领团队经过计算分析和原位试验,反复论证后,推荐北岸桥台采用"地下连续墙+注水泥浆加固的卵石层"复合基础,取得了在16万吨恒载重压下,20个月的卵石地基沉降仅为5.2毫米的世界工程奇迹,完全满足设计要求,为非岩地区建造大跨推力拱桥提供了一个成功范例。

图1　郑皆连院士在合江长江一桥(波司登大桥)照

平南三桥还实现了大型化、装配化、工厂化建造,上部结构工厂制造率达85%,整个上部结构施工实现了无模板化。平南三桥拱桁施工中,一侧拱桁分22段,最大节段质量214吨,长、宽、高分别为37.1米、4.2米、13.0米,采用跨度601米、吊重220吨的缆索起重机吊运。平南三桥建设中,中国工程师还研制了大流动性、自密实、膨胀收缩可设计的混凝土材料,使管内C70混凝土灌注密实与钢管结合紧密,突破了钢管混凝土拱桥发展最重要的质量瓶颈;独创以力主动控制代替传统刚度被动控制吊扣塔位移,不但实现了吊扣塔瘦身,塔顶位移从分米级下降到厘米级;独创斜拉扣索一次张拉不调索,每组扣索一次拆除工法,加快了拱桁悬拼速度和质量。

在施工中,技术团队还创新大型桥梁施工管理范式,打造信息化、规范化施工典范工程。把质量、安全放在首位,坚持文明施工,环境保护。建立施工监控指挥中心和混凝土集控中心,集成BIM技术和其他信息化技术,辅以无人机、鹰眼监控系统、深基坑安全监测系统、大体积混凝土温控系统、塔机安全监控管理系统等十余个智能施工管理系统,实现了对工程质量、安全、进度、费用全天候、多维度的实时监控。在施工监控指挥中心就能完成所有数据采集和生产调度,平南三桥的施工管理水平受到国内外同行的高度赞扬。图2为郑皆连院士在平南三桥加工制造现场照片。

2019年12月8日,以平南三桥为背景成功举办世界大跨度拱桥建设技术大会。在会上,世界拱桥大会永久性学术委员会主席布鲁诺·布利斯杰拉说:"就平南三桥而言,施工现场整洁且建造技术和管理能力在世界上都是一流的。"

平南三桥(图3)已经成为桥梁界的"世界明星",不仅质量优秀,而且建设周期短至28个月,工程造价低(按桥面面积计算,每平方米造价仅为18152元)。平南三桥的成功进一步增强了中国工程师的信心,根据初步论证,我们认为,建造700米级的钢管混凝土拱桥是现实可行的。劲性骨架混凝土拱桥是1898年奥地利工程师约瑟夫·米兰发明的。120年来,国外用此法建成的该类拱桥最大跨径240米。最近30年间,我国把劲性骨架混凝土拱桥的跨径提高到445米。

图2　郑皆连院士在平南三桥加工制造现场照

图3　平南三桥全景图

中国工程师对劲性骨架混凝土拱桥的贡献是多方面的,其中包括用钢管混凝土拱桁代替钢拱桁作劲性骨架,用钢量降低50%;开发了分环、多工作面浇注外包混凝土和斜拉索调载技术,能有效地控制瞬时应力及降低永存应力,从而提高了安全性、经济性,推动其高速发展。

1996年建成的广西邕宁邕江大桥是跨径312米的劲性骨架混凝土肋拱桥,跨径居当时同类桥世界第一,拱肋分3环浇筑,用3组斜拉索调载,实现了底板混凝土连续浇注,至今也是世界唯一实现一环混凝土连续浇注的劲性骨架混凝土肋拱桥。技术攻关团队凭借开发的拱桁悬拼技术和斜拉索调载技术世界领先,摘得国家科技进步二等奖。

2016年建成通车的跨径445米的沪昆高铁北盘江劲性骨架混凝土拱桥,是世界最大跨径的混凝土拱桥。跨径416米的云桂高铁南盘江劲性骨架混凝土拱桥,跨径居客、货共线铁路混凝土拱桥之首。两桥在劲性骨架钢材重量仅为外包混凝土重量的1/15情况下,通过系列调载技术,保证了外包混凝土浇注安全,降低了造价。目前,中国已建成9座跨径超过300米的劲性骨架混凝土拱桥,正在建造跨径600米的广西天峨龙滩劲性骨架混凝土拱桥,预计于2023年建成。

多年来,笔者带领大跨拱桥关键技术研究团队矢志不渝推动拱桥科研和工程技术创新,取得了系列重大成就,赢得了诸如全国创新争先奖牌等殊荣。巨龙飞架,天堑变通途。让我们无比自豪的是,见证并助力一座座雄伟的中华拱桥飞架祖国万里锦绣河山,不仅成为中华民族走向富强的标志性符号,而且为国际桥梁科技进步、提升世界各国交通基础设施建设水平贡献了中国智慧。中国拱桥已经赢得世界声誉,无论是建造技术还是数量,都已挺进到世界前列。

　　科技进步永无止境,科技变革一日千里。中国工程师要奋勇攀登、风雨兼程,把拱桥科技推向新的、更高境界,继续书写中华千年建桥传奇,打造更多当代桥梁经典,更好造福世界。

Feasibility Study and Preliminary Design of Bataan-Cavite Interlink Bridge, Philippines

Naeem Hussain[1]　Sammy Yip[2]

(1. Arup Fellow and Director, Arup, Hong Kong, China; 2. Associate Director, Arup, London, UK)

Abstract　The Bataan-Cavite Lnterlink Bridge (BCIB) is a proposed 32km sea-crossing bridge at the mouth of Manila Bay, Philippines. The BCIB will connect Bataan to Cavite in order to unlock opportunities for economic growth and expansion outside Metro Manila. It comprises of land viaducts, marine viaducts and two cable-stayed navigation bridges of 400m and 900m spans. The BCIB has to cater for extreme conditions of deep water, seismicity, typhoons and ship impact. The feasibility studies, the preliminary design of the link and how the bridge options were assessed in order to achieve an optimum solution are described in this paper.

Keywords　bridges　cable-stayed bridges　design　infrastructure planning　major crossings

E-mail　naeem. hussain@ arup. com

0　Introduction

A new 32km sea crossing is proposed to connect the provinces of Bataan and Cavite in the Philippines by crossing the mouth of Manila Bay, to the west of Metro Manila. The Bataan-Cavite Interlink Bridge (BCIB) will reduce the travel time between the two regions from 5h to 45min. The link will unlock opportunities for expansion and economic growth outside Metro Manila and ease traffic congestion in Metro Manila and the surrounding region. The reduced travel time will lead to socio-economic benefits.

The new crossing comprises an approximately 26km long marine crossing across Manila Bay, 5km of road/bridges on Bataan and a 1km long road on Cavite to join existing local road networks.

Authors Introduction:

Naeem Hussain(1943—), male, DIC, MSc, FIABSE, FICE, FIStructE, FHKIE, FHKEng, FREng.

Sammy Yip(1981—), male, MEng, CEng, MICE, MHKIE.

The marine part of the crossing will traverse two busy navigation channels catering for Manila Port and coastal facilities along the Bataan coast. To ensure shipping will not be restricted by the new bridge, a navigation clearance study was undertaken for the two navigation channels along with navigation simulations. Two long-span cable-stayed bridges with main spans of 900m and 400m have been proposed.

This paper outlines the feasibility study and the preliminary design of the crossing and highlights how the bridge options were assessed in order to achieve optimum solutions.

1 Background

The Republic of the Philippines has seen significant population growth, which has led to increased demand for travel on its already extremely congested road network. The Metro Manila region (the capital) has an under supply of transport facilities, resulting in deteriorating travel times, the severity of which threatens the economic growth of the Philippines.

The impact of population growth on road network congestion is worsened by land use that is not well integrated with the transport system in large parts of the region. Related to this, the challenges are: ①long travel times and congestion; ②lack of economic integration; ③missed opportunities to cater for freight movements.

In line with the United Nations sustainable development goals, in particular goals 8 to 11, the BCIB will provide a permanent road linkage between the provinces of Bataan and Cavite and will also: ①provide an alternative loop road to ease traffic congestion; ②in Metro Manila, south Luzon and north Luzon gateway reduce travel time and vehicle operating costs; ③provide opportunities for expansion outside Metro Manila for economic growth; ④improve profitability and marketability of goods; ⑤improve access to public services and employment within the project proximity.

2 Feasibility study

2.1 Overview

A feasibility study was carried out to plan the BCIB. This included an alignment options study, a traffic study, economic analysis, an environmental assessment, a social safeguards study and preliminary design. These are discussed in the following sub-sections. The preliminary engineering designs for the navigation bridges [South Channel Bridge (SCB) and North Channel Bridge (NCB)] and the marine viaducts of the crossing are discussed in detail in Sections 4 and 5 of this paper respectively.

The key constraints for this project are as follows:

(1) Along the shores of Bataan and Cavite, there are many coastal facilities that need to be retained.

(2) Manila Bay is busy with large amounts of vessel movements into and out of the bay.

(3) The water depth is up to 50m and foundation construction will be challenging.

(4) The link must be designed to withstand extreme conditions such as earthquakes, typhoons

and vessel collisions.

(5) The construction cost is significant and hence cost minimisation was a major consideration in the design.

2.2 Alignment options study

Considering the physical constraints, a number of possible landing points were identified on both Bataan side and Cavite side. Based on these landing points, 12 initial alignment options, including both bridges and immersed tube tunnels, were developed. A high-level assessment was carried out and five options were shortlisted for more detailed consideration.

Each of the options was given a score for various criteria that were identified as key to the success of the project in five categories (technical, financial, economic, environmental and social). Comparing the scores for the options, it was clear that the option with a full-length sea-crossing bridge passing to the east side of Corregidor Island would bring the most benefits. This option was found to be the most suitable with the best overall balance of positive outcomes, cost, ease of implementation and minimal and manageable negative socio-environmental impacts.

The new crossing comprises an approximately 26km long marine crossing in Manila Bay, 5km of road/bridges on Bataan and a 1km long road on Cavite to join to the existing local road network. The marine part of the crossing comprises marine viaducts and two long-span navigation bridges, namely the SCB and the NCB. The two cable-stayed bridges will allow shipping to traverse along the two existing navigation channels. An elevation of the sea crossing is shown in Fig.1.

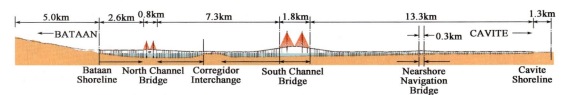

Fig.1　Elevation of the sea crossing

2.3 Traffic study and economic analysis

During the feasibility study, traffic surveys and traffic modelling were conducted. The traffic model was calibrated using the survey data. Traffic forecasting was then carried out for the road network without and with the BCIB for the years 2025 and 2035. The traffic forecast results were then used to assess the number of traffic lanes, which identified that two lanes in each direction would be sufficient. The forecasts were also used to determine the change in traffic on the road network. The forecasts demonstrate a clear reduction of traffic in the north-south corridor of Metro Manila, thus reducing congestion in the region. Based on the traffic forecasts, a traffic impact assessment was carried out to identify any road or junction improvements required as a result of the BCIB road traffic.

The traffic model also provided data about the change in traffic between different locations. These data were then analysed to determine the travel time savings. A cost-benefit analysis was carried out considering the cost and benefits of the project. The main benefit was calculated based on travel time savings and the value of time of different modes of travel. The cost was estimated based on the capital cost of the bridge and other road/junction improvement schemes and recurring costs for operation and maintenance. The cost-benefit analysis demonstrated that the project is economically viable, with a high positive net present value (i.e. economic benefit significantly higher than cost) and a high economic internal rate of return.

2.4 Socio-environmental safeguard study

The socio-environmental impact of the project was studied in detail during the feasibility study. An environmental impact assessment report, a resettlement action plan and a social and gender impact assessment report were evaluated and approved. It was found that the impacts of the project could be mitigated and managed. The mitigating measures and monitoring requirements proposed in the reports need to be instituted throughout the project implementation to minimise the impacts.

While an assessment of the carbon dioxide equivalent foot-print was not a requirement of the feasibility study, an attempt was made to minimise the materials required for construction and this was primarily driven by the lengths of the bridge structure spans. This was achieved by selecting the shortest alignment option, hence involving the shortest structures and the least materials. Further optimisation was carried out in order to minimise both construction costs and embedded carbon dioxide during the preliminary design, as discussed in Section 4.4 of this paper.

A whole-life carbon dioxide equivalent assessment taking into account operational carbon emissions of traffic would be desirable, but this was not evaluated during the feasibility study. Based on the traffic model, with significant travel time savings and reduced travel distances for many of the existing traffic journeys, the bridge will also encourage new economic activities and new journeys. It was found that, despite the significant travel time savings due reduced traffic congestion, there would be a net increase in distances travelled by all modes of traffic. If carbon dioxide emissions are directly proportional to travel distance and independent of travel speed and time, then there would be a net increase in operational traffic carbon emissions.

2.5 Bridge design

As described in Section 2.2 of this paper and shown in Fig. 1, a large portion of the crossing is in Manila Bay. For the bridge design, the main objectives at the feasibility study stage were to ①select an optimal and feasible option that could be developed further at detailed design stage; ② carry out preliminary sizing such that quantity and cost estimates could be undertaken.

The cost estimate of the project was subsequently used in a cost-benefit analysis to evaluate the economic viability of the project. While preliminary design was carried out for all the bridges, the rest of this paper will focus on the design of the SCB and the marine viaducts. Fig. 2 shows the architectural rendering of the BCIB.

Fig. 2　Architectural rendering of the BCIB

3　Design of the navigation bridges

3.1　Overview

The primary function of the navigation bridges is to provide sufficient navigation clearances to ensure the safe passage of all types of vessels that will pass under the bridge whilst minimising cost. The clearances need to be sufficient for shipping operations in various conditions and to reduce the risk of collisions both between vessels and between a vessel and the bridge. However, an increased span length can significantly impact the cost and construction duration of a bridge, and a very high bridge may conflict with other constraints such as airport height restrictions, which will also lead to excessive scale of the approach viaducts.

As a result, before any bridge option study and preliminary design is carried out, it is essential to carry out a navigation clearance study.

3.2　Navigation clearance study

3.2.1　Methodology

The navigation clearance study involved five main steps:

(1) a study of current shipping patterns;

(2) a study of possible future trends in shipping;

(3) a study of metocean conditions, including climate change;

(4) an assessment of horizontal clearance required based on the study (channel width);

(5) an assessment of vertical clearance required based on the study (air draught).

After the initial evaluation of the required minimum clearances, marine simulations were carried out to verify the arrangements. These were useful in assisting the marine authorities in endorsing the scheme and obtaining feedback from vessel pilots on the design of aids to navigation such as channel markings and navigation lighting.

3.2.2　Design vessels

Actual historic vessel movements data from an automatic identification system were acquired and analysed. The results were found to be consistent with the navigation channels marked on Admiralty charts and showed that there are two navigation channels-the North Channel located between Bataan and Corregidor Island and the South Channel between Corregidor Island and Cavite, with the latter more frequently used by larger vessels.

Since there has to be no restrictions on vessels entering and leaving Manila Bay, considering the largest vessels already in Manila Bay and post-Panamax container vessels that may use Manila Port in the future, the design vessel for the South Channel was chosen with a length overall (LOA) of 400m, a beam of 60m and an air draft of 60m. Additional consideration was given for the largest passenger cruise ship which will need to pass under the bridge at the highest point at the centre of the span.

For the North Channel, the design vessel was chosen to allow most of the existing shipping to continue but, in order to limit the overall costs of the project, some vessels will need to divert to the South Channel. The design vessel for the North Channel was LOA = 200m, beam = 32m and air draft = 32m.

3.2.3 Results of desktop study

Based on the chosen design vessels, an assessment was carried out using the navigation clearance methodology of the World Association for Waterborne Transport Infrastructure (PIANC, 2014). The results were presented, discussed and agreed with relevant authorities and stakeholders.

Both channels will have two-way traffic. For the North Channel, the proposed minimum navigation channel is 300m wide and 40.5m above mean sea level (amsl). Any vessels too large for this clearance will need to use the South Channel, where the proposed minimum navigation channel is 750m wide and 72.3m amsl.

The spans and structural clearances of the main bridges are summarised in Tab. 1. The span lengths were chosen in order to reduce the ship impact risk to reasonable level. Ship impact forces to the towers and piers were subsequently determined based on the probability analysis method in the LRFD Bridge Design Specification (AASHTO, 2012). The towers, piers and their foundations were designed to withstand impact forces without additional ship impact protection.

Navigation channel dimensions and span lengths Tab. 1

Channel	Bridge span length: m	Minimum vertical clearance: m amsl
South Channel	900	72.3
North Channel	400	40.5

3.2.4 Marine simulation

Once the bridge spans and profiles were established, marine navigation simulations with pilots were carried out at the simulator centre of the Maritime Academy of Asia and the Pacific, which has a full-mission motion bridge simulator. The simulations were implemented using the proposed navigation aids and accurate environmental factors to allow the pilots to experience realistic conditions while taking vessels under the bridges (Fig. 3). A total of 41 scenarios with combinations of different vessels, directions of travel, weather, current, visibility conditions, amount of nearby vessel traffic, rudder and engine failure were considered.

Fig. 3　Marine simulation

It was confirmed that both the geometry of the navigation channels and the proposed navigation aids were acceptable. To minimise risk, and as recommended by the pilots, the South Channel marked channel width was reduced from 750m to 650m to allow a larger offset between the towers and the navigation channel. Normal navigation speeds were reduced from the typical 12 knots (≈6m/s) to the recommended limit of 10 knots (≈5m/s).

3.3　Design of the SCB

3.3.1　Option selection

The towers of a cable-stayed bridge are the most prominent feature of the bridge. There are a very large number of variations in tower form, proportions and leg sections but these can be broadly categorised into four basic shapes: H-shaped, A-shaped, diamond, and monopole (Fig.4).

Fig. 4　Tower options studied for the SCB(H-shaped, A-shaped, diamond and monopole)

The tower can also affect the road layout and the bridge deck; for example, a monopole tower requires the two carriageways to be separated by the tower, resulting in a split deck arrangement. Apart from the tower, the cable fan arrangement also contributes to the structural action and aesthetics. For example, two fans of cables may be anchored at the two edges of the bridge deck or single/double fan(s) of cables can be anchored at the middle of the bridge deck. The tower and cable arrangements have different effects on the structural behaviour of the bridge and the design.

At option selection stage, the main objective is to select an appropriate option that is technically feasible. For the BCIB, the SCB also needed to be economical and resilient to extreme events such as typhoons, earthquakes and vessel collision. A number of schemes were selected for consideration and two options were studied further.

(1) Option 1: diamond towers with single deck of steel orthotropic boxes.

(2) Option 2: monopole towers with split deck of steel orthotropic boxes.

Preliminary sizing and structural analyses were carried out in order to compare the quantities of materials and aero-dynamic performance. Computational aerodynamic studies were undertaken for the options to determine their aero-dynamic coefficients and aerodynamic stability (galloping and flutter). The options were found to be stable up to mean wind speeds of 110m/s and sufficiently robust for the project site. While physical wind tunnel testing will still be required at detailed design to confirm aerodynamic stability, the results reinforce previous experience on other long-span bridges (e.g. Stonecutters Bridge in Hong Kong) that such a bridge arrangement will be feasible under the severe typhoons at the project location.

Based on preliminary structural analysis and design, it was found that the monopole tower would require a lower concrete volume than the diamond tower. The construction of monopole towers is simpler and the foundation construction for monopole towers is also simpler and quicker. As a result, Option 2 (monopole towers with split steel boxes) was considered cheaper to construct and was taken forward for pre-liminary design.

3.3.2 Preliminary design

Fig. 5 shows the general arrangement of the SCB. The key features are:

(1) 900m main span, 300m + 150m back spans;

(2) octagonal-shaped tapered monopole towers, 304m tall;

(3) steel orthotropic twin box girder deck.

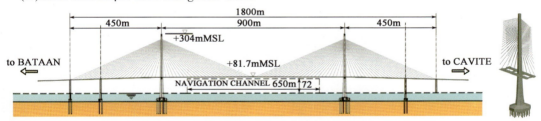

Fig. 5　General arrangement of the SCB

3.3.2.1 Foundation

Tower foundations have to carry significant vertical and horizontal loads from the bridge, earthquakes and potential ship impact. The option of a caisson foundation was initially considered. However, based on interpretation of the ground conditions in the absence of ground investigation, there may be localised weak zones of soil that may be subject to liquefaction. Localised weak soil zones could be missed or not identified even with ground investigations. Compounded with the thick layers of marine deposit and alluvium expected at the seabed and based on available data, it was not possible to prove that any soil strengthening method would be sufficient for a caisson foundation to work, leading to significant risks in the construction and cost estimate.

In order to obtain a robust cost estimate, piled foundations with concrete bored piles were investigated at the preliminary design stage. Unlike viaduct pier pile caps, tower foundations have to resist a significant amount of lateral load. Furthermore, due to the deep water at the site (~45m deep), a traditional bridge pile cap solution would not be an efficient option given the high free-standing length of the piles above the seabed. For this reason, foundation protection using sacrificial dolphins would not be economical either. Submerging the pile cap below water enables piles to resist horizontal impact loads is an option. Such submerged pile caps are common in the offshore energy industry. They can be cast onshore in dry docks and wet docks nearby, floated in and then sunk on top of pre-installed guide piles (Fig.6). Following this, the remaining piles can be installed through socketed sleeves and sealed.

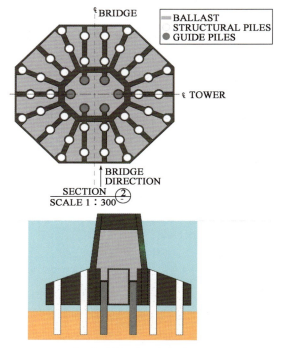

Fig. 6 SCB submerged pile cap

3.3.2.2 Towers

An octagonal cross-section was chosen for the towers for aesthetic reasons and on the basis that the dimensions could be tailored to suit the demand. For the SCB, the section is wider (in the transverse direction) at the tower base while the section is longer (in the longitudinal direction) at the tower stay-cable anchorage zone. A constant section size is maintained at the cable anchorage zone for ease of anchorage detailing. Except for the bottommost stay cables where the cables are anchored on concrete corbels, a steel anchor box will be adopted and will be compositely connected to the concrete tower section.

3.3.2.3 Deck and Stay Cables

A steel orthotropic deck consisting of twin box girders connected by cross-girders was chosen. The cross-girders are spaced at 18m centres to coincide with the stay-cable ancho-rage points. The stay cables connect to the outer edges of the deck. The twin box improves the aerodynamic stability performance and provides the necessary space for the monopole tower. A similar design was successfully adopted for Stonecutters Bridge, with a 1018m main span.

3.4 Design of the NCB

3.4.1 Option selection

Similar to the SCB, monopole towers were found more suitable for the NCB. Given that the main span of the NCB was 400m, a steel composite ladder deck was found to be a more economical solution and was taken forward for preliminary design.

3.4.2 Preliminary design

The preliminary design of the tower and foundation followed similar principles used for the SCB and are not discussed in further detail here. The ladder deck is composed of steel edge girders running in the longitudinal direction and steel floor beams running in the transverse direction, composite with the concrete slab on top. Cable anchors are typically spaced at 12m along the edge girders.

Due to the strong typhoon wind speed in Manila Bay, aerodynamic stability of the ladder beam deck will be critical and will need to be studied in more detail at detailed engineering design stage. Edge details will need to be fine-tuned to maximise the stability against flutter and galloping.

The alternative of a streamlined closed box deck could also be considered. Although in isolation this would be more expensive, when considered in conjunction with the orthotropic steel deck of the SCB, there could be significant efficiencies if both bridges can be constructed under the same contract. The benefits gained from economies of scale and simplifying the supply chain and construction methods will need to be investigated further.

4 Design of marine viaducts

4.1 Overview

As the marine viaducts constitute the longest component and thus form the most significant part of the project cost, careful consideration on the structural design scheme for the marine viaducts was essential in order to identify an efficient and robust design. Compounded with the onerous BCIB site conditions (deep water, poor ground conditions, high seismicity and severe typhoons), structural analysis and verification were essential even at the feasibility study stage.

4.2 Option selection

All feasible options were considered for both the superstructure and the foundations. For the superstructure, it was concluded that prefabrication, speed of construction and a long-span length will be essential, hence concrete or steel-concrete composite box girders were considered to be the most competitive. Piled foundations were considered appropriate for the site conditions. Driven steel piles will be adopted as they are quicker, cheaper and easier to construct than concrete bored piles.

4.3 Seismic design and articulation

Selection of an appropriate earthquake-resisting system is fundamental to adequate seismic performance. Traditionally, energy dissipation through plastic hinges, typically in the pier columns, is a way to prevent bridge collapse. Preliminary analysis revealed that the piles are the most critical elements, mainly due to the deep water and soft marine deposits at the site. These lead to significant free-standing lengths of the piles between the pile cap and the effective point of support in the ground. As such, plastic hinges will form in the piles instead of the pier columns. In order to avoid the formation of plastic hinges below the water level and seabed, which are difficult to access for inspection and repair, seismic isolation with the use of friction pendulum bearings was proposed. Steel piles with unreinforced concrete infill will be provided at potential plastic hinge zones below the seabed such that, under a beyond-design earthquake event, plastic hinges may be formed to avoid collapse of the structure.

During the optimisation study (see Section 4.4), seismic analysis was carried out using response spectrum analysis which included the extra damping and secant stiffness of the friction pendulum bearings. During preliminary design of the selected option, non-linear time history analyses, including the hysteretic behaviour of the friction pendulum bearings, were carried out and these confirmed that the concept and structural design of the piles were feasible.

4.4 Optimisation study

To minimise the cost of the marine viaducts, an optimisation study was carried out to select the optimal span length and deck type.

Structural analyses in Oasys GSA were carried out based on parametric modelling using a combination of Grasshopper, Rhino and Geometry Gym, for a combination of six different deck/span arrangements and three different water depths, making a total of 18 different models. Both static and seismic analyses were carried out in order to estimate the size of the substructure and foundations.

The foundations for the different span and deck types were optimised. Quantities were then estimated for each of the 18 different structures for cost estimation. The costs of different deck types were then compared for each of the three water depths. Fig. 7a) shows the cost comparison for a water depth of 25m. A 100m span with a concrete deck was found to be the most economical option for the BCIB site conditions, and the same was found for the other water depths considered.

Based on the material quantities for the six deck/span arrangements, embodied carbon dioxide equivalent (CO_2e), or ECD calculations were also carried out. The capital carbon dioxide equivalent (or ECD) to practical completion (modules A1-A5) was estimated using the Inventory of Carbon and Energy (Circular Ecology, 2020), assuming UK-specific carbon dioxide factors for concrete/cement and worldwide averages for structural steel and steel reinforcement, because of the lack of data in Asia. Fig. 7b) shows that the 100m span with a concrete deck was also found to be the most optimum solution in terms of ECD.

As a result, the 100m span, concrete deck solution was recommended for further development and analysis. After further design development and optimisation of the chosen arrangement, quantities, costs and ECD were estimated again. The ECD for the marine viaducts was estimated to be 2500kg CO_2e/m^2 with 56% and 34% of this due to the piles and the deck, respectively. The

ECD contribution from the piles is significant due because of the very long piles required due to the deep water and weak soil.

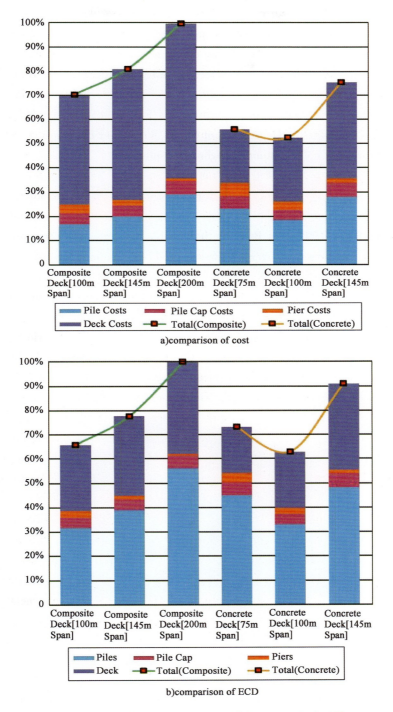

Fig. 7 Options for the marine viaducts considering a water depth of 25m

5 Conclusions

A multi-disciplinary engineering, transport, economics and socio-environmental study was carried out during the feasibility study. This study showed that the BCIB will bring significant travel time savings and economic benefits. Preliminary engineering design was carried out as described in the paper, highlighting how the bridge options were assessed in order to arrive at optimum solutions.

Acknowledgement

The authors acknowledge the Department of Public Works and Highways of the Republic of the Philippines for support and collaboration throughout the project.

References

[1] Schmidt M, Jerebic D. UHPC: Basis for Sustainable Structures-the Gärtnerplatzbrücke Bridge in Kassel [C] // Kassel University Press. 2nd International Symposium on Ultra-high Performance Concrete. Kassel: Kassel University Press, 2008: 619-625.

[2] AASHTO (American Association of State Highway and Transportation Officials) (2012) LRFD Bridge Design Specification 2012 Edition. AASHTO, Washington, DC, USA.

[3] Circular Ecology (2020) Embodied Carbon-The ICE Database. See https://carbon.tips/ice3 (accessed 29/04/2022).

[4] PIANC (World Association for Waterborne Transport Infrastructure) (2014) MarCom WG 121: Harbour Approach Channels Design Guidelines (2014). PIANC, Brussels, Belgium.

管内混凝土钙镁复合膨胀技术研究与应用

徐文[1,2] 李华[1,2] 王毅[1] 刘加平[1*]

（1. 东南大学材料科学与工程学院/江苏省土木工程材料重点实验室　江苏南京　211189；
2. 江苏苏博特新材料股份有限公司/高性能土木工程材料国家重点实验室　江苏南京　211103）

摘　要　避免管内混凝土收缩脱空是保障钢管混凝土拱桥施工质量，促进跨径进一步提升的关键之一。解决这一难题的主要措施之一是利用膨胀剂的收缩补偿性能制备无收缩混凝土。试验研究了掺有不同配比 CaO 和 MgO 膨胀剂的管内混凝土恒温和变温条件下体积变形。结果表明，总掺入比例不变的情况下，20℃恒温时管内混凝土产生了显著的膨胀，膨胀率随 CaO 用量的增加而变大，而在变温条件下较高的 MgO 用量有利于管内混凝土体积稳定性保持。适当选择膨胀组分比例可使管内混凝土产生足够膨胀，以补偿自收缩和温度收缩，温度最终稳定时仍处于微膨胀状态。这一钙镁复合膨胀技术在广西荔玉高速平南三桥等项目中得到成功应用，管内混凝土长龄期超声波速保持在较高水平。

关键词　钢管混凝土拱桥　脱黏脱空　膨胀剂　变形　超声波速

Research and Application of Calcium and Magnesium Oxides-based Expansion Technology for In-tube Concrete

XU Wen[1,2]　LI Hua[1,2]　WANG Yi[1]　LIU Jiaping[1*]

(1. College of Materials Science and Engineering of Southeast University/Jiangsu Key Laboratory of Construction Materials, Nanjing, Jiangsu, 211189, China;
2. Jiangsu Sobute New Materials Co., Ltd/State Key Laboratory of High Performance Civil Engineering Materials, Nanjing, Jiangsu, 211103, China)

Abstract　Ensuring the compactness of the in-tube concrete without de-bonding and separation caused by shrinkage

---

基金项目：国家自然科学基金重点项目(51738004)，江苏省自然科学基金项目(BK20221198)。
作者简介：
徐文(1985—)，男，高级工程师，博士研究生，主要从事混凝土收缩裂缝控制等方面研究。
李华(1987—)，女，高级工程师，博士研究生，主要从事混凝土收缩裂缝控制等方面研究。
王毅(1990—)，男，博士研究生，主要从事钢管混凝土方面研究。
* 刘加平(1967—)，男，教授(院士)，主要从事混凝土收缩裂缝控制和超高性能化等方面研究。

is of importance guaranteeing the construction quality of concrete-filled steel tube (CFST) arch bridge and promoting the further improvement of its span. One of the main measures to solve this problem is to prepare no-shrinkage in-tube concrete by using the shrinkage compensation property of expansive agent. This study investigated the deformation of in-tube concrete containing CaO and MgO-based expansion agents with different mix ratio under both the constant temperature and varying temperature. The results showed that when the total mixing proportion is unchanged, concrete containing CaO and MgO-based expansive agents can produce significant expansion which increases with the increase of CaO addition under the constant temperature of 20℃, while higher MgO addition is conducive to maintain the volume stability of in-tube concrete under the varying temperature. Proper selection of CaO-MgO ratio can produce enough expansion in in-tube concrete to compensate its autogenous and thermal shrinkage, with the concrete still in expansion state when the temperature finally stabilizes. This calcium and magnesium-based expansion technology has been successfully applied in projects such as the Third Pingnan Bridge of Guangxi Liuyu Expressway, and the ultrasonic velocities of in-tube concrete remains at a high level during long age.

Keywords Concrete-filled steel tube (CFST) arch bridge　de-bonding and separation　expansive agent　deformation　ultrasonic velocity

E-mail xuwen@cnjsjk.cn

0　引言

钢管混凝土拱桥是大跨拱桥重要的桥型选择,但管内混凝土与管壁脱黏、脱空问题严重影响结构的刚度和承载能力,是制约其跨径进一步发展的关键因素之一[1-2]。导致上述问题的主要原因之一是管内混凝土早期自收缩和温降收缩等叠加[3-5]。

为解决这一难题,常用的措施包括掺入混凝土膨胀剂[6]、黏度改性剂[7]、轻集料[8]等,其中膨胀剂时最常用的。传统的硫铝酸钙类膨胀剂需水量大,高温下水化产物不稳定[9],不适用于水胶比低、温升高的管内混凝土。近年来,MgO类膨胀剂因其具有水化产物稳定、需水量小,膨胀性能可设计等优点[10],应用范围从水工大体积混凝土,逐步向更多领域扩展[11]。

然而,由于实体结构混凝土处于变温过程中,室温下的性能不能有效地反映其实际作用效果。因此,研究这种膨胀剂在实际温度历程下的作用显得更有价值。此外,由于MgO的早期膨胀率较低,通常与具有较高早期膨胀能但膨胀速度过快的CaO类膨胀剂结合使用,以在早期和中后期均获得更好的收缩补偿效果[12]。本文试验研究了恒温和典型变温历程下不同配比钙镁复合膨胀剂对管内混凝土变形性能的影响,研究结果为工程应用提供了指导。

1　试验研究

1.1　试验方法

试验采用的CaO和MgO膨胀剂化学组成见表1,管内混凝土配合比见表2,掺入了由不同质量比例的CaO和MgO组成的复合膨胀剂取代胶凝材料,总取代比例为6%。混凝土变形测试试验装置如图1所示,采用Q345钢制作,高600mm、外径150mm、壁厚4.5mm。使用该模具,不仅可以用千分表测量管内混凝土竖向和横向变形,还可以预埋应变计测量。为进行比较,同时制作了一种可拆卸式圆柱形钢模,混凝土终凝后拆除钢模,变形不会受到限制。

CaO 和 MgO 膨胀剂化学组成　　　　　　　　　　表 1
The chemical compositions of the CaO-based and MgO-based expansive agent　Tab. 1

No.	Reactivity value (s)	化学组成(wt.%)					
		CaO	MgO	SiO_2	Fe_2O_3	Al_2O_3	Loss
CaO	—	90.3	1.27	2.74	3.19	1.31	0.27
MgO	180 ± 10	1.82	93.60	0.52	1.02	0.18	2.21

管内混凝土配合比(kg/m^3)　　　　　　　表 2
Mix proportions of in-tube concrete (kg/m^3)　Tab. 2

No.	Water	Cement	Fly ash	Slag	Expansive agent (w_{CaO}, w_{MgO})	Sand	Stone
REF	170	410	56	94	0	765	925
C3M1	170	385	53	88	34 (4.5%, 1.5%)	765	925
C1M1	170	385	53	88	34 (3%, 3%)	765	925

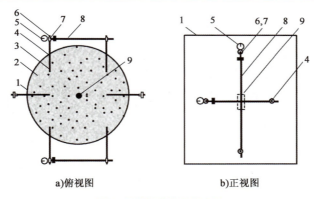

a)俯视图　　　　b)正视图

图 1　变形试验装置示意图

Fig. 1　Sketch map of experimental set-up for deformation test

1-Steel tube；2-Core concrete；3-Φ10 steel bar；4-Φ20 hole；5-Dial gauge；6-Φ4 screw；7-Φ20 bolt；8-Rigid tie rod；9-Strain gauge

1.2　试验结果与分析

1.2.1　20℃恒温条件下管内混凝土变形

采用千分表和应变计测得的管内混凝土20℃恒温条件下的竖向变形如图2所示,结果吻合性很好。采用千分表测得的管内混凝土该条件下的横向变形如图3所示。由图可见,有钢管约束时,管内混凝土膨胀变形明显变小；CaO用量越高,混凝土膨胀变形越大,MgO在常温条件下的膨胀效能则没有有效发挥。这一试验条件与实际工况存在显著差异。

1.2.2　模拟实际变温条件下管内混凝土变形

通过环境模拟试验箱开展管内混凝土变温条件下变形试验,采用的变温历程如图4所示,最大温升近60℃。采用千分表测得的管内混凝土该条件下的竖向和横向变形如图5所示。由图可见,含有更多MgO的管内混凝土在降温阶段产生更大的膨胀,当温度最终稳定时,只有含3% CaO + 3% MgO(C1M1)的管内混凝土横向仍残留了约 20×10^{-6} 的膨胀变形。考虑到测试时变形"零点"选取的延迟,千分表测试结果有约 50×10^{-6} 膨胀损失,实际的管内混凝土残留膨胀变形应更大,有利于组合结构协同受力。

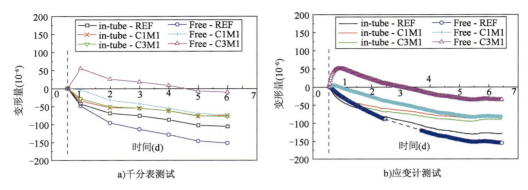

图 2　20℃恒温条件下管内混凝土竖向变形

Fig. 2　Vertical deformation of in-tube concrete under the constant temperature of 20℃

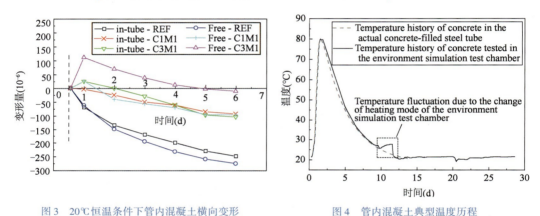

图 3　20℃恒温条件下管内混凝土横向变形

Fig. 3　Transverse deformation of in-tube concrete under the constant temperature of 20℃

图 4　管内混凝土典型温度历程

Fig. 4　Typical temperature history of in-tube concrete

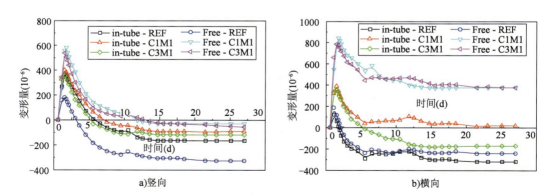

图 5　管内混凝土变温条件下变形

Fig. 5　Deformation of in-tube concrete under varying temperature history

2 工程应用

将上述钙镁复合膨胀技术应用于拉林铁路藏木雅鲁藏布江特大桥、贵州平罗高速大小井特大桥、广西荔玉高速平南三桥等项目,针对每一个项目工况特点分别开展了室内变温变形试验研究,以管内混凝土温度降至常温时仍能保留一部分膨胀变形为目标,设计了管内无收缩混凝土配合比,取得了良好的工程应用效果。图6是平南三桥管内混凝土长龄期超声波速测试结果,可见其总体保持不变或略有增长的趋势,波速平均值超过4800m/s,没有出现与外侧管壁的脱黏乃至脱空现象。

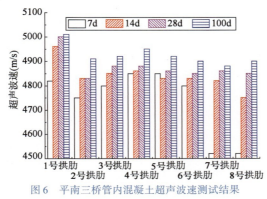

图6 平南三桥管内混凝土超声波速测试结果

Fig.6 Testing results of the ultrasonic velocity of the Third Pingnan Bridge

3 结论

为解决大跨径钢管混凝土拱桥管内混凝土收缩脱黏、脱空难题,本文研究提出了一种CaO与MgO复合膨胀补偿收缩技术。试验结果表明,掺有上述钙镁复合膨胀剂的管内混凝土可以产生显著的膨胀变形。总掺入比例不变时,在20℃恒温条件下,CaO用量越大,管内混凝土膨胀越大,但在模拟实际工况的典型变温历程下,因MgO水化温度敏感性高,其用量越大,管内混凝土降温阶段收缩越小,当温度最终稳定时仍处于膨胀状态。因此,钙镁复合膨胀技术在钢管混凝土中的应用可以有效抑制其收缩脱黏、脱空现象,但应根据结构的实际温度历程合理选择钙镁比例,以充分发挥其补偿收缩的功效。这一技术在广西荔玉高速平南三桥等项目中得到了成功应用。

参 考 文 献

[1] Jielian Zheng, Jianjun Wang. Concrete-Filled Steel Tube Arch Bridges in China[J]. Engineering,2018,4(01):143-155.

[2] 郑皆连.大跨径拱桥的发展及展望[J].中国公路,2017(13):40-42.

[3] 陈宝春,杨亚林.CFST拱桥调查与分析[J].世界桥梁,2006(2):73-77.

[4] 郑皆连.我国大跨径混凝土拱桥的发展新趋势[J].重庆交通大学学报(自然科学版),2016,35(S1):8-11.

[5] 陈宝春,韦建刚,周俊,等.我国 CFST 拱桥应用现状与展望[J].土木工程学报,2017(6):50-61.
[6] 李悦,胡曙光,丁庆军.钢管混凝土的体积形变研究及其膨胀模式的改善[J].河北理工学院学报,1999,21(1):70-75.
[7] Benaicha M, Roguiez X, Jalbaud O, et al. Influence of silica fume and viscosity modifying agent on the mechanical and rheological behavior of self compacting concrete. Construction and Building Materials, 2015(84): 103-110.
[8] Salgar PB, Patil PS. Experimental investigation on behavior of high-strength light weight concrete-filled steel tube strut under axial compression. INAE Letters, 2019, 4(3): 207-214.
[9] Zhou Q, Lachowski EE, Glasser EP, Metaettringite, a decomposition product of ettringite, Cement and Concrete Research, 2004(34): 703-710.
[10] Mo L, Deng M, Tang M, et al. MgO expansive cement and concrete in China: Past, present and future. Cement and Concrete Research, 2014,57: 1-12.
[11] 陶方元,侯维红,杨进波,等.镁质抗裂剂性能及其在混凝土工程中的应用研究[J].中国建筑防水,2016(21):44-49.
[12] 张守治,田倩,郭飞,等.氧化镁复合膨胀剂对高性能混凝土变形特性的影响[J].东南大学学报(自然科学版),2010,40(S2):150-154.

Sustainable Design of CFST Arch Bridges

Bruno Briseghella   XUE Junqing   Alessandro Contento

(College of Civil Engineering, Fuzhou University, Fuzhou, 350104, China)

Abstract Concrete-filled steel tubular (CFST) members and joints gained high interest in the last years due to their widespread use in engineering practice and in particular in Arch Bridges. In meantime, the consumption of construction materials and the pollution caused by their production can be reduced by the use of reliable structures, making Reliability as a Key Driver for a Sustainable Design. Therefore, a reliable prediction of the structural behavior of CFST members and joints is outmost of importance for the assessment of the capacity of new and existing structures. Although considerable research and several experimental tests have been carried out on CFST columns, there is not a probabilistic model for the evaluation of their axial capacity yet. Additionally, the effects of the axial load eccentricity and debonding have received little attention so far. Within this framework, the present research proposes a physics-based probabilistic model to predict the ultimate axial capacity of CFST columns, which is developed as the sum of a deterministic part and a probabilistic correction term, together with two additional corrective models to describe its reduction due to load eccentricity and debonding, which are developed coherently with the axial capacity model as probabilistic correction terms. The accuracy of the proposed models is compared with that of existing capacity equations already in use within technical standards and available literature. Thanks to their very good accuracy and compact form, the proposed models are suitable to be included within technical standards. Moreover, the structural performances of CFST K-joints with and without steel studs are investigated by Finite Element Modelling (FEM) approach with the aim to provide a predictive tool for the design. A comprehensive discussion of the key parameters that govern the FEM procedure as well as the calibration of the FE models is provided to give the basis for a reliable modelling of CFST K-joints with and without studs for the predictions of the load-displacement/strain response and the strength, considering the main failure mechanisms. In this context, in addition to the detailed FEM of CFST

Authors Introduction:

Bruno Briseghella (1971—), male, PhD, Professor, engaged in sustainable design, CFST bridges and seismic research.

XUE Junqing (1985—), male, PhD, Associate Professor, engaged in CFST bridges, integral abutment bridges.

Alessandro Contento (1980—), male, PhD, Associate Professor, engaged in probabilistic analysis.

K joints with steel studs, a simplified equivalent FEM approach is proposed to reduce computational effort keeping the same accuracy.

Keywords　concrete-filled steel tubular　arch bridge　probabilistic capacity models　CFST joints　finite element modelling (FEM)

E-mail　bruno@ fzu. edu. cn

0　Introduction

Concrete-filled steel tubular (CFST) columns are largely employed around the world owing to the fact that they offer two significant advantages. The first one is the composite action of the steel tube and infilled concrete, which enhances the strength and ductility of the columns. The steel tube effectively confines the concrete core, thereby providing a highly ductile response under compression and increasing the overall energy dissipation capacity[2]. The second advantage is the use of the steel tube as a permanent formwork for concrete casting, which helps to reduce construction time and costs. The combination of good structural performances and limited costs makes these structural elements attractive for the design of several structures and infrastructures (particularly arch bridge ribs and bridge piers[2-3]). Truss structures made by concrete-filled steel tubular (CFST) members have been studied and widely used in engineering practice in the last twenty years[6-7]. Motivated by these attractive features, a large amount of experimental, analytical, and numerical studies about CFST columns under axial load have been performed in the last decades, but a probabilistic capacity model has not been proposed yet. Furthermore, there is still a lack of researches about the quantification of the effects due to load eccentricity and debonding[4-5]. Hence, the present study is meant at filling this gap and, to this end, proposed a comprehensive probabilistic model for the axial capacity of CFST columns[6]. Moreover, a reliable simplified FEM approach to overcome the high time-computational costs required by the actual complex FE models keeping the same accuracy is hereby introduced[8]. The developed models can allow to increase the reliability and sustainability of CFST arch bridges.

1　Probabilistic Capacity Model for CFST

The present paper proposes a mechanics-based probabilistic capacity model for the assessment of the ultimate axial capacity of CFST columns. The accuracy of the numerical predictions obtained with the proposed formulation is compared with that of existing capacity equations already in use within technical standards and available in the literature.

1.1　Probabilistic capacity model

The probabilistic model for the axial capacity is derived by means of a Bayesian approach taking into rational account, both, model parsimony and model accuracy.

Following[9], the proposed form of the axial capacity and reduction factors is written as follows (Eq.1):

$$T[C(\boldsymbol{x},\boldsymbol{\Theta})] = T[\hat{C}(\boldsymbol{x})] + \gamma(\boldsymbol{x},\boldsymbol{\theta}) + \sigma\varepsilon \tag{1}$$

Where $T(\cdot)$ is a variance stabilizing transformation, $C(\boldsymbol{x},\boldsymbol{\Theta})$ is the dimensionless capacity, x are the measurable capacity variables, and $\boldsymbol{\Theta} = \{\theta,\sigma\}$ are unknown model parameters. On the right side of

Eq. (1), $C'(x)$ is a deterministic model based on mechanics rules (also borrowed directly from technical standards), $\gamma(x,\theta)$ is a correction term based on mechanics rules and evidence derived from the experimental data. The product $\sigma\varepsilon$ is the model error, with model standard deviation σ and normally distributed random variable ε.

In the case of the axial capacity of CFST, Eq. (1) can be rewritten as:

$$\ln\left[\frac{\tilde{N}_u(\boldsymbol{x}_u,\boldsymbol{\Theta}_u)}{N_c}\right] = \ln(1+\xi) + \gamma_u(\boldsymbol{x}_u,\boldsymbol{\theta}_u) + \sigma_u\varepsilon$$

Through this formulation, the axial capacity of the CFST column is expressed as follows:

$$\tilde{N}_u(\boldsymbol{x}_u,\boldsymbol{\Theta}_u) = N_{pl}e^{[\gamma_u(\boldsymbol{x}_u,\boldsymbol{\theta}_u)+\sigma_u\varepsilon]}$$

Fig. 1 shows the predicted versus measured capacity for each test. The closer the data points are to the 1:1 line (i.e., the continuous lines in the figure), the more accurate are the predictions.

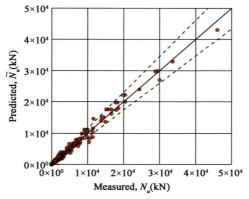

Fig. 1 Predicted versus measured values of the axial capacity: predictions with proposed probabilistic model[5]

1.2 Comparison between standards and literature formulations

The predictive performance of the proposed probabilistic capacity models is compared with existing formulations collected from some available technical standards and previous researches. It can be observed from Tab. 1 that all code-conforming formulations tend to underestimate the axial capacity of CFST columns. The formulations collected from the existing literature show a progressive increment of accuracy in time.

Comparison between literature and technical standards, where S.D stands for Standard Deviation while M.S.E. for Mean Square Error   Tab. 1

Formulation	Mean	S. D.	M. S. E.
EC4	1.084	0.593	0.359
AISC	1.091	0.472	0.231
ACI	1.033	0.453	0.206
Goode et al. (1997)	0.627	0.284	0.219
Giakoumelis and Lam (2004)	1.293	0.546	0.384
Xue et al. (2013)	0.912	0.189	0.044
Ho and Le (2021)	1.188	0.230	0.056
Proposed	1.011	0.155	0.024

2 Simplified equivalent finite element modelling of Cfst K-joints

In this research, the structural performances of CFST K-joints with and without steel studs are investigated by Finite Element Modelling (FEM) approach with the aim to provide a predictive tool for the design. A comprehensive discussion of the key parameters that govern the FEM procedure as well as the calibration of the FE models was provided to give the basis for a reliable modelling of CFST K-joints with and without studs for the predictions of the load-displacement/strain response and the strength, considering the main failure mechanisms. In this context, in addition to the detailed FEM of CFST K joints with steel studs, a simplified equivalent FEM approach is proposed to reduce computational effort keeping the same accuracy.

In Fig. 2 the analyzed K-joint is shown. Moreover, typical stress and strain fields obtained by the FE analyses are introduced in Fig. 3.

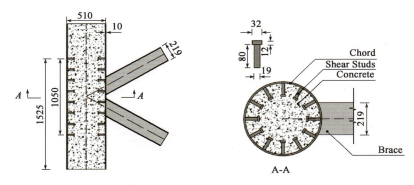

Fig. 2 Details of CFST-S specimens[6]

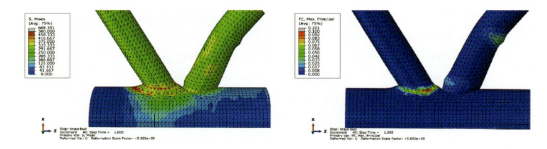

Fig. 3 Stress and strain fields for CFST-8 S specimen[8]

The FE modeling recommendation for CFST K-joints are summarized in the following: ①modelling of steel chord and steel braces including hardening effects, and geometrical non-linearities for the members; ②modelling of the concrete including non-linear behavior if the level of concrete stresses are higher than 50% of the concrete strength; ③modelling of the contact surfaces between steel and concrete by assuming hard contact in the normal direction and Coulomb-friction law with a friction coefficient of 0.5 in the tangential direction.

For the CFST K-joints with studs, it was found that it is possible to employ cohesive-interaction properties by using the contact stiffness coefficients for the normal and the tangential directions to reproduce the contribution provided by the studs in the overall response of the joint. The values of the stiffness coefficients can be related to the density of the studs used to strengthen the inner surface of the chord in the joint region. In doing so, time computational costs resulted to be extremely reduced.

3　Conclusions

Improving reliability in design, in addition to raising availability and direct profits and reducing materials consumption, can also contribute significantly to reducing the risk of catastrophes, negative environmental impact and human injury. This contributes to the environmental and societal components of sustainability. For those reasons, reliability can be considered as the starting point for sustainability. In this study, mechanics-based probabilistic models for the axial capacity of CFST members and reliable FE modelling approaches for CFST k-joints are proposed and discussed.

References

[1] Anderson,J.,Bucher,C.,Briseghella,B.,Ruan,X.,Zordan,T. Sustainable Structural Engineering, Structural Engineering Documents (SED),ISBN 978-3-85748-141-3.

[2] Huang, Y., Briseghella, B., Zordan, T., Wu, Q., & Chen, B. (2014). Shaking table tests for the evaluation of the seismic performance of an innovative lightweight bridge with CFST composite truss girder and lattice pier. Engineering Structures,75,73-86.

[3] Xue,J. Q.,Briseghella,B.,& Chen,B. C. (2012). Effects of debonding on circular CFST stub columns. Journal of Constructional Steel Research,69(1),64-76.

[4] Xue, J. Q., Fiore, A., Liu, Z. H., Briseghella, B., & Marano, G. C. (2021). Prediction of ultimate load capacities of CFST columns with debonding by EPR. Thin-Walled Structures, 164,107912.

[5] Contento, A., Aloisio, A., Xue, J., Quaranta, G., Briseghella, B., & Gardoni, P. (2022). Probabilistic axial capacity model for concrete-filled steel tubes accounting for load eccentricity and debonding. Engineering Structures,268,114730.

[6] Huang,W.,Fenu,L.,Chen,B.,& Briseghella,B. (2015). Experimental study on K-joints of concrete-filled steel tubular truss structures. Journal of Constructional Steel Research,107,182-193.

[7] Huang, W., Fenu, L., Chen, B., & Briseghella, B. (2018). Experimental study on joint resistance and failure modes of concrete filled steel tubular (CFST) truss girders. Journal of Constructional Steel Research,141,241-250.

[8] Ferrotto,M. F.,Fenu,L.,Xue,J. Q.,Briseghella,B.,Chen,B. C.,& Cavaleri,L. (2022). Simplified equivalent finite element modelling of concrete-filled steel tubular K-joints with and

without studs. Engineering Structures,266,114634.
[9] Gardoni,P.,Der Kiureghian,A.,& Mosalam,K. M.(2002). Probabilistic capacity models and fragility estimates for reinforced concrete columns based on experimental observations. Journal of Engineering Mechanics,128(10),1024-1038.

Spatial Arch Bridges: The Conquest of Space

Juan José Jorquera-Lucerga
(Technical University of Cartagena (UPCT), Spain)

Abstract From an aesthetical point of view, spatial arch bridges (SAB) are a consequence of new architectural demands for bridges in urban environments. They also arise to meet unusual functional requirements, such as a horizontally curved deck suspended from an arch. In these bridges, forces, topology and geometry are strongly interdependent, and its structural behavior extends from the original vertical plane to a three-dimensional spatial configuration. Despite the growing number of examples of SABs, little research has been carried out on them. This paper shows some examples of the typological variety of these bridges and briefly describes some of the most distinctive aspects of their structural behavior. This paper also supports the idea that by means of a proper usage of tools such as form-finding methods or approaches based on a correct conceptual design the designer may choose from a wide variety of novel forms that are simultaneously aesthetically pleasing and highly efficient from the structural point of view.

Keywords bridge engineering spatial arch bridge conceptual design structural systems funicularity

E-mail juanjo.jorquera@upct.es

0 Introduction

From an aesthetical point of view, spatial arch bridges (SAB) are a consequence of new architectural demands for bridges in urban environments. They also arise to meet unusual functional requirements, such as the case of an arch being the most suitable structure to support a horizontally curved deck. In these cases, the structural behavior extends from the original vertical plane to a

---

Author Introduction:

Juan José Jorquera-Lucerga (1969—), male, holds a master's degree in civil and structural engineering and a PhD in bridge engineering from the Polytechnic University of Madrid (UPM, Spain). He worked as a structural designer until 2014. In 2010 he joined Polytechnic University of Cartagena (UPCT), where he is currently a full-time associate professor,. His research and teaching focuses on bridge engineering, especially arch and cable-stayed (foot)bridges, conceptual design, structural typologies and historical structures.

three-dimensional spatial configuration.

An arch bridge can be defined as spatial (i.e. it has a spatial structural behavior) when there are vertical loads that induce out-of-plane forces in the arch. Consequently, in longitudinally symmetrical SABs (Fig. 1) spatial behavior appears due to live loads only, whereas, in longitudinally non-symmetrical bridges (Fig. 2) the spatial structural behavior appears both for permanent and live loads. Bridges that are not longitudinally symmetrical are usually spatial.

Fig. 1　Bridge over the River Vinalopo, Elche, Spain
(Photo: CFC www.cfcsl.com)

Fig. 2　La Devesa footbridge, Ripoll, Spain
(Photo: N. Jandberg. www.structurae.net)

Similarly, an arch bridge is spatial if the centerline of the arch cannot be contained within a plane (Fig. 3). In other words, warped arches are also spatial.

Fig. 3　Bridge over the River Galindo
(Photo: Herrad Elisabeth Taubenheim)

Thus, the spatial character of an arch bridge is mainly a matter of geometry. In classical arch bridges, such as the usual tied-arch bridges, the deck is straight, and is suspended, often by means of vertical hangers, from a vertical arch attached to the axis of the deck. In these cases, vertical loads do not induce out-of-plane forces in the arch and the behavior of the bridge should be regarded as "planar", i.e, non-spatial.

Despite the growing number of examples of SABs, little research has been carried out on them[2,3,5,12]. This paper shows some examples of the virtually unlimited variety of these bridges. Then, it briefly describes the most distinctive aspects of their structural behavior. It also shows how the form-finding method used for planar arches can be generalized to spatial geometries. The paper emphasizes the importance of a proper form-selection to achieve bridges that are, simultaneously, very efficient in structural terms and aesthetically pleasing.

1 Examples

The spatial structural behavior appears due to the bridge geometry, which in turn depends on the geometry and the relative position of the arch and the deck.

The most usual SABs are not longitudinally symmetrical. In SABs composed of an arch and a deck, the most frequent causes of spatial behavior appear when the deck alignment is curved (Fig. 4); when the arch is not attached to the centerline of the deck (Fig. 5); when the arch is tilted, i.e. it is rotated about the springing line (Fig. 6); when the arch is rotated about the vertical axis (Fig. 7), which results in a particular type of spatial arch bridge, the so-called diagonal arch bridge (DAB). Two or more of the mentioned causes may appear simultaneously in the same bridge, as it happens in the examples of Fig. 2, 4, 5, 6 or 8. Warped arches are also spatial (Fig. 3 and Fig. 9).

Fig. 4 Tiergarten Brücke, Dessau, Germany (Photo: Peter Stephany. www. structurae. net)

Fig. 5 Campo Volantin footbridge, Bilbao, Spain

Fig. 6 York Millenium footbridge, UK

Fig. 7 Hulme brigde, Manchester, UK[4] (Photo: www. wilkinsoneyre. com)

In longitudinally symmetrical SABs, spatial structural behavior are usually due to the inclination of the hangers (which introduce out-of-plane concentrated loads in the arch under live loads), as in the example shown in Fig. 1 and Fig. 10 or to the inclination of the twin tilting arches (Fig. 11), which introduces out-of-plane loads due to the out-of-plane component of the arch self-weight. Another example is shown in Fig. 12, where the arch is perpendicular to the deck axis.

Fig. 8　Gateshead footbridge, UK.
(Photo: www.wilkinsoneyre.com)

Fig. 9　Ripshorst footbridge. Oberhausen, Germany[13]
(Photo: www.sbp.de)

Fig. 10　Bridge over the River Ebro, Logroño, Spain
(Photo: www.cfcsl.com)

Fig. 11　Butterfly Bridge, Bedford, UK
(Photo: Robin Drayton https://www.geograph.org.uk)

Fig. 12　Margaret Hunt Hill Bridge
(Photo: Brian LoBue. www.structurae.de)

When the spatial arch bridge is used with the architectural intention of creating an urban iconic element, the arch is usually above the deck in order to be visible, as in the cases of Fig. 2, Fig. 5 and Fig. 12, designed by Santiago Calatrava[7,11]. When the approach is based on functionality (Fig. 3 and Fig. 9), the position and/or the form of the arch is chosen to maximize its efficiency.

2 Structural systems

Some structural systems that remain inactive in classical arch bridges under vertical external loads such as self-weight or live loads, become active in SABs. To illustrate this, this Section describes qualitatively the structural behavior of a SAB composed of a planar arch and a curved deck (Fig.13), linked by hangers pinned at both ends. In the example, the displacement of the springings of the arch and the abutments of the deck are restrained.

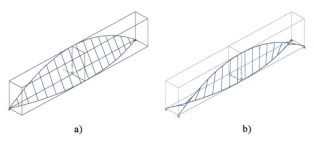

Fig. 13　SABs composed of a vertical planar arch and a curved deck

For permanent loads, it is assumed that the vertical components of the axial prestressing force of the hangers are equal to the vertical reactions obtained at the deck if it were a continuous beam on simple supports at the same locations as the hangers.

It has been assumed the arch cross-section is doubly symmetrical and, therefore, its in-plane and out-of-plane structural behaviors are uncoupled and can be studied separately. Therefore, the in and out-of-plane structural systems (i.e., how the structural elements support the external loads) are governed, respectively, by the in and out-of-plane components in which the axial loads of the hangers can be resolved. Tab. 1 summarizes the structural systems of the bridges shown in Fig. 13. The arch always behaves as a classical arch (with bending and compression) under the in-plane component of the axial loads of the hangers, whereas it behaves as a curved beam under the out-of-plane components. The deck is a horizontally-oriented continuous beam. Under permanent loads, it behaves as if it were simply supported at the hangers' locations, whereas, for live loads, the supports become elastic, their stiffness depending on the arch-cable-deck stiffness. The deck behaves as a horizontal arch under the horizontal components of the hangers.

Structural systems in SABs from Fig. 13　　　　　　　　Tab. 1

Location	Orientation	Structural system
Arch	In-plane	"Classical" planar vertical arch (bending + compressive force)

continued

Location	Orientation	Structural system
Arch	Out-of-plane	Curved beam vertically oriented. (Transversal bending moment + torsion)
Deck	In-plane	Horizontally oriented arch (vertical axis bending + axial force)
Deck	Out-of-plane	Permanent loads: Continuous beam on simple supports (bending + shear + torsion) Vertical live loads: Continuous beam on elastic supports (bending + shear + torsion)

When the springings of the arch coincide with the abutments or the deck, as it happens in Fig. 13a), all the horizontal axial loads of the hangers are at the same side of the arch. Therefore, the transversal bending moments and torsional forces are very high. In this case, the cross-section of the arch should be stiffer, horizontally oriented and wider at springings than at the crown. This is the solution adopted for the cross-sections of the Gateshead footbridge (Fig. 8 and Fig. 14) and the Yuanshan Bridge (Fig. 15).

 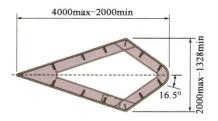

Fig. 14　Gateshead footbridge: Lateral view and cross-section

Fig. 15　Yuanshan footbridge
(Photo: www.sbp.de)

In these cases, the internal forces are very high. When the designer can freely choose the relative arch-deck position, it is preferable to select the optimum location by means of a parametric study rather than simply increasing the arch stiffness.

Fig. 16 shows the bending moments integrated along the arch versus the relative transversal arch-deck position, defined by the distance between the springings and abutments, Y. The curvature of the deck remains unchanged for all the examples. The arrows represent, qualitatively, the magnitude and direction of the out-of-plane components of the axial loads at the hangers. The minimum bending values are obtained when the arch is in an intermediate position, where the horizontal loads act on both sides of the arch. When the location of the arch is properly chosen, its cross-section can be lighter and the displacements under live loads are smaller.

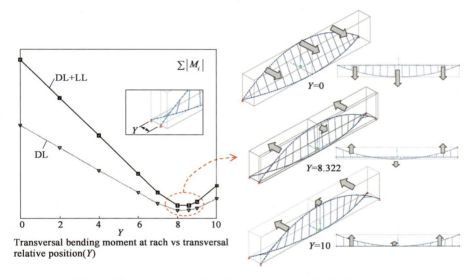

Fig. 16 Bending moment at the arch vs transversal arc deck relative position

Depending on the transversal relative arch-deck location, the deck may be either compressed [as it happens in the Fig. 13a) or Fig. 16, $Y=0$) or tension [Fig. 13b)], Fig. 16, $Y=10$].

Other additional parameters, such as the arch inclination (rotating about the springing line), can also be optimized by means of a more comprehensive parametric study. Then, the curves in Fig. 16 would become three-dimensional surfaces. The results shown so far highlights how the layout of a SAB is not as free as it might seem, and how significant cost savings can be achieved by properly selecting the relative location of the structural elements.

3 Funicularity and form-finding

In a "classical" vertical planar arch bridge subjected only to in-plane loads, its funicular geometry (which is the geometry that results in an equilibrium state free from bending stresses, i.e., simply under axial forces) is contained within a vertical plane. Since SABs support out-of-plane loads, the funicular geometry is warped, i.e. not contained within a plane. Therefore, its design and construction may become more complicated than for classical planar arches. However, these arches can be, simultaneously, very efficient in structural terms and aesthetically pleasing. The great potential of these type of structures has not been fully developed yet. So far, very few theoretical studies have been carried out, and only some design proposals have been eventually built, such as the pioneering Ripshorst footbridge (Fig. 9) or the Galindo Bridge (Fig. 3). Since steel is the most common material used for SABs, the funicular geometry is usually obtained for permanent loads plus half of the live loads.

Several alternative methods can be used to obtain the funicular geometry. Graphic Statics is a well-known tool used traditionally to analyze planar arches or masonry structures. It is based on the construction of the funicular polygon of forces and on the concept that the form of the arch (the thrust line) is the inverted form of a flexible cable[14]. Its scope can be also widened to find the form of funicular three-dimensional geometries by combining two polygons of forces, corresponding to the two projections of the spatial form[8]. An alternative way was used by Schlaich, who obtained the warped geometry of the Ripshorst footbridge as the inverted form of a hanging cable[13]. Beghini et al.[1] obtained a formulation by applying the Rankine Theorem. A variation of the Force Density Method (FDM), a form-finding method originally developed for prestressed cable nets, has been used for form-finding of arches by Lachauer and Block[9]. A simplification of the FDM has also been developed and used by the author[8].

In addition to the form-finding methods mentioned above, the author, along with Prof. Manterola[5-6], developed two form-findings methods, the Local Eccentricities Method (LEM) and the Global Reactions Method (GRM), whose inputs are the internal forces in the arch instead of the axial loads at the hangers. The LEM is based on forcing the arch to pass through the position of the resultant of axial forces at each point of the arch. To do so, the method assumes that the axial force, N (Fig.17), at the arch remains unchanged between iterations, and that the variation of the bending moment at a given point i of the arch, M, depends entirely on the variation of its location with respect to its previous location.

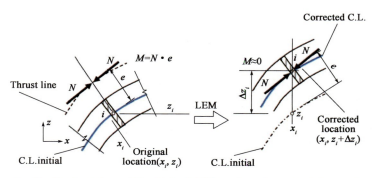

Fig. 17　The Local Eccentricities Method (LEM), shown in a vertical planar arch

The GRM assumes that the reactions at the springing points of the arch, R_X (Fig.18) remain unchanged between iterations and that the variation of the bending moment at a given point i of the arch, M_{xi} (Fig. 18), depends entirely on the variation of its location with respect to the arch springings.

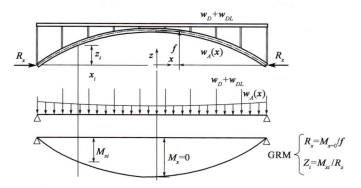

Fig. 18　The Global Reactions Method (GRM) shown in a vertical planar arch

In practical terms, the form-finding process is iterative because the loads acting on the arch depend on its geometry and vice versa. Geometric non-linearity can also be considered. The LEM and the GRM are suitable for computer-aided form-finding algorithms, since the geometry of the arch is iteratively corrected, according to its internal forces (the output from a Finite Element Method (FEM) analysis), until the convergence is achieved. They can be used from the start of the form-finding process or after any of the previously mentioned methods to refine their results.

The precision of form-finding methods can be further improved by using fictitious hydraulic jacks at the springings of the arch during the form-finding iterative process, as it is described in[5,6]. Fig. 19 shows the bending moments, after applying the LEM, obtained from a FEM analysis in a 100m span arch. The funicular geometry has been obtained considering only permanent loads to illustrate how the bending moments of the deck correspond to those of a continuous girder (Fig. 19a). Obviously, the moments in the arch can never be so low, since a certain accidental eccentricity of its axial load is always inevitable, but it illustrates the accuracy of the method.

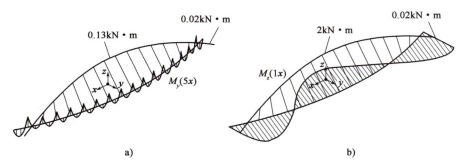

Fig. 19　FEM output after LEM method (internal forces drawn at the same scale for the arch and the deck)

The above-mentioned methods have been used to obtain the warped funicular arches shown in Fig. 20. Besides, it illustrates the aesthetical potential of this type of structures.

41

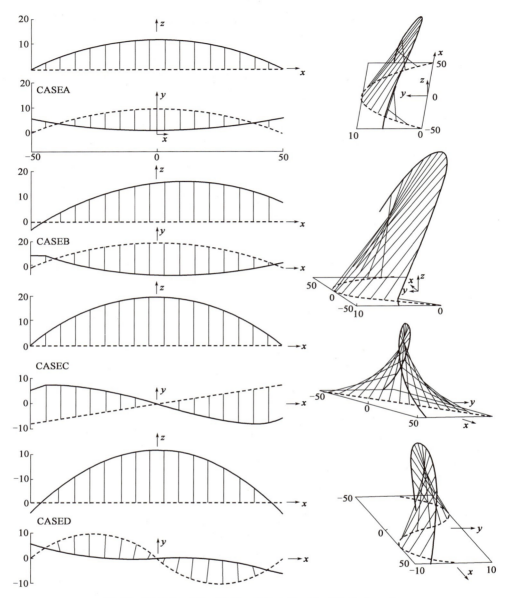

Fig. 20 Examples of form-finding of three-dimensional funicular arches

4 Form selection

The geometry of the funicular arches is very sensitive to the location of the structural elements, as it can be seen in Fig. 20. The funicular geometries shown in Fig. 21 illustrates this fact: the only difference between the bridges is the relative transversal position of the abutments of the deck and the springings of the arch, defined by the distance between them, Y.

In all the funicular forms shown in Fig. 21, the bending moments are extremely low. Therefore, an additional criterion must be defined to select the most efficient form, normally related to serviceability states for different load cases. In Fig. 22, a possible criterion is shown for the bridges obtained in Fig. 21, where the value of Y is defined with the aim of minimizing the vertical deflections at mid-span and quarter-span of the deck under a uniform distributed load (UDL), $q = -10\text{kN/m}$, acting downwards. It is noteworthy that, regarding the deck deflections, for low values of Y, the most adverse load case is not when q acts on half the span, but when q acts upon the whole deck.

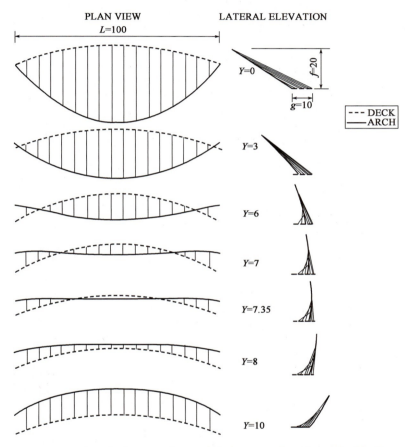

Fig. 21 Antifunicular forms vs relative arch-deck transversal position, defined by Y

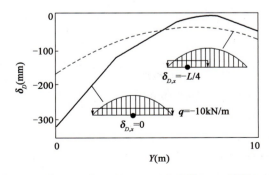

Fig. 22 Vertical deflections at mid-span and quarter-span under UDL $q = -10\text{kN/m}$ for the bridges in Fig. 21

Similarly, Fig. 23 shows a parametric study of the longitudinal reactions at the springins of the arch vs Y, for the bridges of the Fig. 21. As stated above, the deck can be either compressed (drawn in red) or tensioned (drawn in blue) depending on the arch-deck relative position.

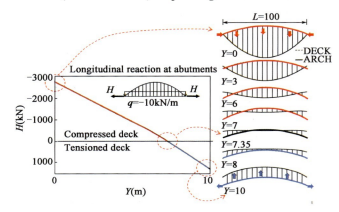

Fig. 23　Longitudinal reaction at the springing vs Y for the bridges in Fig. 21

Any alternative criteria chosen by the designer can be used. This means that, rather than a pure form-finding process, the form and, especially, the position of the arch in a SAB is more a matter of *form-selecting* than of form-finding, since the most suitable form should be selected from among all the studied form-found funiculars.

5　Topology

SABs, as any other structure, must fulfill any functional requirement previously defined by the designer. In SABs the arch and the deck are usually connected by inclined hangers, and it is very common to support the deck by means of cables anchored at one of its edges (rather than at is axis) in order to prevent the hangers from interfering the deck clearance. Fig. 24 shows the eccentrically-supported cross-section ot the deck of the Weinberg-Bridge for the Federal Garden Show 2015 in Rathenow, Germany.

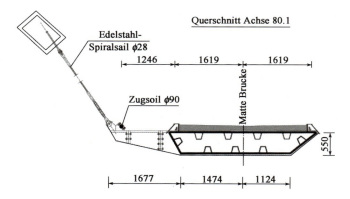

Fig. 24　Cross-section ot the Weinberg-Bridge in Rathenow, Germany(unit:mm)

Therefore, the funicular arches shown in Fig. 20, where the hangers are attached to the axis of the deck, must be corrected accordingly. Fig. 25 shows this correction for the case A, where the centered hangers of the original bridge (Fig. 25a), have been anchored to the inner edge of the deck (Fig. 25b). However, the two hangers located at each end (drawn in red) interfere with the clearance. Thus, in Fig. 25c) it is shown how the topology of the bridge is corrected by anchoring those hangers (drawn in green) at the outer edge of the deck rather than at the inner edge. However, the topology corrected because of functional requirements must be compatible with the aesthetical intention of the designer.

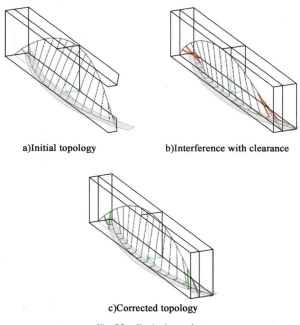

a) Initial topology   b) Interference with clearance

c) Corrected topology

Fig. 25 Funicular arches

Obviously, the eccentricity of the hangers must be considered to obtain the internal forces in the deck. In this case, both for curved and straight decks, deck cross-sections with high torsional stiffness are very common, as that shown in Fig. 24.

It is very interesting to emphasize that the funicular forms of the three arches shown in Fig. 25 are different from each other. The strong interdependence between forms, forces and topology makes the form-finding of a SAB an intrinsically iterative process.

Thus, the form-finding procedure becomes a step of an iterative design process. The form found as the result of the form-finding process will only be acceptable when structural requirements such as structural safety or serviceability states (i.e. ULS or SLS verifications) are fulfilled. The topology of the structure will adapt to this requirements. Thus, the final design is always the product of an iterative process: the structure obtained from the form-finding algorithm, and later modified to fulfill SLS and ULS verifications, becomes the input data in the next iteration. The workflow for this iterative process is described graphically in Fig. 26.

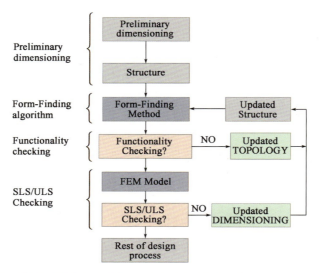

Fig. 26 The form-finding of SABs as a step of the iterative design process workflow

6 Examples of variety

As examples of the typological variety of SABs, two types of bridges are shown that contrast with the classical planar arch bridge.

6.1 The diagonal arch-bridge(DAB)

The first one is the DAB, which is a particular case of SAB where the arch is rotated about a vertical axis passing through its crown so that each springing lies on a different side of the deck (Fig. 7, Fig. 27, Fig. 28).

Fig. 27 Juscelino Kubitschek Bridge, Brasília, Brasil
(Photo: Arne Müseler)

Special attention must be paid to leave enough room to anchor the hangers without interfering with the deck clearance. Fig. 28 clearly shows how this requirement has led to decks with additional width.

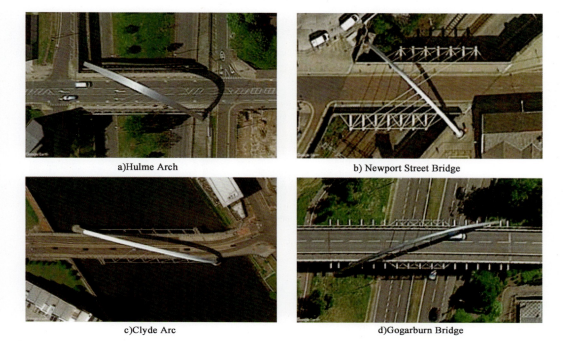

a) Hulme Arch

b) Newport Street Bridge

c) Clyde Arc

d) Gogarburn Bridge

Fig. 28　Diagonal arch bridges

This type of bridge is clearly spatial. The out-of-plane forces on the arch and the deck are represented in Fig. 29.

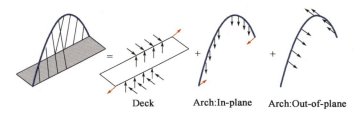

Deck　　Arch:In-plane　　Arch:Out-of-plane

Fig. 29　In and out-of-plane loads in a DAB

The funicular form of DABs is particularly interesting, since the plan of the arch becomes S-shaped [Fig. 20c)] and [Fig. 20d)] because the horizontal loads on the arch have different directions for each half (Fig. 29). An example of these three-dimensional geometries are the proposals by Schlaich, Bergermann and Partner for footbridges in Deizisau and Nine Elms Bridge, and the proposal by José Romo for the Salford Footbridge (Fig. 30).

6.2　The Galindo-type arch-bridge

In the bridge over the River Galindo[10] the horizontally curved deck is supported by a curved warped arch whose plan projection coincide with the axis of the deck (Fig. 3 and Fig. 31). The deck is linked to the upper arch by two sets of hangers (Fig. 32), one vertical, attached to its axis, and the other one, inclined, attached to stiff elements protruding from its inner edge. This is the first time this solution has been used.

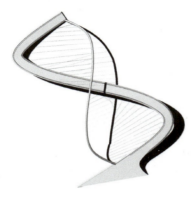

Fig. 30　Proposal for the Salford footbridge
（Photo：courtesy of José Romo）

Fig. 31　Bridge over the River Galindo, Bilbao, Spain
（Photo：www.cfcsl.com）

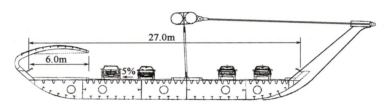

Fig. 32　Bridge over the River Galindo. Cross-section

Regarding conceptual design, the general approach is to make the plan of the funicular arch coincide with the axis of the deck. The problem can be visualized like wrapping a cylinder with a classical planar tied-arch bridge. The arch, now with an imposed curved plan, will not be funicular because the compressive axial force in the curved arch generates an unbalanced outward radial force at each point. Likewise, the axial force at the ends of the deck, now acting as a curved tie, tends to straighten it.

In order to make the arch funicular, it is necessary to introduce radial inward forces opposing the unbalanced outward horizontal forces. This is the purpose of the inclined set of cables. The same set of cables introduce horizontal forces on the deck, at the anchors of the inner face, which push the deck radially outward.

This brings the internal forces of the arch closer to those of a three-dimensional funicular. Nevertheless, the cross-sections of both the arch and the deck must be very stiff given the large live loads (the bridge is over 100m span and 20m wide) and the tight curvature of the bridge.

7　Conclusions

This paper briefly shows the aesthetical possibilities as well as the structural behavior of spatial arch bridges. Their typological variety is far beyond this paper and we can refer to their evolution in the last decades as a genuine conquest of space.

SABs designed at the present time belong to two main and opposing trends. On the one hand, designers tend to optimize structural efficiency, for example when the location and inclination of the arch are a consequence of parametric studies. On the other hand, designers focus on the novel aesthetic qualities of SABs, a priority that generally leads to structurally inefficient solutions, such as the numerous bridges, designed by Calatrava, in which the arch is inclined and attached to the edge of the deck, even for long spans, such as the Valencia or Orleans bridges[7,11].

In SABs forces, topology and geometry are strongly interconnected, i. e. aesthetic, structural and functional aspects are strongly interdependent. Therefore, it is necessary, when proposing a SAB, to analyze thoroughly its structural behavior during the preliminary design stage and always consider the possibility of better alternatives. Failing to do so only leads to inefficient structural behavior, material excess, complications in construction and cost increases.

Proper usage of tools such as form-finding methods or approaches based on a correct conceptual design may allow the designer to choose from a wide variety of novel forms that are both aesthetically pleasing and highly efficient from the structural point of view.

Undoubtedly, the future will require us to sharpen our Engineering judgment to fully develop the aesthetic and structural potential of this type of bridges.

References

[1] Beghini A., Beghini L. L., Schultz J. A., et al. Rankine's theorem for the design of cable structures[J]. Struct. Multidiscip. Optim. 2013,48,877-892.

[2] García-Guerrero J. M. El Puente Arco Espacial Como una Evolución Tipológica (The Spatial Arch Bridge as a Typological Evolution)[D]. UPCT, Cartagena, Spain:2018.

[3] Hudecek. Structural Behaviour of Spatial Arch Bridges[D]. University of Calgary, Calgary, AB, Canada,2017.

[4] Hussain N., Wilson I. The Hulme Arch Bridge, Manchester[J]. Proceedings of the ICE-Civil Engineering,London,UK,1999,132,2-13.

[5] Jorquera-Lucerga J. J. Estudio del comportamiento resistente de los puentes arco espaciales (A study on the structural behaviour of spatial arch bridges) [D]. UPM,Madrid,2007.

[6] Jorquera-Lucerga J. J., Manterola-Armisén J. An iterative form-finding method for antifunicular shapes in spatial arch bridges[J]. Comput. Struct. 2012,42-60,108-109.

[7] Jorquera-Lucerga J. J. Understanding Calatrava's bridges: A conceptual approach to the "La Devesa-type" footbridges[J]. Engineering Structures,2013,56,2083-2097.

[8] Jorquera-Lucerga, J. J. Three-dimensional antifunicular geometries in spatial arch bridges[J]. Proceedings of the 37th IABSE Symposium, Madrid, Spain. 2014,9.

[9] Lachauer L., Block P. Interactive Equilibrium Modelling[J]. Int. J. Space Struct. 2014, 29, 25-37.

[10] Manterola J, Gil MA, Muñoz-Rojas J. Spatial arch bridges over the Galindo and Bidasoa

Rivers[J]. Structural Engineering International,2018, 21(1), 114-121.

[11] Tzonis A., Caso R. Santiago Calatrava: The Bridges; Thames & Hudson: London, UK, 2005.

[12] Sarmiento-Comesías M. Structural Behaviour and Design Criteria of Spatial Arch Bridges [D]. Technical University of Catalonia, Barcelona, Spain, 2015.

[13] Schlaich J, Moschner T. Die Ripshorsterbrücke über den Rheine-Herne-Kanal. (The Ripshorst Bridge over the Rhine-Herne Canal). Bautechnik 1999; 76 [in German].

[14] Wolfe. Graphical Analysis: A Text Book on Graphic Statics. Mc Graw-Hill, 1921.

大跨度拱桥静动力风荷载稳定性

葛耀君[*]

(同济大学桥梁工程系/土木工程防灾国家重点实验室/
桥梁结构抗风技术交通运输行业重点实验室 上海 200092)

摘 要 随着拱桥跨径的不断增长,大跨度拱桥的刚度越来越小,研究受压为主拱桥的静力和动力稳定性越来越重要,特别是风荷载作用下的稳定性。本文采用理论分析、风洞试验和数值分析方法,分析了大跨度钢筋混凝土拱桥施工阶段风荷载失稳原因,研究了三座世界纪录跨度拱桥包括钢箱拱桥、钢管混凝土拱桥和钢管混凝土劲性骨架混凝土拱桥的静动力稳定性,计算了施工阶段和成桥状态的弹性屈曲稳定系数和塑性屈服稳定系数。在此基础上,研究了混凝土拱桥和钢结构拱桥的理论极限跨度,探索了 550m 到 1500m 跨度混凝土拱桥和钢结构拱桥的参数化试设计,验算了 800m 跨度混凝土拱桥和 1200m 跨度钢结构拱桥的强度、刚度和稳定性。

关键词 大跨度拱桥 静力稳定 动力稳定 风荷载 极限跨径

Static and Dynamic Stability of Long Span Arch Bridges under Wind Loading

GE Yaojun[*]

(Department of Bridge Engineering of Tongji University/State Key Laboratory of Disaster Reduction in Civil Engineering/
Key Laboratory for Wind Resistant Technology of Bridges of Ministry of Transport, Shanghai, 200092, China)

Abstract With the ever-glowing span length of arch bridges, the stiffness of long-span arch bridges is getting smaller and smaller. It is more and more important to study the static and dynamic stability of arch bridges under compression, especially the stability under wind loading. In this paper, theoretical analysis, wind tunnel testing and numerical analysis methods are used to analyze the causes of wind load instability of long-span reinforced concrete arch bridges during construction. The static and dynamic stability of three world record span arch bridges, including steel box arch bridge, concrete filled steel tube arch bridge and concrete arch bridges with concrete filled steel tube rigid skeleton are studied. The safety factors of elastic buckling stability and plastic yield stability during construction and after completion are calculated. On this basis, the theoretical limit span of concrete arch bridge and steel structure

---

基金项目:国家自然科学基金项目 51778495 和 51978527 以及科技部国家重点实验室项目 SLDRCE19-A-04 联合资助。
作者简介:
[*] 葛耀君(1958—),男,博士、教授,主要从事桥梁工程和风工程教学科研。

arch bridge is predicted. The parametric trial design of concrete arch bridge and steel structure arch bridge with a main span of 550m to 1500m is explored, and the strength, stiffness and stability of 800m span concrete arch bridge and 1200m span steel arch bridge are carefully checked.

Keywords long span arch bridge static stability dynamic stability wind loading ultimate span
E-mail yaojunge@ tongji.edu.cn

0 引言

拱桥源自于古老的石拱桥。现存最古老的石拱桥是 6m 跨度的希腊 Arkadiko 桥,建于公元前 1300 年;古罗马最著名的石拱桥是建于公元前 18 年的 Gard 桥,长 270m,最大跨度 24.4m;我国的石拱桥建设有着 2000 多年的历史,现存最古老的石拱桥是公元 605 年建成的赵州桥,跨度 37.5m,创造并保持石拱桥跨度世界纪录近 700 年。近代拱桥是以 20 世纪 30 年代建成的两座著名的大跨度钢桁架拱桥为代表,即美国 510m 跨度的贝永大桥和澳大利亚 503m 跨度的悉尼海港大桥,这两座大桥保持拱桥跨度世界纪录达 40 年之久。现代大跨度拱桥始于 1977 年建成的美国 518m 跨度的新河谷大桥,20 世纪 90 年代我国开始建造现代大跨度拱桥,2003 年建成的 550m 跨度的上海卢浦大桥、2009 年建成的 552m 重庆朝天门大桥和 2019 年建成的 560m 跨度广西平南三桥,三次打破了现代大跨度拱桥跨度世界纪录,正在建设的天蛾龙滩特大桥将以 600m 跨度再次刷新拱桥跨度世界纪录[1]。表 1 列出了全世界已经建成的 10 座最大跨度拱桥[2]。

十座世界最大跨度拱桥 表1
Ten longest span arch bridges over the world Tab. 1

序号	桥　名	国　家	跨度(m)	拱　　肋	建成时间(年)
1	平南三桥	中国	560	CFST	2019
2	朝天门大桥	中国	552	钢桁架	2009
3	卢浦大桥	中国	550	钢箱	2003
4	波士顿大桥	美国	530	CFST	2012
5	新河谷大桥	美国	518	钢桁架	1977
6	贝永大桥	美国	510	钢桁架	1931
7	秭归长江大桥	中国	508	CFST	2019
8	悉尼海港大桥	澳大利亚	503	钢桁架	1932
9	巫山大桥	中国	460	CFST	2005
10	官塘大桥	中国	457	钢箱	2018

随着拱桥跨径的不断增加,大跨度拱桥的刚度越来越小,受压为主拱桥的静力和动力稳定性越来越重要,特别是风荷载作用下的静动力稳定性。本文对混凝土拱桥、钢结构拱桥、钢管混凝土拱桥和劲性骨架混凝土拱桥分别进行了弹塑性稳定性分析,评估了施工阶段和成桥状态的弹性屈曲失稳和塑性屈服失稳。在此基础上,研究了拱桥理论极限跨度,通过超大跨度拱桥参数化试设计,探索了 800m 跨度混凝土拱桥和 1200m 跨度钢结构拱桥的静动力稳定性。

1 混凝土拱桥风荷载作用失稳

连接宜宾市和自贡市的宜宾岷江二桥,是一座三跨连续钢筋混凝土拱桥,跨度为 160m,如

图1所示。三跨主拱均由10根钢筋混凝土箱型拱肋组成,每根拱肋宽1.6m,高2.2m,施工时无临时支撑,按照一片一片拱肋从左到右顺序分段架设。在所有三个桥跨上,架设了图2所示横截面的两片钢筋混凝土箱型拱肋后,在1997年6月6日晚上发生了自贡市一侧的边跨和中跨拱肋坍塌坠入河中的事故。为了调查拱肋倒塌事故,施工随即停止。不幸的是,1997年8月29日宜宾市一侧的剩余边跨再次坍塌。

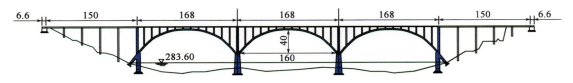

图1 宜宾岷江二桥总体布置图(尺寸单位:m)

Fig. 1 General arrangement of the 2nd Yibin Bridge(unit:m)

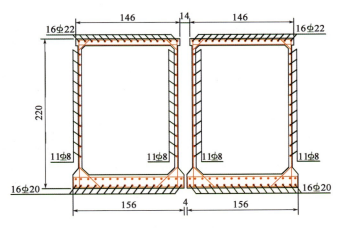

图2 两片钢筋混凝土箱型拱肋横断面(尺寸单位:cm)

Fig. 2 Cross section of two RC box ribs(unit:cm)

为了调查施工中宜宾岷江二桥的两次倒塌事故,进行了深入细致的现场调查、理论分析和风洞试验,特别是静力风荷载和动力风荷载引起的失稳问题,并最终确定出钢筋混凝土箱型拱肋倒塌的原因[3,4]。

1.1 静力风荷载作用

静力风荷载或空气静力三分力,即阻力 F_D、升力 F_L 和升力矩 M_L,可用风轴座标定义如下:

$$F_D = \frac{1}{2} \rho U^2 H C_D \tag{1}$$

$$F_L = \frac{1}{2} \rho U^2 B C_L \tag{2}$$

$$M_L = \frac{1}{2} \rho U^2 B^2 C_M \tag{3}$$

式中,ρ 表示空气质量密度,取 $\rho = 1.225 \text{kg/m}^3$;$U$ 表示平均风速,拱顶高度处 $U = 29$ m/s;B 表示断面宽度,取 $B = 2 \times 1.6 = 3.2$m;H 表示断面高度,取 $H = 2.2$m;C_D、C_L 和 C_M 分别表示阻

力系数、升力系数和升力矩系数,通过图3所示节段模型测力风洞试验识别。

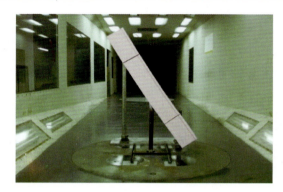

图3 节段模型测力风洞试验
Fig.3 Sectional model force balance testing

根据风轴座标静力风荷载三分力的定义公式(1)~(3),可以确定体轴座标下的静力风荷载三个分量如下

$$W^s_{y,z,\theta}(x) = \bar{W}_{y,z,\theta}\alpha_{y,z,\theta}(x) \tag{4}$$

式中,$\bar{W}_{y,z,\theta}$ 表示静力风荷载三个分量的最大值,节段模型风洞试验确定了水平方向 y、竖直方向 z 和扭转方向 θ 的最大值分别为 $1.53\mathrm{kN/m}$、$-0.061\mathrm{kN/m}$ 和 $0.087\mathrm{kN \cdot m/m}$;$\alpha_{y,z,\theta}(x)$ 表示静力风荷载三个分量的无量纲分布函数,最大值为1。

根据施工阶段拱肋恒载和式(4)中定义的静力风荷载,采用增量迭代法对拱肋三维有限元模型进行静力稳定性分析。图4给出了跨中和四分点处的竖向位移和水平位移,风速增量为10m/s。不难看出,直到拱顶最大风速达到150m/s时,拱肋也没有出现失稳现象。

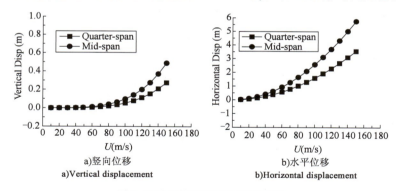

a)竖向位移
a)Vertical displacement

b)水平位移
b)Horizontal displacement

图4 两片钢筋混凝土箱型拱肋位移
Fig.4 Displacements of two RC box ribs

1.2 动力风荷载作用

由于静力风荷载不包括结构风致振动产生的惯性力,因此,还需要考虑动力风荷载作用,即空气动力和气动弹性效应引起的风荷载。为了简化动力风荷载计算,通常将动力风荷载的最大位移响应等效成静力风荷载,然后与静力风荷载进行叠加,为此可以定义体轴座标下的静力和等效静力风荷载三个分量如下:

$$W^e_{y,z,\theta}(x) = \sum_{i=1}^{N} \overline{W}^i_{y,z,\theta} \alpha^i_{y,z,\theta}(x) \tag{5}$$

式中，i 表示拱肋振型阶数，其中 $i=0$ 表示静力风荷载；$\alpha^i_{y,z,\theta}(x)$ 表示等效静力风荷载三个分量的无量纲分布函数，可以采用第 i 阶侧向弯曲振型（y 方向）、竖向弯曲振型（z 方向）和扭转振动振型（θ 方向）表示，当 $i=0,1,2$ 时的 y、z 和 θ 的分布函数如图 5 所示；$\overline{W}^i_{y,z,\theta}$ 表示静力和等效静力风荷载三个分量的最大值，其中等效静力风荷载的最大值为

$$\overline{W}^i_{y,z,\theta} = g^i_{W_{y,z,\theta}} \sigma^i_{W_{y,z,\theta}} = g^i_{W_{y,z,\theta}} \sqrt{1+\mu^i_{W_{y,z,\theta}}} \sigma^i_{W_{r_{y,z,\theta}}} \tag{6}$$

式中，g^i_W 表示峰值因子；μ^i_W 表示拱肋抖振的背景响应与共振响应的比例系数；σ^i_{Wr} 表示拱肋抖振的共振响应均方根值。

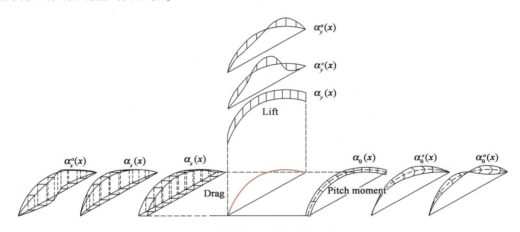

图 5 等效静力风荷载分布函数

Fig. 5 Distribution of equivalent static wind loading

为了风荷载三个分量的最大值，必须首先确定峰值因子 g^i_W、比例系数 μ^i_W 和均方根值 σ^i_{Wr} 三个计算参数，目前最精确可靠的方法是全桥气弹模型风洞试验。根据图 6 中全桥气弹模型风洞试验的三个参数的实测结果，拱肋抖振引起的侧向弯曲（y 方向）、竖向弯曲（z 方向）和扭转（θ 方向）振动前两阶振型的等效静力风荷载最大值见表 2，静力风荷载最大值同时列入了表 2 中。

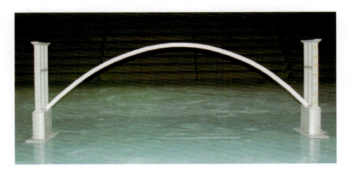

图 6 全桥气弹模型风洞试验

Fig. 6 Full aeroelastic model wind tunnel testing

拱肋静力和等效静力风荷载最大值　　　　　　　　　　　表2
Maximum static and equivalent static wind loading of arch ribs　　　Tab.2

风荷载最大值	$\bar{W}^0_{y,z,\theta}$	$\bar{W}^1_{y,z,\theta}$	$\bar{W}^2_{y,z,\theta}$
$\bar{W}^i_y$（kN/m）	1.53	0.75	0.55
$\bar{W}^i_z$（kN/m）	0.061	0.80	2.10
$\bar{W}^i_\theta$（kN·m/m）	0.087	0.50	0.40

1.3　风荷载作用稳定分析

除了上述静力风荷载和等效静力风荷载之外，施工阶段恒载只有两片拱肋的恒载之和35.45kN/m，考虑P-Δ效应的非线性静力和动力稳定分析，主要基于最不利荷载组合的轴向力N_P等于结构极限承载力N_R。

在拱顶截面，当$N_P=N_R=3,390$kN时，两片拱肋平面内抗弯力矩$M_R=24086$kN·m，远大于规范规定的$M_P=487$kN·m或风洞试验确定的$M_P=849$kN·m；两片拱肋平面外抗弯力矩$M_R=4234$kN·m，虽然大于规范规定的$M_P=2324$kN·m，但是明显小于风洞试验确定的$M_P=6612$kN·m，符合侧向失稳条件。

在拱脚截面，当$N_P=N_R=4963$kN时，两片拱肋平面内抗弯力矩$M_R=23976$kN·m，远大于规范规定的$M_P=64.9$kN·m或风洞试验确定的$M_P=498$kN·m；两片拱肋平面外抗弯力矩$M_R=5534$kN·m，虽然大于规范规定的$M_P=5192$kN，但是远小于风洞试验确定的$M_P=12158$kN，符合侧向失稳条件。

因此，宜宾岷江二桥施工阶段两片钢筋混凝土拱肋状态，结构恒载以及静力和动力风荷载共同作用下，拱顶截面和拱脚截面都有可能出现非线性侧向失稳，实际桥梁出现两次拱肋坍塌的主要原因是没有考虑风荷载的静力和动力作用效应。

2　钢箱拱桥风荷载静动力稳定性

上海卢浦大桥是一座两边跨100m、中跨550m、总长度750m的中承式钢箱拱桥，2003年建成时刷新了保持26年之久的拱桥跨度世界纪录。卢浦大桥有两片跨度550m、高度100m的倾斜钢箱拱肋支撑，钢箱断面采用下端缩小的改进型矩形，拱顶矩形截面宽5m、高6m，拱脚矩形截面宽度不变、高度增大到9m。主梁采用正交异性钢梁，桥面中央设有六车道、两侧各提供一条观光人行道，由拱肋和吊杆及立柱支撑。在750m两道端横梁之间的观光人行道下，设置了16根预应力钢绞线，以平衡中跨拱肋中的恒载水平推力，如图7所示。

2.1　施工阶段风荷载静力稳定性

卢浦大桥施工采用了临时索塔斜拉扣挂悬臂拼装拱肋节段，直至跨中拱肋合拢。由于拱肋合拢后的主梁吊装施工安全性高于成桥状态，所以拱肋悬臂施工特别是最大悬臂状态成为了施工最不利状态，其有限元计算模型如图8所示。由于悬臂施工阶段拱肋的刚度很大，抖振共振响应很小，所以只需要考虑抖振背景响应的静阵风荷载，以及拱肋恒载、临时索塔和拉索索力等施工荷载作用。

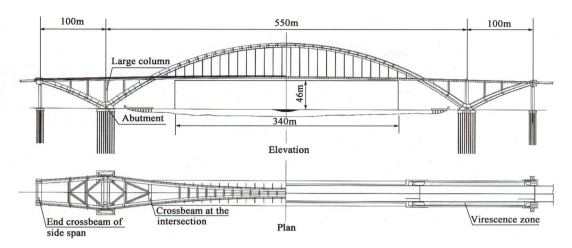

图 7 卢浦大桥总体布置图

Fig. 7 General arrangement of Lupu Bridge

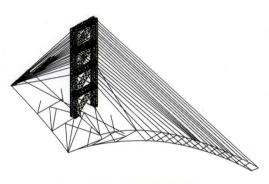

图 8 卢浦大桥拱肋最大悬臂状态

Fig. 8 Maximum cantilever of arch rib of Lupu Bridge

当拱顶高度阵风风速达到设计风速 $U_c = 54\text{m/s}$ 时,拱肋悬臂端位移较小,结构均处于弹性工作阶段。随着风速的增加,拱肋悬臂端位移逐渐增大,当拱顶阵风风速 $U_c = 112\text{m/s}$ 时,拱顶附近一字型风撑最不利截面应力达到屈服,出现弹性失稳现象,此时结构虽未完全失稳,但截面屈服削弱了结构的刚度,位移加速增大;当阵风风速继续增加到 $U_c = 128\text{m/s}$ 时,除了一字型风撑外,拱梁结合处拱肋截面应力达到屈服,结构的承载能力迅速降低;当风速进一步增大到 $U_c = 147\text{m/s}$ 时,拱顶附近一字型风撑和拱梁结合处拱肋全截面进入屈服极限,静风荷载无法继续增加,整个结构出现塑性失稳现象。因此,卢浦大桥施工阶段静动力风荷载稳定性非常高[5]。

2.2 成桥状态风荷载静力稳定性

成桥状态卢浦大桥有限元模型由 669 个节点和 741 个不同类型的单元组成。拱肋、正交异性桥面主梁、支撑和柱由空间梁单元模拟。吊杆和水平后张预应力钢绞线由空间连杆单元模拟。根据几何特征,这些单元可分为 71 种,其中拱肋空间梁单元 37 种,正交异性主梁空间梁单元 2 种,支撑空间梁单元 21 种,横梁空间梁单元 4 种,立柱空间梁单元 4 种,2 种吊杆空间连杆单元和1种钢绞线空间连杆单元。

静力风荷载作用下三维非线性有限元稳定性分析的位移结果如图9所示。当拱顶高度处的风速 U_c 达到设计风速54m/s时，拱肋和正交异性主梁的位移较小，结构处于弹性工作阶段。随着 U_c 的增大，中跨拱肋的位移逐渐增大。当 U_c 为117m/s时，拱脚附近K形支撑的最不利截面应力达到屈服极限，弹性失稳安全系数为2.17，虽然结构并非完全失稳，但截面屈服削弱了结构刚度，加速了变形发展；当 U_c 为131m/s时，拱肋中的屈服段数量迅速增加，包括拱梁节点和K形支撑，结构的承载力急剧下降，塑性失稳安全系数为2.43；当 U_c 进一步增大到149m/s时，拱肋和K形支撑全截面屈服，结构不能承受任何进一步的静风荷载，塑性极限安全系数为2.76[5]。

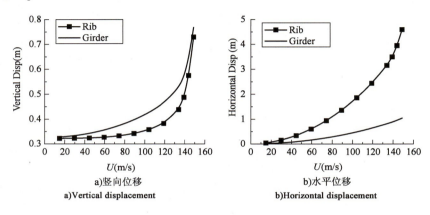

图9　卢浦大桥钢箱拱肋位移

Fig. 9　Displacements of two steel box ribs of Lupu Bridge

2.3　钢箱拱桥风荷载动力稳定性

卢浦大桥两片矩形钢箱截面的拱肋，可能诱发施工阶段和成桥状态的竖向弯曲振型涡激共振。为了确认涡激共振和控制振幅，精心设计制作了1∶100的全桥气弹模型（图10），进行风洞试验，分别模型了拱肋悬臂状态、拱肋合拢状态和成桥状态结构三种状态，全桥气动弹性模型风洞试验种均观察到了涡激振动。

图10　卢浦大桥全桥气弹模型

Fig. 10　Full aeroelastic model of Lupu Bridge

成桥状态全桥气弹模型风洞试验实测的拱肋跨中($L/2$)和四分点($L/4$)的最大涡激振动位移及其相应的风速和频率见表3。

全桥气弹模型拱肋涡激共振最大位移　　表3
Maximum VIV amplitudes of arch ribs　　Tab.3

结构状态	风速(m/s)	频率(Hz)	$L/2$ 位移(m)	$L/4$ 位移(m)
原始拱肋结构	17.5	0.368	0.040	0.164
全封闭隔流板	17.5	0.368	0.067	0.070
半封闭隔流板	17.5	0.368	0.067	0.023

为了控制涡激振动,同时实测了全封闭隔离板和半封闭隔离板的涡振控制效果。其中,原始拱肋结构的涡激共振最大位移为0.164m,设置全封闭隔流板后涡激共振最大位移为0.070m,设置半封闭隔流板后涡激共振最大位移为0.067m,这两种都可以有效减小涡振振幅,见表3[5,6]。

3 钢管混凝土拱桥风荷载稳定性

广西平南三桥是一座主跨560m的钢管混凝土拱桥,2019年建成时再次打破了拱桥跨度的世界纪录。平南三桥两片平行钢管混凝土拱肋的高度140m,每片拱肋由四根$\phi1400$mm的钢管填充C70混凝土组成,主拱肋间通过横联钢管$\phi850$mm和竖向两根腹杆$\phi700$mm钢管连接主弦管而形成矩形截面。

3.1 施工阶段风荷载静力稳定性

平南三桥钢管拱肋节段安装采用"缆索吊装斜拉扣挂"工艺,塔架采用"主扣合一"的结构形式,塔底固结。斜拉扣挂系统由扣索、水平力调节索两部分组成,其中南岸扣挂体系示意如图11所示。

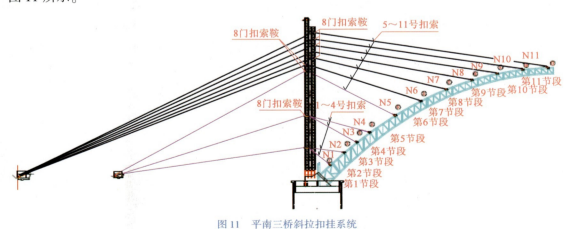

图11　平南三桥斜拉扣挂系统
Fig.11　Cable stayed and buckle system of 3rd Pingnan Bridge

钢管节段斜拉扣挂施工阶段,考虑了风速沿塔架和拱肋高度的修正,塔架上施加了顺桥向和横桥向的风荷载,而拱肋忽略了顺桥向风荷载,横桥向考虑了静阵风荷载的阻力和升力分量。施工工况考虑了塔架施工结束、6号节段施工、9号节段施工、11号节段施工、拱肋合拢等关键状态下在有、无缆风索情况下的静阵风位移响应。施工阶段设计静阵风风速按照20m/s计算,考虑了不同风偏角和风攻角组合。平南三桥钢管拱肋主要施工状态的索塔顶和拱肋端位移,见表4,索塔顶最大顺桥向位移0.264m、最大横桥向位移0.176m,均小于0.5m的要求;拱肋端最大竖向位移0.651m、最大横向位移0.819m,均小于1.0m的要求[7]。

平南三桥钢管拱肋施工时索塔顶和拱肋端位移　　　　　　表4

Displacements of tower top and rib end during construction　　　Tab. 4

钢管拱肋施工状态	索塔顶位移(m)		拱肋端位移(m)	
	顺桥向	横桥向	竖向	横向
裸塔无缆风索	-1.755	-0.293	—	—
裸塔有缆风索	-0.235	-0.175	—	—
6段拱肋无缆风索	-0.264	-0.174	-0.181	0.090
6段拱肋有缆风索	-0.2634	-0.174	-0.186	0.084
9段拱肋无缆风索	-0.239	-0.174	-0.357	0.338
9段拱肋有缆风索	-0.239	-0.174	-0.380	0.289
11段拱肋无缆风索	-0.248	-0.176	-0.588	0.819
11段拱肋有缆风索	-0.247	-0.176	-0.651	0.631
合龙无缆风索	-0.249	-0.175	-0.307	-0.293
合龙有缆风索	-0.249	-0.175	-0.325	-0.262

3.2　成桥状态风荷载静力稳定性

平南三桥成桥状态静力风荷载作用下三维非线性有限元稳定性分析的位移结果如图12所示。当离开水面高度10m处风速达到静风检验风速34.2m/s时,拱肋和主梁位移较小,结构均处于弹性工作阶段;当风速增加至51.3m/s时,下游拱肋拱梁交接处管内混凝土开始屈服,结构达到弹性失效临界状态,安全系数为1.5;当风速增加至96.9m/s时,下游拱肋拱梁交接处全截面达到材料屈服极限,此时结构达到塑性铰极限状态,安全系数为2.8;当风速进一步增加至125m/s时,拱肋拱脚多个截面出现屈服,拱桥结构已经成为机构,以致静风荷载无法进一步增加,整个结构进入塑性失稳极限状态,结构出现失稳,此时安全系数为3.7[7]。

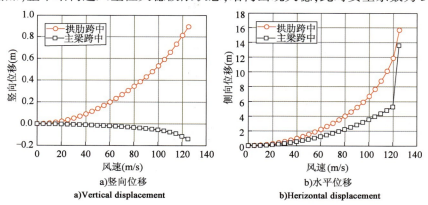

a)竖向位移　　　　　　　　　　b)水平位移
a)Vertical displacement　　　　b)Herizontal displacement

图12　平南三桥钢管混凝土拱肋位移
Fig. 12　Displacements of two CFST ribs of 3rd Pingnan Bridge

4 劲性骨架混凝土拱桥风荷载稳定性

广西天峨龙潭特大桥是主跨600m的劲性骨架混凝土拱桥,2023年建成后将再次打破拱桥跨度的世界纪录。大桥采用上承式钢管混凝土劲性骨架混凝土拱桥,拱轴线采用悬链线,矢高125m,拱轴系数 $m=1.9$,横向设置两片拱肋,呈平行拱形式,拱肋采用6.5m等宽度变高度的混凝土箱型拱肋截面,拱脚处箱肋高度12m、拱顶处箱肋高度8m。拱肋横向中心距16.5m、总宽23m。拱箱腹板标准厚度0.45m,拱脚段渐变至0.95m;顶板标准厚度0.65m;底板厚度由拱顶0.65m渐变至拱脚1.30m,如图13所示。

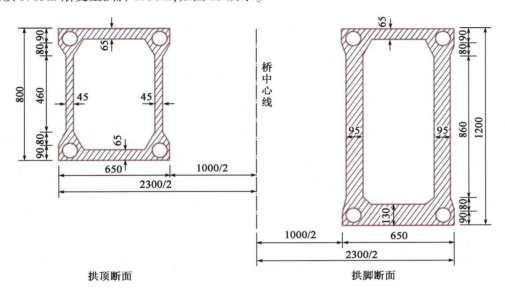

图13 天峨龙滩特大桥拱肋断面(尺寸单位:cm)
Fig. 13 Arch rib cross section of Tiane Longtan Bridge(Unit:cm)

两片箱型断面混凝土拱肋采用埋置式钢管混凝土劲性骨架法施工,首先架设桁式钢管劲性骨架,然后灌注管内混凝土形成钢管混凝土,最后在钢管混凝土劲性骨架上现浇外包混凝土,形成箱型钢筋混凝土拱肋。

4.1 钢管劲性骨架施工阶段稳定性

钢管劲性骨架节段安装采用"缆索吊装斜拉扣挂"工艺,钢管节段斜拉扣挂施工阶段,考虑了风速沿塔架和拱肋高度的修正,塔架上施加了顺桥向和横桥向的风荷载,而拱肋忽略了顺桥向风荷载,横桥向考虑了静阵风荷载的阻力和升力分量。钢管劲性骨架施工控制工况包括钢管最大悬臂状态、钢管合拢状态和合龙后拆除扣索状态等。天峨龙滩特大桥钢管劲性骨架主要施工状态的索塔顶和拱肋端位移,见表5,索塔顶最大顺桥向位移0.094m、最大横桥向位移0.109m,远小于0.5m的要求;设置有缆风索情况下,拱肋端最大竖向位移0.486m、最大横向位移0.938m,均小于1.0m的要求[8]。

天峨龙滩特大桥钢管施工时索塔顶和拱肋端位移　　表5
Displacements of tower top and rib end during steel tube erection　　Tab. 5

钢管施工状态	索塔顶位移(m)		拱肋端位移(m)	
	顺桥向	横桥向	竖向	横向
最大悬臂无缆风索	−0.044	0.109	−0.149	1.566
最大悬臂有缆风索	−0.041	0.109	−0.208	0.909
合拢状态无缆风索	−0.094	0.109	−0.486	0.559
合拢状态有缆风索	−0.094	0.109	−0.474	0.402
拆除扣索无缆风索	0	0	−0.480	0.938
拆除扣索有缆风索	0	0	−0.379	0.564

4.2　灌注管内混凝土施工阶段稳定性

作为埋置式劲性骨架的钢管,悬臂施工至跨中合拢后,进入到8根合拢钢管管内混凝土灌注施工,受压钢管拱肋的弹性稳定性成为了施工阶段的关键问题。为此,需要考虑灌注管内混凝土时是否需要保留缆风索?8根钢管是否可以同时灌注混凝土?

为了确保灌注管内混凝土施工阶段钢管拱肋的稳定性,设定了四个控制工况验算稳定性,即钢管拱肋合拢状态、对称2根钢管灌注混凝土、对称4根钢管灌注混凝土和8根钢管灌注混凝土,采用有限元计算模型,分别计算有无缆风索情况下的平面外弹性稳定系数。天峨龙滩特大桥灌注管内混凝土施工控制工况的弹性稳定系数,见表6。钢管拱肋合拢状态和2根钢管灌注混凝土状态下,缆风索的存在反而不利于侧向稳定性,主要原因是管内混凝土重量较小、但是缆风索拉力却很大;但是,4根和8根钢管灌注混凝土状态下,缆风索是有利的。全部缆风索和部分缆风索的稳定安全系数相差不大,可以不做区分。无缆风索时,8根钢管灌注混凝土状态的稳定安全系数最小为3.95,非常接近于4.0,其他三种状态稳定安全系数均大于4.0。因此,建议灌注管内混凝土时,不用考虑缆风索的作用,同时灌注管内混凝土的钢管数量控制在4根或以下[8]。

天峨龙滩特大桥灌注管内混凝土稳定系数　　表6
Stability factors during pouring concrete in steel tubes of Tiane Longtan Bridge　　Tab. 6

灌注管内混凝土施工	无缆风索	有缆风索	部分缆风
钢管拱肋合拢状态	6.72	5.27	5.30
2根钢管灌注混凝土	5.56	5.43	5.45
4根钢管灌注混凝土	4.76	5.77	5.78
8根钢管灌注混凝土	3.95	4.46	4.46

4.3　现浇外包混凝土施工阶段稳定性

钢管混凝土劲性骨架形成之后,需要在劲性骨架上现浇外包混凝土以便最后形成箱型钢筋混凝土拱肋。箱型拱肋的混凝土一般分成三环在劲性骨架上现浇,第一环是箱型截面的底板,第二环是箱型截面的腹板,第三环是箱型截面的顶板。为此,需要考虑底板、腹板和顶板是否可以一次性现浇混凝土?如果不能一次性现浇混凝土,是否可以每环分成几段现浇?

为了确保现浇外包混凝土施工阶段拱肋的安全性和稳定性。首先分析计算了底板、腹板和顶板一次性现浇施工时的安全性——拱肋最大竖向变形。在无缆风索的情况下，底板一次性浇筑混凝土所产生的最大竖向位移0.566m，腹板一次性浇筑混凝土所产生的最大竖向位移1.146m，顶板一次性浇筑混凝土所产生的最大竖向位移0.470m，按照最大竖向位移不大于1.0m的控制要求，腹板需要至少分成两次以上进行浇筑。然后，分析计算底板、腹板和顶板现浇施工时的稳定性——拱肋弹性稳定安全系数。底板、腹板和顶板一次性浇筑混凝土的拱肋弹性稳定系数分别为2.10、3.01和4.18，见表7，显然底板和腹板不能一次性浇筑混凝土，而必须分段浇筑。根据混凝土拱肋长度和浇筑作业需要，整个拱肋混凝土浇筑均匀分成8个工作面，底板和顶板每个工作面又分6次浇筑混凝土，总共8×6=48个节段，每次混凝土浇筑同时开4个工作面，即4个节段一起浇筑，共分成48÷4=12个施工工况；腹板每个工作面分7次浇筑混凝土，总共8×7=56个节段，每次混凝土浇筑同时开4个工作面，共分成56÷4=14个施工工况。底板、腹板和顶板分段浇筑混凝土时，拱肋稳定安全系数的最大值和最小值见表7，底板分12个工况浇筑混凝土过程中，拱肋最小稳定安全系数4.43，腹板分14个工况浇筑混凝土过程中，拱肋最小稳定安全系数5.05，而顶板即使一次性浇筑混凝土也有4.28的稳定系数，因此，完全能够满足施工阶段稳定性要求[8]。

表7 天峨龙滩特大桥外包混凝土稳定系数

Tab. 7 Stability factors during pouring concrete outside steel tubes of Tiane Longtan Bridge

外包混凝土施工	一次浇筑	分段最小	分段最大
拱肋底板混凝土浇筑	2.10	4.43	5.38
拱肋腹板混凝土浇筑	3.01	5.05	6.45
拱肋顶板混凝土浇筑	4.28	6.71	8.39

4.4 成桥状态风荷载静力稳定性

天峨龙滩大桥成桥状态静力风荷载作用下非线性有限元稳定性分析的位移结果如图14所示，由于天峨龙滩特大桥为上承式拱桥，拱肋跨中位移与主梁跨中位移几乎重合，故图中仅展示拱肋跨中位移。

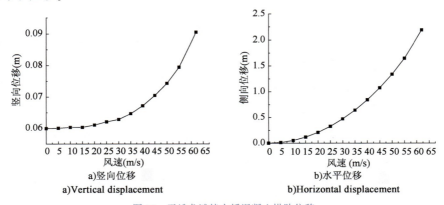

a) 竖向位移
a) Vertical displacement

b) 水平位移
b) Horizontal displacement

图14 天峨龙滩特大桥混凝土拱肋位移

Fig. 14 Displacements of concrete ribs of Tiane Longtan Bridge

当离开水面高度10m处风速达到静风检验风速31.85m/s时，拱肋位移较小，结构均处于弹性工作阶段；当风速增加至45m/s时，下游拱肋外包混凝土开始屈服，结构达到弹性失效临界状态,安全系数为1.41;当风速增加至57m/s时,下游拱肋全截面达到材料屈服极限,此时结构达到塑性铰极限状态,安全系数为1.79;当风速进一步增加至62m/s时,拱肋多个截面出现屈服,拱桥结构已经成为机构,以致静风荷载无法进一步增加,整个结构进入塑性失稳极限状态,结构出现失稳,此时安全系数为1.95。

5 超大跨度拱桥风荷载稳定性

随着施工技术的进步和高性能材料的应用,拱桥正在不断突破自身跨度纪录,迎来超大跨度拱桥发展的新时代。超大跨度拱桥设计主要取决于结构的稳定性和承载力,特别是考虑风荷载静动力效应的整体稳定性和极限承载力。本文旨在通过参数化设计和有限元分析对从现有跨度纪录到理论极限跨度的混凝土拱桥和钢结构拱桥进行方案设计和受力分析,研究拱桥主要参数随跨度增长的规律以及工程可行的跨度极限。

5.1 拱桥理论极限跨度

拱桥理论极限跨度取决于主拱材料的强度和自重之间的关系以及整体稳定性,主要控制条件包括拱肋强度控制方程、面内稳定控制方程和面外稳定控制方程。

5.1.1 拱肋强度控制方程

假设主拱恒载与总荷载的比例系数为λ,主拱结构为等截面,箱形截面面积为A,主拱结构材料容重为γ,恒载集度$q = \gamma A$,材料抗压强度设计值为f_d。《公路桥涵通用设计规范》(JTG D60—2015)规定了拱桥结构重要性系数为1.1、永久作用分项系数为1.2,由此可得基于抛物线和悬链线拱轴的拱肋强度控制方程[9]

$$l_{p1} \leq 6.06\lambda \cdot \frac{n}{\sqrt{1+16n^2}} \cdot \frac{f_d}{\gamma} \tag{7}$$

$$l_{c1} \leq 3.03\lambda \cdot \frac{nk^2}{(m-1)\sqrt{1+4n^2k^2\frac{m+1}{m-1}}} \cdot \frac{f_d}{\gamma} \tag{8}$$

式中,n表示矢跨比;m表示悬链线拱轴系数;k表示与m相关的系数,且

$$k = \ln(m + \sqrt{m^2-1}) \tag{9}$$

5.1.2 面内稳定控制方程

抛物线或悬链线拱在均布荷载作用下,虽然只承受轴向压力而没有弯矩,但是压力沿着拱轴却是变化的,而且拱的曲率也是变化的,因此其平衡微分方程是变系数的,直接求解比较困难。为了简化期间,采用中心压杆临界荷载计算公式,弹性稳定安全系数取$\varphi = 4.0$,由此可得基于抛物线和悬链线拱轴的面内稳定控制方程[9]

$$l_{p2} \leq 0.0114\lambda \cdot \frac{n}{\sqrt{1+4n^2}(1+8n^2/3)^2} \cdot \frac{E}{\gamma} \tag{10}$$

$$l_{c2} \leq 0.00286\lambda \cdot \frac{k^3}{\sinh^2 k \cdot \cosh\frac{k}{2}} \cdot \frac{E}{\gamma} \tag{11}$$

式中,E表示主拱结构材料弹性模量。

5.1.3 面外稳定控制方程

主拱面外稳定临界压力近似采用中心受压直杆临界荷载计算公式,弹性稳定安全系数取 $\varphi = 4.0$,可得抛物线和悬链线拱轴的面外稳定控制方程[9]:

$$l_{p3} \leq 0.205\lambda \cdot \frac{n^3}{\zeta^2 (1 + 4n^2)^{\frac{5}{2}}} \cdot \frac{E}{\gamma} \tag{12}$$

$$l_{c3} \leq 0.0512\lambda \cdot \frac{kn^2}{\zeta^2 \cosh\frac{k}{2}(1 + 4n^2)^2} \cdot \frac{E}{\gamma} \tag{13}$$

式中,ζ 表示面外稳定计算长度系数。

由于上述控制方程都有参数矢跨比 n,因此,统一设定矢跨比 n 为 1/5。对于混凝土拱桥,分别选取 C60、C80、R100、R120 和 R140 五种高强度混凝土;对于钢结构拱桥,分别选取 Q345、Q370、Q420、Q460 和 Q500 五种高强度钢材。采用上述六个控制方程,可以计算出混凝土拱桥和钢结构拱桥的极限跨度分别见表 8 和表 9[9]。

混凝土拱桥理论极限跨度 表 8
Theoretical limit span of concrete arch bridges Tab. 8

混凝土强度等级	C60	C80	R100	R120	R140
抛物线拱轴	627	819	1136	1372	1609
悬链线拱轴	586	766	1062	1283	1505

钢结构拱桥理论极限跨度 表 9
Theoretical limit span of steel arch bridges Tab. 9

钢材强度等级	Q345	Q370	Q420	Q460	Q500
抛物线拱轴	2077	2233	2547	2860	2948
悬链线拱轴	1942	2089	2382	2675	2785

5.2 超大跨度混凝土拱桥安全性分析

超大跨度混凝土拱桥安全性包括强度、刚度和稳定性,基于混凝土拱桥理论极限跨度分析结果,试设计了跨度为 550m、650m、800m、1000m 和 1200m 等五种超大跨度混凝土拱桥,进行参数分析。

超大跨度混凝土拱桥试设计采用双向四车道加两侧紧急停车带,桥面全宽 26.5m。拱桥布置采用上承式,主拱拱轴线为悬链线、矢跨比 1/5,主拱结构为钢筋混凝土单箱三室,拱顶附近三分之一跨度范围内拱箱是等截面的,然后逐渐增加高度和宽度以及壁厚直至拱脚。为了提高整体刚度,拱上建筑采用箱形截面双立柱支撑单箱多室预应力混凝土连续刚构。超大跨度混凝土拱桥有限元计算模型如图 15 所示。

图 15 超大跨度混凝土拱桥计算模型
Fig. 15 Computation model of concrete arch bridge with super-long span

混凝土拱桥安全性分析中考虑了结构恒载、汽车活载、温度影响力、混凝土收缩和徐变、静力风荷载等作用。根据强度控制要求设计的箱形主拱的跨度、高度和壁厚见表10，其中，1000m跨度混凝土拱桥的主拱截面高度拱顶20m、拱脚24m，已经超过了预应力混凝土连续刚构桥的墩顶截面高度。超大跨度混凝土拱桥满足强度要求的前提下，整体刚度很大，汽车活载作用下的挠度很小，见表10，远小于1/1000跨度的拱桥刚度要求。按照拱桥整体结构弹性稳定或一类稳定计算的稳定系数见表10，其中，1000m跨度混凝土拱桥是4.96、1200m跨度混凝土拱桥是4.82，均满足大于4.0的要求；按照拱桥局部结构屈服塑性稳定或二类稳定计算的稳定系数见表10，五种跨度混凝土拱桥的塑性稳定系数均大于2[9]。

超大跨度混凝土拱桥安全性 表10
Safety of concrete arch bridges with super-long spans Tab. 10

主拱跨度(m)	550	650	800	1000	1200
混凝土强度等级	C60	C80	R100	R120	R140
悬链线系数	1.75	1.85	2.30	2.50	2.80
主拱宽度(m)	22/30	22/30	22/35	22/40	30/45
主拱高度(m)	10/12	11/12	14/16	20/24	24/28
平均壁厚(m)	0.65	0.55	0.45	0.50	0.50
活载挠跨比	1/13900	1/7840	1/7930	1/12400	1/13800
弹性稳定系数	9.77	6.40	6.12	4.96	4.82
塑性稳定系数	2.32	2.24	2.40	2.44	2.48

5.3 超大跨度钢结构拱桥安全性分析

超大跨度钢结构拱桥安全性同样包括强度、刚度和稳定性，基于钢结构拱桥理论极限跨度分析结果，设计了跨度为650m、800m、1000m、1200m和1500m五种超大跨度钢结构拱桥，进行参数分析。

超大跨度钢结构拱桥试设计采用双向六车道加两侧紧急停车带，桥面全宽34m。拱桥布置采用中承式，主拱拱轴线为悬链线、矢跨比1/5，主拱结构为提篮式双拱肋，每个拱肋的截面为矩形单箱，拱肋截面宽度不变、高度从拱顶逐渐增大至拱脚，拱肋钢箱壁厚也从拱顶逐渐增大至拱脚。主梁采用正交异性钢箱梁，主梁轴线位置高于拱脚30m，主要通过吊杆与主拱连接。超大跨度钢结构拱桥有限元计算模型如图16所示。

图16 超大跨度钢结构拱桥计算模型
Fig. 16 Computation model of steel arch bridge with super-long span

钢结构拱桥安全性分析中考虑了结构恒载、汽车活载、温度影响力、静力风荷载等作用。根据强度控制要求设计的两片箱形主拱的宽度、高度和壁厚见表11,1200m跨度钢结构拱桥的主拱截面高度拱顶15m、拱脚22m,已经超过了钢结构连续刚构桥的墩顶截面高度。超大跨度钢结构拱桥满足强度要求的前提下,整体刚度虽然比混凝土拱桥小,但是,汽车活载作用下的挠度也较小,见表11,小于1/1000跨度的拱桥刚度要求。按照拱桥整体结构弹性稳定或一类稳定计算的稳定系数见表11,1200m跨度混凝土拱桥是5.25,1500m跨度钢结构拱桥是5.10,均满足大于4.0的要求;按照拱桥局部结构屈服塑性稳定或二类稳定计算的稳定系数见表11,钢结构拱桥塑性稳定系数均大于2[9]。

超大跨度钢结构拱桥安全性 表 11
Safety of steel arch bridges with super-long spans   Tab. 11

主拱跨度(m)	650	800	1000	1200	1500
钢材型号	Q345	Q370	Q420	Q500	Q550
悬链线系数	1.60	1.60	1.80	1.80	1.80
主拱宽度(m)	6.0	7.5	9.0	10.0	14.0
主拱高度(m)	7.5/11.0	9.5/14.5	12/18	15/22	20/28
平均壁厚(m)	0.042	0.042	0.060	0.070	0.085
活载挠跨比	1/1060	1/1190	1/1640	1/1970	1/2770
弹性稳定系数	5.28	5.10	5.29	5.25	5.10

6 结论

本文采用理论分析、风洞试验和数值分析方法,分析了大跨度钢筋混凝土拱桥施工阶段风荷载失稳原因,是静动力风荷载作用引起的拱肋失稳;研究了三座世界纪录跨度拱桥——卢浦大桥钢箱拱桥、平南三桥钢管混凝土拱桥和天峨龙滩特大桥钢管混凝土劲性骨架混凝土拱桥,计算了施工阶段和成桥状态的弹性屈曲稳定系数和塑性屈服稳定系数,静动力风荷载主要影响施工阶段的抗风稳定性,特别是钢管混凝土劲性骨架混凝土拱桥。在此基础上,探索了混凝土拱桥和钢结构拱桥的超大跨度,尽管R140混凝土拱桥的理论极限跨度可以达到1500m,但是试设计表明800m跨度混凝土拱桥才有可行性;同样,尽管Q500钢结构拱桥的理论极限跨度可以达到2500m,但是试设计表明1200m跨度钢结构拱桥才是可行的。

参 考 文 献

[1] 葛耀君.大跨度拱式桥抗风[M].北京:人民交通出版社股份有限公司,2014.

[2] 葛耀君,等.箱形拱桥裸肋状态等效风荷载及抗风稳定性研究[R].上海:同济大学土木工程防灾国家重点实验室,2001.

[3] Ge, Y.J., Yang, Y.X., Pang, J.B. and Xiang, H.F. Wind-induced damages to a three-span, continuous, concrete arch bridge under construction [J]. Journal of Structural Engineering International,2007,17(2):141-150.

[4] 葛耀君,等.超大跨度拱桥风荷载及抗风稳定性研究[R].上海:同济大学土木工程防灾国家重点实验室,2002.

[5] Ge, Y. J., Xiang, H. F. Recent development of bridge aerodynamics in China [C]. 5th International Colloquium on Bluff Body Aerodynamics and Applications, Ottawa, Canada, 2004,11-15.

[6] 葛耀君,等.平南三桥静风响应研究报告[R].上海:同济大学土木工程防灾国家重点实验室,2019.

[7] 葛耀君,等.钢管拱肋施工阶段静风响应研究报告[R].上海:同济大学土木工程防灾国家重点实验室,2022.

[8] 邓卓章.超大跨度拱桥考虑风荷载效应的弹性稳定性和极限承载力[D].上海:同济大学硕士学位论文,2021.

钢管混凝土结构分析理论、标志性工程应用与国家技术标准

韩林海

(广西大学　广西南宁　530004)

摘　要　钢管混凝土是在钢管中填充混凝土而成,且两者共同受力的组合结构形式,性能优越但受力机理复杂。近年来,钢管混凝土逐渐成为我国当代重大土木工程主体结构的优选形式之一,且呈现出超大跨、高耸、重载和在恶劣环境中长期服役等"超常"条件新态势,发展基于全寿命周期的钢管混凝土结构分析理论,成为亟待解决的重大工程技术科学问题。该报告针对钢管混凝土结构这一土木工程关键领域,阐述在新现象发现、特征规律揭示、结构构造发明、实验装置研发、承载力准确计算等方面的研究成果,介绍基于全寿命周期的钢管混凝土结构分析理论。

结合标志性工程实例,阐述大型复杂钢管混凝土主体结构非线性分析与精细化设计的通用本构模型、承载力计算方法、关键构造措施等基础理论与共性技术问题;论述钢管混凝土混合结构概念,阐述其全寿命期分析理论与计算模型,介绍国家标准《钢管混凝土混合结构技术标准》(GB/T 51446—2021)主要内容。

Analytical Theory, Iconic Practical Project Applications and National Technical Standard for CFST Structures

Han Linhai

(Guangxi University, Nanning, Guangxi, 530004, China)

Abstract　Concrete-filled steel tubular (CFST) structure is a type of composite structure formed by filling concrete into a steel tube, which enables the two materials to resist external actions together. It possesses excellent mechanical properties but complex structural mechanisms. In recent years, the CFST structure has gradually emerged as one of the select structural types for the main structural components of major civil engineering constructions in China. These constructions tend to feature a super-long span, a super-large height, to resist super-heavy loads, or to

---

作者简介：

韩林海(1967—),男,教授,主要从事结构工程领域的教学和科研工作。

serve in severe environmental conditions. Thus, the development of a life-cycle-based analytical theory for CFST structure becomes a significant yet urgent scientific issue for engineering applications that needs to be tackled. This presentation focuses on CFST structure, one of the key research fields in civil engineering, and elaborates its life-cycle-based analytical theory. The research outcomes are highlighted with the discovery of new phenomenon, the revealing of characteristic mechanical trends, the invention of structural detailing, the development of novel experimental apparatus, and the accurate calculations of structural resistances.

The fundamental analytical theory and general key techniques, e. g., the universal constitutive models, the calculation methods for structural resistances, and the key detailing, for the nonlinear analysis and the refined design of large-scale and complex CFST main structures, are presented associated with a number of iconic CFST constructions in practice. The concept and life-cycle-based analytical theory and calculation models for CFST hybrid structures are also elaborated. Finally, the newly developed and released Chinese national standard, *Technical Standard for Concrete-Filled Steel Tubular Hybrid Structures*, GB/T 51446—2021, is also introduced in this presentation.

大跨度系杆-撑杆协作抗推拱桥结构体系研究

徐升桥　杨喜文*　李　辉

（中铁工程设计咨询集团有限公司　北京　100055）

摘　要　部分推力拱桥柔性系杆的刚度小，通过主动张拉可以平衡主拱的恒载推力，但对于活载和温度推力的平衡能力弱，因此需要设置大刚度主墩以承担部分主拱推力，大跨度公铁两用桥活载集度大，主墩及其基础设计困难。由拉压相对关系，提出在边跨设置撑杆和锚碇将主墩承担的主拱推力引致两岸锚碇基础，形成系杆-撑杆协作抗推体系拱桥，系杆主要平衡恒载推力，撑杆承担活载和温度推力，以改善主墩及其基础的不利受力状态。依托某拟建长江公铁两用桥对大跨度部分推力拱桥的结构体系和施工方法进行了分析研究，结果表明：与柔性系杆部分推力拱相比，系杆-撑杆协作抗推体系拱的主墩基础反力减小了60%以上，显著改善了主墩及其基础的受力状态；撑杆作为平衡重为大跨度拱桥采用转体法施工提供了便利条件，可以避免拱肋的大节段吊装和高空焊接，有利于改善作业环境和施工质量。

关键词　部分推力拱桥　系杆-撑杆协作抗推体系　撑杆式推力拱　转体施工　钢管混凝土拱桥

中图分类号　U442.5 + 4；U448.22 + 5　　　**文献标识码**　A

Research on the Structural System of Large-Span Tie-Strut Cooperative Anti-Thrust Arch Bridges

XU Shengqiao　YANG Xiwen*　LI Hui

（China Railway Engineering Design and Consulting Group Co., Ltd., Beijing, 100055, China）

Abstract　Flexible tie rods of partial thrust arch bridges have small rigidity, and could balance the dead load thrust of the main arch by active tensioning, with weak ability for live load and temperature, and it is necessary to set a large rigid main pier to bear the arch thrust. This problem is more prominent due to the large live load concentration for large span road-rail bridge. Based on the relationship between tension and compression, it is proposed to set struts

---

基金项目：中国中铁股份有限公司科技研究开发计划（2021-专项-01）。
作者简介：
徐升桥（1966—），男，湖北黄梅人，教授级高工（全国工程勘察设计大师），E-mail：cecql_xsq@qq.com。
通讯作者：
＊杨喜文（1981—），男，河南舞阳人，高级工程师，博士，E-mail：07yxwen@alumni.tongji.edu.cn。

and anchors on the side spans leading the thrust to the anchorage foundations on both banks, forming an arch bridge with a tie-strut cooperative anti-thrust system. The tie rods mainly balance the dead-load thrust. The struts bear live load and temperature thrust to improve the unfavorable stress state of the main pier and its foundation. Based on the proposed Luzhou Yangtze River Road-Rail Bridge, the structural system and construction method of long-span partial thrust arch bridge were analyzed and studied. The results show that: compared with flexible tie-rod partial thrust arch, the reaction force of the main pier foundation of the tie-strut cooperative anti-thrust system arch is reduced by more than 60%, which significantly improves the stress state of the main pier and its foundation; as a counterweight, the strut-rod provides a convenient condition for using swivel construction method, which could avoid large-segment hoisting and high-altitude welding of the arch rib, and is conducive to improving the operating environment and construction quality.

Keywords　partial thrust arch bridge　tie-strut cooperative anti-thrust system　strut thrust arch　swivel construction　concrete-filled steel tube arch bridge

0　引言

拱桥结构形式丰富多样，不同的结构体系适用于不同的地形和地质条件[1-3]。因部分推力和无推力拱桥通过系杆部分或全部平衡了主拱水平推力，大大降低了平原地区或软基地区拱桥下部结构与基础的工程量和造价[4]，使得大跨度拱桥对建设条件的适应能力更强，应用范围更加广泛。按车承方式分类，部分推力和无推力拱桥常见有中承式和下承式两种结构形式。

下承式部分推力拱桥又称刚架拱桥，主拱与主墩固结，在两拱脚之间张拉柔性系杆索平衡主拱的大部分水平推力，目前跨度最大的刚架拱桥分别为主跨300m的广西南宁大桥和主跨约290m的武汉晴川大桥；中承式部分推力拱桥多采用飞燕式结构，中跨为单跨或多跨中承式拱，两边跨为上承式悬臂半拱结构，中拱与边拱的拱脚与主墩或拱座固结，在两边跨端部张拉系杆索平衡主拱的水平推力，目前跨度最大的飞燕式拱桥为主跨550m的卢浦大桥和主跨507m的合江长江三桥[5]；广州新光大桥同样为中承式部分推力拱桥，但却不同于飞燕式拱桥，其结构形式为三联拱，边拱与主梁固结形成刚性系杆无推力拱，中拱通过系杆拉索平衡水平推力，边拱与中拱固结于三角形刚架主墩上，通过边拱的压重平衡中拱在三角形刚架上产生的不平衡弯矩。部分推力拱桥有两个主要特点，一是柔性系杆索轴向刚度小，系杆拉力属于主动平衡力，可以平衡结构恒载产生的水平推力，但被动平衡活载水平推力的能力却很弱；二是需要较大的主墩刚度，活载和温度引起的主拱推力主要由主墩承担。

无推力拱桥为梁拱组合结构，主梁作为刚性系杆，被动平衡主拱的水平推力，结构内部为多次超静定结构，外部则为简支或连续梁结构体系，在恒载、活载和温度作用下不会在桥墩上产生水平推力。目前跨度最大的简支系杆拱为主跨380m的俄罗斯新西伯利亚布格林斯基桥，我国在建的济南齐鲁黄河大桥，简支系杆拱跨度达420m[6]。主跨550m的重庆朝天门大桥是目前跨度最大的中承式梁拱组合无推力拱桥[7]，其结构形式与下加劲连续钢桁梁类似。

受通航、行洪、环保和邻近车站的建站条件限制，某拟建长江公铁两用大桥主跨跨度不小于520m，若采用推力式拱桥方案，则跨度约为750m，技术和经济合理性较差，因此起拱线较高的无推力或部分推力拱桥更适合桥址建设条件。本文依托该拟建长江公铁两用大桥，提出了系杆-撑杆协作抗推体系拱桥方案，研究了主墩刚度受限条件下大跨度部分推力拱桥巨大水平推力的传递和平衡技术。

1 建设条件

拟建长江公铁两用大桥铁路等级为客货共线Ⅰ级铁路,双线,设计时速120km;公路等级为一级公路,双向6车道,设计时速60km,两侧非机动车道各宽3.5m;桥下通航等级为Ⅰ航道。

桥址长江河谷整体呈宽广的U形,枯水期河宽300~500m,洪水期河宽可达900m。年平均气温18.1℃,1月最冷,月平均气温7.7~7.8℃,7~8月最热,月平均气温27.0~28.0℃,极端最低气温-1.0℃,极端最高气温42.1℃。地质岩性以长石砂岩、砂质泥岩、泥质砂岩为主,少量长石石英砂岩、砾岩,岩性比较完整。位于Ⅵ度地震区,基本地震动峰值加速度0.05g,反应谱特征周期0.35s。桥位处于长江上游珍稀、特有鱼类国家级自然保护区的纳溪区河段的实验区范围内。

拟建长江公铁两用桥与既有铁路长江桥并行,位于既有桥下游50m处,既有铁路长江桥主桥为(83.95+3×144+83.95)m连续刚构。

2 拱桥方案设计

2.1 结构体系构思

考虑通航和行洪要求,拟建长江桥需要与既有桥对孔布置,从技术和经济合理的角度,小里程侧主墩与既有桥交界墩对齐,大里程侧主墩与既有桥次中墩的内侧边缘对齐,一跨跨越既有桥的三个通航孔,跨度为520m。拱桥方案的总体布置如图1所示,跨径组合为(169+520+143)m,主拱计算跨径520m,矢高130m,矢跨比1/4,拱轴线为悬链线,拱轴系数$m=1.75$,拱肋为变高度桁式钢管混凝土结构,拱顶和拱脚桁高中心距分别为9.5m和15.0m,钢管外径1.5m,钢材为Q500qD,灌注C70混凝土。主拱与主墩固结,主梁为连续钢桁梁结构,墩-梁之间设置纵向活动支座和阻尼器,采用半漂浮的约束体系。吊杆采用平行钢丝索,间距13.0m。

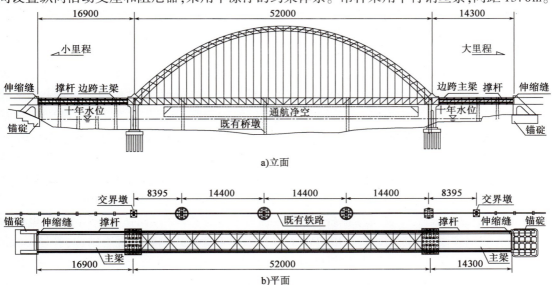

图1 拱桥方案总体布置图(尺寸单位:cm)

该拱桥方案主墩高度 45.6m,为典型的下承式部分推力拱桥,如采用仅设置柔性系杆索的抗推方案,则需要主墩和基础承担较大的水平推力。与既有桥叠加后,主墩尺寸受河道束窄率和通航净空限制,顺桥向宽度为 13.0m,存在设置大刚度基础的困难条件。

由拉和压的相对关系,提出在边跨增设抗推撑杆的系杆-撑杆协作抗推体系,通过柔性系杆索的主动张拉平衡恒载引起的主拱水平推力,刚性抗推撑杆则承担部分恒载以及活载和温度引起的主拱水平推力。撑杆采用桁式钢管混凝土结构,两岸设置锚碇,撑杆支撑在锚碇和主墩之间,为充分发挥撑杆的抗推作用,减小主墩承担的水平推力,主墩采用抗推刚度较小的双薄壁墩结构,通过撑杆和锚碇将部分主拱推力引致岸边基础,从而解决了主墩抗推刚度不足的问题。主梁和撑杆相互分离,主梁两端通过纵向活动支座支撑在反力座横梁上,不承受轴向温度荷载。结构受力体系如图 2 所示。

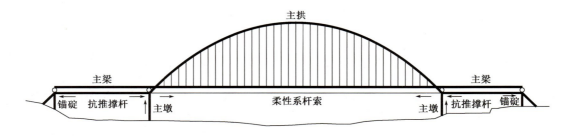

图 2 结构受力原理示意

2.2 抗推体系分析

大跨度拱桥的关键技术问题是主拱水平推力的平衡与传递。为了研究系杆-撑杆协作抗推体系拱桥的受力性能,对三种结构体系的主要分析结果进行了对比分析。三种结构方案分别为柔性系杆索部分推力拱(方案一)、撑杆式推力拱(方案二)和系杆-撑杆协作体系拱(方案三),其中撑杆式推力拱方案在边跨和两岸分别设置撑杆和锚碇,二者与主墩共同组成广义拱座结构,将主拱的水平推力引导至两岸锚碇基础,形成广义的推力式拱桥。

主拱和主梁的延米质量分别为 66.9t 和 51.5t,铁路和公路二期恒载分别为 15t/m 和 8.5t/m;活载包括铁路 ZKH 活载、公路—Ⅰ级车道荷载和人群荷载;温度作用为混凝土和钢管混凝土结构的整体升、降温均取 15℃,钢管混凝土结构的钢管与混凝土之间温差取 5℃,钢结构、吊杆和系杆的整体升降温取 30℃。根据现行《铁路桥涵设计规范》进行荷载组合。

恒载和活载作用下,主拱每端的水平推力分别为 3.64×10^5 kN 和 4.91×10^4 kN。三种方案的关键设计参数均经过分析和优化,方案一的柔性系杆采用 28 束规格为 91-Φ^{s}15.2 的钢绞线,抗拉强度 f_{pk} = 1960MPa;方案二的抗推撑杆采用 4 管桁式钢管混凝土结构,管径 1.4m,灌注 C70 混凝土,每个边跨 2 套抗推撑杆,每个拱肋对应 1 套;方案三的系杆采用 20 束规格为 91-Φ^{s}15.2 的钢绞线,抗拉强度 f_{pk} = 1960MPa,撑杆采用 4 管桁式钢管混凝土结构,管径 1.0m,灌注 C70 混凝土,每个边跨 2 套抗推撑杆,每个拱肋对应 1 套。

主要分析结果见表 1,表中列出了三种方案在恒载、活载、升温和徐变(增量)作用下的墩顶水平位移、基础水平反力、基础底弯矩、撑杆推力、系杆拉力和主拱挠度的分析结果。

抗推体系主要分析结果 表1

项 目	方案一:系杆索部分推力拱				方案二:撑杆式推力拱				方案三:系杆-撑杆协作体系拱			
	恒载	活载	升温	$\Delta_{徐变}$	恒载	活载	升温	$\Delta_{徐变}$	恒载	活载	升温	$\Delta_{徐变}$
墩顶水平位移(mm)	2	−5	−4	1	−5	−11	20	4	−9	−14	11	3
基础水平反力(10^4kN)	−0.1	4.8	4.2	−0.1	−1.1	1.2	−2.6	1.2	−0.2	1.9	−1.6	0.7
基础弯矩(10^4kN·m)	−64.9	225.8	232.5	−9.7	−71.4	66.4	−120.0	81.3	−27.7	85.7	−67.7	32.8
撑杆推力(10^4kN)	—	—	—	—	37.5	3.7	3.0	−1.4	6.9	2.8	3.5	−0.7
系杆拉力(10^4kN)	36.3	0.1	−3.5	0.0	—	—	—	—	29.6	0.24	−1.70	−0.1
主拱挠度(mm)	−640	−139	109	−43	−670	−142	119	−61	−686	−143	100	−62

注:墩顶水平位移和基础水平反力的正方形指向主拱跨中;主拱挠度的正方向向上。

由上表可知:(1)恒载作用下,三种方案均能较好地平衡和传递主拱的水平推力,墩顶位移和基础底反力均较小;(2)活载作用下,方案一的基础底反力是方案二和方案三的2.5~4.0倍;温度作用下,方案一的基础底反力是方案二和方案三的1.6~3.4倍,充分体系出柔性系杆索被动平衡能力弱的特点;(3)方案二因抗推撑杆的轴向刚度更大,温度作用下的墩顶水平位移和基础底反力均大于方案三;(4)混凝土徐变对基础反力影响较大,尤其是方案二和方案三,因方案二撑杆承担大部分主拱水平推力,其混凝土徐变对基础反力的影响与活载相当,是方案三的1.7~2.4倍;(5)恒载和活载作用下,方案二的撑杆反力是方案三的4.2倍,考虑方案二需要的锚碇基础大,撑杆受压失稳的风险高,因此推荐采用方案三的抗推体系。

2.3 主拱管径尺寸优化

与钢拱桥相比,钢管混凝土拱桥用混凝土替代了拱肋中的部分钢材,因此造价较低。但对于大跨度部分推力拱桥而言,拱肋的重量是影响主拱水平推力大小的重要因素,进而影响拱桥的设计难度,因此需要通过参数分析确定合理的拱肋钢管外径。分析参数分别取钢管外径为1.4m、1.5m和1.6m,分析结果包括拱肋延米重、主拱恒载水平推力、钢管应力和结构一阶弹性屈曲稳定系数,分析结果见表2。

主拱钢管外径分析结果 表2

管径(m)	最大壁厚(mm)	拱肋延米重(t)	恒载水平推力(10^4kN)	上钢管应力		下钢管应力		弹性稳定系数
				拱顶	拱脚	拱顶	拱脚	
1.4	62	60.9	35.1	259	273	182	308	7.6
1.5	62	66.9	36.3	243	255	167	288	9.1
1.6	62	73.2	38.0	239	251	166	283	10.3

由分析结果可知:(1)与管径1.4m相比,管径取1.5m和1.6m时拱肋的延米重分别增加9.8%和20.2%,主拱的恒载水平推力分别增加3.4%和8.3%,因此管径的大小对拱肋的重量和恒载水平推力影响显著。(2)在壁厚不变的情况下,随着管径的增加,钢管的最大应力有所减小,与管径1.4m相比,管径取1.5m和1.6m时钢管的最大应力分别减小了6.5%和8.1%,管径由1.5m增加致1.6m的情况下,应力减小并不明显。因此,管径增加到一定程度,增加的用钢量主要用来承受混凝土增加产生的自重。(3)管径的增加对结构的弹性屈曲稳定有一定

程度的改善。综上所述,管径取1.5m较为合适。

主拱结构的应力分析结果如图3所示,根据《铁路桥梁钢管混凝土结构设计规范》(TB 10127—2020)对拱肋弦杆进行的压弯验算结果如图4所示。钢管壁厚为32~62mm,主力+附件力作用下钢管最大压应力288MPa,混凝土压应力为5.3~16.6MPa,拱肋弦杆的压弯强度验算结果均满足要求。

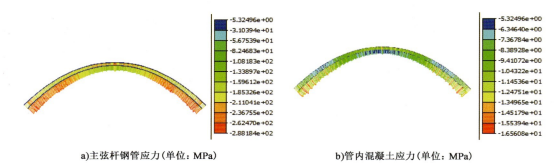

a)主弦杆钢管应力(单位:MPa)　　　b)管内混凝土应力(单位:MPa)

图3　主拱应力结果(主力+附加力组合)

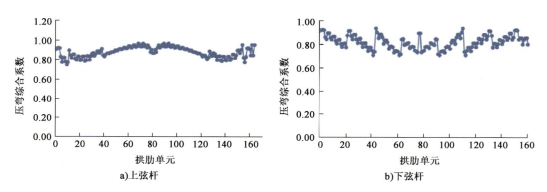

a)上弦杆　　　b)下弦杆

图4　拱肋主弦杆压弯验算结果(主力+附加力组合)

3　主拱施工方案分析

3.1　缆索吊装施工

由我国学者提出的缆索吊节段悬拼加斜拉扣挂的拱桥施工方法是目前最常用的大跨度拱桥成拱方法,该方法成熟可靠[2]。在当前技术水平下,工作跨度为450m、600m、900m的缆索吊机吊重能力分别可达400t、300t和100t[8]。

拟建长江公铁两用桥的缆索吊节段悬拼加斜拉扣挂的施工方案示意图如图5所示。扣塔和缆塔合一,设在主墩顶部,工作跨度为520m。拱脚位置的4个节段每段含一个拱桁节间,其余节段可包含2个拱桁节间,一片拱肋共分为23个节段,最大吊重约为350t。

主拱成拱的主要过程为施工主墩和锚碇;施工撑杆,并将撑杆与主墩和锚碇上的反力座连接;在主墩上设置扣塔和缆塔,建立缆索起重机系统;吊装拱肋节段直至合龙;主拱合龙后拆除扣索,此时由撑杆平衡主拱的水平推力,不需张拉临时系杆索;灌注主拱钢管内的混凝土,混凝土硬化后即完成主拱施工。

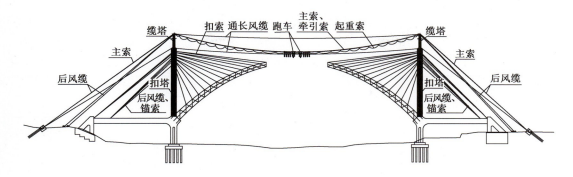

图 5 缆索起重机节段悬拼施工方案示意图

3.2 转体施工

平转和竖转施工同样是成熟可靠的大跨度拱桥的成拱方法,广州丫髻沙大桥在成拱过程中同时采用了竖转和平转施工方法,平转吨位达13680t,大瑞铁路澜沧江大桥则采用了二次竖转的施工方法,两次竖转角度之和为130°,竖转质量为2500t。目前桥梁平转施工的最大吨位已达4.5万t[9]。

系杆-撑杆协作抗推体系拱的撑杆可以作为平衡重实现主拱的转体施工,施工方案示意图如图 6 所示,成拱过程的主要施工步骤包括施工主墩和锚碇,墩底设置平转球铰;在岸边搭设支架,在支架上拼装拱肋和撑杆;在主墩顶部设置扣塔;以撑杆为平衡重实现拱肋竖转;主拱、主墩和撑杆绕墩底球铰平转就位;撑杆合龙,将撑杆和锚碇上的反力座连接;合龙主拱,拆除扣索和扣塔,由撑杆平衡主拱的水平推力;灌注主拱钢管内的混凝土,混凝土硬化后即完成主拱施工。

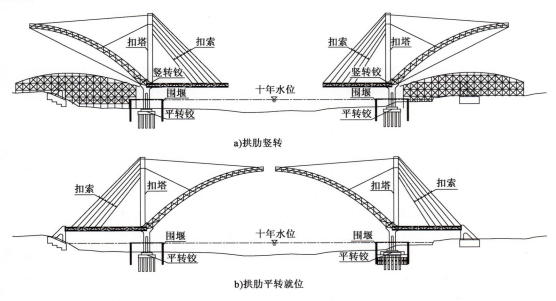

a) 拱肋竖转

b) 拱肋平转就位

图 6 拱肋竖转和平转施工方案示意图

转体施工的主要参数见表3,转体吨位约9万t,球铰直径7.91m,牵引力约10000kN。目前通过球铰的分块制造、运输和现场拼装,解决了大吨位球铰的技术瓶颈,桥梁转体球铰的设计吨位可达10万t[10],因此现有技术可以满足结构的转体施工要求。

主要转体参数 表3

转体质量(t)	球铰直径(m)	总牵引力(kN)	竖转角度(°)	平转角度(°)
90529	7.91	9952	25	180

根据当前的技术水平,两种施工方案均可行且较为成熟,转体施工方案的优点是拱肋钢结构在岸边支架上拼装,可避免大节段钢构件的吊装和高空焊接作业,技术人员的工作环境较好,施工精度和质量更容易保证。

4 结论

(1)针对大跨度部分推力拱桥活载和温度引起的水平推力大,需要设置大刚度主墩,主墩及其基础设计困难的问题,通过在边跨设置抗推撑杆,将部分恒载、活载和温度引起的水平推力引致两岸锚碇,由主墩、撑杆和锚碇共同组成广义拱座,形成系杆-撑杆协作抗推体系拱桥。进一步地,若增加撑杆的抗推能力,由撑杆平衡主拱的水平推力,从而取消中跨柔性系杆,则可以在不增加主拱跨度的情况下形成推力式拱桥,即撑杆式推力拱桥。

(2)与仅设柔性系杆索的部分推力拱相比,系杆-撑杆协作抗推体系拱和撑杆式推力拱由活载和温度引起的主墩基础反力大幅度减小,可改善主墩的受力状态,减小主墩的基础规模;与系杆-撑杆协作抗推体系相比,撑杆式推力拱的撑杆压力和锚碇基础较大,但减少了大吨位系杆索的张拉和后期更换与维护工作。

(3)钢管混凝土拱桥用混凝土替代了钢拱肋的部分钢材,两种材料力学性能互补,造价低廉。但混凝土重量的增加一方面会导致恒载水平推力变大,增加部分推力拱桥的设计难度,另一方面会引起主拱钢管应力的增加,因此需要通过分析比较确定合理的主拱弦杆外径。

(4)将边跨撑杆作为平衡重,为主拱采用转体施工方法提供了便利条件。主拱在岸边支架上拼装,通过竖转和平转就位,可以减小主拱的大节段吊装和高空焊接作业,改善作业环境和施工质量,具体实施方案还需要进一步研究。

参 考 文 献

[1] 周勇政,陈良江,高策.我国高速铁路桥梁设计技术及探索[J].桥梁建设,2018,48(05):11-15.

[2] 郑皆连.我国大跨径混凝土拱桥的发展新趋势[J].重庆交通大学学报(自然科学版),2016,35(1):8-11.

[3] 陈宝春,张梦娇,刘君平,等.我国混凝土拱桥应用现状与展望[J].福州大学学报(自然科学版),2021,49(05):716-726.

[4] 陈宝春,郑怀颖.钢管混凝土飞鸟式拱桥桥型分析[J].中外公路,2006(06):43-51.

[5] 陈宝春,韦建刚,周俊,等.我国钢管混凝土拱桥应用现状与展望[J].土木工程学报,

2017,50(06):50-61.
[6] 陈亮,邵长宇,汤虎,等.济南齐鲁黄河大桥420m跨网状吊杆系杆拱桥设计[J].桥梁建设,2022,52(03):113-120.
[7] 段雪炜,徐伟.重庆朝天门长江大桥主桥设计与技术特点[J].桥梁建设,2010(02):37-40.
[8] 郑皆连,王建军,牟廷敏,等.700m级钢管混凝土拱桥设计与建造可行性研究[J].中国工程科学,2014,16(08):33-37.
[9] 张文学,汪志斌,周玉林,等.超大吨位平面球铰转体斜拉桥多点联合称重技术[J].铁道建筑,2020,49(23):14-17.
[10] 简方梁,徐升桥,高静青,等.超大吨位转体桥梁关键技术研究[J/OL].铁道标准设计,2021,65(11):179-184.

设计与结构分析

钢管混凝土栓焊节点偏压力学性能研究

于 鹏 云惟经 郑皆连*

（广西大学土木建筑工程学院/工程防灾与结构安全教育部重点实验室/
广西防灾减灾与工程安全重点实验室 广西南宁 530004）

摘 要 本文基于大跨钢管混凝土拱桥拱肋节点传统连接形式中切割法兰盘造成拱肋节点应力重分布的问题，提出无须切割法兰盘，保证节点安全并节省工期的新型栓焊节点连接形式。开展了不同连接方式（连续、焊接、栓焊）和偏心距下钢管混凝土柱节点偏心受压缩尺试验，考察了不同连接形式下构件的失效模式、荷载位移曲线等力学性能指标。开展数值模拟，并通过试验数据对有限元模型进行验证。结果表明：建立的数值模型具有准确性，栓焊连接形式可显著提高节点刚度和稳定性，有效避免节点处产生鼓曲变形；小偏心下钢管混凝土栓焊节点较焊接节点承载力更优。

关键词 钢管混凝土拱桥 栓焊节点 偏压 力学性能

Behaviour of Concrete Filled Steel Tube with Bolt-Welded Joint under Eccentric Compression

YU Peng YUN Weijing ZHENG Jielian*

(School of Civil and Architectural Engineering of Guangxi University/Key Laboratory of Disaster Prevention and Structural Safety of the Ministry of Education/Guangxi Key Laboratory of Disaster Prevention and Structural Safety, Nanning, Guangxi, 530004, China)

Abstract Based on the situation of rib joint stress redistribution caused by cutting the joint flange in the traditional connection method, a new bolt-welded connection method for arch ribs of long-span concrete filled steel

---

基金项目：广西创新驱动重大专项、超大跨径钢管混凝土拱桥的材料、装备、设计及施工技术创新与示范（子课题）（桂科 AA18118205）；广西重点研发计划、特大跨劲性骨架混凝土拱桥建造关键技术（桂科 AB22036007）；广西高校引进海外高层次人才"百人计划"。

作者简介：
于鹏（1987—），男，助理教授，博士，主要从事超大跨径拱桥组合构件等方面的研究。
云惟经（1996—），男，硕士研究生，主要从事钢管混凝土方面的研究。
*郑皆连（1941—），男，教授（院士），主要从事大跨桥梁工程研究。

tube(CFST) arch bridge was proposed, which no need to cut flanges, ensuring the safety of the connection joint and saving the construction period. The eccentric compression scale tests of CFST column joints under different connection methods(normal、weld、bolt-welded) and eccentric distances was carried out, and the mechanical properties such as the failure modes and the load-displacement curve were investigated. The numerical simulations were carried out and the finite element model was validated with experimental data. The results show that the established numerical model is precise and the bolt-welded connection method can significantly improve the stiffness, stability and effectively avoid buckling at the joint. The bearing capacity of the CFST bolt-welded joint under small eccentricity is better than that of the welded joint.

Keywords CFST arch bridge　bolt-welded joint　eccentric compression　mechanical properties
E-mail py@gxu.edu.cn

0　引言

钢管混凝土拱桥承载力高、抗风抗震性能好,多用于川藏等地势条件复杂的地区,是工程上强力的竞争桥型之一[1]。由于川藏铁路地区昼夜温差大,低温低压的环境[2]严重影响焊接稳定性和接头质量。传统的拱肋钢管节点施工过程中,易会造成节点应力重分布,严重威胁节点安全,在川藏铁路极端环境下此情况更为突出。因此,有必要对钢管拱肋连接方式进行优化设计,并进行相应力学性能分析,以适应川藏铁路超大跨境拱桥工程需求。

对于钢管混凝土拱桥节点的研究,主要针对桁式拱桥节点[3-5],JIN 等[6-7]提出了新型拱肋 K 形节点盲栓连接形式,其他栓焊节点类型的研究主要针对于梁柱节点[8],对拱肋栓焊节点的研究较少。因此,本文提出一种用于大跨径拱桥拱肋中新型栓焊节点,该节点采用栓、焊混合连接,无须切割拉盘,为验证该节点力学性能的优越性,本文对不同连接形式下(连续、焊接、栓焊)钢管混凝土柱节点开展偏心受压试验及数值研究。

1　试验研究

1.1　试验概况

基于缩尺理论,结合试验室条件,采用缩尺比为 1:4 设计缩尺节点模型。试件的详细尺寸信息见表1,其中"L""S"和"H"分别代表"通长""栓焊"和"焊接",D 为钢管外径,H 为构件高度,t 为钢管厚度,采用 12.9 级 M8 高强螺栓。核心混凝土设计强度为 C80,钢管为 Q420 级钢材。通过材性试验测试得到钢管屈服强度平均值为 623 MPa,核心混凝土立方体抗压强度平均值为 76.66 MPa。

试件参数表　　　　　　　表1
Information of Specimens　　　　Tab.1

序号	试件编号	$D \times H$(mm)	t(mm)	连接方式	偏心距 e_a(mm)
1	L1	219×820	8	连续	8
2	S1	219×820	8	栓焊	8
3	S2	219×820	8	栓焊	40

续上表

序 号	试件编号	$D \times H$(mm)	t(mm)	连接方式	偏心距 e_a(mm)
4	S3	219×820	8	栓焊	70
5	H1	219×820	8	焊接	8
6	H2	219×820	8	焊接	40
7	H3	219×820	8	焊接	70

1.2 试验结果

1.2.1 失效模式

以偏心 8mm 试验结果（图 1）为例，连续钢管（L1）端部及受压侧中部沿轴向往上 5cm 左右处出现明显鼓曲，横向变形不大；焊接（H1）和栓焊钢管（S1）均表现为受压侧中部沿轴向往上 10cm 左右出现鼓曲，横向变形较大，不同之处在于，焊接钢管受拉侧为焊缝断裂，栓焊钢管受拉侧为螺栓受拉断裂。

1.2.2 荷载-位移曲线

试件荷载-位移曲线如图 2 所示，栓焊节点（S1）较焊接节点（H1）表现出更好的延性。偏心距较小时，栓焊钢管承载力高于焊接钢管，且与连续钢管相差甚小，表明栓焊钢管力学性能更优；随着偏心距的增加，试件承载力和延性均会降低。

图 1 失效模式
Fig. 1 Failure Modes

图 2 荷载-位移曲线
Fig. 2 Load-displacement curve

2 数值模拟

2.1 有限元模型

采用 ABAQUS 有限元软件对不同连接形式（连续、焊接、栓焊）钢管混凝土柱偏压力学性能进行分析。其中压头采用离散刚体建模，其余部件均采用实体单元建模。钢材本构采用材性试验数据，混凝土采用 CDP（Concrete Damage Plastic）本构模型，应力-应变关系采用沈聚敏等[9]提出的拉伸本构和韩林海等[10]提出的压缩套箍本构。钢与核心混凝土法向设为"硬接触"，切向摩擦系数取 0.6，压头采用固接，其中一端压头释放轴向位移自由度并施加轴向位移。

2.2 模型验证

以偏心 8mm 模拟结果为例，试验与仿真构件失效模式对比如图 3 所示。仿真模拟失效模式与试验失效模式大体一致。试验中焊接钢管失效表现为节点轴向上方产生鼓曲,仿真钢管鼓曲产生在节点处。栓焊节点失效则以节点处螺栓拉断,焊缝断裂为主,试验钢管变形集中在栓焊节点上部,仿真钢管变形较为均匀,无明显鼓曲变形。试验与仿真荷载-位移曲线对比如图4所示,有限元模拟结果与试验结果较为一致,荷载位移曲线峰值基本相等,且峰值点前曲线重合度较高,仿真曲线在下降段均表现出较好的延性。综上,可认为本文所建立的有限元模型较为准确。

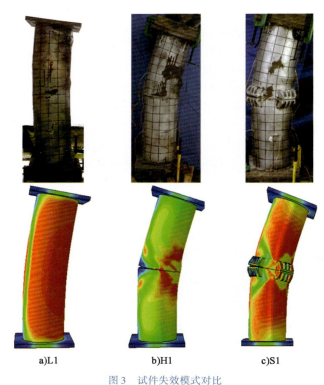

图3 试件失效模式对比

Fig. 3　Comparison of Failure Modes of Specimen

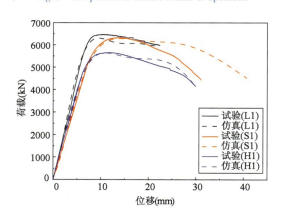

图4 试验与仿真荷载-位移曲线对比

Fig. 4　Comparison of Experimental and Simulated Load-Displacement Curves

3 结论

本文提出一种拱肋新型栓焊节点,通过对不同连接形式下(连续、焊接、栓焊)的钢管混凝土柱开展试验及数值计算研究,发现小偏心距下,栓焊节点柱承载力接近连续柱,大于焊接节点柱;栓焊连接下,焊缝断裂后螺栓仍能继续承载,延缓节点破坏,另外由于加劲肋的存在,钢管节点处稳定性较好,刚度及延性均高于焊接节点,可认为栓焊节点力学性能更优;试验与仿真结果拟合较好,数值模型具有准确性。仿真模拟效果较为理想,构件受力分布较为均匀,结构延性更好。本文研究结果充分验证了小偏心下栓焊连接形式的力学性能强于传统连接形式,能为低温低压等恶劣施工条件下的超大跨径钢管混凝土拱桥拱肋节点设计提供参考依据,避免节点应力重分布的同时节省工期、节约成本,具有极大的实际工程应用价值。

参 考 文 献

[1] 郑皆连,王建军,牟廷敏,等.700m级钢管混凝土拱桥设计与建造可行性研究[J].中国工程科学,2014,16(08):33-37.

[2] 陈正,陈犇,郑皆连,等.青藏高原低气压环境下钢管混凝土的核心混凝土密实性评估方法研究[J].土木工程学报,2021,54(08):1-13.

[3] Hou Chao, Han Linhai, Mu Tingmin. Behaviour of CFDST chord to CHS brace composite K-joints:Experiments[J]. Journal of constructional steel research, 2017, 13597-109.

[4] 庞锦浩.钢管混凝土拱桥K形节点力学性能有限元研究[D].南宁:广西大学,2015.

[5] 卢栋炎.钢管混凝土拱肋K型相贯节点刚度及承载力研究[D].南宁:广西大学,2020.

[6] Jin Dengyiding, Hou Chao, Shen Luming, et al. Numerical investigation of demountable CFST K-joints using blind bolts[J]. Journal of Constructional Steel Research, 2019, 160428-443.

[7] Jin Dengyiding, Hou Chao, Shen Luming, et al. Numerical performance of blind-bolted demountable square CFST K-joints[J]. Journal of Building Engineering, 2021, 33101646.

[8] Zhong Tao, Hassan Md-Kamrul, Song Tianyi, et al. Experimental study on blind bolted connections to concrete-filled stainless steel columns[J]. Journal of Constructional Steel Research, 2017, 128825-838.

[9] 沈聚敏,等.钢筋混凝土有限元与板壳极限分析[M].北京:清华大学出版社,1993.

[10] 韩林海.钢管混凝土结构[M].北京:科学出版社,2004.

大跨度拱桥桩基承台加超长锚索组合地锚系统研究

马少坤[1]，李旭锋[1]，李卓峰[1]*，侯凯文[2]，黄震[1]，刘莹[1]，付晓茜[1]，高峰[1]，曹琛[1]

（1. 广西大学土木建筑工程学院　广西南宁　530004；
2. 广西路桥工程集团有限公司　广西南宁　530004）

摘　要　大跨度拱桥桩基承台加超长锚索组合地锚系统是一种新型的地锚系统，主要应用在采用斜拉挂扣法的大跨度拱桥，本论文采用有限元软件Plaxis3D进行数值模拟，在验证模型正确性基础上研究锚索数量、尾索力大小和尾索力施加顺序对于地锚系统的影响。锚索数量越多，总体预应力越大，初始阶段位移、剪力和弯矩变幅大，阶段位移、剪力和弯矩变幅相应减小；尾索力小，则地锚系统的承台位移、桩身最大弯矩和剪力相应变小；调整尾索力施加顺序对于地锚系统施工中间阶段的受力是有利的。

关键词　桩基承台　超长锚索　组合地锚系统　Plaxis3D　尾索力

中图分类号　U445.464　　　　**文献标识码**　A

Research on Combined Ground Anchor System of Long-span Arch Bridge Pile Foundation Cap and Super-long Anchor Cable

MA Shaokun[1]，LI Xufeng[1]，LI Zhuofeng[1]*，HOU Kaiwen[2]，HUANG Zhen[1]，LIU Ying[1]，FU Xiaoxi[1]，GAO Feng[1]，CAO Chen[1]

（1. College of Civil Engineering and Architecture, Guangxi University, Nanning, Guangxi, 530004, China；
2. Guangxi Road and Bridge Engineering Group Co., Ltd., Nanning, Guangxi, 530004, China）

Abstract　The long-span arch bridge pile foundation cap and super-long anchor cable combined ground anchor system is a new type of ground anchor system, which is mainly used in long-span arch bridges using the cable-stayed hook method. This paper used the finite element software Plaxis3D for numerical simulation. On the basis of verifying

---

作者简介：

马少坤（1972—），男，博士，教授，主要从事地下工程、隧道工程、地基、物探、边坡方面的研究。

李旭锋（1999—），男，硕士研究生，主要从事地下工程方面的研究。

*李卓峰（1992—），男，博士，讲师，主要从事特殊土基本性质、地下空间工程等研究。

the correctness of the model, the influence of the number of anchor cables, the size of the tail cable force and the order of the application of the tail cable force on the ground anchor system was studied. The greater the number of anchor cables, the greater the overall prestress, the greater the amplitude of initial phase displacement, shear and bending moment, and the corresponding decrease of stage displacement, shear and bending moment When the tail cable force is small, the displacement of the ground anchor system, the maximum bending moment of the pile body and the shear force correspondingly decrease. Adjusting the order of force application of the tail cable is beneficial to the force in the middle stage of the construction of the ground anchor system.

Keywords pile foundation cap super-long anchor cable combined ground anchor system Plaxis3D tail cable force

0 引言

现有的拱桥施工技术主要包括支架法、转体法和缆索吊装斜拉扣挂法等,其中,缆索吊运斜拉扣挂施工技术凭借施工便捷、适应性好和经济性好等优点,在工程中应用最为普遍[1,2]。千斤顶斜拉扣挂法一般由索塔系统和扣挂系统两部分组成。索塔系统包括主塔、悬索、锚索;扣挂系统包括扣塔、扣索、锚索[3]。地锚是缆索吊装施工中必不可少的结构。目前拱桥施工常用的后锚主要有重力式锚碇和岩锚两种形式,也有桩基承台锚和桩式地锚等形式[5,6,7]。

锚索、承台、桩基组成的组合地锚系统,将桩基承台水平抗力和预应力锚索预张拉产生的水平力有效结合,共同抵抗尾扣索传递的水平分力;将预应力锚索预张拉产生的竖向力与桩基承台自重相结合,共同抵抗尾扣索传递的竖向分力。在地质条件较差的情况下,如桥位地形陡峻、高山河谷地带中有很好的作用,具有较高的经济性,因此对其进行研究有重要意义。本文以天峨龙滩特大桥为依托,建立有限元模型,通过数值模拟分析结果和监测结果的对比,验证模型正确性,进而研究锚索数量、尾索力施加顺序对墩台水平位移、桩身弯矩、桩身剪力的影响,分析组合地锚系统整体受力特点。

1 工程概况

1.1 工程地质概况

桥位区位于龙滩水库(红水河)库区,属剥蚀低山丘陵地貌,桥址库区河槽呈"U"形,水库流向自北西向南东,两岸山体走向总体与河槽一致。特大桥两岸拱座均坐落于"U"形岸坡山体半坡,岸坡沟谷多基岩裸露,岩性主要为三叠系碎屑岩类,岩石抗风化力较弱;山坡表层以粉质黏土混碎石、粉质黏土、碎石土为主,场地内地层主要由第四系洪积层角砾土、残坡积层粉质黏土和碎石土、崩积层块石土和古滑坡堆积层碎石土、块石土;三叠系中统砂岩、三叠系下统粉砂质泥岩地层组成。

1.2 地锚布置概况

锚索均为10束,直径15.2mm高强度低松弛钢绞线,钢绞线标准强度不小于1860MPa,每根锚索预应力设计值1200kN,锚孔直径130mm。钢垫板尺寸40×40cm,厚4cm。

2 有限元模型及模型验证

2.1 有限元模型

本模型利用有限元软件 Plaxis3D 来模拟,以南丹岸 3 号墩、4 号墩为例构建数值模型,模型大小为 900m×100m×600m。其中,碎石土、岩质堆积体、强风化砂岩夹泥岩、页岩运用小应变土体硬化模型(HSS Small)模拟,中风化岩石采用线弹性模型模拟。3 号墩实际施工锚索 40 束,4 号墩实际施工锚索 21 束。采用点对点锚杆单元模拟锚索自由段,采用嵌入桩单元模拟锚杆的锚固段,采用嵌入桩单元模拟桩基。3 号墩采用 17 根直径为 2.0m 的钢筋混凝土桩基,桩长 38.0m,并布置 5 排地锚。4 号墩台共采用 18 根直径为 2.0m 的钢筋混凝土桩基,桩长 35.0m,并布置 3 排地锚。将桩作为弹性材料,弹性模量为 $3×10^4$MPa,密度为 25kN/m^3,3 号墩台桩和 4 号墩台桩的轴向侧摩阻力分别为 314kN/m 和 440kN/m。与此同时,采用施加集中荷载的方法来模拟尾索力。数值模型如图 1 所示。

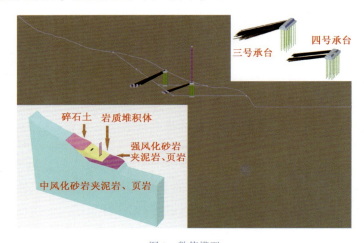

图 1 数值模型
Fig. 1 Numerical Models

2.2 模型验证

与现场试验不同,有限元模拟的是理想状态,即不受到材料不均匀性、现场环境变化、测量仪器精度及人为因素等影响,因此,有限元得到的位移曲线与现场监测测量结果有一定的差别,但两者在总体趋势及数值上比较接近,说明有限元计算时所取的土体参数基本上能够反映现场的实际情况。因此,有限元能够反映大跨度拱桥桩基承台加超长锚索组合地锚系统真实的工作性状。在此基础上进行了组合地锚系统的仿真模拟。

3 地锚系统影响因素分析

3.1 锚索数量

为了研究锚索数量对于桩基承台加超长锚索组合地锚系统的影响,取锚索数量分别为 3 号墩 5 排 61 根锚索、4 号墩 3 排 42 根锚索和 3 号墩 2 排 30 根锚索、4 号墩无锚索。施工顺序如下:施工桩基承台、张拉 3 号墩和 4 号墩锚索(锚索施加 1200kN 预应力)、4 号墩施加 2 号~

7号尾索力、3号墩施加8号~12号尾索力。

图2a)为不同锚索数量下承台位移图。图2b)为不同锚索数量下桩身最大剪力图。图2c)为不同锚索数量下桩身最大弯矩图。

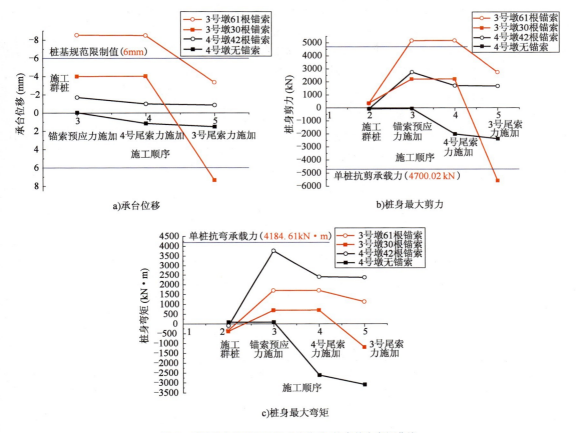

图2 不同锚索数量的地锚系统位移、桩身剪力弯矩曲线

Fig. 2 Displacement of Ground Anchor System, Shear Force and Bending Moment Curve of Pile Body with Different Number of Anchor Cables

图2说明了不同锚索数量下的曲线趋势接近。锚索施加预应力阶段,将造成承台位移增加和桩身最大剪力、最大弯矩增加,并且增加锚索数量对上述响应影响也越大。在施加尾索阶段,作用力与锚索预应力相互抵消,可以减小承台位移和桩身最大剪力、最大弯矩。在低锚索数量的工况下,施加尾索后,承台位移和桩身最大剪力、最大弯矩将出现方向倒转现象。这样的受力方向突变,对桩身受力不利,对桩身配筋设计和施工也带来不利。因此,在施工过程中,应合理选择锚索张拉数量,既要保障初始承台位移和桩身受力,又要尽量降低受力方向突变。

3.2 尾索力施加顺序

为了研究尾索力施加顺序对于桩基承台加超长锚索组合地锚系统的影响,取尾索力施加顺序分别为在3号墩第二排锚索预应力施加前施加11号尾索力和在3号墩第二排锚索预应力施加后施加11号尾索力。锚索数量为3号墩2排30根锚索、4号墩无锚索。尾索力大小取表5尾索力2,施工顺序如下:施工桩基承台、4号墩施加2号~7号尾索力、张拉3号墩第一排锚索(锚索施加1200kN预应力)、3号墩施加8号~11号(8号~10号)尾索力、张拉3号墩第二排锚索、3号墩施加12号(11号~12号)尾索力。

图3为不同尾索力施加顺序下承台位移、桩身最大剪力、桩身最大弯矩图。调整3号墩尾索力施加顺序对于4号墩的影响很小,可以忽略。调整尾索力施加顺序,可以更好的限制3号墩承台位移,能更好的控制3号墩桩身剪力和弯矩的变化幅度及方向。张拉锚索在不同尾索力施加顺序下对于组合地锚系统的影响是相同的,调整尾索力施加顺序,充分发挥地锚预应力作用,对于组合地锚系统受力是有利的。

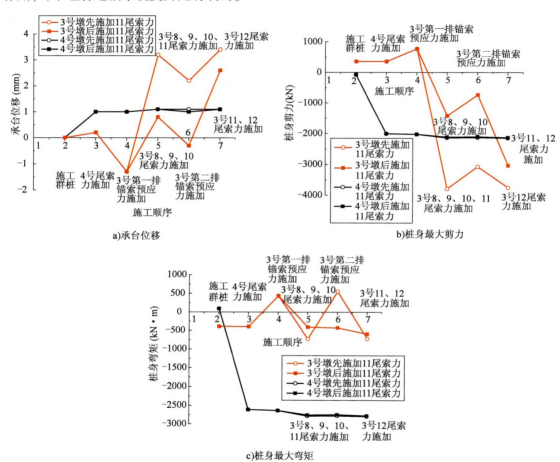

图3 不同尾索力施加顺序地锚系统位移、桩身剪力弯矩曲线

Fig. 3 Displacement of Ground Anchor System, Shear Force and Bending Moment Curve of Pile Body with Different Tail Cable Forces

4 结论

以天峨龙滩特大桥为背景,对桩基承台加超长锚索组合地锚系统进行分析,得到以下结论:

(1)在低锚索数量的工况下,施加尾索后,承台位移和桩身最大剪力、最大弯矩将出现方

向倒转现象,对桩身受力不利。施工过程中,应合理选择锚索张拉数量,降低桩身力方向倒转现象。

(2)优化尾索力施加顺序能够降低承台位移和桩身最大弯矩、最大剪力的变化幅度。

参 考 文 献

[1] 陈宝春,韦建刚,周俊,等.我国钢管混凝土拱桥应用现状与展望[J].土木工程学报,2017,50(6):50-61.

[2] 陈宝春,刘福忠,韦建刚.327座钢管混凝土拱桥的统计分析[J].中外公路,2011,31(3):96-103.

[3] 戴森.大跨度拱桥安装扣挂系统结构分析[D].南京:河海大学,2006.

[4] 严德育.大吨位钢管拱吊装扣锚系统组合式桩基承台锚施工技术研究[J].铁道建筑技术,2017(06):72-74+107.

[5] 方乃平,许鑫,王帅.秭归长江公路大桥重型缆索吊机设计[J].桥梁建设,2022,52(01):116-123.

[6] 肖玉德,俞高明,王春礼,等.拱桥施工中桩式地锚的力学行为分析[J].安徽建筑工业学院学报(自然科学版),2001(03):16-20+41.

笛卡儿坐标系下拱结构面内非线性应变

胡常福[1*]　胡　星[1]　罗文俊[1,2]　李诚斌[3]　韩春光[3]

（1. 华东交通大学土木建筑学院　江西南昌　330013；
2. 华东交通大学江西省防灾减灾及应急管理重点实验室　江西南昌　330013；
3. 中铁建大桥工程局集团第一工程有限公司　辽宁大连　116033）

摘　要　极坐标系下圆弧拱的面内非线性弹性屈曲与后屈曲已被广泛研究，但笛卡儿坐标系下拱的面内非线性弹性屈曲问题尚未引起足够的重视，尽管笛卡儿坐标系下的拱已被广泛应用于实际拱桥工程中。本文基于 Timoshenko 梁假设，推导了笛卡儿坐标系下拱的面内非线性压缩应变、弯曲应变与剪切应变表达式；根据非线性应变表达式，推演了填料自重荷载下悬链线拱的面内非线性弹性屈曲与后屈曲，得到了非线性稳定解析解。与有限元计算结果对比表明，本文提出的解析解与有限元数值解吻合较好，所提出的平面内非线性应变可用于推导笛卡儿坐标系下拱结构非线性稳定解析解。

关键词　非线性应变　笛卡儿坐标系　非线性稳定　解析解

中图分类号　U441　　　　**文献标识码**　A

In-plane Nonlinear Strains for Nonlinear Elastic Stability of Arches in Cartesian Coordinate System

HU Changfu[1*]　HU Xing[1]　LUO Wenjun[1,2]　LI Chengbin[3]　HAN Chunguang[3]

（1. School of Civil Engineering and Architecture, East China Jiaotong University, Nanchang, Jiangxi, 330013, China;
2. Jiangxi Key Laboratory of Disaster Prevention-mitigation and Emergency Management, East China Jiaotong University, Nanchang, Jiangxi, 330013, China;
3. China Railway Construction Bridge Engineering Bureau Group First Engineering Co. Ltd., Dalian, Liaoning, 116033, China）

Abstract　The in-plane nonlinear elastic buckling and post-buckling of circular arches have been investigated extensively and the corresponding problems of arches in the Cartesian coordinate system have not attracted enough attention although these arches are applied extensively in the arch bridge engineering. This paper explored the

---

基金项目：国家自然科学基金项目（52168017，51568020）。

作者简介：

＊胡常福（1980—），男，博士，副教授，主要从事拱桥力学方面的研究。

in-plane nonlinear membrane strain, bending strain and shear strain for curve arches in the Cartesian coordinate system based on the Timoshenko beam hypothesis, and the in-plane nonlinear elastic buckling and post-buckling of catenary arches subjected to infill gravity are investigated based on these nonlinear strains and analytical solutions for the stability are derived. Comparisons with finite element method results show that the analytical predictions are in good agreement with numerical solutions, and the proposed in-plane nonlinear strains can be applied to derive analytical solutions for the nonlinear stability of arches in the Cartesian coordinate system.

Keywords　　Nonlinear strain　　Cartesian coordinate system　　Nonlinear stability　　Analytical solution
E-mail　　changfu.hu@ecjtu.edu.cn

0　引言

随着拱桥跨径的不断增大,拱桥结构的非线性屈曲问题越来越受到研究人员的关注,极坐标系下圆弧拱和笛卡儿坐标系的非圆弧拱的面内屈曲问题已有大量研究成果。

针对极坐标系下圆弧拱的面内非线性稳定,Bradford 和 Pi[1-2]研究了均布荷载和集中荷载作用下圆弧浅拱的面内非线性屈曲和后屈曲。Liu 等[3-4]研究了功能梯度材料圆弧拱的面内非线性稳定与局部荷载作用下的非线性屈曲行为。Tong 等[5-6]的研究指出,对于薄壁结构的非线性屈曲,应考虑剪切应力的影响。Babaei 等[7]研究了考虑剪切变形的功能梯度材料浅拱在力和温度荷载作用下的几何非线性行为。Lu 等[8-9]在 Timoshenko 梁假设的基础上研究了圆弧浅拱的弯扭屈曲问题。Zhang 等[10]研究了考虑剪切变形的叠层拱非线性屈曲问题。

针对笛卡儿坐标系下非圆弧拱的面内非线性稳定性,Bradford 等[11-13]对抛物线浅拱的面内非线性稳定进行了研究,并进行了实验验证。Hu 等[14-17]基于 Euler-Bernoulli 梁假设,推导了抛物线深拱、连拱和梁拱组合结构在笛卡儿坐标系下的面内非线性应变表达式和面内非线性弹性稳定解析解。

以上研究中,缺乏关于笛卡儿坐标系中考虑剪切变形的拱面内非线性弹性稳定性的研究。为了填补这一领域的空白,本文提出了一种在笛卡儿坐标系下推导拱面内非线性应变的理论方法。基于 Timoshenko 梁假设,推导了非圆弧拱面内非线性应变-位移表达式,根据推导的非线性应变表达式和虚功原理,得到了悬链线拱面内非线性弹性屈曲和后屈曲的解析解。最后,将解析解与有限元计算结果进行了比较,验证了所提出的非线性应变。

1　面内非线性平衡方程

1.1　基本假定

为指导理论分析,本文基于以下基本假定:
(1)基于 Timoshenko 梁理论,剪应变为线性应变;
(2)只考虑平面内变形,不涉及面外位移和扭转;
(3)拱结构所用材料在整个屈曲过程中始终处于线弹性范围内;
(4)拱为承受填料自重荷载的理想拱结构。

1.2 面内非线性应变

图 1 为悬链线拱几何示意图，对悬链线拱分别建立了整体坐标系 oyz 和局部坐标系 $o*y*z*$。图 1a)中，f 为矢高；L 为拱的跨径；g 为填料自重荷载。图 2 为拱结构微元的变形图，其中 w 和 v 分别表示拱的水平位移和竖向位移；ψ、γ 和 ϕ 分别表示弯曲导致的转角、剪切变形导致的转角和结构总的转角；s 和 $s*$ 分别表示变形前曲线微元弧长和变形后曲线微元弧长。

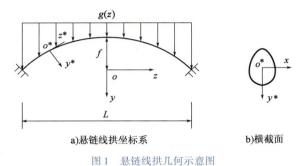

图 1　悬链线拱几何示意图
Fig. 1　Geometry of catenary arches

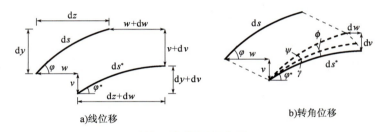

图 2　拱结构微元变形
Fig. 2　Deformation of differential element for arches

基于 Timoshenko 梁理论，拱结构的曲线微元的压缩应变 ε_m 可表示为

$$\varepsilon_m = \frac{\mathrm{d}s^* - \mathrm{d}s}{\mathrm{d}s} \tag{1}$$

根据变形前后曲线微元两端的位置变化关系可推导出拱的压缩应变-位移表达式为

$$\varepsilon_m = \frac{1}{1+y'^2}\left(w' + \frac{1}{2}v'^2 + v'y'\right) \tag{2}$$

式中：$(\cdot)' = \mathrm{d}(\cdot)/\mathrm{d}z$。

拱结构曲线微元的弯曲变形可表示为

$$\varepsilon_b = -y^* \Delta K \tag{3}$$

式中：ΔK——变形前后拱结构曲线微元的曲率变化，其表达式为

$$\Delta K = \frac{\mathrm{d}\varphi + \mathrm{d}\psi}{\mathrm{d}s^*} - \frac{\mathrm{d}\varphi}{\mathrm{d}s} \tag{4}$$

将式代入式，略去高阶小量，则弯曲应变-位移的表达式为

$$\varepsilon_b = -y^* \frac{\psi'}{(1+y'^2)^{1/4}} \tag{5}$$

拱结构曲线微元的转角 ϕ 由两部分组成,一部分是弯曲导致的转角 ψ,另一部分是剪切变形导致的转角 γ,因此结构转角位移的表达式可写成

$$\phi = \gamma + \psi \tag{6}$$

从图 2 可以看出,转角位移是变形前后曲线微元与水平线之间夹角的变化量,根据曲线微元与水平线夹角的几何定义,转角位移又可表示为

$$\phi = \arctan\frac{dy + dv}{dz + dw} - \arctan\frac{dy}{dz} \tag{7}$$

将式代入式,采用泰勒展开方法,则剪切应变可近似化简为

$$\gamma \approx \frac{v' - \psi}{(1 + y'^2)^{1/4}} \tag{8}$$

1.3 面内非线性平衡方程

在图 1 所示的全局坐标系 oyz 下,悬链线拱的拱轴线方程可表示为

$$y = \frac{f}{m-1}\left(\text{ch}\frac{2kz}{L} - 1\right) - f \tag{9}$$

式中:ch(·)——双曲余弦函数;
　　　m——悬链线拱轴系数,表达式为 $m = g_e/g_c$,g_e 和 g_c 分别表示填料自重荷载在悬链线拱脚和跨中位置的荷载集度;
　　　k——悬链线方程参数,表达式为 $k = \ln(m + \sqrt{m^2 - 1})$。基于虚功原理,笛卡儿坐标系下拱的面内非线性平衡微分方程为

$$\delta\Pi = \int_V \sigma_m \delta\varepsilon_m dV + \int_V \sigma_b \delta\varepsilon_b dV + \int_V \tau\,\delta\gamma dV - \int_{-\frac{L}{2}}^{\frac{L}{2}} g(z)\delta v dz = 0 \tag{10}$$

式中:$\delta(\cdot)$——(·)的变分;
　　　Π——悬链线拱总能量;
　　σ_m 和 σ_b——压缩应力和弯曲应力,表达式分别为 $\sigma_m = E\varepsilon_m$ 和 $\sigma_b = E\varepsilon_b$;
　　　E——拱材料的杨氏模量;
　　　V——悬链线拱的体积,且 $dV = Ads$;
　　　s——悬链线拱的轴线长度,且 $ds = \sqrt{1 + y'^2}\,dz$;
　　　A——悬链线拱横截面面积;
　　　τ——剪切应力,$\tau = \kappa G\gamma$;
　　　κ——横截面剪切系数;
　　　G——材料的剪切模量;
　　　g——悬链线拱的填料自重荷载,表达式为

$$g(z) = g_c \text{ch}\frac{2kz}{L} \tag{11}$$

$$\delta\Pi = \int_{-\frac{L}{2}}^{\frac{L}{2}} -\left(\frac{EA\varepsilon_m}{\sqrt{1+y'^2}}\right)'(\delta w)dz + \int_{-\frac{L}{2}}^{\frac{L}{2}}\left[-EI_x\psi'' - \kappa GA(v'-\psi)\right](\delta\psi)dz + \\ \int_{-\frac{L}{2}}^{\frac{L}{2}}\left[-\left(\frac{EA\varepsilon_m v'}{\sqrt{1+y'^2}}\right)' - \left(\frac{EA\varepsilon_m y'}{\sqrt{1+y'^2}}\right)' - \kappa GA(v''-\psi') - g_c\text{ch}\frac{2kz}{L}\right](\delta v)dz = 0 \tag{12}$$

式中:I_x——x轴的截面惯性矩,可表示为 $I_x = \int_A y^{*2} dA$。基于虚位移 δw、δv 和 $\delta \psi$ 的任意性原理,可从式中推导得到水平方向的平衡微分方程

$$-\left(\frac{EA\varepsilon_m}{\sqrt{1+y'^2}}\right)' = 0 \tag{13}$$

竖直方向的平衡方程

$$-\left(\frac{EA\varepsilon_m v'}{\sqrt{1+y'^2}}\right)' - \left(\frac{EA\varepsilon_m y'}{\sqrt{1+y'^2}}\right)' - \kappa GA(v'' - \psi') - g_c \text{ch}\frac{2kz}{L} = 0 \tag{14}$$

和转动方向的平衡方程

$$-EI_x \psi'' - \kappa GA v' + \kappa GA \psi = 0 \tag{15}$$

式中,$(\cdot)'' = d^2(\cdot)/dz^2$。基于悬链线拱理论,根据水平方向的平衡微分方程式,可以得到

$$\begin{cases} N = -EA\varepsilon_m \\ \dfrac{EA\varepsilon_m}{\sqrt{1+y'^2}} = -H = \text{constant} \end{cases} \tag{16}$$

式中:N——悬链线拱的非线性轴力;

H——悬链线拱拱脚非线性水平反力。可得考虑剪切变形的悬链线拱面内非线性平衡微分方程

$$\begin{cases} \dfrac{1}{\mu^2}\psi''' + \psi' = \dfrac{\overline{\omega}}{p}\text{ch}\dfrac{2kz}{L} \\ v' = \psi - \chi\psi'' \end{cases} \tag{17}$$

式中,$(\cdot)''' = d^3(\cdot)/dz^3$;$\chi = EI_x/\kappa GA$;$p = (m-1)(L/2k)^2/f$;$\overline{\omega} = (pg_c - H)/H$;$\mu = \sqrt{(H/EI_x)[1/(1-H/\kappa GA)]}$。对于悬链线无铰拱,边界条件为

$$w|_{z=\pm\frac{L}{2}} = 0, \quad v|_{z=\pm\frac{L}{2}} = 0, \quad \psi|_{z=\pm\frac{L}{2}} = 0 \tag{18}$$

基于无铰拱的边界条件式,考虑剪切变形的悬链线拱面内非线性平衡微分方程的解为

$$\begin{cases} \psi = \dfrac{\overline{\omega}\mu^2 L^3}{2kp(4k^2+L^2\mu^2)}\left(\text{sh}\dfrac{2kz}{L} - \dfrac{\text{sh}k\sin\mu z}{\sin\theta}\right) \\ v = \dfrac{\overline{\omega}\theta L^2}{pk^2(4k^2+4\theta^2)}\left[\theta\left(\text{ch}\dfrac{2kz}{L} - m\right)\left(1 - \dfrac{4\chi k^2}{L^2}\right) + k\text{sh}k\left(1 + \dfrac{4\chi\theta^2}{L^2}\right)\left(\dfrac{\cos\dfrac{2\theta z}{L} - \cos\theta}{\sin\theta}\right)\right] \end{cases} \tag{19}$$

式中:$\theta = \mu L/2$;

sh($\cdot$)——双曲正弦函数。

式中存在互相耦合的未知参数 μ 和 ω,需另一个方程进行求解。根据式计算得到的压缩应变必须与式在跨径 $-L/2$ 至 $L/2$ 上计算得到的平均压缩应变相等,基于此应变相等原则可以得到另一方程为

$$\int_{-\frac{L}{2}}^{\frac{L}{2}} -\frac{H}{EA}(1+y'^2)^{3/2} dz = \int_{-\frac{L}{2}}^{\frac{L}{2}} \left(w' + \frac{1}{2}v'^2 + v'y'\right) dz \tag{20}$$

基于 Hu[18] 提出的近似曲线积分方法,则将面内非线性平衡方程求解可得到

$$A\bar{\omega}^2 + B\bar{\omega} + C = 0 \tag{21}$$

式中:系数 A、B 和 C 分别为

$$A = \frac{k^2\theta^4}{8(m-1)^2(k^2+\theta^2)^2}\left[\left(1+\frac{\theta^2}{\eta}\right)^2\frac{(2\theta-\sin2\theta)\operatorname{sh}^2k}{4\theta\sin^2\theta} - \left(1-\frac{k^2}{\eta}\right)^2\frac{2k-\operatorname{sh}^2k}{4k} - \left(1-\frac{k^2}{\eta}\right)\left(1+\frac{\theta^2}{\eta}\right)\frac{2\operatorname{sh}k}{k^2+\theta^2}(mk-\theta\cot\theta\operatorname{sh}k)\right] \tag{22}$$

$$B = \frac{k^2\theta^2}{4(m-1)^2(k^2+\theta^2)}\left[\left(1-\frac{k^2}{\eta}\right)\left(\frac{\operatorname{sh}^2k}{4k}-\frac{1}{2}\right) - \left(1+\frac{\theta^2}{\eta}\right)\frac{\operatorname{sh}k}{k^2+\theta^2}(mk-\theta\cot\theta\operatorname{sh}k)\right] \tag{23}$$

$$C = \frac{\xi}{1+\theta^2/\eta}\left(\frac{\theta}{\lambda}\right)^2 \tag{24}$$

式中:λ——悬链线拱的修正长细比,$\lambda = 2f/i_x$;

i_x——横截面对 x 轴的回转半径,$i_x = \sqrt{I_x/A}$;

η——剪切效应参数,定义为 $\eta = \kappa GA(L/2)^2/EI_x$;

ξ——矢跨比相关参数,表达式为

$$\xi = \frac{a}{6L}\left(9\operatorname{sh}\frac{L}{2a} + \operatorname{sh}\frac{3L}{2a}\right) \tag{25}$$

2 有限元验证

为验证提出的笛卡儿坐标系下拱结构面内非线性压缩应变、弯曲应变和剪切应变,将推导得到的解析解与有限元结果进行比较。以箱形截面悬链线拱为例,箱形截面的高度、宽度、腹板厚度和顶底板厚度分别为 500mm、400mm、40mm 和 30mm;悬链线拱的拱轴线系数为 $m = 1.988$,矢跨比为 $f/L = 1/8$,剪切效应参数为 $\eta = 500$;材料的杨氏模量为 $E = 210$GPa,泊松比为 $v = 0.2$。提出的解析方法和有限元方法得到的无量纲荷载位移曲线和屈曲行为曲线的比较如图 3 所示。图 3 中 N_{E2} 为考虑剪切变形影响的同跨径等效固接柱体的二阶失稳临界力。

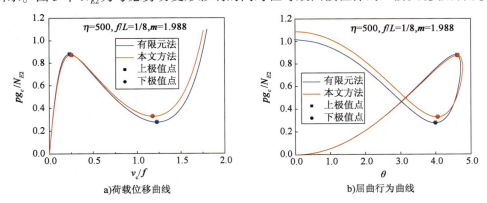

a) 荷载位移曲线   b) 屈曲行为曲线

图 3 验证提出的解析

Fig. 3 Verification of proposed solutions

从图3中可以看出,对于屈曲前的非线性平衡路径,本文提出的解析方法与有限元方法的计算结果吻合较好;屈曲后,随着位移的不断增大,本文提出的解析法与有限元法的误差逐渐增大,达到后屈曲阶段则误差较大,与有限元结果存在较为明显的偏离。对于实际拱桥工程,屈曲前拱的状态是我们关注的重点,本文提出的近似解析可以高精度预测拱在屈曲前的位移与内力状态,能够满足实际工程需要,具备一定的实用价值。

为进一步验证本文提出的非线性应变与解析解,在如表1所示的更大参数范围内将本文方法与有限元方法的结果进行对比,表1所示的参数范围较大,可以包含实际拱桥工程中常用的拱。对比结果如图4所示,从图4可以看出,在大参数范围内,本文提出的解析方法与有限元结果吻合较好,本文提出的非线性应变具有足够的精度,在考虑剪切变形的情况下,可以在笛卡儿坐标系下推导出足够精确的拱结构面内非线性稳定解析解。

参 数 验 证 范 围　　　　　　　表1
Parameter ranges of verification　　Tab.1

参　数	f/L	η	m
上限值	1/7	2000	2.814
下限值	1/12.5	87	1.167

注:f/L为矢跨比;η为剪切效应参数;m为拱轴线系数。

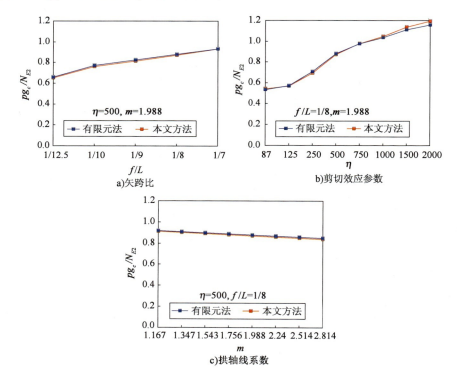

图4　大参数范围验证
Fig.4　Verification in large parameter range

3　结论

（1）推导得到了笛卡儿坐标系下拱的面内非线性压缩应变、弯曲应变与剪切应变表达式；

（2）基于得到的非线性应变表达式，可以推导出笛卡儿坐标系下考虑剪切变形的拱结构面内非线性稳定解析解；

（3）基于非线性应变表达式推导的拱结构面内非线性稳定解析解具有较高的精度，可以准确预测拱屈曲前的状态，能够满足实际工程需要。

参 考 文 献

[1] Pi Y L, Bradford M A, Uy B. In-plane stability of arches[J]. International Journal of Solids and Structures, 2002, 39(1):105-125.

[2] Bradford M A, Uy B, Pi Y L. In-plane elastic stability of arches under a central concentrated load[J]. Journal of Engineering Mechanics, ASCE, 2002, 128(7):710-719.

[3] Lu H W, Liu A R, Pi Y L, et al. Localized loading and nonlinear instability and post-instability of fixed arches[J]. Thin-Walled Structures, 2018, 131:165-178.

[4] Yang Z C, Huang Y H, Liu A R, et al. Nonlinear in-plane buckling of fixed shallow functionally graded graphene reinforced composite arches subjected to mechanical and thermal loading[J]. Applied Mathematical Modelling, 2019, 70:315-327.

[5] Tong G S, Zhang L. The transverse stresses in thin-walled beams and its effect on strength and stability[J]. Advances in Structural Engineering. 2003, 6(2):159-167.

[6] Tong G S, Pi Y L, Bradford M A, et al. In-plane nonlinear buckling analysis of deep circular arches incorporating transverse stresses[J]. Journal of Engineering Mechanics. 2008, 134(5):362-373.

[7] Babaei H, Kiani Y, Eslami M R. Geometrically nonlinear analysis of shear de-formable FGM shallow pinned arches on nonlinear elastic foundation under mechanical and thermal loads[J]. Acta Mechanical. 2018, 229:3123-3141.

[8] Lu H W, Liu A R, Pi Y L, et al. Flexural-torsional buckling of steel arches under a localized uniform radial-load incorporating shear deformations[J]. Journal of Structural Engineering, ASCE, 2019, 145(10):04019117.

[9] Lu H W, Liu A R, Pi Y L, et al. Lateral-torsional buckling of arches under an arbitrary radial point load in a thermal environment incorporating shear deformations[J]. Engineering Structures. 2019, 179:189-203.

[10] Zhang Z X, Liu A R, Yang J, et al. Nonlinear in-plane buckling of shallow laminated arches incorporating shear deformation under a uniform radial loading[J]. Composite Structures, 2020, 252:112732.

[11] Bradford M A, Wang T, Pi Y L, et al. In-plane stability of parabolic arches with horizontal spring supports. I: Theory[J]. Journal of Structural Engineering, ASCE, 2007, 133(8):

1130-1137.

[12] Wang T, Bradford M A, Gilbert R I, et al. In-plane stability of parabolic arches with horizontal spring supports. Ⅱ: Experiments[J]. Journal of Structural Engineering, ASCE, 2007,133(8):1138-1145.

[13] Bradford M A, Pi Y L, Yang G T, et al. Effects of approximations on non-linear in-plane elastic buckling and postbuckling analyses of shallow parabolic arches[J]. Engineering Structures,2015,101:58-67.

[14] Hu C F, Pi Y L, Gao W, et al. In-plane non-linear elastic stability of parabolic arches with different rise-to-span ratios[J]. Thin-Walled Structures,2018,129:74-84.

[15] Hu C F, Huang Y M. In-plane nonlinear elastic stability of pin-ended parabolic multi-span continuous arches[J]. Engineering Structures,2019,190:435-446.

[16] Hu C F, Li Z, Liu Z W, et al. In-plane non-linear elastic stability of arch-es subjected to multi-pattern distributed load[J]. Thin-Walled Structures,2020,154:106810.

[17] Hu C F, Li Z, Hu Q S. On non-linear behavior and buckling of arch-beam structures[J]. Engineering Structures,2021,239:112214.

[18] Hu C F, Wan Y, Shangguan X. A new practice in the design of arch axis[C]//Chen B C, Wei J G. Proceedings of the 6th International Conference on Arch Bridges. Fuzhou,2010: 709-715.

设计与结构分析

600m级劲性骨架混凝土拱桥足尺模型试验

黄 酉　罗小斌　沈 耀　匡志强

(广西路桥工程集团有限公司　广西南宁　530011)

摘　要　以天峨龙滩特大桥外包混凝土施工分项工程为主,依托模型试验,验证外包混凝土施工工艺、模板设计及操作流程的可行性。试验方式采用足尺模型试验,同时严格按照实际施工流程,进行管内混凝土灌注及外包混凝土的施工,实时记录数据,形成影像资料。试验结果表明,采用已有的模板与施工工艺,基本能够满足天峨龙滩特大桥外包混凝土的施工,但仍需优化模板设计,细化施工操作,精化施工流程。本次足尺模型试验,为天峨龙滩特大桥外包混凝土施工提供了施工经验,指明了模板设计、施工工艺优化方向,对实际施工有很好的指导作用。

关键词　600m级劲性骨架混凝土拱桥　足尺模型　外包混凝土　模板设计　施工流程

中图分类号　TU398[+].9　　**文献标识码**　A

Full-scale Model Test of 600m-level Rigid Skeleton Concrete Arch Bridge

HUANG You　LUO Xiaobin　SHEN Yao　KUANG Zhiqiang

(Guangxi Road and Bridge Engineering Group Co., Ltd., Nanning, Guangxi, 530011, China)

Abstract　Focusing on the sub-project of outsourcing concrete construction of Tian'e Longtan Bridge, relying on model tests to verify the feasibility of outsourcing concrete construction technology, formwork design and operation process. The test method adopts a full-scale model test, and at the same time, in strict accordance with the actual construction process, the concrete pouring in the pipe and the construction of the outsourcing concrete are carried out, the data is recorded in real time, and the image data is formed. The test results show that the existing formwork and construction technology can basically meet the construction of the outsourcing concrete of the Tian'e Longtan Bridge, but it is still necessary to optimize the formwork design, refine the construction operation, and refine the construction process. This full-scale model test provides construction experience for the outsourcing concrete construction of Tian'e

---

作者简介：
黄酉(1998—),男,学士,助理工程师,主要从事大跨度拱桥施工技术研发及管理方面的研究。
罗小斌(1985—),男,学士,高级工程师,主要从事大跨度拱桥施工技术研发及管理方面的研究。
沈耀(1978—),男,学士,高级工程师,主要从事大跨度拱桥施工技术研发及管理方面的研究。
匡志强(1991—),男,学士,工程师,主要从事大跨度拱桥施工技术研发及管理方面的研究。

Longtan Bridge, points out the direction of template design and construction process optimization, and has a good guiding role for actual construction.

Keywords 600m-level rigid skeleton concrete arch bridge full-scale model outsourced concrete template design construction flow

E-mail 1484567051@qq.com

0 引言

天峨龙滩特大桥主桥为跨径600m上承式劲性骨架混凝土拱桥(图1),矢高125m,矢跨比$f=1/4.8$,是世界第一跨度的劲性骨架钢管混凝土拱桥,建成后将刷新世界拱桥建造纪录(图1)。主拱圈外包混凝土设计强度C60,总方量近3万m^3,体量位居同类桥型之冠。钢筋混凝土拱桥具有原材料价格低廉、后期养护费用低、潜在承载力大等优点,是今后拱桥朝大跨径发展的一个方向[1]。钢筋混凝土拱桥向大跨径发展面临着有两个关键问题:一是混凝土自重大,因此有效地减轻结构自身重量是重要的研究方向;二是施工方法,混凝土拱桥施工方案的合理性和可行性直接影响拱桥方案能否成立、能否被采用[2]。

天峨龙滩特大桥施工难度大,且缺乏可借鉴经验。故展开足尺模型试验,在验证方案可行性的同时,也从实际施工中汲取不足,进一步优化方案,为实桥施工打下坚实的基础。

图1 天峨龙滩特大桥效果图
Fig. 1 Rendering of Tian'e Longtan Bridge

1 工程背景

1.1 桥梁概况

天峨龙滩特大桥跨径600m,矢高125m,外包混凝土采用C60,设计方量28000m^3;主桥拱圈为左右单独拱肋箱室,拱脚截面径向高12m,拱顶截面径向高8m,箱宽6.5m,肋间横向中心距16.5m,总宽23m;左右箱室通过箱型横联及横撑连接成整体。

1.2 足尺节段模型施工方案

根据桥梁结构形式,选取了拱顶13m段劲性骨架作为试验节段进行1∶1足尺模型试验。试验节段长13m、高8m、宽6.5m,安装角度15°,配筋及钢管材质、尺寸与实桥相同。试验总用钢量59.6t,管内C80混凝土用量34m^3,外包C60混凝土用量240m^3。

其中模型外包混凝土施工亦按照主桥方案,分底板、腹板、顶板三环施工。

施工地点于南天5标向阳服务区,先将劲性骨架片装运送至向阳服务区,并在向阳服务区进行焊接总成,然后在C30混凝土基础上进行施工。施工完成后对足尺节段模型进行切割,验证管内及外包混凝土是否密实,或者出现何种缺陷,以此优化混凝土配合比、施工操作(图2、图3)。

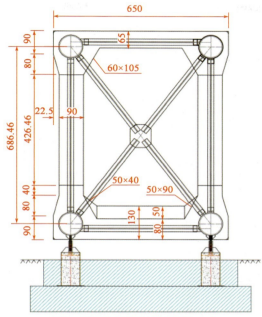

图2 模型横断面图(尺寸单位:cm)
Fig. 2 Model section view(Unit:cm)

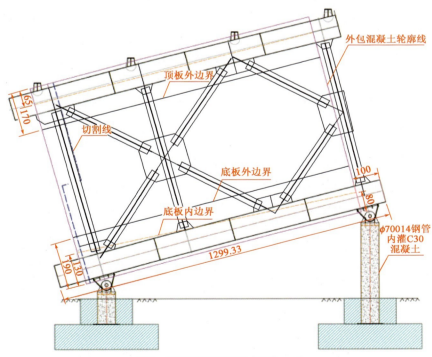

图3 模型纵断面图(尺寸单位:cm)
Fig. 3 Model vertical Section(Unit:cm)

105

2 主要研究内容及成果

2.1 C60外包混凝土性能

通过室内及现场试验,考察水胶比、胶凝材料总量、水泥用量、矿物掺和料比例、砂率,以及膨胀剂掺入等因素对混凝土性能的影响,以及原材料优选等措施,提出主拱管内及外包高性能混凝土制备方法,获得满足工作性能、抗裂性能等要求混凝土配合比。

现场试验混凝土配备比基本满足施工要求,工作性能较好,且混凝土外观平整,对于混凝土抗压强度及弹性模量均符合设计要求(图4、图5)。

试验段混凝土抗压强度				
序号	试验部位	取样日期	28d抗压强度(MPa)	60d抗压强度(MPa)
1	C60外包混凝土底板	2022/3/18	68.4	76.2
2	C60外包混凝土腹板	2022/4/11	68.8	
3	C60外包混凝土顶板	2022/5/25	62.3	

图4 混凝土抗压强度监测

Fig. 4 Concrete compressive strength monitoring

序号	混凝土标号	取样日期	技术要求	3d弹性模量(MPa)	7d弹性模量(MPa)	11d弹性模量(MPa)	14d弹性模量(MPa)	28d弹性模量(MPa)	60d弹性模量(MPa)
1	C60外包混凝土	2022/3/18	≥36000	35900	39800	42100	43500	44000	47900
			抗压强度	51.3	53.6	55.1	56.2	64.1	72.0

图5 混凝土弹性模量监测

Fig. 5 Monitoring of elastic modulus of concrete

2.2 模板施工

基于主桥实际情况,研究制定足尺模型的试验方案,提出底板环、腹板环、顶板环一整套模板体系。

试验结果表明,现有模板体系基本满足施工要求,但对于拱脚端模需要进行加强处理,防止漏浆;腹板端压模则需要做简化处理,方便浇筑振捣后及时安装。

底板箱内模板横梁过重,试验段施工虽然有随车吊辅助施工,并不困难,但实桥施工塔吊任务过于繁重,难以满足频繁的搬运工作,故需对横梁进行改进。现将横梁进行分段处理,采用三段式横梁(图6),倒角连接处通过螺栓紧固的形式进行连接,极大方便工人搬运及施工。

腹板大块模板背楞连接,试验段采用的是螺栓连接的方式,这种连接方式在实际施工中,受到多种因素的影响,往往导致孔洞难以对齐,从而造成施工过于繁琐。经与劳务队商讨,现进行优化,改螺栓连接为贴钢板焊接,施工完成后进行切割,此施工方式受制约因素较少,简单有效,省去了开孔的繁琐。

顶板模板施工时,由于先安装模板再安装钢筋,试验段施工往往出现钢筋抵住模板的情况。

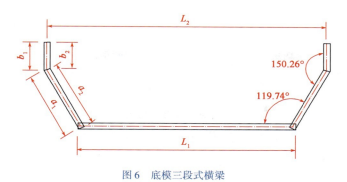

图6 底模三段式横梁

Fig. 6 Three section cross beam of bottom formwork

2.3 施工平台

首先对吊架进行优化,在不影响施工操作空间的前提下,缩小吊架的尺寸,同时对结构进行优化,主承重桁片斜杆使用方通,减轻吊架的自重,不仅能够节省材料,提高效益,还能方便吊运安装。同时吊架横梁原设计采用型钢,经过优化后采用圆管的形式,方便吊架的横移,满足安装钢筋及模板,对施工空间不同的需求(图7)。

对于顶板施工悬挂平台,原设计采用焊接的方式,这样不利于平台的拆卸和周转使用。后续调整为平台与顶横梁连接由焊接设计改为螺栓固定,方便平台的拆卸及调整。

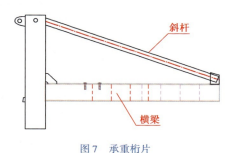

图7 承重桁片

Fig. 7 Load bearing member

3 结论

天峨龙滩特大桥足尺节段试验模型,得出的结论如下:
(1)C60混凝土配合比满足施工要求,可以运用到实桥上。
(2)现有外包混凝土施工方案对于实桥的施工可行性较高,基本可以满足实际施工要求。
(3)设计的模板体系经受住了考验,基本满足施工要求,但仍需进行优化,解决漏浆、模板桁架过重的问题。

参 考 文 献

[1] 项海帆.高等桥梁结构理论[M].北京:人民交通出版社.2001.
[2] 朱波.大跨径钢筋混凝土拱桥悬臂浇筑施工控制技术研究[D].重庆:重庆交通大学,2012.

核心混凝土初始缺陷下钢管混凝土栓焊节点偏压力学性能研究

云惟经　于　鹏*

（广西大学土木建筑工程学院/工程防灾与结构安全教育部重点实验室/
广西防灾减灾与工程安全重点实验室　广西南宁　530004）

摘　要　基于钢管混凝土拱桥拱肋新型栓焊连接设计及管内核心混凝土两种常见脱空形式，进行了不同核心混凝土初始缺陷（球冠形、月牙形）和偏心距下钢管混凝土栓焊节点偏压缩尺试验，考察失效模式、荷载-位移曲线等力学性能指标。建立了有限元模型，并通过试验结果验证其准确性。结果表明：建立的数值模型具有准确性；球冠形、月牙形脱空试件失效模式较为相近；脱空率、偏心率越大，荷载降低程度越大。

关键词　钢管混凝土　栓焊节点　初始缺陷　偏压　力学性能

Effects of Core Concrete Initial Imperfection on Performance of Eccentrically Loaded CFST with Bolt-Welded Joint

YUN Weijing　YU Peng*

(School of Civil and Architectural Engineering of Guangxi University/Key Laboratory of Disaster Prevention and Structural Safety of the Ministry of Education/Guangxi Key Laboratory of Disaster Prevention and Structural Safety, Nanning, Guangxi, 530004, China)

Abstract　Based on the new bolt-welded connection method for arch ribs of long-span concrete filled steel tube (CFST) arch bridge and two common gap forms of core concrete in tubes of arch ribs, this paper conducted eccentric

---

基金项目：广西创新驱动重大专项，超大跨径钢管混凝土拱桥的材料、装备、设计及施工技术创新与示范（桂科 AA18118055）；广西重点研发计划，特大跨劲性骨架混凝土拱桥建造关键技术（桂科 AB22036007）；广西高校引进海外高层次人才"百人计划"；青年人才托举工程（YESS20210178）。

作者简介：
云惟经（1996—），男，硕士研究生，主要从事钢管混凝土方面的研究。
于鹏*（1987—），男，助理教授，博士，主要从事超大跨径拱桥组合构件等方面的研究。

compression scale tests of CFST column joints under different core concrete initial imperfection (spherical-cap imperfection and interfacial imperfection) and eccentric distances, and the mechanical properties such as the failure modes and the load-displacement curve were investigated. The numerical simulations were carried out and the finite element model was validated with experimental data. The results show that the established numerical model is precise, and the failure modes of the CFST bolt-welded joint with spherical-cap imperfection and interfacial imperfection are relatively. The greater the gap ratio and eccentricity, the greater the load reduction.

Keywords CFST bolt-welded joint initial imperfection eccentric compression mechanical properties

E-mail guoxiao7868@163.com

0 引言

在钢管混凝土拱桥施工过程中,由于核心混凝土灌注方量较大,且拱圈倾斜,管内核心混凝土密实性较难保证,容易出现管内核心混凝土脱空现象,而对于钢管混凝土拱桥拱肋,常见脱空类型主要为球冠形脱空和月牙形脱空[1]。对于核心混凝土脱空的研究,针对钢管混凝土竖直构件主要研究缺陷为周边脱空[2-4];对于拱肋及桁架结构,主要研究球冠型脱空[5-6]。其中叶勇等[7]提出了不同脱空率下钢管混凝土构件抗剪计算方法;Chen 等[8]同时研究了拱肋球冠形和月牙形两种脱空缺陷,提出了随机初始缺陷的可靠性和相关的系统阻力系数。

随着拱桥在低温低压的川藏地区[9]的广泛应用,拱肋新型栓焊节点设计方案得以提出,而关于脱空缺陷对此节点力学性能的影响的研究较少,因此本文开展了两种脱空缺陷下(球冠形、月牙形)钢管混凝土栓焊节点偏压力学性能研究,讨论不同缺陷对构件偏压力学性能的影响(图1)。

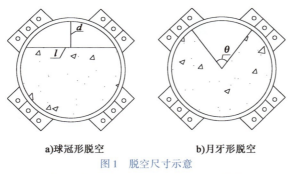

a) 球冠形脱空　　　　　b) 月牙形脱空
图1 脱空尺寸示意
Fig.1 Size of concrete imperfection in CFST

1 试验研究

1.1 试验概况

试件的尺寸信息如表1所示,其中 D 为钢管外径,H 为构件高度,t 为钢管厚度,d 为钢管内壁到脱空处的垂直距离,l 为脱空长度。球冠形脱空采用 PVC 板放置在钢管内,浇筑混凝土时起到隔板作用;月牙形脱空采用钢管内壁涂油处理[10],使核心混凝土与钢管脱黏。钢管强度 Q420,混凝土强度 C50,通过材性试验测得钢管屈服强度 623MPa,混凝土立方体抗压强度 50.44MPa。脱空尺寸示意如图1所示。

试 件 信 息 表　　　　　　表1
Information of Specimens　　　Tab. 1

编 号	$D×t$(mm)	$d×l$(mm)	脱空率$χ$(%)	脱空角度$θ$(°)	偏心距e(mm)	H(mm)
W1	219×8	—	—	—	40	810
S1	219×8	5×63	2.3	—	40	810
S2	219×8	10×88	4.6	—	40	810
S3	219×8	15×106	6.9	—	40	810
I1	219×8	—	—	180	8	810
I2	219×8	—	—	180	40	810
I3	219×8	—	—	180	70	810

1.2 试验结果

1.2.1 失效模式

以偏心40mm为例,试件失效模式如图2所示。球冠形、月牙形脱空缺陷的破坏形态与无缺陷相似,试件均为中上、下部及端部鼓曲为主,中部因法兰和加劲板的存在,节点强度、刚度提升,鼓曲转移至中上部及中下部,可见节点失效模式主要取决于外部钢管及栓焊节点。

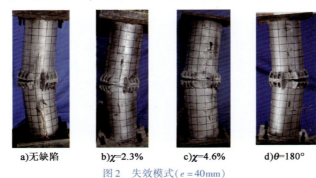

a)无缺陷　　b)$χ$=2.3%　　c)$χ$=4.6%　　d)$θ$=180°

图2　失效模式(e=40mm)
Fig. 2　Failure Modes(e=40mm)

1.2.2 荷载-位移曲线

不同核心混凝土脱空缺陷下钢管混凝土栓焊节点偏压试验结果如图3所示。月牙形脱空缺陷的荷载-位移曲线弹性段相似,只是峰值荷载有所不同,偏心距越大,峰值荷载越低;球冠形脱空下,脱空率越大,荷载降低程度越大。

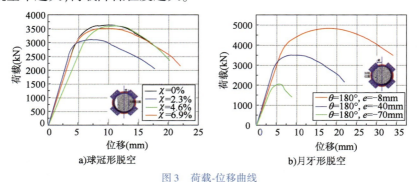

a)球冠形脱空　　　　　　b)月牙形脱空

图3　荷载-位移曲线
Fig. 3　Load-displacement curve

2 数值模拟

2.1 有限元模型

采用 ABAQUS 有限元软件对不同核心混凝土脱空(无缺陷、球冠形脱空、月牙形脱空)钢管混凝土柱偏压力学性能进行分析。模型如图 4 所示。钢管本构采用材性试验数据,混凝土采用 CDP 模型,拉伸模型采用沈聚敏等[11]提出的本构,压缩采用韩林海等[12]提出的套箍本构。钢与混凝土法向为"硬接触",切向摩擦系数 0.6,对于月牙形脱空,脱空位置设置为无摩擦,以模拟脱黏情况;压头采用固接,其中一端压头释放轴向位移自由度并施加位移。

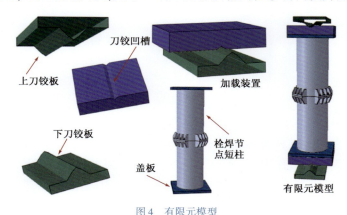

图 4 有限元模型
Fig. 4 Finite Element Model

2.2 模型验证

试验与仿真失效模式及荷载-位移曲线对比如图 5、图 6 所示,模型节点受拉破坏情况与试验现象拟合较好,荷载-位移曲线拟合情况较好。由于仿真模型材质较为均匀,未发生局部明显鼓曲的情况,且模型承载力及延性均高于试验结果。

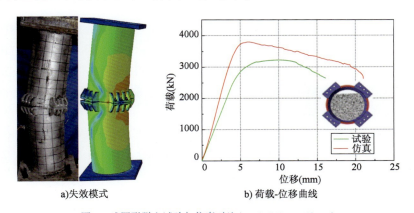

a)失效模式   b)荷载-位移曲线

图 5 球冠形脱空试验与仿真对比($x=2.3\%$, $e=40mm$)
Fig. 5 The comparison between the test and simulation of the spherical-cap imperfection ($x=2.3\%$, $e=40mm$)

月牙形脱空模型节点失效模式及荷载-位移曲线均与试验结果拟合较好。由于仿真模型材质较为均匀,刚度更大,仿真曲线弹性段斜率大于试验曲线,且仿真承载力及延性均高于试验结果。综上可认为本文所建立的数值模型有一定的准确性。

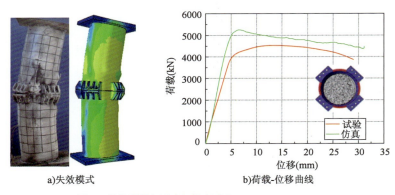

a)失效模式 b)荷载-位移曲线

图6　月牙形脱空试验与仿真对比($\theta=180°$, $e=8$mm)

Fig. 6　The comparison between the test and simulation of the interfacial imperfection($\theta=180°$, $e=8$mm)

3　结论

本文通过对比拱桥常见两种脱空形式(球冠形、月牙形)对栓焊节点偏压力学性能的影响,得到以下结论:偏心荷载作用下,随着脱空率、偏心距的大,钢管混凝土栓焊连接短柱峰值荷载逐渐减小;栓焊节点失效模式主要与栓焊节点及钢管有关,脱空形式对构件失效模式影响不大;本文建立的数值模型具有一定的准确性,可为后续核心混凝土脱空下的钢管混凝土节点力学性能研究提供参考。

参 考 文 献

［1］郑皆连,等. 500米级钢管混凝土拱桥建造创新技术［M］. 上海:上海科学技术出版社,2020.

［2］Lu Zhengran, Guo Chao, Li Guochang. Air void and ring gap effect on CFST arch bridges dynamic performance［J］. Journal of Constructional Steel Research, 2021, 177106418.

［3］Liao Feiyu, Han Linhai, He Shanhu. Behavior of CFST short column and beam with initial concrete imperfection: Experiments［J］. Journal of constructional steel research, 2011, 67(12): 1922-1935.

［4］Liao Feiyu, Han Linhai, Tao Zhong. Behaviour of CFST stub columns with initial concrete imperfection: Analysis and calculations［J］. Thin-walled structures, 2013, 7057-69.

［5］Han Linhai, Yong Ye, Liao Feiyu. Effects of Core Concrete Initial Imperfection on Performance of Eccentrically Loaded CFST Columns［J］. Journal of Structural Engineering, 2016, 142(12).

［6］Ye Yong, Li Wei, Liu Xiaojuan, et al. Behaviour of concrete-filled steel tubes with concrete imperfection under axial tension［J］. Magazine of Concrete Research, 2021, 73(14): 743-756.

［7］叶勇,韩林海,陶忠.脱空对圆钢管混凝土受剪性能的影响分析［J］.工程力学,2016,33

(S1):62-66.
[8] Chen Silin, Hou Chao, Zhang Hao, et al. Structural behaviour and reliability of CFST trusses with random initial imperfections[J]. Thin-Walled Structures, 2019, 143.
[9] 陈正,陈犇,郑皆连,等.青藏高原低气压环境下钢管混凝土的核心混凝土密实性评估方法研究[J].土木工程学报,2021,54(08):1-13.
[10] Huang Yonghui, Liu Airong, Fu Jiyang, et al. Experimental investigation of the flexural behavior of CFST trusses with interfacial imperfection[J]. Journal of Constructional Steel Research, 2017, 137:52-65.
[11] 沈聚敏,等.钢筋混凝土有限元与板壳极限分析[M].北京:清华大学出版社,1993.
[12] 韩林海.钢管混凝土结构[M].北京:科学出版社,2004.

A Study on the Strength and Fatigue Properties of Seven-Wire Strands in Hangers under Lateral Bending

ZHOU Yiming[1] DENG Nianchun[1,2,3]* YANG Tao[1,2,3]*

(1. College of Civil Engineering and Architecture, Guangxi University, Nanning, Guangxi, 530004, China;
2. Guangxi Key Laboratory of Disaster Prevention and Engineering Safety, Nanning, Guangxi, 530004, China;
3. Key Laboratory of Disaster Prevention and Structural Safety of Ministry of Education, Nanning, Guangxi, 530004, China)

Abstract Hangers are important tensile members in half-through arch bridges and through arch bridges (HTABs and TABs). The floating deck structures of HTABs and TABs will commonly produce longitudinal deformation and rotate under the effect of temperature and the temperature gradient, which will cause bending deformation at anchorages of fixed-end hangers. This bending deformation can generate adverse bending stress for hangers and decrease the strength and fatigue properties of the seven-wire strands in the hangers. Firstly, theoretical derivation and finite element analysis are conducted to study the bending stress of hangers that is caused by bending deformation. We find that bending stress of hangers is mainly generated by lateral bending caused by the difference in longitudinal displacement at both ends of the hangers under the effect of temperature. Subsequently, the ultimate tensile strength of the seven-wire strands under lateral bending is obtained by FEM and an experimental study. The ultimate tensile strength of the seven-wire strands could decrease by 23.3% when lateral bending is considered. Moreover, the relationship between the fatigue properties of the seven-wire strands and lateral bending is obtained based on observing the ultimate tensile strength under lateral bending. Lateral bending significantly influences the fatigue properties of the seven-wire strands. When the lateral bending angle reaches about 50 mrad, the fatigue resistance of the seven-wire strands drop by almost 40%. The considerable decrease in the strength and fatigue properties of the seven-wire strands indicates that lateral bending has a significant adverse influence on hangers that consist of seven-wire strands. Finally, it is advised to use the tied arch structure for HTABs and TABs to mitigate the adverse influence of lateral bending on hangers.

Keywords hangers lateral bending seven-wire strands strength fatigue properties
E-mail yiming. zhou@ research. uwa. edu. au

0 Introduction

In half-through and through arch bridges (HTABs and TABs), bridge decks are connected to arch ribs by hangers. Hangers transfer loads from the bridge decks to the arch ribs and they are arranged evenly along the longitudinal directions of bridges to transmit the load on the bridge decks to the arch ribs uniformly. HTABs and TABs have long been considered to be safe and reliable structural patterns. However, in the past few decades, many HTABs and TABs with floating deck structures have failed due to the sudden failure of their hangers[1-3], such as Nanmen Bridge (2001) (as shown in Fig. 1a), Peacock River Bridge (2011), Gongguan Bridge (2011), and Nanfang'ao Bridge (2019).

It is clear that corrosion and fatigue are the main factors that lead to the fracture of tension-resisting elements in hangers and further cause the sudden failures of bridge hangers[4-7]. In recent years, some scholars have suggested that, besides corrosion and fatigue, the bending deformation of bothend-fixed hangers might be an important factor in the sudden failure of hangers[8-10]. The bending stress that is caused by the bending deformation (as shown in Fig. 1b) of hangers could accelerate the corrosion rates of the tension-resisting elements in hangers and, therefore, shorten the lives of hangers significantly[11-13]. However, bending stress is difficult to correctly measure in hangers using sensors and few numerical studies have been conducted on bending stress. Therefore, it remains di cult to further study the effect of bending on the corrosion and fatigue of hangers. Besides bending stress, the strength and fatigue properties of tension-resisting elements under bending are poorly understood; these elements may be greatly weakened by bending deformation, but only a few scholars have studied this topic. The neglect of the decrease on properties of tension-resisting elements in hangers might lead the safety of hangers is overrated under bending.

a) Fracture of hangers of half-through and through arch bridges (HTABs and TABs)

b) Hangers under lateral bending

Fig. 1 Complicated loading states of hangers in HTABs and TABs

According the above literature review, it is of great necessity to conduct a detailed study on the bending stress of hangers and the strength and fatigue properties of tension-resisting elements in hangers under bending deformation. In this paper, the types of hangers, the boundary conditions, and arch bridge structures are first discussed. We propose that end-fixed hangers consisting of parallel seven-wire strands (or hangers could be simplified as both end-fixed hangers) have sucient bending stiffness to bear the bending moment. Moreover, it is found that HTABs and TABs with floating deck structures can cause a significant lateral bending to hangers. Therefore, the bending stress of HTAB and TAB hangers with floating deck structures and the strength and fatigue properties of seven-wire strands are studied.

Subsequently, the theoretical formulations for the bending angles and maximum bending stress of hangers caused by the effects of temperature and the temperature gradient are developed. The finite element method (FEM) then verifies the accuracy of the formulas for bending angles and the maximum bending stress of the hangers. Based on an analysis of the hangers of a real TAB with a floating deck structure, we find that the bending of hangers is mainly caused by the difference in longitudinal displacement between the arch and the deck under the effect of temperature. Thus, the following study is conducted under the consideration of lateral bending of hangers that is caused by the difference in longitudinal displacement between the arch and the deck. Based on an analysis of the mechanical model of hangers, it is concluded that, besides the maximum bending stress σb in hangers, the ultimate tensile strength σu of the seven-wire strand under lateral bending is also the primary influential factor of the safety of hangers when hangers have lateral bending deformation. The influence of lateral bending deformation on the ultimate tensile strength of the seven-wire strands is obtained, according to finite element analysis and tests on the seven-wire strands. It is found that the ultimate tensile strength of the seven-wire strands under lateral bending decreases significantly. Thus, a method for checking the strength of the seven-wire strands in hangers under lateral bending is proposed. In addition, the S-N curve of the seven-wire strands under lateral bending can also be obtained based on the ultimate tensile strength under lateral bending. The fatigue properties of seven-wire strands will be weakened with an increase in lateral bending θ according to the S-N curve of the seven-wire strands under lateral bending. When the lateral bending θ is over 40 mrad, the fatigue properties of seven-wire strands will fall dramatically.

In conclusion, lateral bending can exert a significant adverse influence on the seven-wire strands in hangers, so it is advised to take several measures to mitigate this adverse influence, such as using a tied arch structure as much as possible, replacing the fixed connections with hinged connections for short hangers, and using a jointless bridge structure. Using a tied arch structure for HTABs and TABs might have fewer side effects when compared with using the other methods above, so using a tied arch structure is more strongly recommended.

1　Study on the Main Bending Form of Hangers

The theoretical formulation for the lateral bending angles and maximum bending stress of hangers is conducted here. Presently, bearings that allow for bridge decks to have longitudinal deformation of their bridges and rotate (such as rubber bearings) are widely used in HTABs and TABs with floating deck structures[13]. Under the effect of temperature and the temperature gradient, bridge decks can produce longitudinal deformation and rotate. The longitudinal deformation of bridges is related to the temperature changes of the whole bridge, and the rotation of bridge decks is related to the temperature gradient throughout the bridge sections.

Based on the analysis above, the lateral bending angle of hangers consists of two parts. One is the bending angle (θ_1) that is caused by the longitudinal deformation of the bridge decks, and the other part is the bending angle (θ_2) that is caused by the rotation of the bridge decks[19] (shown in Fig. 3). We theoretically deduce the formulas to describe the bending angle caused by the longitudinal deformation of bridge decks and the bending angle caused by the rotation of the bridge decks, according to the analysis above.

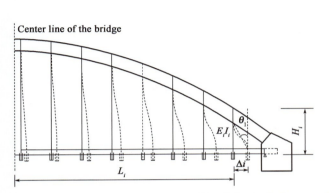

Fig. 2　Lateral bending angles caused by the longitudinal deformation of bridge decks

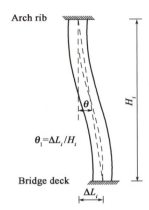

Fig. 3　Lateral bending deformation of the hangers under the longitudinal deformation of bridge decks

2　Finite Element Analysis and Experimental Study on the Ultimate Tensile Strength of Seven-Wire Strands under Lateral Bending

The main form of the bending of hangers is the lateral bending deformation that is caused by temperature, according to the analysis of the previous section. Fig. 4 shows the stress state of hangers under lateral bending.

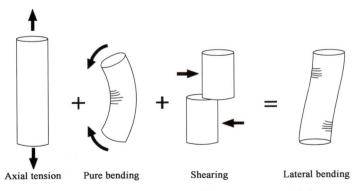

Fig. 4　Peak stress of the main arch under different arch axis coefficients m

117

3 Conclusions

(1) We conclude that end-fixed hangers consisting of parallel seven-wire strands of HTABs and TABs with a floating deck structure can produce significant bending deformation based on the investigations of types of hangers, boundary conditions, and arch bridge structures. The bending deformation of hangers can exert an adverse influence on the strength of the hangers.

(2) We propose that lateral bending causes the uneven loading of the parallel seven-wire strands in hangers based on the study of the mechanical model of hangers under lateral bending deformation. The seven-wire strand that is located at the outer edge of the hangers will bear the maximum bending stress and it can be regarded as under the most unfavorable loading conditions in all the parallel seven-wire strands. The properties of the seven-wire strands under the most unfavorable loading conditions and the maximum bending stress that they bear decide the safety of the hangers.

(3) FEM developed and verified the theoretical formulation for the lateral bending angle and maximum bending stress in hangers. According to the results of the calculations using the formulas and FEM, the bending of hangers is mainly caused by the different displacements along the longitudinal direction of the bridge at both ends of the hangers and the bending that is caused by the rotation of the bridge deck can be ignored. Moreover, FEM and tests obtained the ultimate tensile strength of the seven-wire strands under lateral bending. The S-N curve that could reflect the fatigue properties of seven-wire stands under lateral bending is also obtained based on the ultimate tensile strength of the seven-wire strands under lateral bending. It was found that the ultimate tensile strength and fatigue properties of the seven-wire strands significantly decrease when lateral bending is considered. Therefore, the adverse influence of lateral bending on hangers cannot be ignored, and a method for checking the strength of seven-wire strands in hangers considering lateral bending is proposed.

(4) Several measures are proposed for mitigating the adverse influence of lateral bending on hangers, such as using tied arch structures as much as possible, replacing fixed connections with hinged connections for short hangers, and using a jointless bridge structure. Synthetically speaking, using tied arch structures might produce fewer side effects is more strongly recommended than using other methods.

References

[1] Liu, J. F., Li, Y. B., Zhang, Q. W. Mechanical behavior of damaged strand suspender with asymmetric broken wires in arch bridges[J]. J. Tongji Univ. 2019, 47, 451-457.

[2] Zhong, S. T. The Concrete-Filled Steel Tubular Structures [M]. Tsinghua University Press Publishers: Beijing, China, 2003.

[3] He, W., Chen, H. Characteristics and Related Research of through and Half through Arch

Bridges in China[J]. Appl. Mech. Mater. 2014, 488-489, 509-512.

[4] Li, Y., Lv, D. G., Sheng, H. F. Fatigue Reliability Analysis of the Stay Cables of Cable-Stayed Bridge under Combined Loads of Stochastic Traffic and Wind[J]. Key Eng. Mater. 2011, 456, 23-35.

[5] Qu, Y., Zhang, H., Zhao, R., Liao, L., Zhou, Y. Research on the Method of Predicting Corrosion width of Cables Based on the Spontaneous Magnetic Flux Leakage[J]. Materials 2019, 12, 2154.

[6] Winkler, J., Georgakis, C., Fischer, G., Wood, S., Ghannoum, W. Structural Response of a Multi-Strand Stay Cable to Cyclic Bending Load[J]. Struct. Eng. Int. 2015, 25, 141-150.

[7] Sophianopoulos, D. S., Michaltsos, G. T., Cholevas, H. I. Static and dynamic responses of suspended arch bridges due to failure of cables[J]. Arch. Appl. Mech. 2019, 89, 2281-2312.

[8] Wang, D., Yang, Q., Liu, Y. Analysis of cable bending stiffness effect on test accuracy of anchor span tension for long-span suspension bridge[J]. J. Comput. Mech. 2015, 32, 174-179.

[9] Zheng, W. Bending Stress of Stay Cables of Cable-stayed Bridges and Probe into Control Countermeasures[J]. Technol. Highw. Transp. 2013, 5, 90-93.

[10] Huang, B., Li, Y., Zhu, L., Zhang, W. Effects of Towers' Random Sectional Bending Stiffness on Dynamic Characteristics of Large-Span Cable-Stayed Bridge[J]. J. Southwest Jiaotong Univ. 2014, 49, 202-207.

[11] Xu, J., Zhou, J., Lei, S. Wire Stress Distribution among Damaged Cable Based on FEM Analysis[J]. In Proceedings of the 2014 7th International Conference on Intelligent Computation Technology and Automation, Changsha, China, 25-26 October 2014; pp. 995-997.

[12] Guo, Y. L. Cable Corrosion Analysis and Damage Monitoring[J]. Appl. Mech. Mater. 2014, 578-579, 1302-1305.

[13] Zhu, J. S., Yi, Q. Non-uniformity of stress impact factor of suspenders on half-through or through arch bridges[J]. J. Vib. Shock 2012, 31, 5-10.

[14] Chen, W. F., Lian, D. Bridge Engineering Handbook: Superstructure Design[M]. Taylor & Francis: Boca Raton, FL, USA, 2014.

[15] Gimsing, N. J., Georgakis, C. T. Cable Supported Bridges, Concept & Design, 3rd ed. [M]. John Wiley & Sons: New York, NY, USA, 2012.

[16] Habib, T. Inspection and Maintenance of Bridge Stay Cable Systems[M]. Transportation Research Board: Washington, DC, USA, 2005.

[17] Cu, V. H., Han, B., Nguyen, T. N. Optimal parameters of viscous damper for hanged cables in arch bridges[J]. KSCE J. Civ. Eng. 2016, 20, 847-854.

[18] Chen, B., Su, J., Lin, S., Chen, G., Zhuang, Y., Tabatabai, H. Development and

Application of Concrete Arch Bridges in China. J[J]. Asian Concr. Fed. 2017, 3, 12-19.

[19] Shiu, K. N., Tabatabai, H. Measured thermal response of concrete box-girder bridge[J]. Transp. Res. Record 1994, 1460, 94-105.

[20] Zhang, C. Study on thermal expansion coefficient of bridge decks[J]. Shanxi Sci. Technol. Transp. 2008, 2, 52-55.

[21] Li, P. J., Wang, R. H., Zhang, Y., et al. Precisely Identifying Method for Geometric Stiffness of Section of Cable Strut; Guangxi Transportation Research Institute: Nanning, China, 2012.

[22] Timoshenko, S. P., Gere, J. M. Theory of Elastic Stability[M]. McGraw Hill: New York, NY, USA, 1961.

[23] Cheng, Y. L., Xu, H. C., Yu, Y. G. Accident analysis of lowered/half supported tied arch bridges and enlightments for bridge detection[J]. J. FuJian Univ. Technol. 2013, 11, 213-217.

[24] Hawileh, R., Rahman, A., Tabatabai, H. 3-D FE modeling and low-cycle fatigue fracture criteria of mild steel bars subjected to axial and bending loading. In Proceedings of the McMat, Joint ASME/ASCE/SES Conference on Me-chanics and Materials, Baton Rouge, LA, USA, 1-3 June 2005.

[25] Ministry of Transport of the People's Republic of China. JTG D60—2004 General Code for Design Highway Bridges and Culverts [S]. China Communications Press: Beijing, China, 2004.

[26] Yu, Y., Chen, Z., Liu, H., Wang, X. Finite element study of behavior and interface force conditions of seven-wire strand under axial and lateral loading[J]. Constr. Build. Mater. 2014, 66, 10-18.

[27] Li, H. The Determination of Friction Coefficient between Parallel Wires in Stay Cables[J]. Appl. Mech. Mater. 2013, 351-352, 250-253.

[28] ANSYS Help Documents. SAS IP, Inc.: Cary, NC, USA, 2015. Chen, Y.; Meng, F.; Gong, X. Parametric modeling and comparative finite element analysis of spiral triangular strand and simple straight strand[J]. Adv. Eng. Softw. 2015, 90, 63-75.

[29] Hayashi, Y., Nakano, M., Shirahama, S., Yoshihara, N. Characteristics of Developed High-Strength Prestressing Strand. In Proceedings of the Third International Conference on Sustainable Construction Materials and Technology, Kyoto, Japan, 18-21 August 2013.

[30] Wu, Z. J., Ding, Z., Sun, C. P., Zhang, L. M. Finite element analysis of section stress and failure mode of steel strand[J]. China Sci. 2018, 13, 2623-2628.

[31] Bao, Y., Wierzbicki, T. On fracture locus in the equivalent strain and stress triaxiality space [J]. Int. J. Mech. Sci. 2004, 46, 81-98.

[32] Xie, K. Z., Wang, H., Guo, X., Zhou, J. X. Study on the safety of the concrete pouring process for the main truss arch structure in a long-span concrete-filled steel tube arch bridge [J]. Mech. Adv. Mater. Struct. 2019, 1-10.

[33] Tabatabai, H., Ciolko, A. T., Dickson, T. J. Implications of Test Results from Full-Scale Fatigue Tests of Stay Cables Composed of Seven-Wire Prestressing Strands. In Proceedings of the Fourth International Bridge Engineering Conference, San Francisco, CA, USA, 28-30 August 1995; Volume 1, pp. 266-277.

[34] Qin, S. Q. Control Method of Stress-Free Status for Erection of Cable-Stayed Bridges. Bridge Constr. 2003, 2, 31-34.

[35] Liao, Y., Zhan, J. H., Li, C. Application of Stress-Free Status Control Method in Bridge Construction Control. Appl. Mech. Mater. 2014, 587-589, 1412-1415.

[36] Technical Code for Concrete-Filled Steel Tube Arch Bridges; Ministry of Housing and Urban-Rural Development of the People's Republic of China; Chinese Planning Press: Beijing, China, 2013. (In Chinese)

[37] Pang, J. C., Li, S. X., Zhang, Z. F. General relations between S-N curve parameters and tensile strength of steels with a wide strength range. In Proceedings of the 12th Cross Strait Conference on Destructive Science and Material Testing, Beihai, China, 17 November 2018.

[38] Hawileh, R. A., Rahman, A., Tabatabai, H. Evaluation of the Low-Cycle Fatigue Life in ASTM A706 and A615 Grade 60 Steel Reinforcing Bars. J. Mater. Civ. Eng. ASCE 2010, 22, 65-76.

[39] Vukelic, G., Vizentin, G. Damage-induced stresses and remaining service life predictions of wire ropes. Appl. Sci. 2017, 7, 107.

[40] Hawileh, R. A., Tabatabai, H., Abu-Obeidah, A., Balloni, J., Rahman, A. Evaluation of the Low-Cycle Fatigue Life in Seven Steel Bar Types. J. Mater. Civ. Eng. ASCE 2015.

[41] Ma, L. Study on fatigue performance of domestic 1860 MPa low relaxation prestressed steel strand. Rail Stand. Desk 2000, 20, 21-23.

[42] Lee, Y., Pan, J., Hathaway, R., Barkey, M. Fatigue Testing, Analysis, and Design: Theory and Applications; Elsevier's Science & Technology: Burlington, VT, USA, 2004.

[43] Gu, A. B., Xu, J. L. Structural Analysis of Short Suspenders of Half Through or Through Arch Bridge. Highway 2002, 5, 8-10.

[44] Sun, H., Ma, J., Yu, B. Study on Suspender's Fatigue Performance of Half-through CFST Arch Bridge due to Vehicular Loads. Adv. Eng. Forum 2012, 5, 189-194.

[45] Lin, J., Briseghella, B., Xue, J., Tabatabai, H., Huang, F., Chen, B. Temperature Monitoring and Response of Deck-Extension Side-by-Side Box Girder Bridges. J. Perform. Constr. Facil. ASCE 2020, 34, 04019122.

[46] Huang, F., Shan, Y., Chen, G., Lin, Y., Tabatabai, H., Briseghella, B. Experiment on Interaction of Abutment, Steel H-Pile and Soil in Integral Abutment Jonitless Bridges (IAJBs) under Low-Cycle Pseudo-Static Displacement Loads. Appl. Sci. 2020, 10, 1358.

[47] Briseghella, B., Zordan, T. An innovative steel-concrete joint for integral abutment bridges. J. Traffic Transp. Eng. 2015, 2, 209-222.

特大跨拱桥拱肋子结构长期荷载作用下的变形分析

李松林[1]　安永辉[1]　马丹阳[2]*　钟锦祥[3]

(1. 大连理工大学建设工程学部　辽宁大连　116023；
2. 北京航空航天大学交通科学与工程学院　北京　100191；
3. 广西大学土木建筑工程学院　广西南宁　530004)

摘　要　针对钢管混凝土加劲混合结构研究中多个部件内力难以同时测量的问题，本文提出一种新型长期荷载下加载-量测试验装置，实现对钢管混凝土加劲混合结构分阶段施加长期荷载，同时分别量测内置钢管混凝土和外包钢筋混凝土的内力，并在混凝土徐变发展过程中开展长期监测。通过10个第一阶段的长期荷载试验结果，发现此新型实验装置能够很好地单独对钢管混凝土部分施加轴向荷载，试验装置具有安装便捷性、荷载稳定性、位置可调性等多方面的优点。钢管混凝土试件在长期荷载作用下前期发生部分徐变变形，但远小于素混凝土徐变模型计算结果。

关键词　长期荷载试验装置　长期荷载　混凝土徐变
中图分类号　U445.4　　**文献标识码**　A

Analysis of Deformation Development Law of Super Long-span ArchRib Under Long-term Load

LI Songlin[1]　AN Yonghui[1]　MA Danyang[2]*　ZHONG Jinxiang[3]

(1. Faculty of Infrastructure Engineering, Dalian University of Technology, Dalian, Liaoning, 116023, China;
2. School of Transportation Science and Engineering, Beihang University, Beijing, 100191, China;
3. College of Civil Engineering and Architecture, Guangxi University, Nanning, Guangxi, 530004, China)

基金项目：国家优秀青年科学基金项目(52122803)。
作者简介：
李松林(1998—)，男，大连理工大学在读硕士生，主要从事大跨径拱桥在长期荷载作用后的抗震性能研究。
安永辉(1986—)，男，博士，大连理工大学教授，博导，主要从事土木工程新型与智能结构研究。
*马丹阳(1993—)，男，博士，北京航空航天大学助理教授，硕导，主要从事钢管混凝土加劲混合结构研究。
钟锦祥(1998—)，男，广西大学在读硕士生，主要从事大跨径拱桥在长期荷载作用后的抗震性能研究。

Abstract For the stiffened concrete-filled steel tube composite structure, to solve the problem of measuring the internal forces of multiple components simultaneously, this paper presents a new type of loading-measuring experimental device under long-term load, which applies the long-term load to the hybrid structures by stages. The internal forces of the inner circular concrete-filled steel tube and the outer reinforced concrete could be measured at the same time, and long-term monitoring is carried out during the creep development of the concrete. Based on the results of 10 long-term load tests in the first stage, it is found that the new experimental device can efficiently apply axial load on the concrete-filled steel tube alone. The test device has many advantages, such as convenient installation, load stability, and position adjustment. The inner circular concrete-filled steel tube specimens behaved creep deformation at the early stage, which is lower than the predicted results of plain concrete.

Keywords　　Long-term Experimental Device　　Long-term Load　　Creep of Concrete

E-mail　　madanyang@buaa.edu.cn

0　引言

钢管混凝土加劲混合结构具有承载力高，抗震性能好，结构稳定，耐腐蚀性好等多方面优点，被广泛地用于特大跨拱桥建设中。但在长期荷载作用下，混凝土因其本身的材料特性，会发生显著的徐变效应，对大跨径拱桥而言，混凝土的徐变会导致结构内力重分布，对结构的受力产生非线性影响，严重影响结构的受力和变形。

以往的学者对混凝土及钢管混凝土的徐变已经做了大量的研究。Lennart[1]等对不同水胶比的混凝土进行蠕变试验，对普通混凝土早期蠕变的数学建模方法进行了探讨。Li[2]等制作了3组除结合材料类型之外，配料比相同的高性能混凝土（HPC），根据GBJ82-85研究了3组混凝土的蠕变特性，比较了超细磨砂状高炉矿渣（GGBS）和硅粉（SF）对HPC蠕变和干燥收缩的影响，并分析了其机理。姚宏旭[3]等进行了高强混凝土徐变试验研究，测试并绘出了混凝土徐变发展曲线，提出了高强混凝土徐变系数的近似估算式。Forth[4]等进行了6个阶段的测试，探查了加载龄期、施加的应力水平、材料混合成份、相对湿度等多方面因素对混凝土拉伸蠕变的影响。Ichinose[5]等采用三种加载条件对非复合的素混凝土柱和复合的钢管混凝土试件进行研究，发现日本公路桥梁规范（JSHB）给出蠕变系数值是相对保守的，钢管混凝土结构的蠕变系数是远小于混凝土结构的，通过测量还发现，钢管混凝土试件的收缩徐变量约为混凝土试件的9%，在设计上可以忽略不计。张治成[6]采用"龄期调整的有效模量法"得到的混凝土徐变方程式，推导出钢管核心混凝土的换算弹性模量计算公式，并通过有限元软件ANSYS进行了验证；Zhang[7]等设计了经历长期荷载后的钢管混凝土试件轴压破坏试验，研究了长期荷载对钢管混凝土试件的抗压强度、弹性模量以及应力应变关系的影响，同时基于混凝土蠕变的微预应力凝固理论和混凝土的塑性模型，提出了一个预测CFST柱蠕变后力学性能的分析模型。试验结果和模型分析结果都表明，蠕变后CFST柱的弹性模量增加，而抗压强度略下降。

对于钢管混凝土加劲混合结构，不少学者已经对其开展了长期荷载作用下的研究，但以往的研究都是把钢管混凝土加劲混合结构作为一个整体进行受力分析，很少将外围钢筋混凝土部分和内置钢管混凝土部分单独进行受力分析。Li[8]等在不同的加载阶段和加载条件下对28个试件进行测试，研究了钢管混凝土加劲混合构件在联合预荷载和长期荷载作用下的结构性能，并提出了一种预测联合预荷载和长期荷载作用后的钢管混凝土加劲混合构件极限强度的简化方法。Ma[9]等通过有限元模型分析，对长期荷载试验结果进行验证，通过有限元模型，分析了钢管混凝土加劲混合构件的力学性能,如全程应变发展、不同构件之间的内力分布、钢管与混凝土之间的约束效应等,并通过参数分析,研究了钢管混凝土加劲混合构件各种参数对其自身强度退化的影响,并给出计算表,用于评估钢管混凝土加劲混合构件在长期荷载后的极限强度。

本文取特大跨拱桥中的拱肋节段作为研究对象,其截面为钢管混凝土加劲混合结构,针对缺少内置钢管混凝土部分和外包钢筋混凝土部分在长期荷载下实测结果的问题。提出一种新型试验量测装置,以研究该类结构的内力重分布规律,深入分析了其在长期荷载作用下的变形能力。同时,运用已有的素混凝土徐变模型进行对比分析,为之后提出考虑多重约束作用下的混凝土徐变模型提供依据。

1 长期荷载试验

1.1 试验方案及设计

第一期长期荷载的试验对象为未浇筑外围混凝土的钢管混凝土试件,长期荷载作用下的轴压比 $N_{l1}=0.15$,轴压比即对试件施加的荷载 N 和试件的极限承载力 N_u 的比值,此时的 N_u 为钢管混凝土试件的极限承载力。

1.2 试件设计

本阶段试件设计成 3 个尺寸,见表 1,一共 10 个未浇筑外围混凝土的钢管混凝土试件。其中 CFST-1-1、CFST-2-1、CFST-3-1 为不进行长期加载的对照试件,CFST-2-2 为后期试验的主要研究对象,共设置了 5 个同一型号的试件。

阶段性长期加载试件 表 1
Periodic long-term loading of specimens Tab. 1

试件编号	钢管外径 D(mm)	钢管厚度 t(mm)	试件长度 L(mm)	数量(个)
CFST-1-1	89	4.5	666	1
CFST-1-2	89	4.5	666	1
CFST-2-1	89	4.5	444	1
CFST-2-2-1~5	89	4.5	444	5
CFST-3-1	89	4.5	333	1
CFST-3-2	89	4.5	333	1

1.3 材料特性

本试验试件钢管内浇筑的混凝土为高强混凝土,前期对试配的 4 种配合比的混凝土立方体标准试件进行材性试验,见表 2。根据试配结果不断调整配合比,以实现合适的强度和工作性能。最终实配混凝土每平方米用料为:415kg 水泥,55kg 石灰石粉,80kg 矿粉,633kg 砂,440kg 小石,660kg 大石,132kg 水,19kg 减水剂,混凝土的水胶比为 0.24。钢管内浇筑混凝土的同时,各浇筑 6 个棱柱体和 6 个立方体材性试件,试验试件和材性试件在相同的条件下进行养护。测得 28d 混凝土立方体抗压强度 f_{cu} 为 73.2MPa,弹性模量 E_c 为 34635MPa。试验用的钢管为外径 89mm,厚度 4.5mm 的钢管,其屈服强度 f_y 为 357.8MPa,抗拉强度 f_u 为 497.1MPa,断后伸长率为 24.76%,弹性模量 E_s 为 181370MPa。

试配混凝土配比信息表(kg/m³) 表2
Mix proportion information of trial concrete(kg/m³) Tab. 2

编号	水泥	石灰石粉	矿粉	砂	小石	大石	水	外加剂	水胶比	7d抗压强度 f_{cu7}(MPa)
A1	377	68.5	100.5	705	413.2	619.8	136	18.5	0.25	44.0
A2	377	68.5	100.5	705	413.2	619.8	131	18.5	0.24	52.4
A3	377	68.5	100.5	705	413.2	619.8	125	18.5	0.23	48.1
A4	377	68.5	100.5	705	413.2	619.8	120	18.5	0.22	39.2

1.4 加载装置及加载方式

本试验采用新提出的加载装置对试件施加长期荷载,试验装置的最终装配图见图1,此阶段长期荷载试验并不包括外包混凝土部分。

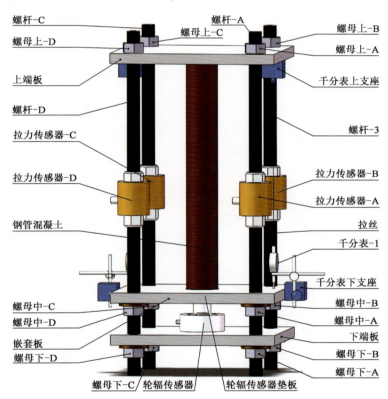

图1 试验装置装配图
Fig. 1 Assembly drawing of test device

试验装置安装过程包括:①将钢管和上端板焊接;②安装螺杆和拉力传感器;③安装嵌套版;④安装轮辐传感器和轮辐传感器垫板;⑤安装下端板;⑥安装千分表支座和千分表。第④步安装之前先将传感器垫板通过 M32×1.5 螺纹和轮辐传感器固定,然后使用胶水将传感器垫板和试件的端部进行黏接。第⑤步安装完下端板后要将加载装置调平,调平时先将下端板调平,之后调节嵌套板,再对上端板进行水平验证,以确定加载装置在安装过程中各接触面是否接触完好。在每个试件中部钢管外表面各粘贴一个横向应变片和纵向应变片，用以监测试件的蠕变。

第一阶段长期荷载比 $N_{l1}=0.15$，根据混凝土和钢管的力学性能，计算出钢管混凝土试件的极限承载力为 681.34kN，去除自重影响，各试件的长期荷载值见表3。加载时为了保证试件轴心受压，对每个试件的4个螺母（螺母上-A～D）采用对角拧紧的方式加载，保证4根螺杆上的拉力相等。4个螺杆上的荷载以及整个试件的荷载通过采集端采集到的4个拉力传感器和轮辐传感器的读数进行确定。

表3 试件长期荷载值

Tab.3 The long-term load value of specimen

试件编号	试件持荷 N_1 (kN)
CFST-1-2	101.62
CFST-2-2-1～5	101.79
CFST-3-2	101.87

2 结果分析

对前一周的长期采集数据进行分析，分析了3个型号试件的应变变化规律，其应变随时间的变化如图2所示，环境因素对应变产生的影响已根据对照试件的应变变化进行消除。

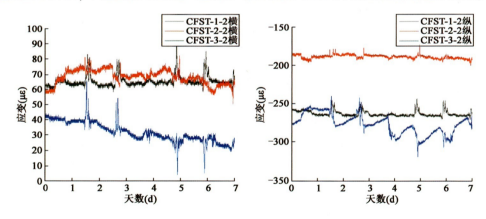

图2 试件表面应变变化

Fig.2 Strain changes on the specimen surface

给试件施加荷载时试件会产生一个瞬时应变，见表4中，根据分析，CFST-1-2、CFST-2-2、CFST-3-2三个型号的试件在第一周内由于持荷而产生的实测徐变量分别为其初始瞬时变形的3.85%，3.74%，2.15%，对应表4中的R1。根据ACI209[10]计算同样几何尺寸的素混凝土试件在相同条件下7天的理论徐变值，如图3所示。通过对比发现，试验试件的实测徐变值分别为对应尺寸的素混凝土理论徐变值的17.88%，12.51%，10.73%，对应表4中的R2。由于钢管的约束作用及组合截面的内力重分布，一定程度上制约了钢管内核心混凝土徐变的发展。

徐 变 分 析 表　　　　　　　　　　　　表4
Specimen Creep Analysis Table　　　　　　　Tab.4

试件编号	瞬时应变(με)	实测徐变(με)	素混凝土理论徐变(με)	R_1(%)	R_2(%)
CFST-1-1	260	10	100.86	3.85	17.88
CFST-2-1	187	7	140.17	3.74	12.51
CFST-3-1	278	6	159.86	2.15	10.73

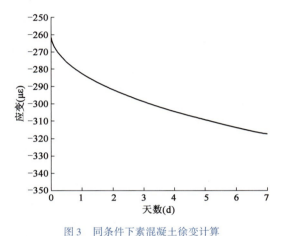

图3　同条件下素混凝土徐变计算
Fig.3　Theoretical creep of plain concrete columns under the same conditions

3　结论

（1）本文提出一种新型加载装置，其具有安装便捷性、荷载稳定性、位置可调性等优点，能独立测量出钢管混凝土加劲混合构件的内置钢管混凝土和外围混凝土的受力状况，以便于对拱桥中常用的钢管混凝土加劲混合结构做进一步的力学性能研究。

（2）对拱桥构件进行初步长期荷载试验，加载初期试件纵、横向都有较明显的应变变化，因混凝土徐变引发的变形为施加荷载时的初始瞬变形量的3.85%、3.74%和2.15%，分别为ACI209规范中预测的同等型号的素混凝土试件在相同加载下同周期内徐变的17.88%、12.51%和10.73%，说明钢管对其内部混凝土的徐变有很大的约束作用。

参 考 文 献

［1］Lennart Østergaard, David A. Lange, Salah A. Altoubat, et al. Tensile basic creep of early-age concrete under constant load［J］. Cement and Concrete Research, 2001, 31(12):1895-1899.

［2］Li Jianyong, Yao Yan. A study on creep and drying shrinkage of high performance concrete［J］. Cement and Concrete Research, 2001, 31(8):1203-1206.

［3］姚宏旭,陈政清,唐小弟. 高性能混凝土徐变试验分析［J］. 中南林学院学报, 2006, 26(03):113-116.

[4] Forth J. P. Predicting the tensile creep of concrete [J]. Cement and Concrete Composites, 2015,55:70-80.

[5] Ichinose L. H, Watanabe E, Nakai H. An experimental study on creep of concrete filled steel pipes [J]. Journal of Constructional Steel Research,2001,57(4):453-466.

[6] 张治成. 大跨度钢管混凝土拱桥的徐变分析[J]. 工程力学,2007(05):151-160.

[7] Zhang Dian Jie, Ma Yi Shuo, Wang Yuanfeng. Compressive behavior of concrete filled steel tubular columns subjected to long-term loading [J]. Thin-Walled Structures, 2015, 89: 205-211.

[8] Li Yongjin, Li Gen, Hou Chao, et al. Long-term experimental behavior of concrete-encased CFST with preload on the inner CFST [J]. Journal of Constructional Steel Research, 2019, 155:355-369.

[9] Ma Dan-Yang, Han Lin-Hai, Li Wei, et al. Behaviour of concrete-encased CFST stub columns subjected to long-term sustained loading [J]. Journal of Constructional Steel Research, 2018, 151:58-69.

[10] American Concrete Institute. ACI 209R-92 (2008) Prediction of Creep, Shrinkage, and Temperature Effects in Concrete Structures [S].

Flexural Behaviour of Pultruded Circular Tubular GFRP Composite Truss Bridges with Novel Non-corrosive Connections

Thumitha Mandula Higgoda[1]　Mohamed Elchalakani[1]　Mehrdad Kimiaei[2]
Adam Wittek[3]　YANG Bo[4]*

(1. Department of Civil, Environmental and Mining Engineering, The University of Western Australia,
35 Stirling Highway, Perth, WA 6009, Australia;
2. Oceans Graduate School, The University of Western Australia, 35 Stirling Highway, Perth, WA 6009, Australia;
3. Intelligent Systems for Medicine Laboratory, Department of Mechanical Engineering,
The University of Western Australia, 35 Stirling Highway, Perth, WA 6009, Australia;
4. School of Civil Engineering, Chongqing University, Chongqing, 400045, China)

Abstract　Five multiplanar truss bridges (MTBs) made of glass-fibre reinforced polymer (GFRP) circular tubular profiles incorporating different innovative non-metallic connections with adhesives, grouted GFRP rods and GFRP laminate wrapping are proposed. These MTBs were tested under flexure with static loading, and their performance surpassed the design load demands required by pedestrian bridges. One of the MTBs showed sufficient load capacity for heavy load platforms in Australian road bridge applications. Failure of the MTBs was triggered by member connections, and no damage such as local or member buckling of the individual members was observed. It was found that the combined effect of GFRP rods and GFRP wrapping on the connections increased the ultimate strength and the ductility of the MTBs. The capacity of the members and connections for the MTBs were calculated using available design guidelines and analytical equations which were compared and discussed with the experimental results.

Keywords　multi-planar truss bridge　non-metallic connections　GFRP　circular tubular members　GFRP wrapping reinforcement　GFRP rods

0　Introduction

Fibre-reinforced polymers (FRP) are known for their superior char-acteristics such as high strength to weight ratio, lightweight and resis-tance to corrosive and harsh environments[1].

Among all the differentfibres used in FRP, glass fibre-reinforced polymers (GFRP) are preferred for being more economical and pre-senting reduced life cycle costs[2,3]. The pultrusion manufacturing process, which involves pulling unidirectional fibres impregnated in resin through a heated die, is the most preferred choice for open and closed FRP profiles with constant cross-section along its length[4,5]. Circular hollow sections are well known for their high torsional resis-tance and bending resistance in all directions through their cross-section. Furthermore, circular hollow sections are preferred in offshore structures as they minimize hydrodynamic forces imparted on its surface due to its lower drag coefficient and exposed surface area from its geometry[6,7].

Marine offshore structures such as jetties and piers constructed from traditional building materials such as reinforced concrete and steel are subjected to rapid ongoing deterioration in strength and stiffness. Steel structures in marine environments are prone to corrosion, and factors such as seawater salinity are known to accelerate this process[8]. Reinforced concrete marine structures are subjected to chloride attacks, which reduce the alkalinity of concrete and result in corrosion of the reinforcing steel[9]. Consequently, the maintenance and rehabilitation costs for marine and coastal infrastructure is very high and could be a severe economic burden. For example, in Australia between 2010 and 2024, it is estimated that there would be a shortfall of $17.6 billion for maintenance expenditure on civil infrastructure[10].

FRP composites such as carbonfibre reinforced polymers (CFRP) have been widely used to strengthen and repair deteriorated reinforced concrete marine structures[11-14]. However, the use of FRP as a base material for structural elements in marine infrastructure has been limited due to the lack of engineering standards[15,16]. Consequently, FRP structural materials cannot be used widely yet in the design of marine structural systems.

Consideration of FRP materials in bridges has been subjected to ongoing research since the early 1970s[17]. FRP structural systems for bridges can be categorized into three types: Truss bridges with relatively small-sized pultruded profiles around 75-150 mm, cable-stayed bridges incorporating non-metallic cables and smaller sized pultruded profiles and girder bridges comprising of relatively large profiles[17]. The first-ever FRP pedestrian bridge was built in 1975[18], and since the 1980s, the use of FRP in pedestrian bridges was adopted by countries in North America, Asia and Europe such as the Aberfeldy cable-stayed footbridge[19] in Scotland (built in 1992), the Pontresina truss footbridge[20] in Switzerland (constructed in 1997), and the Lleida truss footbridge[21] in Spain (completed in 2001, see Fig.1). However, the member con-nections in these truss bridges comprised of both mechanical fastened metallic connections as well as adhesively bonded connections due to the lack of confidence and experience in using glued joints with adhe-sives alone[22].

Member connections in trusses are vital as they determine how the external forces acting on the trusses are distributed to its members. This re-distribution of member forces inherently adds stiffness and rigidity to the truss[23], which is beneficial especially for GFRP structures due to its low elastic modulus compared to steel[24]. Moreover, given that pultruded FRP tubes are dominant in their longitudinal direction in terms of strength and rigidity, they are ideal to be used as axial members in trusses[25]. In the past couple of decades, research has shifted to incorporate metallic connections into large scale FRP frames and trusses to provide extra ductility to the structure given that FRP itself is a brittle material. It will be shown herein that non-metallic connections can have excellent ductility if carefully designed.

Fig. 1 Lleida footbridge in Spain[22]

Studies on GFRP truss systems with circular members are limited in the literature. No previous studies have focused on multiplanar circular tubular GFRP truss systems with non-metallic member connections. Furthermore, additional research is still required to explore new and innovative types of FRP truss system connections to enhance their load-bearing capacities[15]. This paper presents five 3-D multiplanar truss bridges (MTBs) comprising pultruded GFRP circular members and different types of non-metallic member connections incorporating structural adhesives, grouted GFRP rods and GFRP laminate wrapping. Each MTB comprises the same geometric truss configuration and member sizes and are only distinguished by the connections of its members. The bridges were simply supported at the ends and were loaded up to their failure point, and their associated load-displacement behaviour and failure modes are discussed in detail.

1 Experimental program

As shown in Fig. 2, a 3-D truss configuration was adopted with pultruded GFRP circular hollow members. The top of the MTB comprises two chords with outer diameter of 114 mm and thickness of 6.4 mm, which are connected by horizontal braces in the XY plane with outer diameter of 50.8 mm and thickness of 3.2 mm. The top chords of the MTB are connected to a bottom chord by vertical braces of the same dimensions as the horizontal braces. Moreover, the structure is symmetric about the YZ plane located at the midspan of the MTB. In total, there are 19 joints involving the chord interface and the braces. Five different MTBs consisting of different member connections were constructed with the same truss geometry as depicted in Fig. 2 and Fig. 3. All joints within each MTB are identical in design.

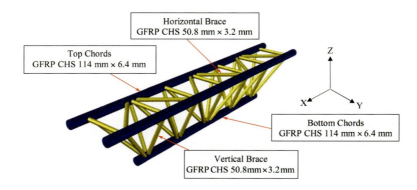

Fig. 2　MTB design isometric view

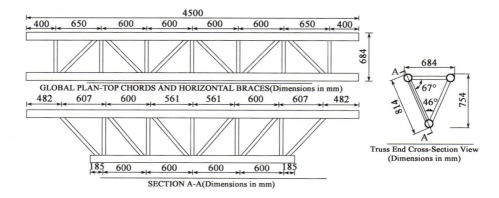

Fig. 3　MTB-plan and section views. References

2　Experimental setup

The top chords of each MTB rested on saddles which were located 230mm from the ends of each top chord. The saddles were connected to roller supports which were secured to a strong reaction Uframe bolted to the ground. A single-acting ENERPAC hydraulic ram with a capacity of 20 tons was used to apply the load to each MTB at a force-controlled loading rate of 4kN/min. The load from the hydraulic ram was distributed to 8 designated joints (C5, C13, C6, C14, C9, C16, C10, C17) on each MTB using a series of cylindrical rollers, SHS primary and sec-ondary beams (see Fig.4). Strain gauges were attached to selected braces and chords (due to symmetry) located at the extreme ends and the midspan of the truss owing to the maximum shear force and bending moments respectively. All strain gauges were installed along the longitudinal axis along the member to measure the axial strain in each member. For MTBs 1 and 2, the strain gauges were attached directly on the GFRP members while for MTBs 3-5, the strain gauges were attached onto the outermost layer of GFRP laminate wrapping. String pots were attached below the bottom chords at C3, C1 and C19 to measure the vertical displacement.

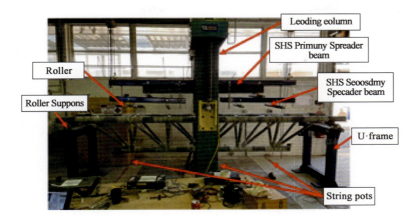

Fig. 4　Experimental set-up for the MTBs

3　Conclusions

(1) All the five MTBs showed an initial linear elastic behaviour up to the first failure point followed by a drop in load due to partial or com-plete failure in the connections between the chord and the brace. No individual member failures or localized failure in chords such as chord punching shear or ovalisation was observed. Once the brace is detached from the chord, this excess load is transferred to the adjacent brace, which provokes progressive failure in the MTB as inferred from the global load-displacement behaviour of each MTB.

(2) Using grouted GFRP rods for member connections increased the ul-timate load by approximately 71 % by comparing MTB 1 and MTB 2. The use of glass fibre laminated wrapping at the chord and member connections was found to increase the ultimate failure load of MTBs. MTB 5 incorporating 16 mm GFRP rods and 1 layer of glass fibre laminate wrapping exhibited superior strength with an ultimate load of 118 kN which is 238 % more than that of MTB 1. Moreover, MTB 5 was found to meet the ultimate load demand for the structural design of road bridges based on Australian design codes.

(3) Four different performance indices were calculated from all five MTBs relative to MTB 1 based on their global load-displacement behaviour for comparison of strength and ductility. MTB 2 incor-porating 32 mm grouted GFRP rods was found to be the most ductile bridge followed by MTB 5 incorporating 16 mm GFRP rods and a single layer of glass fibre laminate wrapping.

(4) Using existing guidelines and research results with some simplifying assumptions, analytical calculations for member and connections capacities were conducted. Analytical member capacity calculations were found to be consistent with the fact that no member failures occurred for all the MTBs. Furthermore, analytical localized connection capacities for all MTBs were predicted and were found to be consistent with the axial loads generated from the beam element model.

References

[1] Keller T. Recent all-composite and hybrid fibre-reinforced polymer bridges and buildings. Prog Struct Eng Mater 2001;3(2):132-40. https://doi.org/10.1002/pse.66.

[2] Lee SW, Hong KJ, Park S. Current and Future Applications of Glass-Fibre-Reinforced Polymer Decks in Korea. Struct Eng Int 2010;20(4):405-8. https://doi.org/10.2749/101686610793557672.

[3] Nystrom HE, Watkins SE, Nanni A, Murray S. Financial Viability of Fiber-Reinforced Polymer (FRP) Bridges. J Manage Eng 2003;19(1):2-8. https://doi.org/10.1061/(ASCE)0742-597X(2003)19:1(2).

[4] Bakis CE, Bank LC, Brown VL, Cosenza E, Davalos JF, Lesko JJ, et al. Fiber-Reinforced Polymer Composites for Construction—State-of-the-Art Review. J Compos Constr 2002;6(2):73-87.

[5] Bank LC. Composites for construction: structural design with FRP materials. Hoboken, N.J: John Wiley & Sons;2006.

[6] Chen WF, Sohal IS. Cylindrical members in offshore structures. Thin-Walled Struct 1988;6(3):153-285. https://doi.org/10.1016/0263-8231(88)90010-9.

[7] Wardenier J, Packer J, Zhao XL, Vegte G, "Hollow sections in structural applications," Jan. 2010.

[8] Alc'antara J, de la Fuente D, Chico B, Simancas J, Díaz I, Morcillo M. Marine Atmospheric Corrosion of Carbon Steel: A Review. Materials (Basel) 2017;10(4):406. https://doi.org/10.3390/ma10040406.

[9] Verma SK, Bhadauria SS, Akhtar S. Evaluating effect of chloride attack and concrete cover on the probability of corrosion. Front Struct Civ Eng 2013;7(4):379-90.

[10] GHD, "Infrastructure maintenace: a report for Infrastructure Australia." 2015.

[11] Pellegrino C, Maiorana E, Modena C. FRP strengthening of steel and steel-concrete composite structures: an analytical approach. Mater Struct 2009;42(3):353-63. https://doi.org/10.1617/s11527-008-9386-6.

[12] George JM, Kimiaei M, Elchalakani M, Fawzia S. Underwater strengthening and repairing of tubular offshore structural members using Carbon Fibre Reinforced Polymers with different consolidation methods. Thin-Walled Struct 2022;174:109090. https://doi.org/10.1016/j.tws.2022.109090.

[13] George JM, Kimiaei M, Elchalakani M, Fawzia S. Experimental and numerical investigation of underwater composite repair with fibre reinforced polymers in corroded tubular offshore structural members under concentric and eccentric axial loads. Eng Struct 2021;227:111402. https://doi.org/10.1016/j.engstruct.2020.111402.

[14] George JM, Kimiaei M, Elchalakani M, Efthymiou M. Flexural response of underwater offshore structural members retrofitted with CFRP wraps and their performance after exposure to real

marine conditions. Structures 2022;43:559-73. https://doi.org/10.1016/j.istruc.2022.06.075.

[15] R. M. Hizam, A. C. Manalo, and W. Karunasena, "A review of FRP composite truss systems and its connections".

[16] Gira~o Coelho AM, Mottram JT. A review of the behaviour and analysis of bolted connections and joints in pultruded fibre reinforced polymers. Mater Des 2015;74:86-107.

[17] Bank L, "Application of FRP Composites to Bridges in the USA," Japan Society of Civil Engineers (JSCE), Proceedings of the International Colloquium on Application of FRP to Bridges, January 20, pp. 9-16, Jan. 2006.

[18] Hollaway LC. A review of the present and future utilisation of FRP composites in the civil infrastructure with reference to their important in-service properties. Constr Build Mater 2010;24(12):2419-45. https://doi.org/10.1016/j.conbuildmat.2010.04.062.

[19] Skinner JM, "A Critical Analysis of the Aberfeldy Footbridge, Scotland." 2009.

[20] Keller T. Towards Structural Forms for Composite Fibre Materials. Struct Eng Int 1999;9(4):297-300. https://doi.org/10.2749/101686699780481673.

[21] Sobrino JA, Pulido MDG. Towards Advanced Composite Material Footbridges. Struct Eng Int 2002;12(2):84-6. https://doi.org/10.2749/101686602777965568.

[22] "International award for innovative GRP footbridge | Fiberline." https://fiberline.com/cases/bridges/international-award-for-innovative-grp-footbridge (accessed Nov. 01, 2021).

[23] Lan TT, "Space Frame Structures," 1999:59.

[24] Yang X, Bai Y, Ding F. Structural performance of a large-scale space frame assembled using pultruded GFRP composites. Compos Struct 2015;133:986-96. https://doi.org/10.1016/j.compstruct.2015.07.120.

[25] Hizam RM, Manalo AC, Karunasena W, Bai Y. Behaviour of pultruded GFRP truss system connected using through-bolt with mechanical insert. Compos B Eng 2019;168:44-57. https://doi.org/10.1016/j.compositesb.2018.12.052.

[26] Green AK, Phillips LN. Crimp-bonded end fittings for use on pultruded composite sections. Composites 1982;13(3):219-24. https://doi.org/10.1016/0010-4361(82).

GFRP 管约束钢管混凝土加劲混合柱轴压与偏压力学性能试验研究

李双蓓[1,2]　苏全福[1]　曾钧柯[1]　潘星年[1]　梁睿[1]

(1. 广西大学土木建筑工程学院　广西南宁　530004；
2. 广西大学工程防灾与结构安全教育部重点实验室　广西南宁　530004)

摘　要　GFRP 管约束钢管混凝土加劲混合柱是一种力学性能优良的新型组合柱,能够适应现代特大跨劲性骨架混凝土拱桥的发展需要,但是其力学性能的研究仍处于相对空白阶段。为研究 GFRP 管约束钢管混凝土加劲混合柱的轴压和偏压力学性能,本文以 GFRP 管厚度、箍筋间距、荷载偏心率为设计参数,对 GFRP 管约束钢管混凝土加劲混合柱进行了轴压试验和偏压试验。结果表明:(1)GFRP 管厚度越厚,混凝土受到的环向约束作用越大,FCECFST 的轴压承载力越高,二次强化越明显,第二峰值荷载也就越高;(2)FCECFST 的箍筋间距越密,箍筋对外围混凝土的环向约束作用越大,混凝土的膨胀开裂就越受限,荷载下降的幅度越小,试件的剩余承载力越高,同时试件的整体变形能力提高;(3)荷载偏心率越大,FCECFST 的荷载-挠度曲线的前期刚度和峰值荷载越小,荷载-位移曲线曲线的初始斜率和峰值点下降显著。

关键词　GFRP 管　钢管混凝土加劲混合柱　轴压　偏压　承载力
中图分类号　TU398[+].9　　**文献标志码**　A

Experimental Study on the Mechanical Properties of GFRP Tubed Confined Concrete-encased CFST Columns

LI Shuangbei[1,2]　SU Quanfu[1]　ZENG Junke[1]　PAN Xingnian[1]　LIANG Rui[1]

(1. College of Civil Engineering and Architecture, Guangxi University, Nanning, Guangxi, 530004, China;
2. Key Laboratory of Disaster Prevention and Structural Safety of Ministry of Education, Nanning, Guangxi, 530004, China)

作者简介:
李双蓓(1963—),女,博士,教授,主要从事钢与混凝土组合结构、智能材料结构及其工程应用等。
苏全福(1996—),男,硕士研究生,主要从事钢与混凝土组合结构研究。
曾钧柯(1998—),男,硕士研究生,主要从事钢与混凝土组合结构研究。
潘星年(1997—),男,硕士研究生,主要从事钢与混凝土组合结构研究。
梁睿(1995—),男,硕士研究生,主要从事钢与混凝土组合结构研究。

Abstract GFRP tubed confined concrete-encased CFST column has excellent mechanical properties and is a new type of composite column, able to adapt to the development of modern extra-large span stiffened skeleton concrete arch bridges, but its mechanical properties research is still in the relatively blank stage. For the study of GFRP tubed confined concrete-encased CFST column axial compression and mechanical properties of the bias, Based on the design parameters of GFRP pipe thickness, stirrup spacing and load eccentricity, axial compression tests and bias tests are carried out on the concrete filled steel tubular stiffened mixed column with GFRP pipe constraint. The results show that (1) the thicker the GFRP pipe is, the greater the circumferential constraint on concrete is, the higher the axial bearing capacity of FCECFST is, the more obvious the secondary strengthening is, and the higher the second peak load is. (2) The greater the hoop constraint effect of the stirrup on the peripheral concrete, the more restricted the expansion and cracking of concrete, the smaller the decrease in load, the higher the residual bearing capacity of the specimen, and the higher the overall deformation ability of the specimen. (3) With the increase of load eccentricity, the earlier stiffness and peak load of FCECFST's load-deflection curve are smaller, and the initial slope and peak point of the load-displacement curve decrease significantly.

Keywords GFRP　Concrete-encased concrete-filled steel tubular columns　Axial compression　Eccentric compression　Bearing capacity

E-mail lsbwh90@163.com

0　引言

随着我国土木工程的飞速发展，工程结构逐渐向大跨度、重荷载、超高层方向发展，对构件力学性能的要求不断提高，传统的钢筋混凝土结构已难以满足现代工程应用需求，而钢与混凝土组合结构因其突出的力学性能，受到众多学者的研究，越来越受到土木行业的青睐[1-3]。近年来，众多学者对纤维增强复合材料（Fiber Reinforced Polymer, FRP）开展了相应的研究，其中将FRP与传统结构形式进行优化组合是一大热门，受到学术界以及工程界的广泛关注[4-7]。为了充分发挥构件的力学性能，各学者将钢材、FRP与混凝土这三种材料进行组合，形成了钢管混凝土加劲混合柱（CECFST）[8-10]、GFRP管约束钢筋混凝土柱（FRC）[11-12]、GFRP约束钢管混凝土加劲混合柱（FCECFST）[13]等构件，各构件的力学性能也不尽相同。

钢管混凝土劲性骨架拱桥拱肋部分本质上是钢管混凝土加劲混合构件，一般以受压为主，因此可以将劲性骨架钢筋混凝土拱桥的拱肋当作受压作用下的钢管混凝土加劲混合构件进行研究。实际工程中，CECFST的承载力较高，但构件破坏时外围钢筋混凝土剥落程度严重，延性较差，CECFST的核心混凝土与外围混凝土能否共同工作至破坏是亟待解决的问题[14-16]。FRC能有效提高组合柱的承载力、刚度以及延性，但FRP属于脆性材料，当FRP约束混凝土轴压短柱达到极限承载力时，内部混凝土达到抗压强度，侧向变形的速度加快，FRP容易出现突然断裂的情况，表现出一定的脆性特征，这对于结构整体来说是不利的[17-18]。FCECFST的外围混凝土受到GFRP管和钢管的双重约束，受力状态变为三向受压，裂缝发展放缓，抗压性能提高。在GFRP管的环向约束作用下，普通钢管混凝土加劲混合柱的外围混凝土的强度和延性得到了有效提高，有效缩短了钢管内外混凝土之间的性能差距，使FRP、混凝土和钢材三种不同材料的优点得到充分发挥，从而使新型组合构件具有较高的承载力和延性[13]。

由此可知，FCECFST更能够适应现代特大跨劲性骨架混凝土拱桥的发展需要，鉴于国内外对GFRP管约束钢管混凝土加劲混合短柱的轴压力学性能研究较少，为了给今后该类新型组合构件的研究、设计和施工提供参考依据，促进其在实际工程结构中的应用，本文开展GFRP管约束钢管混凝土加劲混合柱轴压和偏压试验，通过对荷载-变形曲线、荷载-应变曲线进行分析，研究箍筋间距、GFRP管厚度以及偏心率对FCECFST力学性能的影响。

1 试验概况

1.1 试件设计与制作

本试验共设计了12个GFRP管约束钢管混凝土加劲混合构件和2个普通钢管混凝土加劲混合构件。其中，试件截面宽度$B=300\,\mathrm{mm}$，柱长$L=900\,\mathrm{mm}$，试件长宽比为$L/B=3$；试件端部设置20mm厚的高强钢端板用来定位GFRP管、钢管和纵筋；GFRP管的倒角半径为30mm，钢管采用Q355低合金高强度钢无缝钢管，外径$D=159\,\mathrm{mm}$，壁厚$t=5\,\mathrm{mm}$；纵筋、箍筋均采用直径12mm与8mm的HRB400钢筋，并在试件两端的150mm区域设置箍筋加密区，加密区的箍筋间距$s=50\,\mathrm{mm}$；试件钢管内外混凝土设计强度分别为C60和C30。

制作时，采用高强低碳钢端板与钢管以及绑扎好的钢筋笼进行定位焊接，按照试验设计方案粘贴应变片并采取保护措施，将GFRP管作为钢管外围混凝土浇筑模板并与底板进行固定；试件采用立式浇筑的方式，分期分层浇筑钢管内外混凝土，先浇筑钢管内核心混凝土，待混凝土强度达到75%设计强度后再浇筑钢管外围混凝土；试件养护完成后，采用高强无收缩灌浆料及高强石膏进行封顶补平，焊接顶部钢板，试件制作过程如图1所示。

a)钢骨架制作　　　　　b)固定钢管和GFRP管位置　　　　　c)混凝土分期浇筑

图1　GFRP管约束钢管混凝土加劲混合柱制作过程

Fig.1　FCECFST production process

设计主要考虑GFRP管厚度t_g、箍筋间距s和荷载偏心率e/r（e为初始偏心距，$r=B/2$，B为截面边长，$B=300\,\mathrm{mm}$）三个变化参数。具体设计参数见表1。

试件参数　　　　　　　　　　表1

Specimen parameters　　　　　Tab.1

序号	试件编号	FRP管厚t_g(mm)	箍筋间距s(mm)	偏心率e/r
1	FCE-0-150-0-Ⅰ/Ⅱ	0	150	0
2	FCE-3-150-0-Ⅰ/Ⅱ	3	150	0
3	FCE-6-150-0-Ⅰ/Ⅱ	6	150	0
4	FCE-3-100-0-Ⅰ/Ⅱ	3	100	0

续上表

序号	试件编号	FRP管厚 t_g(mm)	箍筋间距 s(mm)	偏心率 e/r
5	FCE-3-200-0-Ⅰ/Ⅱ	3	200	0
6	FCE-3-150-0.3-Ⅰ/Ⅱ	3	150	0.3
7	FCE-3-150-0.6-Ⅰ/Ⅱ	3	150	0.6

注：从左往右第一个数字代表GFRP管厚度，第二个数字代表箍筋间距，第三个数字代表偏心率，Ⅰ/Ⅱ代表相同参数的试件有两根。

1.2 材料性能

试件所有混凝土均为同批次混凝土。在试件浇筑时不同强度等级混凝土各预留了1组标准立方体试块，试块与试件同龄期同条件养护，实测钢管内外混凝土立方体抗压强度分别为63.91MPa与42.94MPa。钢材与GFRP管按照相关标准进行测定，结果如表2、表3所示。

钢材的力学性能指标　　　　　　　　　　　　　　表2
Mechanical property index of steel　　　　　　　Tab. 2

材料类型	厚度（直径）mm	屈服强度 f_y(MPa)	抗拉强度 f_u(MPa)	弹性模量 E_s(MPa)
钢管	5	386.05	538.67	1.98×10^5
钢筋	8	380.98	536.44	2.00×10^5
	12	404.55	569.63	2.03×10^5

GFRP的力学性能指标　　　　　　　　　　　　　　表3
Mechanical property index of GFRP　　　　　　　Tab. 3

取样方向	抗拉强度 f_g(MPa)	弹性模量 E_g(GPa)	断裂应变 ε_g(μɛ)
环向	379.15	38.2	9925
轴向	19.35	9.1	2180

1.3 加载与测量方案

试件加载装置采用广西大学12000kN微机控制电液伺服大型多功能结构试验系统（WAW-J12000J）。采用位移控制加载方式，加载速度为0.5mm/min。试件GFRP管、钢管、纵筋和箍筋的应变值通过柱中截面粘贴应变片测取，试件柱中截面形式与应变测点布置见图2。设计并使用轴压偏压通用的端部钢夹具，以实现端部的加固作用及保证加载偏心距准确，如图3所示。试件的轴向位移和侧向挠度采用位移计测量，加载装置及位移计布置见图4。

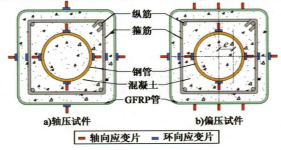

图2　试件截面形式与应变测点布置
Fig. 2　Sectional form of specimens and arrangement of strain measuring points

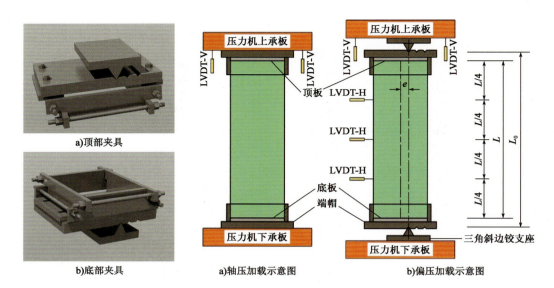

图 3 偏压装置三维效果图
Fig. 3 Three-dimensional rendering of eccentric loading device

图 4 试验加载装置与位移计布置
Fig. 4 Test loading deviceand arrangements of displacement meters

2 试验结果

2.1 试件破坏形态

2.1.1 轴压

不同参数的 GFRP 管约束钢管混凝土加劲混合柱的破坏现象和破坏形态相似,如图 5 所示,该类组合柱的破坏形式基本不受 GFRP 管厚度、箍筋间距的影响,均表现为 GFRP 管中截面附近的角部最先拉裂随后纤维多处断裂破坏,以 FCE-3-150-0-Ⅰ 为例对 FCECFST 柱在轴压作用下的破坏过程进行描述。

a)FCE-3-150-0-I

b)FCE-3-150-0-II

c)FCE-6-150-0-I

d)FCE-6-150-0-II

图 5

e)FCE-3-100-0-I　　　　f)FCE-3-100-0-II　　　　g)FCE-3-200-0-I　　　　h)FCE-3-200-0-II

图 5　GFRP 管约束钢管混凝土加劲混合柱破坏形态
Fig. 5　Failure modes of FCECFST

对试验观察发现,加载初期试件变形增长缓慢,荷载达到峰值荷载约 85% 后,GFRP 管和钢管中间的夹层混凝土挤压开裂,GFRP 管发生微小的横向膨胀;荷载达到峰值点时,夹层混凝土压碎,荷载发生短暂下降,柱中截面 GFRP 管发生微小鼓起,产生环向褶皱和白纹,并伴随着树脂开裂声;此后,荷载缓慢上升,柱中截面 GFRP 管外鼓现象加剧,倒角处产生明显的环向褶皱和白纹并向中部发展,发展速度逐渐变快直至环向贯通,且数量不断增加,伴随着噼叭的纤维撕裂声,响声由小到大、由疏至密;荷载上升至第二峰值时,伴随着巨大的纤维炸裂声后,柱中区域 GFRP 管倒角处局部产生明显的裂缝并迅速沿轴向扩展,条状断裂大幅外翘,压碎的夹层混凝土脱落,荷载迅速下降,结束加载。

2.1.2　偏压

图 6a)和图 6b)给出了偏心率为 0.3 的偏压短柱在加载后的破坏形态。加载初期侧向挠度增长缓慢,试件无明显变化;荷载达到峰值荷载约 75%,试件挠曲变形不明显,挠度增长速度依旧缓慢。荷载达到峰值荷载约 85% 时,侧向挠度值增长加快,受压侧中部倒角处 GFRP 管产生环向褶皱和白纹,受拉侧从中部陆续出现多条环线泛白,可听到些许纤维断裂声和树脂开裂声;随后受压侧环向褶皱和白纹向试件两侧发展,相邻皱褶汇集成带状,直至纤维断裂声逐渐增大且愈发频繁,受压侧带状褶皱中部明显可见断裂纤维束,荷载达到峰值;峰值荷载后,试件侧向挠度增长迅速,挠曲变形明显加快,试件中部受拉区树脂断裂,受压区带状褶皱加速汇集,纤维断裂口数量沿轴向不断增加;荷载下降到峰值荷载的 95% 左右,试件中部受压区约 20cm 范围内纤维断裂口汇集大幅外翘,内部混凝土剥落,荷载下降速度明显加快,夹层混钢筋混凝土逐步退出工作,承载力由核心钢管混凝土提供,试件挠度明显加快,结束加载。偏心率为 0.3 的短柱主要发生受压破坏,受压区 GFRP 管纤维成块脆断是其破坏的标志。

图 6c)和图 6d)给出了偏心率为 0.6 的偏压短柱在加载后的破坏形态。偏心率为 0.6 的偏压短柱和偏心率为 0.3 的偏压短柱的变化基本相似,不同的是,偏心率为 0.6 的偏压短柱受

压侧多条纤维断口发展汇集并大幅外翘时对应的荷载为90%峰值荷载,并且挠曲变形更明显。

a)FCE-3-150-0.3-I   b)FCE-3-150-0.3-II   c)FCE-3-150-0.6-I   d)FCE-3-150-0.6-II

图6 偏压短柱破坏形态

Fig.6 Failure appearance of short columns under eccentrically compression

2.2 荷载-变形关系曲线

2.2.1 轴压

GFRP管约束钢管混凝土加劲混合柱的荷载-位移曲线如图7所示。从图中可以看出,在加载达到第二个峰值荷载点之前相同参数试件的曲线十分接近,这说明该类组合柱的力学性能较为稳定,离散型较小。

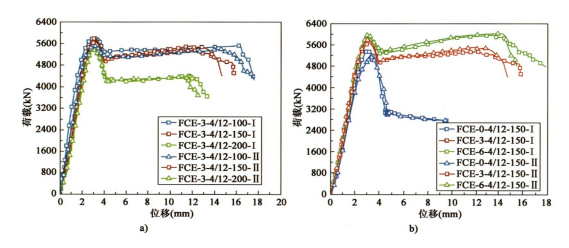

图7 GFRP管约束钢管混凝土加劲混合柱荷载-位移曲线

Fig.7 Load-displacement curves of FCECFST

通过观察不同参数下GFRP管约束钢管混凝土加劲混合柱的荷载-位移曲线可以知道,各FCECFST试件的荷载-位移曲线趋势基本一致,均呈上升-下降-上升-失效的形式[13],与

CECFST(FCE-0-150-0-Ⅰ/Ⅱ)的荷载-位移曲线有着较大的区别,原因如下:

(1)在加载前期,FCECFST 与 CECFST 的曲线变化相似,这是由于在加载前期 FCECFST 的 GFRP 管尚未发挥其约束作用,因此此时的 FCECFST 与 CECFST 并无天大区别。

(2)当达到峰值荷载后,FCECFST 与 CECFST 的荷载-位移曲线的趋势开始发生明显变化,这是由于 CECFST 的外围钢筋混凝土部分达到抗压强度被压碎,与内部钢管混凝土脱离,无法提供有效的承载力,此时 CECFST 的承载力主要由内部钢管混凝土部分提供,因此出现承载力大幅度下降的情况;而 FCECFST 在外围钢筋混凝土部分被压碎后,承载力出现小幅度下降,但是由于 GFRP 管的约束作用使得钢筋混凝土处于三向受压的受力状态,钢筋混凝土部分仍然能够继续承载。

(3)在加载后期,由于 GFRP 管的存在,FCECFST 的钢筋混凝土部分的承载力逐渐恢复,荷载-位移曲线出现二次强化现象,最终达到第二峰值点,且 GFRP 管越厚,则对钢筋混凝土部分的约束力越强,第二峰值点就越高;而 CECFST 的外围钢筋混凝土部分由于没有受到约束,随着加载的进行外围钢筋混凝土的脱落程度越大,但是由于钢管混凝土的存在承载力下降幅度减小。

2.2.2 偏压

偏压试件加载全过程的荷载-柱中挠度(N-f)曲线分别图 8 所示,在荷载发生骤降之前相同参数的试件 N-f 曲线十分接近,说明试件制作及试验数据测量过程对误差的控制良好,试验数据具有较高的可靠度。根据各偏压试件 N-f 曲线的发展趋势,并结合试验现象,将 GCECFST 的 N-f 曲线划分为四个阶段,如图 9 所示。

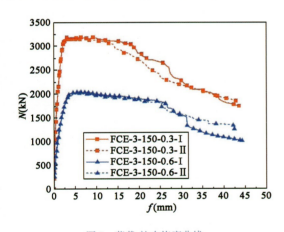

图 8 荷载-柱中挠度曲线　　　　　　图 9 荷载-柱中挠度典型曲线
Fig. 8 Load-deflection curves　　　　Fig. 9 Typical load-deflection curve

弹性阶段(OA):从加载开始至 $0.8N_u$ 左右,曲线近似于直线发展,柱中截面受拉侧混凝土边缘可能出现拉应变,受压状态仍然是截面大部分区域的状态,此时钢管、纵筋及箍筋变形协调,挠曲变形极小,试件表面无明显可见现象,GFRP 管环向应变小,套箍作用不明显,构件处于弹性阶段。

弹塑性阶段(AB):当荷载达到 $0.8N_u$ 左右,柱中挠度增长速度逐渐加快,且增长速度逐渐大于荷载的增长速度,曲线斜率逐渐减小,荷载与挠度呈非线性关系,此时受压区应变显著增大,外部 GFRP 管受压侧开始出现皱褶、受拉侧出现白纹,构件进入弹塑性阶段;随着荷载的增大,柱中区域 GFRP 管受压侧开始外鼓,套箍作用明显,GFRP 管受拉侧白纹处开始产生环向裂纹,受压侧夹层混凝土压碎,不足以承受继续增加的荷载,荷载达到峰值。

塑性下降段(BC):峰值荷载后试件挠曲变形明显加快,荷载逐渐下降,曲线表现为缓慢下降趋势,此时在 GFRP 管的约束作用下夹层压碎混凝土逐渐压密,GFRP 管受压侧环向应变提高明显,纤维断裂增多,受拉侧 GFRP 管环向裂缝增多,承载力由核心钢管混凝土和 GFRP 管约束受损的夹层混凝土提供。

失效阶段(CD):随着荷载的继续增大,夹层混凝土横向膨胀致使柱中区域 GFRP 管受压侧环向纤维大部分到达极限抗拉强度,纤维断裂外翘,夹层已受损混凝土剥落,承载力迅速下降,且仅由内部核心混凝土提供,构件组合性能失效。

2.3 荷载-应变关系曲线

2.3.1 轴压

图 10 为 GFRP 管约束钢管混凝土加劲混合柱轴压试验所测得的试件中部截面 GFRP 管、纵筋、箍筋以及钢管的荷载-纵向/横向应变曲线,图中数据以拉应变为正,压应变为负。

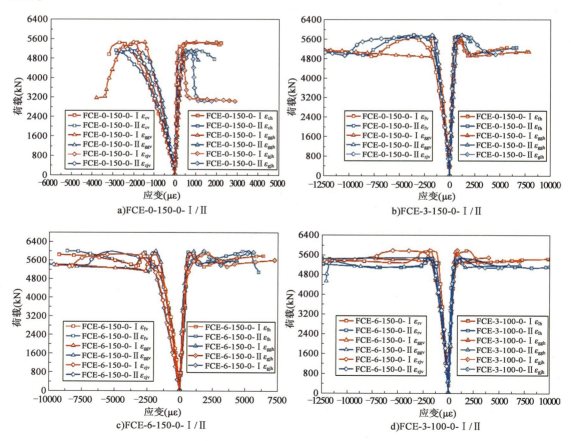

图 10

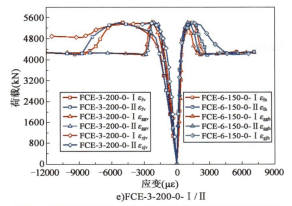

图 10　GFRP 管约束钢管混凝土加劲混合柱荷载-应变曲线

Fig. 10　Load-strain curves of FCECFST

加载初始阶段,因试件的前期刚度较大,各部件的应变发展缓慢并随着荷载线性增加,试件明显处于弹性阶段。当 GFRP 管与钢管的荷载-环向应变曲线的斜率出现降低,说明试件加载达到了弹塑性阶段,混凝土在该阶段出现侧向膨胀,其变形受到 GFRP 管和钢管的限制,两管的环向约束作用逐渐开始显现。部分钢管的横向变形稍大于 GFRP 管的原因主要是,钢管的变形被外围混凝土中的裂缝孔隙或者集料错动所吸收,导致钢管的横向变形尚未完全传递到 GFRP 管。当纵筋应变达到 0.002 左右之后,其应变快速增长,纵筋逐渐发生屈服,荷载接近第一个峰值点,而此时 GFRP 管以及钢管的环向应变均没有达到 0.002,这表明,试件荷载在达到第一个峰值荷载前 GFRP 管和钢管起到的约束效果还很小。当加载至第一个峰值点后,纵筋与箍筋的应变骤增,其原因主要是外围钢筋混凝土部分的强度已达到抗压极限,外围混凝土开裂变形,钢筋完全发生了屈服。紧接着,GFRP 管与钢管的环向变形增加,应变增长速率明显加快,两者对混凝土的约束作用显著提高,试件展现出明显的强化特点,承载力持续上升。

在 GFRP 管的约束作用下,FCECFST 各组试件的纵向应变和横向应变曲线趋势基本一致,在弹性阶段和弹塑性阶段曲线基本重合,说明试验所测得的应变数据结果较为稳定、可靠,试件各部件之间有着良好的协同变形作用。

2.3.2　偏压

图 11 为偏压试件轴向应变测点布置图,图 12 为偏压试件 GFRP 管和钢管柱中截面测点的荷载-轴向应变关系曲线。

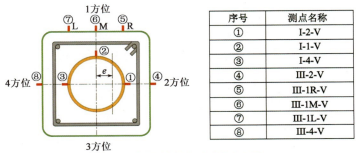

图 11　偏压试件轴向应变测点布置

Fig. 11　Axial strain measuring point layout of eccentric compression specimen

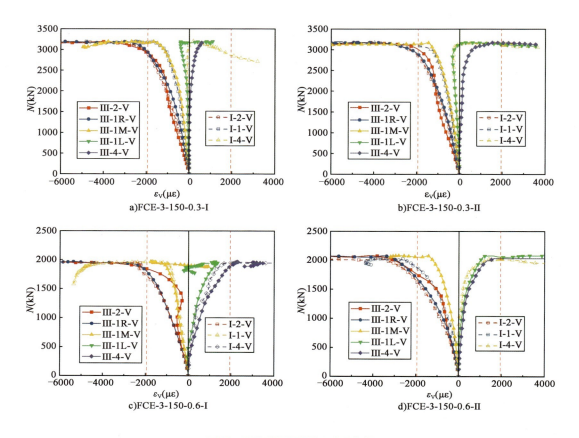

图 12 偏压试件荷载-轴向应变曲线

Fig. 12 Load-axial strain curves of eccentric compression specimen

从图 12 中可以看出：

（1）无论是外部 GFRP 管还是内部钢管，测点的应变值均明显呈现出受压区大于受拉区的现象，这是因为 GFRP 管和钢管的约束作用为核心混凝土和外围混凝土提供了围压，使得混凝土处于三向受压状态，抗压能力大大提高，进而使得试件截面受压区抗变形能力较受拉区优异。

（2）加载初期，GFRP 管和钢管的轴向应变与荷载之间呈线性关系，且应变发展较慢，为典型的弹性特征；随着荷载增大至峰值荷载约 80% 时，受压区轴向应变增长加快，受压侧钢管开始逐渐屈服，试件进入弹塑性阶段；峰值荷载后，受拉侧 GFRP 管荷载-轴向应变曲线较短，偏心率较大的试件甚至出现受拉侧 GFRP 轴向应变骤降的情况，原因是受拉侧树脂开裂沿环向发展，减弱了轴向应变的传递。

（3）峰值荷载后，大部分试件的荷载轴向应变曲线下降缓慢，钢管在荷载保持不变时应变继续增大，表明内部钢管混凝土的延性性能得到了充分发挥。

图 13 为偏压试件环向应变测点布置图，图 14 为偏压试件 GFRP 管和钢管柱中截面测点的荷载-环向应变关系曲线。

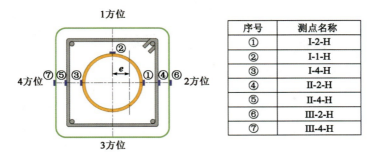

图 13 环向应变测点布置

Fig. 13 Circumferentia strain measuring point layout

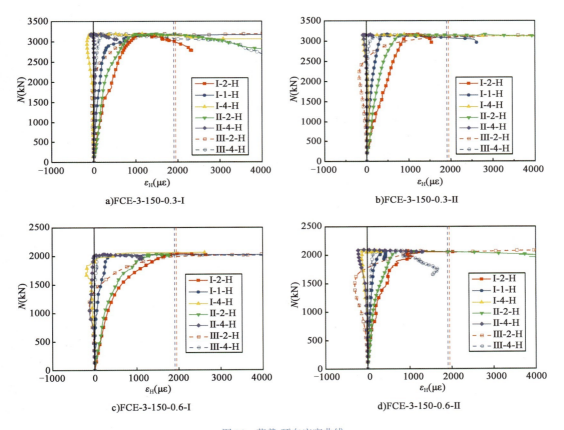

图 14 荷载-环向应变曲线

Fig. 14 Load-circumferential strain curves

从图 14 中可以看出:

(1)受压侧环向应变明显大于受拉侧环向应变,表明受压区环向应力值大于受拉区环向应力值,尤其是加载前期 GFRP 管的环向应变微小,甚至受压侧出现拉应变,当荷载达到峰值荷载约 85% 时,受压侧 GFRP 管环向应变发展增长显著,与试验中试件破坏前受压侧鼓起到环向纤维断裂的试验现象相符。

（2）加载初期，钢管和箍筋的环向应变与荷载呈线性关系，随着荷载的增大，受压侧各测点的荷载环向应变曲线逐渐发生偏转，其中钢管和 GFRP 管的应变增长较快，箍筋次之，原因可能是外围混凝土开始产生裂缝，而箍筋提供的约束为间断约束，其约束作用体现不如钢管和 GFRP 管；对于受拉侧来说，环向应变均远小于相同材料受压侧测点应变值，约束作用分布主要体现在受压侧。

（3）荷载加载至峰值时，绝大部分钢管和箍筋的环向应变距离屈服应变仍有较长距离，说明峰值荷载时，钢管和箍筋对混凝土的约束作用仍有较为充足的富余量，对试件达到极限状态之前的延性性能具有保障作用；峰值荷载后，环向应变的发展速度大大提高，表明约束混凝土横向膨胀变形加快，约束部件的约束作用得到显著的发挥。

3 力学性能分析

3.1 箍筋间距的影响

为探讨箍筋间距对 GFRP 管约束钢管混凝土加劲混合柱轴压力学性能的影响，本文设计了三组不同箍筋间距的试件，分别为 100mm、150mm 和 200mm，为方便对比分析，绘制了相应的荷载-位移曲线，如图 15 所示。

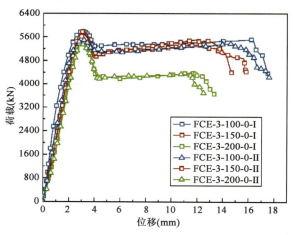

图 15 不同箍筋间距试件的荷载-位移曲线

Fig. 15 Load-displacement curves of specimens with different stirrup spacing

结合图 15 可以看出：

（1）三组不同箍筋间距试件的曲线走势相同，箍筋间距越密，试件的前期刚度越高。由此可见，在一定范围内，当 FCECFST 的箍筋间距减小，试件的第一个峰值荷载呈升高趋势，增幅较小。

（2）试件曲线进入塑性下降阶段后，荷载下降至谷点，FCE-3-100-0-Ⅰ/Ⅱ组试件的承载力下降幅度最小，FCE-3-150-0-Ⅰ/Ⅱ组试件次之，FCE-3-200-0-Ⅰ/Ⅱ组试件的承载力下降最明显。由此可见，FCECFST 的箍筋间距不宜过大，当箍筋间距越密时，外围混凝土的裂缝发展以及侧向变形均受到限制，荷载下降的幅度越小，试件的剩余承载力越高。

（3）相对于 FCE-3-200-0-Ⅰ/Ⅱ组试件，FCE-3-150-0-Ⅰ/Ⅱ组试件和 FCE-3-100-0-Ⅰ/Ⅱ组

试件的第二峰值荷载均有了显著提升。这再次表明，FCECFST的箍筋间距不宜过大。当箍筋间距处于一个较为合理的范围时，FCECFST的第二个峰值荷载基本不受该因素的影响。

3.2 GFRP管厚度的影响

对于GFRP管约束钢管混凝土加劲混合柱来说，GFRP管厚度是关键的设计参数之一，该参数代表着对混凝土约束刚度的大小。为考察GFRP管厚度对组合柱轴压力学性能的影响，本文设计了三组不同GFRP管厚度的试件，分别为0mm、3mm和6mm，为方便对比分析，绘制了相应的荷载-位移曲线，如图16所示。

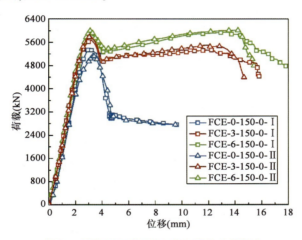

图16 不同GFRP管厚度试件的荷载-位移曲线

Fig. 16 Load-displacement curves of specimens with different thickness of GFRP tubes

结合图16可以看出：

（1）在采用GFRP管约束钢管混凝土加劲混合柱后，试件的前期刚度有所提升，荷载达第一个峰值点前，外围混凝土的侧向变形被GFRP管所限制而处于三向受压状态，随着GFRP厚度的增加，外围混凝土受到的环向约束作用增大，其强度有一定提高。

（2）第一个峰值点过后，试件曲线进入塑性下降阶段，外围钢筋混凝土部分达到极限强度而开始破坏，荷载从第一个峰值点下降至谷点，无GFRP管增强的FCE-0-150-0-Ⅰ/Ⅱ组试件的承载力下降最明显；而在GFRP管的围箍作用下，FCE-6-150-0-Ⅰ/Ⅱ组试件的承载力仅平均下降幅度最小，FCE-3-150-0-Ⅰ/Ⅱ组试件次之。由此可见，普通钢管混凝土加劲混合柱在加载过程中会出现外部混凝土保护层破碎剥落导致试件承载力骤降的问题；而FCECFST则具有良好的整体稳定性，当GFRP管厚度越大，承载力在塑性下降段的降低幅度越小，曲线谷点对应的荷载值越高，试件具有更高的剩余承载力。

（3）在GFRP管的约束作用下，FCECFST中各部件的性能得以充分发挥，试件加载进入强化阶段后承载力持续上升出现第二个峰值点；而CECFST的承载力持续缓慢下降，加载后期试件荷载几乎仅由核心钢管混凝土承担，外围混凝土破损严重。当加载至第二个峰值点时，FCE-3-150-0-Ⅰ/Ⅱ组试件的第二个峰值荷载略低于第一个峰值荷载；FCE-6-150-0-Ⅰ/Ⅱ组试件的第二个峰值荷载则几乎与第一个峰值荷载持平；且FCE-6-150-0-Ⅰ/Ⅱ组试件的第二个峰值荷载高于FCE-3-150-0-Ⅰ/Ⅱ。由此可见，FCECFST试件曲线中的第二个峰值荷载会随着

GFRP 管厚度的增大而增大。

3.3 偏心率的影响

为了探究偏心率对 FCECFST 力学性能的影响,本文设计了偏心率分别为 0、0.3、0.6 的三组 FCECFST 试件,其荷载-轴向位移(N-Δ)曲线如图 17 所示,荷载-柱中挠度(N-f)曲线如图 8 所示。

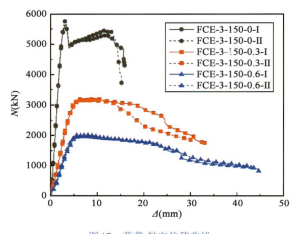

图 17 荷载-轴向位移曲线
Fig. 17 Load-displacement curves

从图 8 和图 17 和可知：

(1)随着荷载偏心率 e/r 的增大,N-Δ 曲线的初始斜率和峰值点下降显著。当荷载达到峰值后,轴压($e/r=0$)试件夹层混凝土压碎,荷载骤降,在 GFRP 管的约束作用下,压碎后的混凝土逐渐压密,曲线进入强化上升段,到达第二峰值荷载时柱中 GFRP 管大面积环向纤维断裂外翘,荷载骤降,试件失效。而偏压试件在到达峰值荷载后无骤降现象,而进入缓慢下降段,其中荷载偏心率较大的试件下降段较长。

(2)荷载偏心率的变化对 N-f 曲线弹性段斜率和峰值荷载影响显著,随着荷载偏心率的增大,试件的峰值荷载大幅降低,但下降段较缓慢且下降过程较长。

4 结论

基于本文中 GFRP 约束钢管混凝土加劲混合柱的轴压和偏压试验结果,主要得出以下结论：

(1)FCECFST 外部的 GFRP 管有效地限制了混凝土的侧向变形,使外围混凝土处于三向受压状态,强度、延性得以提升,有效解决了传统 CECFST 因钢管内外混凝土性能差异较大,外围钢筋混凝土保护层被过早压裂剥落,承载力骤降而试件破坏失效的问题。

(2)相同设计参数下的 GFRP 管约束钢管混凝土加劲混合柱的荷载-位移曲线和荷载-应变曲线较为接近,组合柱的轴压力学性能较为稳定,在试验加载后期,FCECFST 进入强化阶段,承载力二次上升出现第二个峰值,表明 GFRP 管及核心钢管混凝土的性能得到充分发挥,试件各部分能够有效协同工作至破坏,充分体现了 FCECFST 优异的承载能力和变形能力。

（3）FCECFST外围混凝土的裂缝发展及侧向变形受到GFRP管限制，随着GFRP管厚度的增大，混凝土受到的环向约束作用越大，FCECFST的轴压承载力提高；FCECFST的箍筋间距越密，箍筋对外围混凝土的环向约束作用越大，混凝土的裂缝发展和侧向变形就越受限；随着荷载偏心率的增大，FCECFST试件的前期刚度和峰值荷载大幅降低，但下降段较缓慢且下降过程较长。

参 考 文 献

[1] 韩林海,李威,王文达,等.现代组合结构和混合结构-试验和理论和方法[M].2版.北京:科学出版社,2017.

[2] Zhang S,Li X,Chen X,et al. Behavior of circular-steel-tube-confined square CFST short columns under axial compression-ScienceDirect[J]. Journal of Building Engineering.

[3] Han L H,An Y F. Performance of concrete-encased CFST stub columns under axial compression[J]. Journal of Constructional Steel Research,2014,93(5):62-76.

[4] 于冬雪,于化杰,黎红兵,等.FRP建筑材料的结构性能及应用综述[J].材料导报,2021,35(S2):660-668.

[5] Wang Y L,Liu P,Cao Q,et al. Comparison of monotonic axial compressive behavior of rectangular concrete confined by FRP with different rupture strains[J]. Construction and Building Materials,2021,299:124241.

[6] Teng J G,Wang Z H,Yu T,et al. Double-tube concrete columns with a high-strength internal steel tube: Concept andbehaviour under axial compression[J]. Advances in Structural Engineering,2018,21(10):1585-1594.

[7] Le Huang,Tao Yu,Shi-Shun Zhang,et al. FRP-confined concrete-encased cross-shaped steel columns:Concept and behaviour[J]. Engineering Structures,2017,152:348-358.

[8] 韩林海,李成君,牟廷敏.钢管混凝土混合结构设计原理及其在桥梁工程中的应用[J].土木工程学报,2020,53(5):24.

[9] 牛海成,高锦龙,吉珈琨,等.钢管高强再生混凝土叠合柱轴压性能[J].复合材料学报,2022,39:1-12.

[10] 陈港,包超,车佳玲,等.钢管-纤维增强水泥基复合材料混凝土叠合柱轴压性能[J].科学技术与工程,2021,21(07):2823-2829.

[11] 王吉忠,赵海波,王苏岩.纤维增强复合材料(FRP)加固高强混凝土柱的研究现状和展望[J].工业建筑,2007(S1):1.

[12] Turgay T,Polat Z,Köksal H O,et al. Compressive behavior of large-scale square reinforced concrete columns confined with carbon fiber reinforced polymer jackets[J]. Materials and Design,2010,31(1):357-364.

[13] 李双蓓,潘星年,陈宇良,等.GFRP管约束钢管混凝土加劲混合柱轴压力学性能试验研究[J].混凝土,2022(05):31-36.

[14] 孔令旭,闫维明,慈俊昌.大尺寸钢管混凝土叠合柱轴压承载力计算方法研究[C]//2020

年工业建筑学术交流会论文集(上册).

[15] 闫维明,孔令旭,慈俊昌,等.大径宽比钢管混凝土叠合柱轴压试验[J].建筑科学与工程学报,2020,37(06).

[16] Park H G,Lee H J,Choi I R,et al. Concrete-Filled Steel Tube Columns Encased with Thin Precast Concrete[J]. Journal of Structural Engineering,2015,141(12):04015056.

[17] 杨俊杰,周涛,章雪峰.FRP管实心混凝土柱承载力的轴压试验研究[J].建筑结构,2014,44(22):72-75+89.

[18] Saleem S,Pimanmas A,Qureshi I,et al. Axial Behavior of PET FRP-Confined Reinforced Concrete[J]. Journal of Composites for Construction,2020,25(1):1-17.

超大跨度劲性骨架混凝土拱桥主拱圈构造参数优化分析

李芳园* 刘梦麟 张晓宇

(广西交通设计集团有限公司 广西南宁 530029)

摘 要 以主跨600m的天峨龙滩特大桥为例,利用有限元软件对不同主拱圈构造参数进行优化分析。本桥在给定其他构造参数的前提下,结果表明:拱轴系数 $m=1.9$ 时,主拱峰值应力相对较低;考虑到路线总体设计需求,矢跨比 $f/L=1/4.8$(即矢高125m)为最佳矢跨比;拱圈高度 $h=8\sim12$m 时,全桥整体稳定性明显优于拱圈高度 $h=6\sim10$m、$7\sim11$m;底板板厚 t_b、腹板板厚 t_f 对底板、腹板峰值应力的敏感性影响明显大于顶板板厚 t_u,这主要与外包混凝土的浇筑顺序有关,从构造需求考虑,推荐顶板板厚 t_u 为65cm,从峰值应力考虑,推荐腹板板厚 t_f 为 45cm+45cm~95cm,底板板厚 t_b 为 65cm+80cm+80cm~130cm。

关键词 600m级拱桥 主拱圈构造参数 峰值应力 优化分析

中图分类号 U443 **文献标识码** A

Optimization Analysis of Structural Parameters on the Main Arch Ring of the Super-large-span Concrete Arch Bridge with Stiff Skeletons

LI Fangyuan* LIU Menglin ZHANG Xiaoyu

(Guangxi Communications Design Group Co. Ltd, Nanning, Guangxi, 530029, China)

Abstract Take Tian'e Longtan bridge with a main span of 600m as an example, different structural parameters of the main arch ring are optimized by using finite element software. Given other structural parameters, the results show that: when the arch axis coefficient of this bridge is $m=1.9$, the peak stress of the main arch is relatively low; considering the overall design requirements of the route, the rise-span ratio $f/L=1/4.8$ (that is, the rise height is 125m) of this bridge is the best rise span ratio; when the arch ring height of this bridge is $h=8\sim12$m, its

---

作者简介:
* 李芳园(1994—),女,硕士研究生,主要从事大跨径复杂型桥梁研究。
刘梦麟(1987—),男,硕士研究生,主要从事大跨径复杂型桥梁研究。
张晓宇(1989—),男,硕士研究生,主要从事大跨径复杂型桥梁研究。

overall stability is obviously better than that of the arch ring height $h = 6 \sim 10\mathrm{m}$ and $7 \sim 11\mathrm{m}$; the sensitivity of the bottom plate thickness t_b and the web thickness t_f to the peak stress of the bottom plate and the web is obviously greater than that of the top plate thickness t_u, which is mainly related to the pouring sequence of the wrapped concrete. Considering the structural requirements of this bridge, the recommended top plate thickness t_u is 65cm. Considering the peak stress of this bridge, the recommended web plate thickness t_f is 45cm + 45cm ~ 95cm, and the bottom plate thickness t_b is 65cm + 80cm + 80cm ~ 130cm.

Keywords　600m arch bridge　structural parameters of the main arch ring　peak stress　optimization analysis
E-mail　2476327981@qq.com

0　引言

随着跨径的增大，劲性骨架混凝土拱桥逐渐成为混凝土拱桥发展的方向，大跨度劲性骨架混凝土拱桥成为发展强势的重要桥型[1-3]。劲性骨架混凝土拱桥是指拱圈以钢管混凝土和型钢连接构件组成的桁架结构作劲性骨架，钢管内灌注管内混凝土，其外包裹混凝土的钢筋混凝土拱桥[4-5]。

然而，当拱桥的跨径达到600m级或更大时，将给混凝土拱桥设计和施工带来更大的挑战[6]。尽管已形成一些可指导混凝土拱桥设计的标准，如四川省地方标准《钢筋混凝土箱形拱桥技术规程》、国家铁路局发布的行业标准《铁路桥涵混凝土结构设计规范》等，但主拱圈构造直接关系结构的受力性能和经济性能，600m级的劲性骨架混凝土拱桥主拱圈构造尚无经验可循，因此必须开展专门的参数化分析来确定最优的构造参数。

1　项目概况及模型简介

天峨龙滩特大桥为主跨600m的上承式劲性骨架混凝土拱桥，横桥向设置两片平行拱肋，拱肋箱宽6.5m，横向中心距16.5m，总宽共23m。拱肋弦管钢材采用Q420qD，管内灌注C80自密实微膨胀混凝土，拱肋外包混凝土采用C60。主拱圈外包混凝土在纵向分八个工作面对称同步浇筑，竖向分为3环：底板环、腹板环和顶板环。浇筑顺序为：分段浇筑底板混凝土直至合龙，待底板混凝土达到强度后，再分段浇筑腹板混凝土直至合龙，最后分段浇筑顶板混凝土。

采用有限元软件Midas/Civil建立天峨龙滩特大桥梁板模型，即劲性骨架采用梁单元模拟，外包混凝土采用板单元模拟，扣背索采用桁架单元模拟。梁板模型先后模拟劲性骨架吊装成拱、管内混凝土灌注、外包混凝土底板浇筑、外包混凝土腹板浇筑、外包混凝土顶板浇筑、上构施工等施工阶段。

2　主拱圈构造参数分析

2.1　拱轴系数 m

本桥拱轴线选择为悬链线，对比分析拱轴系数 $m = 1.7$、1.9及2.1时的主拱峰值应力。在其他构造参数一定的前提下，由图1a)可知，从弦管和管内混凝土峰值应力方面考虑，建议 m 取1.7或1.9；由图1b)可知，从外包混凝土峰值应力方面考虑，建议 m 取1.9或2.1。综合考虑，最终本桥将拱轴系数 m 拟定为1.9。

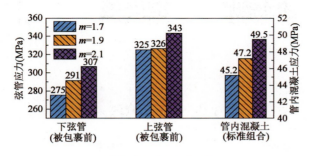

a) 弦管和管内混凝土峰值应力

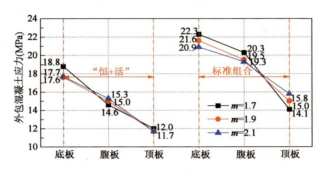

b) 外包混凝土峰值应力

图 1　不同拱轴系数 m 下，主拱峰值应力

Fig.1　Peak stress of the main arch under different arch axis coefficients m

2.2　矢跨比 f/L

本桥主跨 $L=600$ m，以下对比分析矢跨比 $f/L=1/5$、$1/4.8$ 及 $1/4.44$ 下的主拱峰值应力。在其他构造参数一定的前提下，由图 2a) 可知，从弦管和管内混凝土峰值应力方面考虑，建议 f/L 取 $1/4.44$；由图 2b) 可知，从外包混凝土峰值应力方面考虑，建议 f/L 取 $1/4.44$。因此，矢跨比 $f/L=1/4.44$（即矢高135m）时，拱圈的受力更有利。考虑到增大矢跨比将影响路线纵坡的总体设计以及桥头隧道的设计，从而增加整条线路的工程造价，故最终将矢跨比 f/L 拟定为 $f/L=1/4.8$（即矢高125m）。

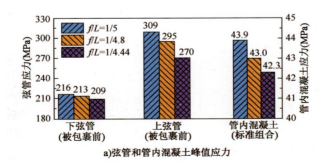

a) 弦管和管内混凝土峰值应力

图 2

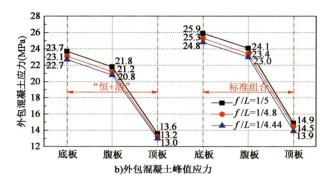

图2 不同矢跨比 f/L 下,主拱峰值应力

Fig. 2 Peak stress of the main arch under different rise-span ratios f/L

2.3 拱圈高度 h

本桥采用变截面形式,对比分析拱圈高度 $h = 6 \sim 10m$、$7 \sim 11m$ 及 $8 \sim 12m$ 时的主拱峰值应力。在其他构造参数一定的前提下,由图3a)可知,从弦管和管内混凝土峰值应力方面考虑,建议拱圈高度 h 取 $7 \sim 11m$;由图3b)可知,从外包混凝土峰值应力方面考虑,建议拱圈高度 h 取 $7 \sim 11m$ 或 $8 \sim 12m$。由于拱圈高度 h 会影响主拱刚度,现对比分析运营阶段下一阶弹性整体稳定系数 k。其中:拱圈高度 $h = 6 \sim 10m$、$7 \sim 11m$ 及 $8 \sim 12m$ 时,一阶弹性整体稳定系数 k 分别对应 3.07、3.99 及 4.79。《公路钢管混凝土拱桥设计规范》规定,主拱弹性整体稳定系数不应小于 4.0,因此拱圈高度 $h = 8 \sim 12m$ 时,整体稳定性才满足要求。综上,从弦管、管内混凝土及外包混凝土应力综合考虑,并结合弹性稳定计算结果,最终拱圈高度 h 拟定为 $8 \sim 12m$。

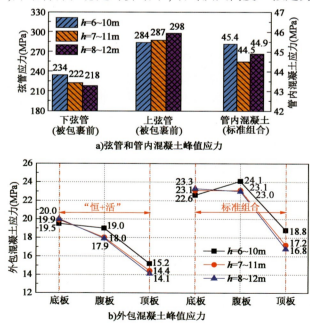

图3 不同拱圈高度 h 下,主拱峰值应力

Fig. 3 Peak stress of the main arch under different arch ring heights h

2.4 拱肋板厚 t

拱圈外包混凝土一方面要满足截面构造要求,另一方面要根据结构实际受力确定各个截面处的顶板、底板及腹板厚度[7]。首先,采用单变量方法初步分析拱肋板厚 t 对主拱应力的影响;然后,再根据初步分析得到的规律,对主拱应力较大处局部调整板厚。

2.4.1 拱肋板厚 t 初步分析

在其他构造参数一定的前提下,顶板板厚 t_u 对主拱峰值应力的影响很小;腹板板厚 t_f 对主拱峰值应力的影响较大,且随着腹板板厚 t_f 的增大,主拱峰值应力呈下降趋势(图4);底板板厚 t_b 对主拱峰值应力的影响较大,且随着底板板厚 t_b 的增大,主拱峰值应力呈下降趋势(图5)。

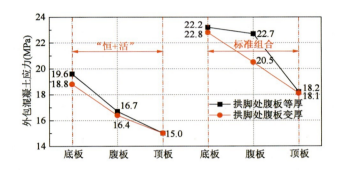

图 4　腹板板厚 t_f 局部调整前后,主拱峰值应力

Fig. 4　Peak stress of the wrapped concrete before and after the local adjustment of the web thickness t_f

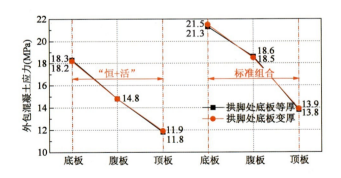

图 5　底板板厚 t_b 局部调整前后,主拱峰值应力

Fig. 5　Peak stress of the wrapped concrete before and after the local adjustment of the bottom plate thickness t_b

同一拱圈构造参数下,底板、腹板峰值应力明显高于顶板峰值应力。以下将外包混凝土峰值应力随板厚变化汇总于表1,可知顶板板厚变化对外包混凝土峰值应力影响很小,腹板、底板板厚变化对外包混凝土峰值应力影响较大。这主要与外包混凝土的浇筑顺序有关,即先浇筑底板,再浇筑腹板,最后浇筑顶板,先浇筑的最先受力,对应的板厚也需相应增加。

外包混凝土峰值应力随板厚变化率   表1
Change rate of peak stress of wrapped concrete with plate thickness   Tab. 1

板厚变化率(%)	"恒+活"工况下峰值应力降低率			"标准组合"工况下峰值应力降低率		
	底板	腹板	顶板	底板	腹板	顶板
顶板板厚提高50	0.0%	0.0%	1.3%	1.3%	1.3%	0.6%
腹板板厚提高22	3.5%	4.9%	0.0%	5.5%	4.0%	0.0%
底板板厚提高83	13.7%	12.4%	0.7%	12.2%	9.1%	9.4%

2.4.2 拱肋板厚 t 局部调整

经过上述拱肋板厚 t 初步分析后，考虑到顶板板厚 t_u 对主拱峰值应力的影响很小，故顶板板厚可尽可能小。但受骨架被包裹所需最小板厚构造要求限制，最终顶板板厚 t_u 拟定为65cm。

经过不断优化后，1#立柱至拱脚处底板应力仍较大，而上述初步分析证明腹板板厚 t_f 可有效降低底板应力。因此，将拱脚处腹板板厚由等厚改为变厚，此时底板峰值应力有所改善（减小0.8MPa）。故最终腹板板厚组合 t_f 拟定为 45cm+45cm~95cm。

经过不断优化后，1#立柱至拱脚处底板板厚 t_b 为130cm，底板太厚可能会带来水化热太大易开裂等问题，因此将130cm等厚改为由拱脚130cm线性渐变至1#立柱80cm，此时主拱峰值应力影响很小。故最终底板板厚组合 t_b 拟定为 65cm+80cm+80cm~130cm。

3 结论

(1) 在给定其他构造参数的前提下，本桥拱轴系数 m 的优化组合值为1.9。

(2) 在给定其他构造参数的前提下，本桥主拱峰值应力随着矢跨比 f/L 的减小而增大，对应的优化组合值为1/4.44（即矢高135m），但考虑到矢跨比增大过多会导致整条线路的工程造价相应增加，故推荐矢跨比 f/L =1/4.8（即矢高125m）。

(3) 考虑到本桥拱圈高度 h = 6~10m、7~11m 时，运营阶段一阶弹性稳定系数较低（分别为3.07、3.99），而本桥拱圈高度 h = 8~12m 时，运营阶段一阶弹性稳定系数相对较高（为4.79），因此在给定其他构造参数的前提下，本桥拱圈高度 h 的优化组合值为 8~12m。

(4) 同一拱圈构造参数下，底板、腹板峰值应力明显高于顶板峰值应力，且顶板板厚 t_u 对主拱峰值应力的影响很小，而腹板板厚 t_f 及底板板厚 t_b 对主拱峰值应力的影响较大。这主要与外包混凝土的浇筑顺序有关，即先浇筑底板，再浇筑腹板，最后浇筑顶板，先浇筑的最先受力，对应的板厚也需相应增加。本桥从构造需求考虑，推荐顶板板厚 t_u 为65cm，本桥从峰值应力考虑，推荐腹板板厚 t_f 为 45cm+45cm~95cm，底板板厚 t_b 为 65cm+80cm+80cm~130cm。

参 考 文 献

[1] 郑皆连. 我国大跨径混凝土拱桥的发展新趋势[J]. 重庆交通大学学报(自然科学版)，2016，35(增1)：8-11.

[2] 郑皆连,王建军,牟廷敏,等.700m级钢管混凝土拱桥设计与建造可行性研究[J].中国工程科学,2014,16(8):33-37.
[3] 陈宝春,刘君平.世界拱桥建设与技术发展综述[J].交通运输工程学报,202,20(1):27-41.
[4] 胡伦.大跨度钢管混凝土劲性骨架拱桥施工控制及工序优化[D].成都:西南交通大学,2014.
[5] 麦梓浩.劲性骨架拱桥受力特点分析[D].广州:华南理工大学,2016.
[6] 邵旭东,何广.800m级钢-UHPC组合桁式拱桥概念设计与可行性研究[J].中国公路学,2020,33(02):73-82.
[7] 谢海清.特大跨度铁路劲性骨架混凝土拱桥结构选型及关键力学问题研究[D].成都:西南交通大学,2012.

超大跨径劲性骨架混凝土拱桥抗震性能研究分析

刘丽芳 陈 鑫 张晓宇

(广西交通设计集团有限公司 广西南宁 530029)

摘 要 以一座600m跨径的劲性骨架钢管混凝土拱桥——天峨龙滩特大桥为例进行研究。利用ABAQUS建立桥梁三维弹塑性模型,分析主桥的动力特性,采用时程分析方法对该桥的地震响应进行分析,并对主桥拱肋、拱上立柱等关键截面进行抗震验算。研究结果表明:一阶振型为面外横向侧弯振动,表明结构的横向刚度较小,地震时容易发生横向失稳,因此大跨度劲性骨架肋拱桥设计时应注意增强拱肋横向刚度或肋间横向联系;分环浇筑施工过程导致主拱肋的截面初始应力分布不均匀,不满足平截面假定,推荐采用叠合单元法计算截面的承载能力;在E1及E2两种地震强度作用下,主拱肋和立柱均在安全范围之内,能需比均大于1。

关键词 劲性骨架拱桥 叠合单元法 动力特性 地震响应时程分析

中图分类号 U441   **文献标识码** A

Study on the Seismic Performance of Super-large-span Concrete Arch Bridges with Stiff Skeletons

LIU Lifang CHEN Xin ZHANG Xiaoyu

(Guangxi Communications Design Group Co., Ltd., Nanning, Guangxi, 530029, China)

Abstract A 600m span concrete-filled steel tube arch bridge with stiff skeletons, the Tian'e Longtan Super Large Bridge, was studied as an example in this paper. A three-dimensional elastoplastic model of the bridge was established by ABAQUS to analyze the dynamic characteristics of the main bridge. The time course analysis method was used to analyze the seismic response of the bridge. Seismic tests on the key sections of the main bridge, such as the arch ribs and columns on the arch, were carried out. The results show that the first-order vibration pattern is out-of-plane transverse lateral bending vibration, which indicates that the transverse stiffness of the structure is small and is prone to transverse instability during earthquakes. Therefore, the transverse stiffness of the arch ribs or the transverse connection

---

作者简介:

刘丽芳(1992—),女,硕士研究生,主要从事大跨径复杂桥梁研究。

陈鑫(1987—),男,硕士研究生,主要从事大跨径复杂桥梁研究。

张晓宇(1989—),男,硕士研究生,主要从事大跨径复杂桥梁研究。

between the ribs should be enhanced in the design of long-span arch bridges with stiff skeletons. The construction process of the split-loop pouring causes the initial stress distribution of the main arch rib section to be uneven, which does not meet the assumption of a flat section. The superimposed element method is recommended to calculate the bearing capacity of the section. In the case of earthquake intensities E1 and E2, the main arch rib and column all meet safety requirements, and the energy-to-demand ratio is greater than 1.

KEYWORDS　Stiff-skeleton arch bridge　Superimposed element method　Dynamic characteristics　Time history analysis of seismic response

　　E-mail　1348506903@ qq. com

0　引言

钢管混凝土劲性骨架拱桥兼有钢管混凝土拱桥和钢筋混凝土拱桥的优点,具有良好的延性和抗剪能力,动力性能及抗震性能优越。近年来,随着设计理论和施工工艺的逐渐成熟,愈加广泛地应用于我国桥梁建设中,尤其是大跨径劲性骨架混凝土拱桥的发展异常迅猛[1-5]。但国内外缺乏专门的大跨度拱桥抗震规范,现有规范适用跨径有限,对大跨度拱桥的抗震设计和抗震分析研究的指导较为有限[6]。本文以一座600m跨径的劲性骨架钢管混凝土拱桥为例进行研究,该桥拱上建筑采用12跨一联的T梁方案,拱上建筑联合受力对支座布置形式提出了较高的要求,针对其特殊性,本文对主桥支座进行了专项设计;然后利用ABAQUS建立桥梁三维弹塑性模型,分析主桥的动力特性,采用时程分析方法研究该桥的地震响应,并对主桥拱肋、拱上立柱等关键截面进行抗震验算。

1　工程背景

天峨龙滩特大桥为目前在建的世界最大跨度拱桥。大桥全长2557m,其中主桥长624m,桥面总宽24.5m,采用上承式劲性骨架混凝土拱桥方案,桥面主梁采用12×40m预应力混凝土先简支后连续T梁,主桥两侧采用跨径组合为(72+135+72)m预应力混凝土连续刚构(图1)。

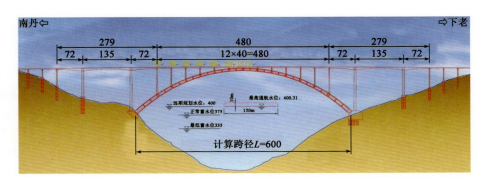

图1　主桥总布置图(尺寸单位:m)
Fig.1　General layout of main bridge (Unit:m)

2　计算模型

采用ABAQUS软件建立三维弹塑性模型,其中主桥部分主拱肋与拱上立柱、主拱肋与拱肋横联采用节点耦合连接,桩基、连续刚构与拱桥的交界墩底部以及拱座底部为完全固支的边界条件,即6个自由度完全锁定,桩基采用土弹簧和固定节点连接。在进行时程分析时,所有固定边界条件施加对应的加速度时程,即可模拟从基础输入给结构的地震动(图2)。

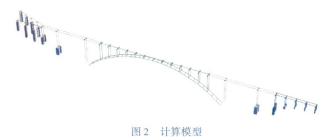

图2 计算模型

Fig. 2 Computational Model

劲性骨架钢管混凝土拱桥在分环浇筑施工过程主拱肋的截面初始应力的不均匀分布[10],不满足平截面假定,使得截面的承载能力与普通截面不同,故往常的计算方法不再适用,推荐采用叠合单元法(图3)。

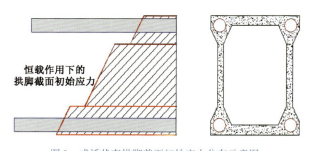

图3 成桥状态拱脚截面初始应力分布示意图

Fig. 3 The schematic diagram of initial stress distribution of arch foot section in completed bridge state

2.1 动力特性分析

模态分析是地震响应的基础。基于上述静力模型,采用子空间迭代法计算了本桥前300阶模态,得到其基本周期为7.35s,并且横向前2阶周期分别为7.35s和4.44s,纵向前2阶周期分别为4.279s和2.867s。天峨龙滩特大桥的横向纵向的前2阶自振特性均为拱桥的经典振动模态。一阶振型为面外横向侧弯振动,表明结构的横向刚度较小,地震时容易发生横向失稳,因此超大跨度劲性骨架肋拱设计时应考虑增强拱肋横向刚度或横向联系(表1)。

动力特性 表1

Dynamic characteristics Tab. 1

振型阶数	周期(s)	频率(Hz)	振型特征
1	7.350	0.136	主拱对称侧弯振型(横向)
2	4.440	0.225	主拱和刚构对称侧弯振型(横向)
3	4.279	0.234	反对称竖弯伴随纵飘振型(纵向)
4	2.867	0.349	连续刚构纵飘振型(纵向)

2.2 截面抗震验算

在 E1 及 E2 两种地震强度作用下,主拱肋和立柱均在安全范围之内,能需比均大于 1（表 2）。

主拱肋和拱上立柱内力验算表　　表 2
The internal force checking calculation table of main arch rib and column on arch　Tab. 2

地震水平	拱肋位置	最小轴力（kN）	纵向弯矩（kN·m）	横向弯矩（kN·m）	屈服弯矩（kN·m）	能需比
E1 纵向	拱脚	46389	493552	159695	209924	1.3
E1 横向+竖向	1/4 截面	34492	168420	2867	710268	4.2
	拱顶	17251	12033	51545	159938	3.1
E1 纵向+竖向	1#立柱	−25439	18434	4419	35540	1.9
	2#立柱	−23795	18771	2443	41370	2.2
	3#立柱	−17426	18788	2263	29480	1.5
E2 纵向+竖向	4#立柱	−19616	18181	1809	31490	1.7
	5#立柱	−17130	13597	1523	24730	1.8

3 结论

采用 ABAQUS 软件建立一座 600m 跨径的劲性骨架钢管混凝土拱桥,基于地震响应分析,主要结论如下:

(1) 一阶振型为面外横向侧弯振动,表明结构的横向刚度较小,地震时容易发生横向失稳,因此大跨度劲性骨架肋拱桥设计时应注意增强拱肋横向刚度或肋间横向联系。

(2) 分环浇筑施工过程导致主拱肋的截面初始应力分布不均匀,不满足平截面假定,其截面的承载能力与普通截面不同,故往常的计算方法不再适用,推荐采用叠合单元法。

(3) 在 E1 及 E2 两种地震强度作用下,主拱肋和立柱均在安全范围之内,能需比均大于 1。

参 考 文 献

[1] 郑皆连.我国大跨径混凝土拱桥的发展新趋势[J].重庆交通大学学报(自然科学版), 2016,35(1):8-11.

[2] 郑皆连,王建军,牟延敏.700m 级钢管混凝土拱桥设计与建造可行性研究[J].中国工程科学,2014(8):33-37.

[3] 郑皆连,王劼耘,徐凤云.一种劲性混凝土拱桥的施工方法:201510143960.8[P].2015-12-20.

[4] 陈宝春,刘君平.世界拱桥建设与技术发展综述[J].交通运输工程学报,2020,20(1):27-41.

[5] 赵人达,张正阳.我国钢管混凝土劲性骨架拱桥发展综述[J].桥梁建设,2016,46(06):45-50.

[6] 刘德文.大跨度劲性骨架拱桥抗震性能分析[D].南宁:广西大学,2017.

[7] 贺坤龙,许伟,户东阳.基于行波效应的大跨度上承式劲性骨架拱桥抗震性能分析[J].铁道建筑.2020.60(10):21-24.

[8] 夏修身,戴胜勇,刘尊稳.大跨度拱桥抗震概念设计方法[J].地震工程与工程振动,2017(2):92-98.

[9] 唐堂,钱永久.既有大跨度混凝土拱桥震害机理分析[J].地震工程学报.2016,38(05):701-706.

[10] ZHAO C H, DUAN J H, CHENG T. Seismic Performance Analysis of CFST Stiff Skeleton Concrete Arch Bridge considering Non-planar Sectional Stress Induced by Balanced Ring-casting Construction[J]. Journal of Earthquake Engineering. 2021(27).

大跨度劲性骨架混凝土拱桥非线性稳定性分析

凌塑奇* 张晓宇 黎栋家

（广西交通设计集团有限公司　广西南宁　530029）

摘　要　以天峨龙滩特大桥为背景，进行非线性稳定性分析，并讨论多种因素对其影响。分析采用考虑双重非线性的有限元方法，建立精细化的主拱有限元模型，对其逐级增加荷载直至结构破坏。分析中针对非线性因素（几何非线性和材料非线性）、初始缺陷和车载布载方式等多种因素设置了不同的工况。通过对比不同工况的非线性稳定系数，讨论影响因素对分析的重要程度。分析发现，仅考虑几何非线性或仅考虑材料非线性的分析结果与考虑双重非线性的相差很大；考虑初始缺陷模型的非线性稳定系数比不考虑的略有下降；车载不同的布载方式中满布车载的非线性稳定系数最高，使得拱顶弯矩最大的车载工况的最低，但是相差不大。结果表明，几何非线性和材料非线性的影响不可忽略；大桥的非线性稳定性主要受恒载控制，其他因素例如初始缺陷、车载布载方式等对分析的影响较小。

关键词　大跨度拱桥　劲性骨架　稳定　非线性　极限承载力

中图分类号　TU398[+].9　　**文献标识码**　A

Nonlinear Stability Analysis of the Long-span Stiff Skeleton Concrete Arch Bridge

LING Suqi* ZHANG Xiaoyu LI Dongjia

(Guangxi Communications Design Group Co., Ltd., Nanning, Guangxi, 530029, China)

Abstract　Based on the Tian'e Longtan Bridge, a nonlinear stability analysis was carried out, and the influence of various factors on its nonlinear stability was discussed. An elaborate FE model considering dual nonlinearity of the main arch was built, and loads applied to it were increased gradually until it met the ultimate capacity. In the analysis, different working conditions are set for various factors such as nonlinear factors (geometrical nonlinearity and material nonlinearity), initial imperfection, and vehicle loading methods. By comparing the nonlinear stability factors of different working conditions, the importance of the influencing factors is discussed. The analysis results considering

---

作者简介：

*凌塑奇（1994—），男，工程师，主要从事大跨径复杂型桥梁研究。

张晓宇（1989—），男，工程师，主要从事大跨径复杂型桥梁研究。

黎栋家（1982—），男，高级工程师，主要从事大跨径复杂型桥梁研究。

only geometric nonlinearity or only material nonlinearity are very different from the one considering dual nonlinearity; Considering initial imperfection in model result in slightly lower nonlinear stability factor than ignoring; among various vehicle loading methods, the highest nonlinear stability factor comes from the one with full-span distributed load, while the lowest comes from the one makes the largest bending moment in arch crown, but the difference is small. It can be concluded that the influence of dual nonlinearity cannot be ignored; the nonlinear stability of the bridge is mainly controlled by dead load, other factors such as initial imperfection and vehicle loading methods have little impact on the analysis.

KEYWORDS   long-span arch   stiff skeleton   stability   nonlinear   ultimate capacity
E-mail   Lingsuqi@ 126. net

0 引言

近年来涌现了大量跨径超过300m的拱桥,如何准确地分析大跨度拱桥的承载能力已经成为学者们广泛讨论的问题[1-3]。其中大部分采用的是非线性稳定性分析,即考虑双重非线性(几何非线性和材料非线性)、利用有限元方法求解结构的极限承载能力。这样的分析同时考虑了结构的屈服后性能和大位移对结构刚度及其分布的影响[4],能够准确地了解结构在给定荷载下的安全储备,为其安全施工和运营管理提供依据和保障。

然而,大跨度拱桥的非线性稳定性分析受到多种因素的影响。不仅分析本身的非线性因素(即几何非线性和材料非线性)对结果有很大的影响,其他的因素例如初始缺陷和施加的荷载等都可能对结构的非线性稳定性有所影响。文献[5-8]认为几何非线性对结构的非线性稳定性影响较小,而材料非线性影响较大。程进等[6]对大跨度钢拱桥进行非线性稳定性的结果中,半中跨均布车载的极限承载能力明显低于满跨均布车载;张建民等[9]对大跨度钢管混凝土拱桥的非线性稳定性分析中发现半桥均布活载工况下,结构破坏时的活载比全桥均布活载工况要小30%。由此可见,荷载的布置方式对大跨度拱桥的非线性稳定性分析的影响值得深入讨论。上述研究大多是对钢管混凝土拱桥的研究,对钢管混凝土劲性骨架混凝土拱桥的研究较少。有必要针对该桥型开展非线性稳定性分析影响因素的研究。

天峨龙滩特大桥是一座跨径600m的钢管混凝土劲性骨架混凝土拱桥,建成后将成为世界上最大跨度的拱桥。本文依托天峨龙滩特大桥作为工程背景,进行非线性稳定性分析,讨论非线性因素、初始缺陷和车载布载方式等多种因素对大跨度劲性骨架混凝土拱桥的非线性稳定性分析的影响,分析其中主要的影响因素,为今后的设计提供参考和依据。

1 分析方法

1.1 工程背景

天峨龙滩特大桥为上承式劲性骨架混凝土拱桥,拱轴线采用悬链线,主跨600m,矢高125m,矢跨比1/4.8,拱轴系数 $m=1.9$。主拱横向设置两片拱肋,呈平行拱形式。拱肋采用等宽度变高度的混凝土箱肋拱截面,截面尺寸如图1所示。每片拱肋采用四管式钢管混凝土桁架结构作为劲性骨架,桁架弦管管径 $\phi900mm$,壁厚30~35mm,内灌注自密实微膨胀混凝土。主拱肋采用劲性骨架法施工,即先架设桁式劲性骨架,然后在骨架上现浇外包混凝土,形成钢筋混凝土箱肋拱(图1)。

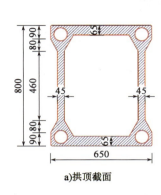
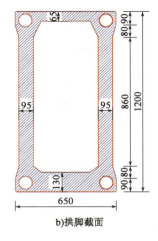

a) 拱顶截面   b) 拱脚截面

图1 主拱肋横断面图(尺寸单位:cm)

Fig.1 Cross section of the main arch(Unit:cm)

1.2 计算模型

本项目为上承式拱桥,拱上建筑主要起传力作用。因此,本文仅建立主拱的有限元模型,将拱上建筑作为荷载考虑其影响。采用通用有限元分析软件ABAQUS建立主拱有限元模型,模型如图2所示。

有限元模型采用不同的单元来模拟主拱圈的构件,利用实体单元(C3D8R)模拟外包混凝土和管内混凝土,壳单元(S4)模拟钢管,梁单元(B32)模拟劲性骨架腹杆、平联杆和肋间横撑等型钢杆件以及杆单元(T3D2)模拟钢筋。

图2 有限元模型

Fig.2 Finite element model

模型的边界条件为拱顶设置对称约束,拱脚设置固定约束。模型施加的荷载包括结构自重、立柱传递的荷载(包括拱上建筑的自重、二期恒载和移动荷载等)和肋间横联的荷载等。

2 影响因素

2.1 非线性因素

为了分析几何非线性和材料非线性对于结构非线性稳定性的影响,分别进行了不考虑几何非线性和不考虑材料非线性的计算。结果如图3所示。

根据荷载系数-拱顶位移曲线,仅考虑几何非线性模型在荷载倍数大于7.13后进入平台段,非线性稳定系数为7.13,相比双重非线性模型的3.05升高了133%;仅考虑材料非线性模型在荷载倍数大于4.00后进入拐点,非线性稳定系数为4.00,相比双重非线性模型的3.05升高了31%。显然这两种非线性因素都对结果有较大影响,相对而言,材料非线性的影响更大。

2.2 初始缺陷

不同初始缺陷类型的荷载系数-拱顶位移曲线如图4所示。不考虑初始缺陷的模型非线性稳定系数为2.84。考虑初始缺陷的模型非线性稳定系数为2.76,与不考虑初始缺陷的模型相比降低2.8%。由此可见,初始缺陷对结构的非线性稳定性影响较小。

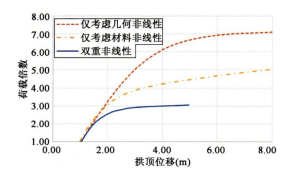

图3　不同非线性因素的荷载倍数-拱顶位移曲线

Fig. 3　Loading magnitude-displacement on top of the arch curves for various nonlinear factors

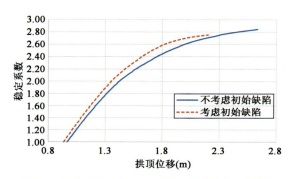

图4　是否考虑初始缺陷的荷载倍数-拱顶位移曲线对比

Fig. 4　Contrast of the Loading magnitude-arch crown displacement curves for considering initial imperfection or not

2.3　车载布载方式

如表1所示,不同的车载工况作用下的结构非线性稳定系数最低为 $L/8$ 截面最大弯矩工况和拱脚截面最大弯矩工况,稳定系数为2.75;最高为拱顶截面最大轴力工况、$L/4$ 截面最大轴力工况、$L/8$ 截面最大轴力工况和满布车载工况,稳定系数为2.88。最低的稳定系数比最高的降低4.5%。由此可以看出,车载布载方式对结构的非线性稳定影响较小。

不同车载工况的稳定系数　　表1

Stability factors for various vehicle loading methods　　Tab. 1

工况	稳定系数	工况	稳定系数
拱顶截面最大弯矩	2.85	拱顶截面最大轴力	2.88
$L/4$ 截面最大弯矩	2.83	$L/4$ 截面最大轴力	2.88
$L/8$ 截面最大弯矩	2.75	$L/8$ 截面最大轴力	2.88
拱脚截面最大弯矩	2.75	拱脚截面最大轴力	2.85
满布车载	2.88	—	—

3 结论

(1) 对于非线性稳定性的影响因素的讨论,几何非线性和材料非线性的影响不可忽视,准确地考虑几何非线性和材料非线性对结构的非线性稳定性分析尤为重要。

(2) 相比而言,钢管混凝土劲性骨架混凝土拱桥的非线性稳定性主要由恒载控制,初始缺陷和车载布载方式的影响较小。车载的最不利布载方式是拱顶截面产生最大弯矩的车载。

参 考 文 献

[1] 郑皆连,牟廷敏,韩玉,等. 500米级钢管混凝土拱桥建造创新技术[M]. 上海:上海科学技术出版社,2020.

[2] Zlatko Savor, Jelena Bleiziffer. Long span concrete arch bridges of Europe[C] // Proceedings of Chinese-Croatian Joint Colloquium on Long Span Arch Bridges. Brijuni Islands, Croatia, 2008:171-180.

[3] 赵人达,张正阳. 我国钢管混凝土劲性骨架拱桥发展综述[J]. 桥梁建设,2016,46(6):45-50.

[4] 项海帆. 高等桥梁结构理论[M]. 2版. 北京:人民交通出版社,2013.

[5] 崔军,王景波,孙炳楠. 大跨度钢管混凝土拱桥非线性稳定性分析[J]. 哈尔滨工业大学学报,2003,35(7):876-879.

[6] 程进,江见鲸,肖汝诚,等. 大跨度拱桥极限承载力的参数研究[J]. 中国公路学报,2003,16(2):45-47.

[7] 严定国. 大跨度钢管混凝土拱桥非线性稳定性研究[D]. 武汉:华中科技大学,2005.

[8] 谢尚英,钱冬生. 劲性骨架混凝土拱桥施工阶段的非线性稳定分析[J]. 土木工程学报,2000,33(1):23-26.

[9] 张建民,郑皆连,肖汝诚. 钢管混凝土拱桥的极限承载能力分析[J]. 中南公路工程,2004,29(4):25-28.

大跨度下承式拱桥面内自由振动的传递矩阵法

康厚军[1,2,3,4]　邓力铭[1]*　丛云跃[1,2,3,4]

(1. 广西大学土木建筑工程学院　广西南宁　530004；
2. 广西大学工程防灾与结构安全教育部重点实验室　广西南宁　530004；
3. 广西大学工程力学研究中心　广西南宁　530004；
4. 广西大学防灾减灾与工程安全广西重点实验室　广西南宁　530004)

摘　要　为弥补高维工程结构有限元分析在结构参数优化设计等的局限，本文基于 Euler-Bernoulli 梁理论与传递矩阵法，研究大跨度拱桥面内自由振动问题，考虑整桥力学模型吊杆位置具体分布情况，将结构离散为多个拱梁段单元，结合拱梁自然边界条件与耦合边界条件，推导多跨下承式拱桥传递矩阵理论。以一座四跨下承式拱桥的平面力学模型，求解其面内自由振动时的固有频率与振型，并将所得结果与用同样参数建模的有限元分析结果对比，证明传递矩阵法对求解该类问题的有效性与精确性。此外，在传递矩阵法基础上通过改变整桥各跨矢跨比、吊杆截面面积、拱肋惯性矩分析面内自振频率变化趋势。结果表明：随着拱桥矢高增大，系统固有频率减小，因拱桥质量的快速增加，对整桥面内刚度影响显著；增大吊杆截面面积可在一定程度内增大拱桥的面内刚度，导致系统频率值在一定范围内增大，但容易引起 Veering 现象，造成整桥模态与能量的快速交换；伴随拱肋惯性矩增大，系统各阶频率增大，且拱肋惯性矩对低阶频率影响显著，对高阶频率影响不大。根据参数分析结果，在现有研究基础上，建立该类桥型竖弯刚度评估方法，为大跨度拱桥健康监测与损伤评估提供相关理论依据。

关键词　下承式拱桥　面内自由振动　传递矩阵法　频率　振型
中图分类号　U441　　　　**文献标识码**　A

作者简介：

康厚军(1977—)，男，博士，教授，主要从事大跨度桥梁结构动力学、工程结构静动力学、非线性动力学等研究。

* 邓力铭(1998—)，男，硕士研究生，主要从事大跨度桥梁结构动力学研究。

丛云跃(1991—)，男，博士，助理教授。主要从事结构动力学研究。

Transfer Matrix Method for In-plane Free Vibration of Long-span Through Arch Bridge

KANG Houjun[1,2,3,4]　　DENG Liming[1]*　　CONG Yunyue[1,2,3,4]

(1. College of Civil Engineering and Architecture, Guangxi University, Nanning, Guangxi, 530004, China;
2. Key Laboratory of Disaster Prevention and Structural Safety of Ministry of Education, Guangxi University, Nanning, Guangxi, 530004, China;
3. Scientific Research Center of Engineering Mechanics, Guangxi University, Nanning, Guangxi, 530004, China;
4. Guangxi Key Laboratory of Disaster Prevention and Engineering Safety, Guangxi University, Nanning, Guangxi, 530004, China)

Abstract　To make up for the limitations of finite element analysis of high-dimensional engineering structures in the optimization design of structural parameters, based on Euler Bernoulli beam theory and transfer matrix method, this paper studies the in-plane free vibration of long-span arch bridges. Considering the specific distribution of suspender positions in the mechanical model of the whole bridge, the structure is discretized into multiple arch beam segment elements, and the transfer matrix theory of multi-span through arch bridges is derived by combining the natural boundary conditions and coupling boundary conditions of arch beams. Based on the plane mechanical model of a four-span through arch bridge, the natural frequency and vibration mode of its free vibration in the plane are solved, and the results are compared with the finite element analysis results modeled with the same parameters, which proves the effectiveness and accuracy of the transfer matrix method in solving this kind of problems. In addition, based on the transfer matrix method, the variation trend of in-plane natural frequency is analyzed by changing the rise span ratio of each span, the cross-sectional area of suspenders, and the moment of inertia of arch ribs. The results show that with the increase of the rise height of the arch bridge, the natural frequency of the system decreases, and the rapid increase of the quality of the arch bridge has a significant impact on the stiffness of the whole bridge deck; Increasing the cross-sectional area of the suspender can increase the in-plane stiffness of the arch bridge to a certain extent, resulting in the increase of the system frequency within a certain range, but it is easy to cause the veering phenomenon, resulting in the rapid exchange of mode and energy of the whole bridge; With the increase of the moment of inertia of the arch rib, the frequency of each order of the system increases, and the moment of inertia of the arch rib has a significant effect on the low order frequency, but has little effect on the high order frequency. According to the results of parameter analysis, based on the existing research, the vertical bending stiffness evaluation method of this type of bridge is established, which provides the relevant theoretical basis for the health monitoring and damage evaluation of long-span arch bridges.

Keywords　through arch bridge　in-plane free vibration　transfer matrix method　frequency　mode shape
E-mail　2543131871@qq.com

0　引言

目前拱作为一种常见结构形式,因其拥有良好的力学特性和优美的造型在土木工程、机械工程和航空航天工程等领域中得到广泛应用。拱桥在建成运营中,除承受自身静载作用外,人群车辆荷载、风荷载及地震作用等使得桥梁产生振动,此时结构实际内力高于结构体系按静力计算得出的内力,即存在动内力,易使构件发生局部变形,严重时威胁桥梁安全。因此对大跨拱桥动力学行为相关研究有十分重大的意义。作为非线性振动研究的重要基础,理清结构的自由振动特性对研究车桥耦合振动[1]、地震作用[2]、结构抗风稳定性[3]等具体工程设计至关重要。

众多学者[4-6]对拱桥动力性能研究多集中在有限元分析法,但对于大跨桥梁结构,有限元建模过程烦琐,计算成本高,且不利于模型的参数分析。在结构动力学领域,LI 等[7-8]、KANG 等[9-10]、ZHU 等[11]的研究表明,传递矩阵法能很好解决各类拱动力学问题,为传递矩阵法在拱桥力学计算方面的应用开辟了前景,但用于多跨拱式组合体系桥梁动力学的研究尚未见到。

鉴于此,本文基于多跨下承式拱桥平面力学模型,据圆拱与梁的面内自由振动动力学方程,结合相应边界条件,推导多跨拱桥传递矩阵理论,求解其面内自由振动问题;重点分析拱桥矢跨比、吊杆截面面积、拱肋惯性矩三个参数对整桥系统面内自振频率的影响,得到多跨拱桥相应自振特性,为实际工程提供理论依据。

1 多跨拱桥构型及假设

图1为多跨下承式拱桥的力学模型。将主梁视作不考虑轴力的 Euler-Bernoulli 梁;主拱肋视作圆弧拱;吊杆视作无质量弹簧。引入以下基本假定:(1)为更明确自振特性研究,忽略阻尼 c 的影响。(2)忽略拱与梁的横向转动惯量与剪切变形。(3)拱轴线不可压缩。

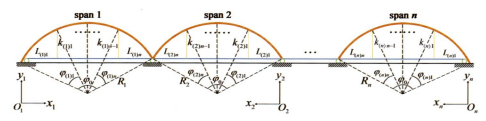

图1 多跨下承式拱桥的力学模型
Fig 1 Mechanical model of multi-span through arch bridge

2 结论

基于多跨拱桥力学模型的特点,在折纸式传递方式基础上,推导多跨拱桥的传递矩阵理论,以一座四跨下承式拱桥为例,求解其频率与振型,并对整桥动力特性进行参数分析,相关结论如下:

(1)在圆拱与梁的自振微分方程求解基础上,本文引入一种半解析法——传递矩阵法求解多跨拱桥的面内自由振动问题,并与有限元软件 ANSYS 进行对比,相对误差的绝对值可控制在8%以内,充分证明传递矩阵解的正确性与可行性。

(2)拱梁刚度比的取值会显著影响高阶模态的振动形状,为避免主拱肋或主梁振幅过大,工程中需对拱梁构件材料与截面形式进行合理设计。

(3)随着矢跨比的增大,拱圈弧度变陡,在施工过程中会使用更多建材,一定程度上加大整桥质量,而此时整桥面内刚度处于增势不明显乃至于呈减小的态势,结合一般自振频率计算公式可知,频率值会逐步减小,工程中应选取合适的矢高与拱桥半径进行施工。

(4)随着拱桥吊杆截面面积的增大,会增大吊杆对拱肋与主梁的约束作用,进而增大系统面内刚度;但是各阶频率间极易发生 Veering 现象,工程设计时应避免相应频率不稳定区间导致的内共振现象产生。

（5）随着拱肋惯性矩的增大，使得拱部可抵抗更大的变形，进而在一定程度上提高整桥面内刚度。工程中一般采取提高拱截面高度或根据实际情况采取更加合理的截面形式等方法提高拱肋惯性矩。

（6）本文在多跨拱桥传递矩阵法应用中所得技术方法还可用于拱桥横向面外振动的分析。

（7）因本文在进行建模分析时引入了一系列假设，例如吊杆等效为无质量弹簧，实际工程中，整体系统的振动会包括吊杆的弯曲，在后续工作中应着重对此进行深入研究。

参 考 文 献

[1] 贺煊博,郭增伟,徐华.车桥耦合振动下中承式拱桥吊杆汽车冲击效应[J].噪声与振动控制,2022,42(01):206-213.

[2] 李小珍,杨得海,雷康宁,等.大跨度连续梁拱桥多点多维地震响应分析[J].西南交通大学学报,2021,56(02):221-228.

[3] 李松敖.大跨度钢管混凝土拱桥吊装施工稳定性分析及抗风研究[D].南宁:广西科技大学,2019.

[4] 韩洪举,张基进.大跨度钢筋混凝土拱桥施工阶段动力特性分析[J].中外公路,2020,40(05):165-167.

[5] 谢裕平.桥面系连接刚度对中承式钢管混凝土拱桥动力特性和稳定性的影响[J].公路,2019,64(05):106-108.

[6] 计静,林钰博,姜良芹,等.双跨钢管高强混凝土拱桥模态分析与对比[J].低温建筑技术,2021,43(12):83-87.

[7] 滕兆春,李万春.变曲率平面拱的自由振动分析[J].兰州理工大学学报,2017,43(02):167-172.

[8] 李万春,滕兆春.变曲率FGM拱的面内自由振动分析[J].振动与冲击,2017,36(09):201-208.

[9] KANG Houjun, ZHAO Yueyu, Zhu H P. Out-of-plane free vibration analysis of a cable-arch structure[J]. Journal of Sound and Vibration, 332 (2013) 907-921.

[10] ZHAO Yueyu, KANG Houjun. In-plane free vibration analysis of cable-arch structure[J]. Journal of Sound and Vibration 312 (2008) 363-379.

[11] 康厚军,朱国敬,苏潇阳.拱桥悬臂施工过程中面内特征值的传递矩阵法[J].计算力学学报,2022,39(02):198-208.

大跨拱桥施工阶段动力学建模与自振特性研究

丁 文[3] 康厚军[1,2,3,4]* 丛云跃[1,2,3,4] 苏潇阳[1,2,3,4]

（1. 广西大学工程防灾与结构安全教育部重点实验室 广西南宁 530004；
2. 广西大学工程力学研究中心 广西南宁 530004；
3. 广西大学土木建筑工程学院 广西南宁 530004；
4. 广西大学防灾减灾与工程安全广西重点实验室 广西南宁 530004）

摘 要 为准确评估拱桥在斜拉扣挂法施工阶段的动力学特性；基于其施工特点，建立了梁-弹簧-拱动力学模型；依据系统边界条件、连续性条件，基于Hamilton原理推导模型的面内自由振动控制微分方程，并采用传递矩阵法对微分方程进行求解。基于所提出的模型和方法，计算吊装完成1/4跨、1/2跨与合龙时模型系统的各阶频率和模态解析解，并与有限元结果对比。最后，分析扣索数、拱截面惯性矩、初始索力及合龙后扣索拆除对结构振动特性的影响。研究表明：理论计算结果的误差在5%以内，建立的模型和计算方法能有效反映施工过程中桥塔与拱肋的自振特性；系统的频率随拱肋吊装数的增加而降低；拱肋分段数与合龙后拆索数在特定范围内对系统的频率影响显著；随参数变化，系统相邻阶频率均出现Veering现象，工程中需合理设计避免系统内共振的发生。

关键词 施工阶段 梁-弹簧-拱模型 Hamilton原理 传递矩阵法 自振特性

中图分类号 U441 **文献标识码** A

作者简介：

丁文（1995—），男，博士研究生，主要从事大跨度桥梁结构动力学研究。

*康厚军（1977—），男，博士，教授，主要从事大跨度桥梁结构动力学、工程结构静动力学、非线性动力学等研究。

丛云跃（1991—），男，博士，助理教授，主要从事结构动力学研究。

苏潇阳（1994—），男，博士，助理教授，主要从事结构动力学研究。

Dynamics Modeling and Free-vibration Characteristics Analysis of Large-span Arch Bridge During Construction Phases

DING Wen[3]　KANG Houjun[1,2,3,4]*　CONG Yunyue[1,2,3,4]　SU Xiaoyang[1,2,3,4]

(1. Key Laboratory of Disaster Prevention and Structural Safety of Ministry of Education, Guangxi University, Nanning, Guangxi, 530004, China;

2. Scientific Research Center of Engineering Mechanics, Guangxi University, Nanning, Guangxi, 530004, China;

3. College of Civil Engineering and Architecture, Guangxi University, Nanning, Guangxi, 530004, China;

4. Guangxi Key Laboratory of Disaster Prevention and Engineering Safety, Guangxi University, Nanning, Guangxi, 530004, China)

Abstract　To accurately evaluate the dynamic characteristics of arch bridges during the construction phase with the cable-stayed buckle method, the beam-spring-arch dynamics model was established according to its construction characteristics. Based on the boundary and continuity conditions of the system, the governing differential equations for in-plane free vibration of the model were derived from Hamilton's principle. Then, the transfer matrix method was used to solve the differential equations. Therefore, the analytical solutions for each-order frequencies and mode shapes were calculated when the lifting was completed 1/4 span, 1/2 span, and closing, and compared with FEM results. Finally, the influences of buckling cables number, the arch cross-section inertia moment, the initial cable force, and the removal of the buckling cables after closing on the structure vibration characteristics were analyzed. The results show that: the established model and calculation method can effectively reflect the self-vibration characteristics of the bridge tower and arch during the construction phases. The results show that: The error of the theoretical calculation result is within 5%, and the established model and calculation method can effectively reflect the self-vibration characteristics of towers-arch during the construction phases. With the arch lifting number increasing, the system frequency decreases. The arch ribs segment number and dismantled cables number after closure have a significant effect on the system frequency in a specific range. With the parameters change, the 'Veering' phenomenon occurred between adjacent frequencies. The parameters need to be reasonably considered to avoid the internal resonance occurring.

Keywords　construction phases　beam-spring-arch model　Hamilton principle　transfer matrix method　free-vibration characteristics

E-mail　HJKang@ gxu. edu. cn

0　引言

目前，大跨度钢管混凝土(CFST)拱桥与劲性骨架拱桥拱圈主要采用斜拉扣挂法[1]吊装施工，悬臂施工阶段，结构稳定性差，对索力要求高，在风、雨等环境荷载作用下，拱肋合龙前后的动力学行为不容忽视[2]。

国内外学者对拱桥的研究内容主要集中在施工阶段的吊装、浇筑、索力计算等各项施工技术[3]以及成桥后各项力学性能[4-5]研究，缺少施工阶段拱桥动力特性的相关研究。在桥梁工程领域，Kang 等[6]、Su 等[7-8]的研究表明，传递矩阵法对解决不同桥型的动力特性问题具有很好的适用性。

鉴于此，本文基于斜拉扣挂法施工的拱桥结构特点，建立梁-弹簧-拱动力学模型；采用Hamilton 原理构建系统的面内自由振动控制微分方程，利用传递矩阵法求解系统特征值；重点分析扣索数、拱肋截面惯性矩、扣索拆除等参数对系统频率的影响,得到不同施工阶段系统的自振特性,以期为工程设计提供参考。

1 梁-弹簧-拱动力学模型及控制微分方程

图 1 为天峨龙滩大桥斜拉扣挂施工现场图。将桥塔视作考虑轴力影响的 Euler-Bernoulli 梁;将索简化为无质量弹簧;主拱肋视为圆弧拱,简化后的梁-弹簧-拱模型如图 2 所示。引入如下基本假定:(1)忽略拱和桥塔的横向剪切变形、转动惯量、扭转惯量、扭转刚度和剪切刚度;(2)忽略拱肋与塔自身重力,运动方程基于动平衡位置建立。

图 1 天峨龙滩大桥斜拉扣挂法施工现场

Fig. 1 Construction Site of Tian'e Longtan Bridge With Cable-Stayed Buckle Method

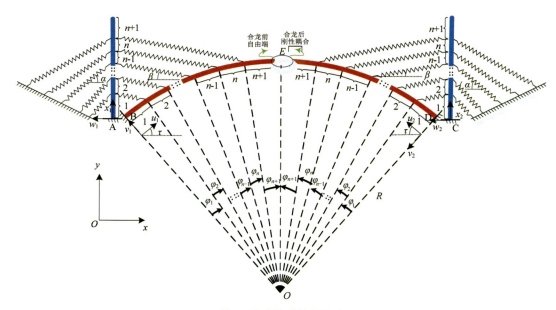

图 2 梁-弹簧-拱简化模型

Fig. 2 Simplified Beam-spring-arch Model

根据 Hamilton 原理得到系统的控制微分方程式(1)、(2)。

$$m_b \frac{\partial^2 w}{\partial t^2} + E_b I_b \frac{\partial^4 w(x,t)}{\partial x^4} + N \frac{\partial^2 w(x,t)}{\partial x^2} - \sum_{i=1}^{n} \delta(x_i - X_i) k_{1,i} w(x,t) \cos\alpha_i \cos\alpha_i +$$

$$\sum_{i=1}^{n}\delta(x_i-X_i)\delta(s_i-S_i)k_{2,i}[u(s,t)\cos(\tau_i+\beta_i)-v(s,t)\sin(\tau_i+\beta_i)+w(x,t)\cos\beta_i]\cos\beta_i+$$
$$\sum_{i=1}^{n}\delta(x_i-X_i)P_{1,i}\cos\alpha_i-\sum_{i=1}^{n}\delta(x_i-X_i)\delta(s_i-S_i)P_{2,i}\cos\beta_i=0 \tag{1}$$

$$\frac{\partial^5 v(\varphi,t)}{\partial\varphi^5}+2\frac{\partial^3 v(\varphi,t)}{\partial\varphi^3}+\frac{\partial v(\varphi,t)}{\partial\varphi}+\frac{m_a R^4}{E_a I_a}\frac{\partial^3 v}{\partial t^2 \partial\varphi}-\sum_{i=1}^{n}\delta(x_i-X_i)\delta(s_i-S_i)P_{2,i}\sin\beta_i-$$
$$\sum_{i=1}^{n}\delta(x_i-X_i)\delta(s_i-S_i)k_{2,i}[u(s,t)\cos(\tau_i+\beta_i)-v(s,t)\sin(\tau_i+\beta_i)+w(x,t)\cos\beta_i]\sin\beta_i=0 \tag{2}$$

2 结论

基于大跨拱桥施工特点,建立大跨拱桥施工过程的梁-弹簧-拱模型;采用传递矩阵法求解系统的面内自振频率及模态,并对拱桥施工阶段动力特性进行参数分析,得到的主要结论如下:

(1)随拱桥斜拉扣挂施工推进,合龙前系统刚度与频率降低;模态由桥塔、拱肋交替振动变为拱肋振动为主。合龙后系统前两阶频率交合龙前有所增大;第6阶模态为桥塔、拱肋共同振动。

(2)拱肋分段数与合龙后拆索数在特定范围内对系统自振特性影响显著,工程中需合理设计。

(3)系统频率随拱肋-桥塔截面惯性矩比增大而增大。拱截面面积一定时,可增大截面惯性矩提高系统刚度。

(4)随着拱肋吊装数、拱肋分段数、拆索数与拱肋-塔截面惯性矩比的改变,系统相邻频率均出现 Veering 现象。工程中需合理设计避免系统产生模态内共振。

参考文献

[1] 胡大琳,陈定市,赵小由,等.大跨径钢筋混凝土拱桥悬臂浇筑施工控制[J].交通运输工程学报,2016,16(1):25-36.

[2] JIN C, LI Q S. Reliability analysis of a long span steel arch bridge against wind-induced stability failure during construction[J]. Journal of Constructional Steel Research, 2009, 65(3):552-558.

[3] 郝聂冰,顾安邦.500m 级钢管混凝土拱桥施工控制[J].西南交通大学学报,2015,50(4):635-640.

[4] A J C, B J J J, A R C X, et al. Wind-induced load capacity analysis and parametric study of a long-span steel arch bridge under construction[J]. Computers & Structures, 2003, 81(26-27):2513-2524.

[5] LIU C, WANG Y, WU X, et al. In-Plane Stability of Fixed Concrete-Filled Steel Tubular Parabolic Arches under Combined Bending and Compression[J]. Journal of Bridge Engineering, 2016, 22(2):4016111-4016116.

[6] KANG H J, XIE W D, GUO T D. Modeling and parametric analysis of arch bridge with trans-

fer matrix method[J]. Applied Mathematical Modelling, 2016, 40(23-24): 10578-10595.

[7] SU X Y, KANG H J, GUO T D. A novel modeling method for in-plane eigen problem estimation of the cable-stayed bridges[J]. Applied Mathematical Modelling, 2020, 87.

[8] 苏潇阳,康厚军,丛云跃.混合体系多塔斜拉桥竖弯刚度评估动力学理论[J].动力学与控制学报,2020,18(4):26-32.

钢纤维对 UHPC 单轴受压损伤本构关系的影响

杨 简[1,2] 李 洋[2] 徐 港[1,2*] 邓金岚[2] 包逍逍[2] 李 聪[3] 田秀娟[2]

(1. 防灾减灾湖北省重点实验室 湖北宜昌 443002；
2. 三峡大学土木与建筑学院 湖北宜昌 443002；
3. 广西大学土木与建筑工程学院 广西南宁 530004)

摘 要 本文对不同钢纤维体积率及长径比的超高性能混凝土(UHPC)棱柱体试件进行单轴受压试验,分析了钢纤维体积率和长径比对 UHPC 破坏形态、抗压性能和本构关系的影响。结果表明:随着钢纤维体积率或长径比的增大,轴压强度和峰值压应变提高,脆性破坏得到明显改善。此外,进一步探究了钢纤维长径比和体积率对 UHPC 单轴受压损伤本构关系的影响,建立了考虑钢纤维影响,包含钢纤维参数的 UHPC 单轴受压试件损伤本构模型。

关键词 超高性能混凝土 单轴受压 本构关系 钢纤维参数
中图分类号 TU528.572   **文献标识码** A

Influence of Steel Fibers on the Damage Constitutive Relationship of UHPC under Uniaxial Compression

YANG Jian[1,2] LI Yang[2] XU Gang[1,2*] DENG Jinlan[2] BAO Xiaoxiao[2] LI Cong[3] TIAN Xiujuan[2]

(1. Hubei Key Laboratory of Disaster Prevention and Mitigation, Yichang, Hubei, 443002, China;
2. College of Civil Engineering & Architecture, China Three Gorges University, Yichang, Hubei, 443002, China;
3. College of Civil Engineering and Architecture, Guangxi University, Nanning, Guangxi, 530004, China)

Abstract Uniaxial compression tests were carried out on ultra-high performance concrete (UHPC) specimens with different steel fiber volume fraction and aspect ratio. The influence of volume fractions and aspect ratio of steel fibers on the failure mode, compressive performance and constitutive relationship of UHPC were analyzed. Results showed that with the increase of steel fiber volume fractions or aspect ratio, the uniaxial compressive strength and strain at peak stress of UHPC increased, and the brittle failure mode was significantly improved. Moreover, the influence of steel fiber on the damage constitutive relationship of UHPC under uniaxial compression was explored. The UHPC uniaxial compression damage constitutive model considering the influence of steel fiber was established.

Keywords　ultra-high performance concrete　uniaxial compression　constitutive relationship　steel fiber parameter

0　引言

超高性能混凝土(Ultra-high performance concrete, UHPC)是一种具有超高抗压强度、优异耐久性能和较好抗拉性能的新型水泥基复合材料,其抗压强度超过120MPa[1-2]。UHPC凭借优异的力学性能,目前已应用于桥梁工程、海洋工程等领域[3-4]。拱是桥梁工程中常用的一种结构形式。作为典型的受压构件,所用材料的抗压强度越高,拱结构的承载能力和耐久性就越好。因此,具有超高抗压强度的UHPC被认为是拱结构中最理想的材料。然而,UHPC单轴受压本构模型研究的不足,限制了结构的非线性设计。UHPC单轴压应力-应变关系作为结构非线性计算的重要依据,是UHPC性能研究的重点,也是难点之一。

国内外学者已经通过对普通混凝土(NC)或高强混凝土(HPC)本构模型进行修正,以及对UHPC单轴受压的试验数据直接拟合等方法,围绕UHPC单轴受压(轴压)本构关系展开了部分研究[5-10]。但仍然存在一些问题:①不能直观体现UHPC因为纤维的桥联作用而展现出特殊的受压损伤演化过程;②数据拟合得到的UHPC单轴受压本构方程中所确定的系数缺乏明确的物理意义,本构模型选择缺乏物理依据,并且本构关系的可靠性高度依赖于样本数量,导致模型的普遍适用性不高。此外,一些学者通过损伤理论分析UHPC材料的单轴受压过程,构建出具有理论基础的损伤本构关系方程。Zhang等[11]基于Lee[12]提出的塑性损伤模型,以割线模量的损伤定义UHPC损伤因子,基于UHPC的损伤因子与非弹性应变存在一阶指数衰减关系的假定,提出了UHPC单轴受压本构关系。Cheng等[13]基于应变等效原理构建损伤因子,并采用weibull分布函数作为损伤因子的演化方程,推导得到了UHPC单轴受压条件下的本构模型。Hashim等[14]针对掺入3种不同种类纤维的UHPC展开单轴受压试验,以割线模量定义损伤因子,基于试验结果认为损伤演化符合多项式分布,从而建立了3种不同纤维UHPC材料的损伤本构模型。损伤本构具有理论基础,能准确地反映UHPC的轴压过程[15-16]。但现有研究中,钢纤维对UHPC单轴受压损伤本构方程影响的研究还较少,并且围绕纤维对UHPC单轴受压本构关系影响的研究大多停留在单因素阶段,缺乏多因素的综合分析。需要进一步研究UHPC单轴受压本构关系,并探究纤维参数对UHPC单轴受压本构方程的影响。

本研究对9种不同钢纤维体积掺量及长径比的UHPC开展了棱柱体试件单轴受压(轴压)试验,分析了纤维体积掺量、长径比对UHPC破坏形态以及抗压性能的影响,基于损伤理论分析建立UHPC的单轴受压本构关系方程,并进一步探究纤维参数对本构方程系数的影响。

1　试验

1.1　UHPC配合比及原材料

试验中UHPC采用统一的基体配合比和原材料,具体配合比见表1。原材料为:P.C42.5

水泥,性能指标满足国家标准《通用硅酸盐水泥》(GB 175—2007)[17]的要求;硅灰,粒径0.1～0.2μm,比表面积18920m²/kg,密度2000kg/m³,SiO_2含量97.57%;减水剂采用聚羧酸系高效减水剂,减水率为30%;集料采用经级配设计后的3种石英砂和石英粉混合构成;钢纤维采用圆直形镀铜微细钢纤维,其原丝弹性模量为200GPa,抗拉强度2850MPa。

UHPC 配合比设计　　　　　　　　　　　表1

The mix proportion of UHPC　　　　　Tab. 1

水泥	硅灰	石英砂	高效减水剂	水
1.00	0.18	1.18	0.02	0.19

以钢纤维体积率及长径比为变量,选用长径比为:43(直径0.30mm、长度13mm)、65(直径0.20mm、长度13mm)、100(直径0.20mm、长度20mm)的三种钢纤维;分别设计3种体积掺量:1.0%、2.0%和3.0%。共设计并制备9种UHPC材料,并对其进行单轴受压试验。

以"U-纤维长径比-纤维掺量"的形式对试件进行命名,例如U1001.0表示在基体中掺入1.0%的长径比为100的钢纤维制备出的UHPC试件。

1.2 浇筑及养护制度

制备UHPC时,先将称量好的石英砂、硅灰、水泥按顺序加入搅拌锅中干拌5min,再将减水剂加入水中混合均匀后缓慢倒入搅拌锅,继续搅拌至混合物呈浆体状(约5min)。分批加入钢纤维搅拌5min,直至钢纤维被浆体包裹并分布均匀。搅拌完成后,采用沿长度方向分批、分层浇筑的方式入模,浇筑完成后模外振动密实。

在试件表面覆盖塑料薄膜,静置8～24h后脱模。脱模后将试件放入蒸养室,在90℃蒸汽环境下蒸养72h。蒸养完成后,自然养护至28d龄期进行单轴受压试验。

1.3 轴压试验方法

每组UHPC浇筑3个尺寸为100mm×100mm×300mm的棱柱体试件,用于UHPC单轴受压试验。同批浇筑3个100mm×100mm×100mm的立方体试件,测试其抗压强度。参照规范《活性粉末混凝土》(GB/T 31387—2015)[18]进行抗压性能检测,加载设备为300kN的液压伺服微机控制万能试验机,加载方式为力和位移混合加载,先以0.25kN/s的速度连续加载至30kN;然后以0.1mm/min的加载速度连续加载至试件发生破坏。在棱柱体试件纯压段的两侧面布置100mm应变片和标距为100mm的引伸计。正式试验前进行预加载,调试试验机、引伸计、应变片至功能正常,并通过应变片对试件进行对中。

2 试验结果及分析

2.1 破坏形态

试验得到单轴受压状态下,掺入不同长径比、不同体积率钢纤维时试件的破坏形态。以钢纤维长径比为65的UHPC单轴受压试件为例,不同钢纤维体积率条件下UHPC单轴受压试件的破坏形态如图1所示。

随着钢纤维体积率增加,UHPC轴压试件的破坏形态逐渐由脆性破坏转变为延性破坏。不掺钢纤维时,试件爆裂解体;掺入钢纤维后,试件沿若干条竖向裂纹开裂破坏,但在钢纤维的桥联作用下试件各部分依旧为一个整体。这是因为钢纤维在基体中乱向分布,从而形成纤维网骨架,纤维提供的界面黏结力和摩擦力限制了微裂缝的发展以及宏观裂缝的产生和扩展,进而增强了基体的塑性变形能力,使试件表现为延性破坏。

 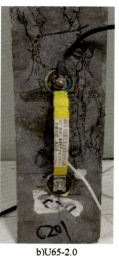

a)U65-1.0　　　　　　　　b)U65-2.0

图 1　不同钢纤维体积率的 UHPC 单轴受压试件破坏形态

Fig. 1　Failure Mode of UHPC Uniaxial Compression Specimens with Different Steel Fiber Volume Fractions

2.2　抗压性能

钢纤维体积率及长径比不同时,9 组 UHPC 的弹性模量、轴压强度以及轴压峰值应变如图 2 所示。钢纤维长径比相同时,随着体积率的增加,UHPC 的弹性模量、轴压强度及轴压峰值应变均有不同程度的增大,其中对弹性模量的影响最小。另外,当钢纤维体积率超过 2.0% 时,抗压性能的增长量下降。钢纤维对 UHPC 抗压性能的增强主要有两方面原因,一方面,钢纤维作为高弹性模量、高抗压强度的组分(可视为集料),对毗邻影响区内基体具有增强作用,提高了影响区基体的弹性模量和轴压强度;另一方面,主要原因是试件开裂后钢纤维的桥联作用约束了试件的竖向裂纹扩展,宏观表现为限制了试件沿竖向裂纹横向膨胀,从而提高了核心基体的强度,间接增强了轴压强度。但当钢纤维体积率较高、纤维过多时,材料制备过程中容易出现搅拌不均匀、纤维成团的现象,导致材料内部孔隙率增大,弹性模量及轴压强度的增长率减小。

当钢纤维体积率不变时,UHPC 的弹性模量、轴压强度和轴压峰值应变随钢纤维长径比的增大而增大。当体积率一定时,钢纤维越细(半径越小)则竖向裂纹处单位面积内钢纤维的平均数量越多,能够更好地约束裂缝扩张;钢纤维越长与基体接触面积越大、锚固长度越长,可提供更强的桥接力,更有效地约束竖向裂纹的扩张。综合钢纤维长度和直径的影响,以长径比作为钢纤维尺寸的参数,表明长径比大的钢纤维对基体增强作用更显著。此外,UHPC 轴压峰值应变试验值范围为 $2908.6 \sim 4152.3 \times 10^{-6}$,超过工程常用钢筋的屈服应变(约 2000×10^{-6}),表明受压时 UHPC 与钢筋的协同性较好,受压区的钢筋能充分发挥其抗压强度。

2.3　轴压应力-应变关系

试验得到各组 UHPC 单轴受压时的应力-应变曲线。但由于试验机自身刚度的限制,本文仅测试到 UHPC 单轴受压应力-应变曲线的上升段,如图 3 所示。

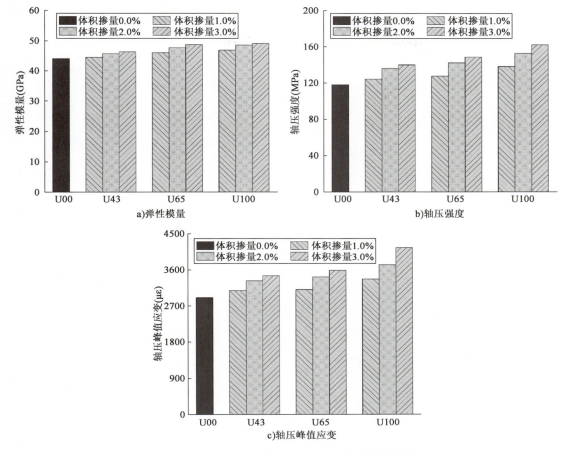

图 2 钢纤维长径比及体积率对 UHPC 抗压性能的影响

Fig. 2 Effects of aspect ratio and volume fraction of steel fiber on compressive performance of UHPC

对比各组试件的应力-应变曲线,发现钢纤维长径比相同时,试件的峰值应力和峰值应变随着体积率的增加逐渐增大,试件的延性提高。而体积率相同时,钢纤维的长径比越大,试件的延性越强。这是因为在 UHPC 单轴受压破坏的过程中,钢纤维与基体间的粘结、滑移以及拔出的过程,会吸收大量能量,体积率或长径比越大时,与基体的接触面积越大,需要耗散的能量越多,则试件的峰值强度越高、延性越强。

3 UHPC 单轴受压损伤本构模型

本文采用塑性损伤理论推导 UHPC 单轴受压时的上升段本构方程。根据 Lemaitre[19] 提出的应变等效原理,得到单轴受力状态下材料的损伤本构关系:

$$\sigma = (1-D)E_0\varepsilon \tag{1}$$

式中,D 为损伤因子;E_0 为初始弹性模量;σ、ε 分别为材料的应力和应变。

对式(1)进行无量纲处理,两端同除峰值应力 $\sigma_p = E_c\varepsilon_p$,其中 σ_p 为峰值应力,E_c 为峰值割线模量,ε_p 为峰值应变。

$$\frac{\sigma}{E_c \varepsilon_p} = \frac{E_0}{E_c}(1-D) \cdot \frac{\varepsilon}{\varepsilon_p} \tag{2}$$

令 $A = E_0/E_c$，表示初始弹性模量与峰值割线模量的比值。则式(2)可表示为：

$$y = A(1-D) \cdot x \tag{3}$$

式中，x,y 分别为无量纲化的峰值应变和峰值应力（$x = \varepsilon/\varepsilon_p, y = \sigma/\sigma_p$）。

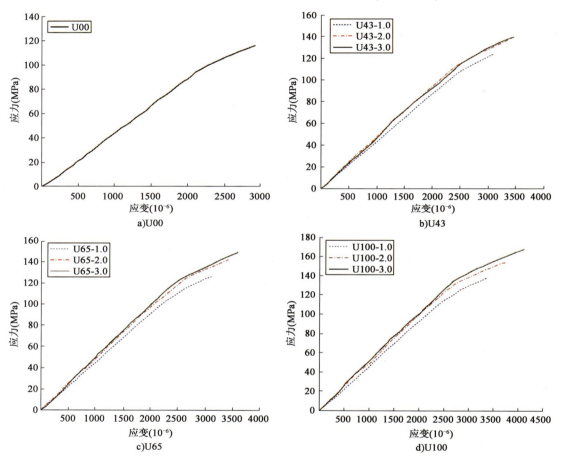

图 3　UHPC 单轴受压应力-应变曲线
Fig. 3　UHPC Uniaxial Compressive Stress-Strain Curves

现有 UHPC 单轴受压本构关系的理论模型主要是根据塑性损伤理论结合 Weibull 分布推导得到的。Weibull 分布认为在要素串联时薄弱要素是整体的决定要素，契合 UHPC 薄弱位置决定整体强度和应变的特点，因此诸多学者将其作为本构分析时的细观单元体极限应变分布函数。本文采用 Weibull 分布来描述 UHPC 单轴受压过程中材料的损伤演化规律，拟定损伤因子 D 与 x 之间的关系符合 Weibull 分布函数，即：

$$D(x) = 1 - \exp(-(x/a)^b) \tag{4}$$

已知材料损伤是一个不可逆的热力学过程，因此本构关系模型必须满足热力学第二定律不等式，损伤变量函数需为单调增函数，即 $D' > 0$。已知 $x > 0, a > 0, b > 0$ 时，$D' = b(x/a)^{b-1}$

$\exp(-(x/a)^b)>0$ 成立。因此,基于 Weibull 分布函数建立的损伤演化方程适用于描述 UHPC 单轴受压本构关系中应力-应变曲线上升段损伤历程。

将式(4)代入式(3)中,得到 UHPC 单轴受压时应力-应变曲线上升段的本构方程为:

$$y = Ax \cdot \exp(-(x/a)^b) \quad (5)$$

结合边界条件,对本构方程表达式进行进一步简化。单轴受压应力-应变关系的等量边界条件为:

(1)应变为 0 时,应力为 0,即:$x=0$ 时,$y=0$;

(2)应变为 0 时,应力-应变曲线的切线斜率为初始弹模,即 $x=0$ 时,$\dfrac{dy}{dx}=E_0$;

(3)应变为单轴受压峰值应变时,应力为单轴受压强度,即 $x=1$ 时,$y=1$;

(4)峰值点为应力-应变曲线极值点,即:$x=1$ 时,$\dfrac{dy}{dx}=0$。

引入边界条件,得到本构方程表达式(6)。

$$y = \sqrt[n]{e}x \cdot \exp\left(-\frac{x^n}{n}\right), n = \frac{1}{\ln A} \quad (6)$$

式中,e 为自然对数底数,A 定义与前文相同。通过峰值应力、峰值应变和初始弹性模量进行估算,得到本构方程系数 n,结果见表 2。将通过式(6)拟合得出的理论曲线与实测曲线进行对比,由表 3 可知,拟合判定系数均大于 0.94,表明本文所建立的上升段 UHPC 单轴受压损伤本构模型能够与试验曲线较好吻合。

UHPC 单轴受压试件损伤本构模型的相关参数　表 2
Relevant parameters of damage constitutive model of UHPC uniaxial compression specimens　Tab. 2

试件编号	初始弹模 E_0（GPa）	纤维体积掺量 ρ(%)	纤维长径比	纤维特征参数 λ	系数 n	判定系数 R^2
U43-1.0	44.5	1.0	43	0.43	9.97	0.971
U43-2.0	45.8	2.0	43	0.86	8.89	0.966
U43-3.0	46.3	3.0	43	1.29	7.51	0.942
U65-1.0	46.1	1.0	65	0.65	8.58	0.987
U65-2.0	47.8	2.0	65	1.30	7.26	0.982
U65-3.0	48.8	3.0	65	1.95	6.14	0.943
U100-1.0	46.9	1.0	100	1.00	7.42	0.986
U100-2.0	48.6	2.0	100	2.00	5.90	0.945
U100-3.0	49.2	3.0	100	3.00	4.37	0.966

在确定文中所建立的上升段损伤本构方程适用于不同基体 UHPC 的基础上,进一步探究钢纤维长径比及体积率对 UHPC 单轴受压应力-应变关系的影响,为准确量化钢纤维的影响,引入钢纤维参数 λ:

$$\lambda = V_f \cdot l_f/d_f \quad (7)$$

式中,V_f 为钢纤维的体积率;l_f/d_f 为钢纤维的长径比。式(6)所示损伤本构方程仅与系数

n 相关,由表3中数据可知,n 值随钢纤维参数 λ 的变化趋势如图4所示。

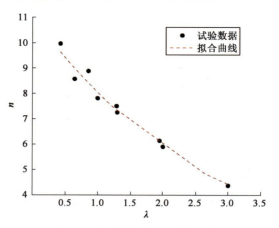

图4 纤维参数对系数 n 的影响趋势
Fig. 4　Influence of Steel Fiber Parameters on Coefficient n

在 $0 < \lambda \leq 3$ 的范围内,n 值随钢纤维参数 λ 的增加而降低,通过数值回归分析得到 n 的估算式见式(8),回归曲线判定系数为0.96,表明 n 与 λ 的函数相关性显著。

$$n = 0.38\lambda^2 - 3.33\lambda + 11 \tag{8}$$

将式(8)带入式(6)得到含钢纤维参数 λ 的 UHPC 单轴受压上升段损伤本构方程:

$$y = \sqrt[0.38\lambda^2-3.33\lambda+11]{ex} \cdot \exp\left(-\frac{x^{0.38\lambda^2-3.33\lambda+11}}{0.38\lambda^2 - 3.33\lambda + 11}\right) \tag{9}$$

通过式(9)对掺入不同体积率和长径比钢纤维的9组 UHPC 的单轴受压应力-应变曲线进行非线性回归,得到相应的拟合判定系数均大于0.93,表明式(9)得出的拟合曲线与试验数据吻合良好。

4　结论

(1)认为峰值应力前 UHPC 单轴受压损伤演化规律符合 Weibull 分布函数,结合损伤理论,得到 UHPC 单轴受压损伤本构方程。对试验数据进行回归分析,得到钢纤维参数 λ 与 UHPC 单轴受压损伤本构关系上升段方程系数 n 的函数关系式,进而建立了考虑钢纤维体积率和长径比综合影响的 UHPC 单轴受压上升段损伤本构方程。

(2)随着钢纤维的掺入,UHPC 单轴受压试件逐渐由脆性破坏变为延性破坏。并且,不同裂缝发展阶段钢纤维发挥的作用也有所不同。初裂前,钢纤维凭借自身的高弹模特性,在材料中主要作为集料组分参与承受压应力,从而提高了 UHPC 的抗压性能;初裂后,钢纤维通过桥接作用限制试件中竖向微裂纹的产生与拓展,抑制试件的横向膨胀,间接增强 UHPC 抗压性能。

(3)UHPC 的弹性模量、轴压强度和轴压峰值应变随着钢纤维长径比或体积率的增大而增大,弹性模量的增强最不显著。掺入3.0%的长径比为100的钢纤维时,UHPC 轴压强度和轴压峰值应变提高最明显。轴压强度提高值为47MPa,约为 UHPC 基体的34.8%;轴压峰值应变达到了 4152.3×10^{-6},相较 UHPC 基体约提高了41.7%。

参 考 文 献

[1] Azmee N M, Shafiq N. Ultra-high performance concrete: From fundamental to applications[J]. Case Studies in Construction Materials, 2018, 9: e197.

[2] Abhyankar S, Ralegaokar R V. State of the Art: Ultra-High-Performance Concrete: From Fundamental to Applications[J]. Lecture Notes in Civil Engineering, 2022, 172: 351-363.

[3] Zhou M, Lu W, Song J, et al. Application of ultra-high performance concrete in bridge engineering[J]. Construction and Building Materials, 2018, 186: 1256-1267.

[4] Shaikh F U A, Luhar S, Arel H S, Luhar I. Performance evaluation of Ultra-high performance fiber reinforced concrete-A review[J]. Construction and Building Materials, 2020, 232: 117-152.

[5] Abbas S, Nehdi M L, Saleem M A. Ultra-high performance concrete: Mechanical performance, durability, sustainability and implementation challenges[J]. International Journal of Concrete Structures and Materials, 2016, 10(3): 271-295.

[6] Yoo D, Banthia N. Mechanical properties of ultra-high-performance fiber-reinforced concrete: A review[J]. Cement and Concrete Composites, 2016, 73: 267-280.

[7] Naeimi N, Moustafa M A. Compressive behavior and stress-strain relationships of confined and unconfined UHPC[J]. Construction and Building Materials, 2021, 272: 121844.

[8] Yu X, Fu B, Chen S. Compression constitutive relationship of RPC with different steel fiber content[C]//Journal of Physics: Conference Series. IOP Publishing, 2020, 1635(1): 012084.

[9] Prabha S L, Dattatreya J K. Stress strain behavior of ultra-high-performance concrete under uniaxial compression[J]. International Journal of Civil Engineering and Technology (IJCIET), 2014, 5(3): 187-194.

[10] Graybeal B A. Compressive behavior of ultra-high-performance fiber-reinforced concrete[J]. ACI Materials Journal, 2007, 104(2): 146.

[11] 张燎军,马天骁. 超高性能混凝土的损伤力学模型及其在水利工程中的应用[J]. 华北水利水电大学学报(自然科学版),2019,40(04):10-14.

[12] Lee J, FENVES G. L. Plastic-damage model for cyclic loading of concrete structures[J]. Journal of engineering mechanics, 1998, 124(8): 892-900.

[13] 程臻赟. 活性粉末混凝土单轴受压本构模型研究[J]. 中国水运(下半月),2012,12(12):87-88,90.

[14] Hashim D. T, Hejazi F, Lei V. Y. Simplified constitutive and damage plasticity models for UHPFRC with different types of fiber[J]. International Journal of Concrete Structures and Materials, 2020, 14(1): 1-21.

[15] Othman H, Marzouk H. Applicability of damage plasticity constitutive model for ultra-high performance fibre-reinforced concrete under impact loads[J]. International Journal of Impact Engineering, 2018, 114: 20-31.

[16] Shafieifar M, Farzad M, Azizinamini A. Experimental and numerical study on mechanical properties of ultra high performance concrete (UHPC)[J]. Construction and Building Materials, 2017, 152:402-411.

[17] 全国水泥标准化技术委员会. GB 175—2007 通用硅酸盐水泥[S]. 北京:中国标准出版社, 2008.

[18] 全国混凝土标准化技术委员会. GB/T 31387—2015 活性粉末混凝土[S]. 北京:中国标准出版社, 2015.

[19] Lemaitre J. A continuous damage mechanics model for ductile fracture[J]. Engineering Materials and Technology, 1985, 107(1):83-89.

不同循环加载路径下焊钉连接件抗剪性能退化规律

何东洋[1]　刘玉擎[2]　杨涛[1]　徐晓青[2]

（1. 广西大学土木建筑工程学院　广西南宁　530004；
2. 同济大学桥梁工程系　上海　200092）

摘　要　地震引起的循环荷载作用具有随机性和复杂性。为探明不同循环加载路径下，焊钉连接件抗剪性能退化规律，本文开展6个焊钉连接件的低周循环荷载试验。本试验考察双侧反复循环加载、单侧重复循环加载、不同等级循环荷载的加载次序等加载路径对焊钉连接件破坏模式、抗剪承载力、抗剪刚度以及能量耗散等抗剪性能的影响。结果表明：试件均发生典型的焊钉剪切破坏；双侧反复、单侧重复循环荷载试验的滞回曲线均较为饱满，且捏缩现象较轻，滞回性能良好；不同的加载路径对试件最大抗剪承载力的影响较小，但是单侧重复循环加载试件的屈服位移和极限位移均大于双侧反复加载试件，尤其极限位移是双侧反复加载试件的1.92~2.96倍；6种加载路径下的试件环线刚度（K）随焊钉相对滑移增大的退化规律基本一致，且退化速率先大后小；加载路径基本不影响每次循环的残余位移与极限位移比例关系；不同等级循环荷载的加载次序对试件的刚度退化过程和损伤累积过程影响较大，较早进行大荷载循环加载会增大试件的刚度退化速率以及累积损伤程度。

关键词　焊钉连接件　加载路径　低周循环　抗剪性能　刚度退化
中图分类号　TU398$^+$.9　　**文献标识码**　A

Study on the Degradation Law of Shear Performance of Headed Stud Shear Connectors Under Different Loading Paths

HE Dongyang[1]　LIU Yuqing[2]　YANG Tao[1]　XU Xiaoqing[2]

(1. College of Civil Engineering and Architecture, Guangxi University, Nanning, Guangxi, 530004, China;
2. Department of Bridge Engineering, Tongji University, Shanghai, 200092, China)

作者简介：
何东洋(1996—)，男，博士研究生，主要从事组合结构桥梁方向的研究。
刘玉擎(1962—)，男，博士，教授，主要从事组合结构桥梁方向的研究。
杨涛(1979—)，男，博士，副教授，主要从事结构抗震性能方向的研究。
徐晓青(1990—)，男，博士，助理教授，主要从事组合结构桥梁方向的研究。

Abstract The cyclic loading caused by earthquakes is random and complex. In order to explore the degradation law of shear performance of headed stud shear connectors under different cyclic loading paths, the low cyclic loading tests of six headed stud shear connectors were carried out in this paper. The effect of loading paths such as bilateral repeated cyclic loading, unilateral repeated cyclic loading, and loading sequences of different levels of cyclic loading on the failure mode, shear capacity, shear stiffness, and energy dissipation of headed stud shear connectors were investigated. The results show that the typical headed stud shear failure occurs in all specimens. The hysteresis curves of bilateral repeated and unilateral repeated cyclic loading tests are relatively plump and the pinching phenomenon is slight, which shows good hysteretic behavior. The influence of different loading paths on the maximum shear capacity of the specimen is small, but the yield displacement and the ultimate displacement of the unilateral repeated cyclic loading specimen are greater than those of the bilateral repeated cyclic loading specimen, especially the ultimate displacement is 1.92-2.96 times that of the bilateral repeated specimen. The degradation law of loop stiffness (K) with the increase in relative slip under six loading paths is basically the same, and the degradation rate is great and then small. The loading path essentially does not affect the proportional relationship between the residual displacement and the ultimate displacement of each cycle. The loading sequence of different levels of cyclic loading has a great influence on the stiffness degradation process and damage accumulation process of the specimen. The earlier large-load cyclic loading will increase the stiffness degradation rate and cumulative damage degree of the specimen.

Keywords headed stud shear connector   loading path   low cyclic   shear performance   stiffness degradation
E-mail 2210402031@st.gxu.edu.cn

基于 IDA 方法的上承式钢管混凝土拱桥地震易损性分析

孙宝印[1]　张达[2]　申伟[2*]　孙天舒[3]

（1. 河海大学土木与交通学院　江苏南京　210098；
2. 广西大学土木建筑工程学院　广西南宁　530004；
3. 大连理工大学建设工程学部　辽宁大连　116024）

摘　要　为了从概率角度定量地描述上承式钢管混凝土拱桥的抗震性能，本文以某座 500 米跨径上承式钢管混凝土拱桥为研究对象，基于增量动力分析（IDA）法进行地震易损性分析。考虑材料非线性，利用 OpenSees 建立桥梁的三维有限元模型；以地面峰值加速度为地震动强度参数，采用变形破坏准则，以拱脚、拱顶截面为最不利截面所对应的曲率为损伤指标，定义四级损伤状态；基于 IDA 方法对符合条件的 10 条地震波进行调幅，对桥梁模型进行非线性时程分析，得到主拱各构件的地震响应；通过最小二乘法进行概率地震需求模型参数估计，进一步通过拟合，建立了主拱在不同破坏状态下的易损性曲线。综合对比主拱各部位地震作用下的损伤概率，结果显示拱脚为最易破坏部位。

关键词　钢管混凝土拱桥　地震易损性　增量动力分析　概率地震需求模型　抗震性能评估

中图分类号　U24　　**文献标识码**　A

基金项目：广西科技基地和人才专项（桂科 AD21220050）；广西重点研发计划（桂科 AB22036007）。
作者简介：
孙宝印（1989—），男，博士，讲师，主要从事建筑与桥梁结构非线性分析方面的研究。
张达（1999—），男，硕士研究生，主要从事拱桥抗震方面的研究。
＊申伟（1988—），男，博士，助理教授，主要从事结构智能监测与性能评估、特大跨桥梁结构设计理论与计算方面的研究。
孙天舒（1988—）男，博士，博士后，主要从事建筑与桥梁结构抗震减震分析与设计方面的研究。

Seismic Vulnerability Analysis of Deck-type CFST Arch Bridge Based on IDA Method

SUN Baoyin[1]　　ZHANG Da[2]　　SHEN Wei[2]*　　SUN Tianshu[3]

(1. College of Civil and Transportation Engineering, Hehai University, Jiangsu, Nanjing, 210098, China;
2. College of Civil Engineering and Architecture, Guangxi University, Nanning, Guangxi, 530004, China;
3. Faculty of Infrastructure Engineering, Dalian University of Technology, DaLian, Liaoning, 116024, China)

Abstract　To quantitatively describe the seismic performance of deck-type CFST arch bridge from the perspective of probability, a 500 meter long-span deck-type CFST arch bridge was taken as the research object to conducts seismic vulnerability analysis based on the incremental dynamic analysis (IDA) method. Considering the material non-linearity, the three-dimensional finite element model of the bridge was established by using OpenSees. Taking the peak groud acceleration as the seismic strength parameter and according to the deformation failure criterion, the curvature of the arch foot and arch crown sections, which are the most unfavorable sections, was defined as damage index, and then the fourth level damage state was defined. Based on IDA method, amplitude modulation is carried out for 10 qualified seismic waves, and the nonlinear time history analysis was carried out to obtain the seismic response of each component of the main arch. The parameters of the probabilistic seismic demand model were estimated by linear regression with the least square method, and then the vulnerability curves of the main arch under different failure states are further established by fitting. By comparing the damage probability of each part of the main arch under earthquake, the results show that the arch foot is the most vulnerable part.

Keywords　CFST arch bridge　Seismic vulnerability　Incremental dynamic analysis　Probabilistic seismic demand model　Seismic performance evaluation

E-mail　shenwei431@ gxu. edu. cn

0　引言

大跨度钢管混凝土（Concrete-filled Steel Tubular, CFST）拱桥因其优越的结构风格和跨越能力强等优势而在我国被广泛接受并迅速建造,以往的研究大多致力于钢管混凝土拱桥混凝土和钢材的静力行为、热和蠕变效应、结构构件形式或施工技术[1]。由于近些年地震频发,地震对人类及其现有环境造成了灾难性的破坏,虽然在理论上,钢管混凝土拱桥的整体抗震性能较好,但根据多次震害后统计结果,大跨度钢管混凝土拱桥中仍有局部构件产生损伤,目前国内外对钢管混凝土拱桥抗震性能的研究还很少,尤其是从概率角度定量地描述 CFST 的抗震性能更是匮乏。

作为目前抗震理论研究的热点问题,美国太平洋地震工程研究中心（PEER）于 2005 年提出新一代基于性能的地震工程研究框架,其中地震易损性分析为该框架的重要环节和热点之一。桥梁地震易损性分析提供了一种评估桥梁地震损伤的方法。该方法通过整个结构或某些结构构件在给定的地震动强度下达到或超过一定的破坏水平的条件概率来评估桥梁的抗震性能。这对于我国公路网的建设、灾害评估、地震加固和灾后应急响应决策等有指导意义。在目前的文献研究中,已经提出了不同的地震易损性评估方法。它们可以分为两大类:经验性和分析性,并且这两个类别可以在混合方法中合并。经验方法通过将已发生的大量地震动与对其已经观测到的损伤程度相关联来评估地震易损性（统计方法）,而分析方法使用的有限元模型再现了结构的主要特征,并估计了结构的地震动能能力和地震动所施加的需求水平(定量方法)。由于目前大跨径桥梁结构的地震破坏数据和抗震试验还极少,所以,理论分析法往往是得到其地震易损性曲线的唯一可行方法,在分析易损性分析方法中,已经使用了几种技术来开发桥梁的易损性曲线,例如蒙特卡洛模拟,贝叶斯方法和人工神经网络(ANN)等[2]。

针对目前对钢管混凝土拱桥地震易损性研究较少的状况,本文以某500m大跨径上承式钢管混凝土拱桥为研究对象,由于主拱肋为钢管混凝土拱桥最主要的受力构件,所以建立其主拱的三维有限元模型,并采用IDA方法建立其理论地震易损性曲线,确定主拱在地震中最易损伤构件。

1 地震易损性分析基本流程

结构的地震易损性是指结构在地震作用下的破坏概率,首先采用增量动力分析(IDA)方法来建立概率地震需求模型(PSDM),这是地震易损性函数的基础。地震易损性可以表示为结构的条件概率,该概率 P_f 是超过IM的假定破坏水平的概率,可以在式(1)中定义结构的超过概率[3]。

$$P_f = P(D \geq C \mid \mathrm{IM} = x) \quad (i = 1, 2, \cdots, n) \tag{1}$$

式中,P_f 为超过概率;D 为地震需求,C 为结构容量;IM代表地震记录的强度度量。

文献[10]表明,桥梁的地震需求和结构实际的承载能力的对数值符合正态分布的分布规律,由此可推之桥梁结构的损伤超越概率也同样为正态分布,某一极限状态的超越概率可由式(1)得到式(2)。

$$P_f = \Phi\left[\frac{1}{\sqrt{\sigma_{\ln D}^2 + \sigma_{\ln C}^2}} \ln\left(\frac{\mu_D}{\mu_C}\right)\right] \tag{2}$$

式中,μ_D 为地震需求的中值估计;μ_C 为地震容量的中值估计;$\sigma_{\ln D}$ 为以地震动强度度量(IM)为条件的地震需求的对数正态标准差,$\sigma_{\ln C}$ 为地震容量的对数正态标准差,并且(Cornell等人)假设 μ_C 和IM具有公式(3)的幂函数或者对数关系关系:

$$\mu_D = a\mathrm{IM}^b \text{ or } \ln(\mu_D) = \ln a + b\ln(\mathrm{IM}) \tag{3}$$

本文主要分两个步骤进行分析,首先,建立合理的桥梁有限元模型,分别进行静力分析和非线性时程分析,对于上承式钢管混凝土拱桥构件较多,一般无法直接确定其易损位置及其破坏模式,为此,确定主拱在地震组合下的易损部位;其次,确定适当的损伤指标并进行量化,进行IDA分析,通过最小二乘法进行线性回归分析,采用PSDM进行拟合,建立了主拱在不同破坏状态下的易损性曲线,确定其损伤概率,图1中的流程图显示了本文建立易损性曲线的基本流程。

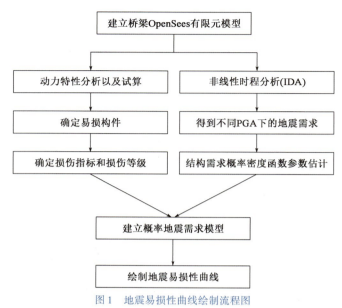

图 1 地震易损性曲线绘制流程图
Fig. 1 Seismic vulnerability curve drawing flowchart

2 桥梁有限元模型

2.1 工程概况

本文以某大跨度上承式钢管混凝土拱桥为研究对象,根据图纸以及设计资料可知,该桥位于四川省甘孜自治州白玉县和西藏自治区昌都市贡觉县之间,桥址区为典型高山深切"V"形峡谷地貌,坡陡谷深,基岩为花岗闪长岩,场地基本烈度为7°。该桥为四线铁路桥,各线线间距为5.0m,主桥采用500m跨径上承式钢管混凝土拱桥,主拱结构为双拱肋提篮拱,拱肋结构形式为变截面高度的钢管混凝土桁式混合结构,拱轴线采用悬链线,主拱的跨径为500m,拱肋矢高 $f=105m$,矢跨比 $f/L=1/4.76$;拱肋弦杆直径在拱脚56.2m区段内为1.8m,其他区段内为1.6m。拱肋弦杆在立面通过工字钢腹杆连接,拱肋间通过方、圆钢管连接,主拱结构各主要构件的横截面形式与尺寸、材料特性见表1。

主要构件的横截面形式与尺寸、材料特性   表1
Cross section form, size and material characteristics of main components   Tab. 1

构件名称	横截面形式	材料种类	横截面尺寸(mm)
弦杆	圆形钢管混凝土	钢管:Q500qENH 核心混凝土:C70	$D \times t$:1600×(24~44) 1800×(40~64)
腹杆	工字钢 方形钢管	Q370qENH	$H \times B \times t$:900×700×32 $H \times B \times t$:900×1100×(32~36)
平联斜杆	圆形钢管	Q370qENH	$D \times t$:1600×(24~44)
平联直杆	圆形钢管	Q370qENH	$D \times t$:1100×(20~30)
横联腹杆	圆形钢管	Q370qENH	$D \times t$:(700~800)×14=32
拱顶直杆与斜杆	方形钢管	Q370qENH	$H \times B \times t$: 800×(900~1320)×(28~40)

注:D、H 和 B 分别表示横截面的直径、高度和宽度,t 表示壁厚。

2.2 有限元模型的建立

基于开源软件平台 OpenSees 建立该拱桥主拱有限元模型,如图 2 所示,并考虑材料非线性,在有限元分析模型中,主拱共划分为 808 个单元、274 个节点。Open Sees 主拱有限元模型(X 和 Y 方向)见图 3。分析中考虑除弯矩以外的截面内力对结构破坏过程的影响以及双向弯曲变形的影响,选择纤维模型对两种构件的截面进行定义。为了建立精细化弹塑性纤维单元模型,主拱上下弦杆、腹杆等其他构件均采用基于刚度法的 3 个高斯点纤维单元进行模拟(即 OpenSees 中提供的 dispBeamColumn 单元),并且每个积分点采用 Gauss-Legendre 积分方案。该纤维单元将钢管和混凝土离散为纤维,假设纤维之间完全黏结,且满足平截面假定。

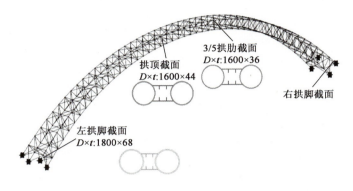

图 2　OpenSees 主拱有限元模型
Fig. 2　OpenSees finite element model of main arch

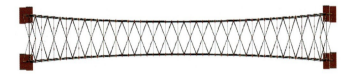

图 3　OpenSees 主拱有限元模型(X 和 Y 方向)
Fig. 3　OpenSees finite element model of main arch (XY direction)

3 地震易损性分析结果

目前对于理论易损性分析常用的表示方法为绘制地震易损性曲线。首先,选择 10 个地震波并将其缩放到不同的 IM,通过使用 IDA 方法在不同 IM 下获得主拱的动力响应,然后,使用 IDA 方法获得并计算地震需求 D 和 IM 的关系,同时得到概率地震需求模型(PSDM)。根据上述流程可以得到基于拱脚截面曲率,主拱结构在不同损伤状态的地震易损性曲线,如图 4 所示。

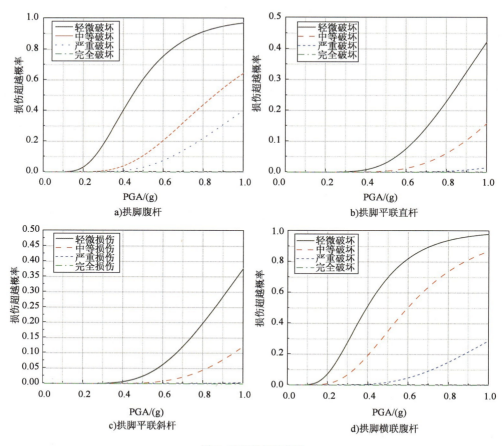

图 4 地震易损性曲线
Fig. 4 Seismic vulnerability curve

4 结论

本文对某大跨度上承式钢管混凝土拱桥主拱进行地震易损性分析。首先,采用 OpenSees 软件建立该拱桥主拱有限元模型,同时,确定了主拱的损伤指标和损伤极限状态,并将其纳入地震易损性分析。然后,基于非线性时程分析(IDA 方法),模拟了主拱在地震作用下的损伤过程,获得地震概率需求模型的回归参数,最后得到了一系列地震激励下主拱结构的地震易损性曲线,并将其用于评估主拱的破坏状态。本研究的结论总结如下:

(1)主拱的拱脚各连接杆件截面曲率服从对数正态分布,可以选择作为主拱地震易损性的损伤指标,通过计算定义四个损伤指标来表示地震作用下主拱的破坏状态。

(2)钢管混凝土拱肋具有较高的地震强度安全储备,尤其对于上下弦杆一般不会因地震作用而出现损伤;同时,对于 1/4 拱肋单元、3/4 拱肋单元、拱顶在地震动低于 1.0g 时的损伤状态也可以忽略,但是对拱脚处的连接杆件发生破坏的概率远大于其他杆件。当 PGA 低于 0.1g 时,拱脚各连接杆件均未发生破坏;当 PGA 超过 0.1g 时,主拱结构开始发生轻微破坏,对于对于 PGA 超过的 0.2g 的地震动,主拱结构开始发生中等破坏。可对拱脚连接杆件采取必要的加强措施,以保证拱脚具有良好的抗震性能。但可以发现,在可预料的地震作用下主拱结构几乎不会发生完全破坏。

(3)依据各连接杆件地震易损性曲线分析可知,各构件在不同损伤状态对应的地震易损性差异较大。通过对比拱脚各杆件不同损伤状态下的地震易损性曲线可以发现,在各级损伤状态下,横联腹杆的破坏概率是最大的,拱脚腹杆的损伤概率略低于横联腹杆,但都大于平联直杆和斜杆,平联直杆和斜杆的损伤概率。

本文研究仍存在以下不足之处:目前本研究只输入了10条地震波,后续的研究需要增加地震波数量,以便获得更多地震响应,提高数据的普遍性。另外,本文只考虑截面曲率这一个损伤指标,后续研究可以重点放在使用不同破坏准则来确定以及量化损伤指标。

参 考 文 献

[1] ZHANG Deyi,WEI Xili,YAN Ming,et al. Stochastic seismic analysis of a concrete-filled steel tubular (CFST) arch bridge under tridirectional multiple excitations[J]. Engineering Structures,52(2013):355-371.

[2] Moustafa Moufid Kassem,Fadzli Mohamed Nazri,Ehsan Noroozinejad Farsangi. The seismic vulnerability assessment methodologies:Astate-of-the-artreview[J]. Ain Shams Engineering Journal,11,(2020):849-864.

[3] Tavares D H,Suescun J R,Paultre M,et al. Seismic Fragility of a Highway Bridge in Quebec[J]. Bridge Engineering,2013,18(11):1131-1139.

[4] 黄飞鸿,何沛祥,吴腾飞.下承式钢管混凝土拱桥地震易损性分析[J].合肥工业大学学报(自然科学版),2022,45(06):801-807.

[5] 钟剑,庞于涛,袁万城.斜拉桥易损性分析的合理地震动强度指标评估[J].同济大学学报(自然科学版),2016,46(09):1340-1346,1370.

[6] PANG Yutao,WU Xun. SHEN Guoyu,et al. Seismic Fragility Analysis of Cable-Stayed Bridges Considering Different Sources of Uncertainties[J]. Bridge Engineering,2014,19(4):04013015.

[7] Hwang H,Jemigan J B,Lin Y W. Evaluation of seismic damage to memphis bridges and highway system[J]. Journal of Bridge Engineering,2000,5(4):322-330.

[8] Susanthakas,GE H,Usami T. Uniaxial stress-strain relationship of concrete confined by various shaped steel tubes[J]. Engineering Structures,2001,23:1331-1347.

[9] 夏修身,杜骞,戴胜勇.大跨度钢管混凝土拱桥抗震性能指标研究[J].世界地震工程,2019,35(01):110-116.

[10] 薛挥杰.基于IDA方法的连续刚构桥地震易损性分析[D].昆明:昆明理工大学,2021.

基于纤维模型的特大跨拱桥受力分析

钟锦祥[1]　安永辉[1,2]　马丹阳[3]*　李松林[2]

（1. 广西大学土木建筑工程学院　广西南宁　530004；
2. 大连理工大学建设工程学部　辽宁大连　116023；
3. 北京航空航天大学交通科学与工程学院　北京　100191）

摘　要　针对钢管混凝土加劲混合结构在特大跨桥梁工程中的推广应用，本文分别建立了直线型构件和拱形结构的纤维模型，模型中考虑了混凝土受压损伤退化规律和钢材的塑形发展规律。对于箍筋和钢管约束混凝土，模型考虑了约束程度对混凝土强度和延性的提升作用。在平衡计算精度与计算效率基础上，采用直线型构件的荷载位移曲线进行验证。进一步建立了特大跨拱桥中拱肋和拱上立柱的纤维模型，并开展竖向荷载作用下荷载位移曲线、应力应变曲线以及弯矩分布情况的分析。分析结果揭示了该特大跨拱桥的受力状态、变形发展规律以及关键验算截面。

关键词　特大跨拱桥　有限元分析　纤维模型　内力分析
中图分类号　U445.4　　　　**文献标识码**　A

Mechanical Analysis of Super Long-Span Arch Bridge based on the Fiber Model

ZHONG Jinxiang[1]　　AN Yonghui[1,2]　　MA Danyang[3]*　　LI Songlin[2]

(1. College of Civil Engineering and Architecture, Guangxi University, Nanning, Guangxi, 530004, China;
2. Faculty of Infrastructure Engineering, Dalian University of Technology, DaLian, Liaoning, 116023, China;
3. School of Transportation Science and Engineering, Beihang University, Beijing, 100191, China)

Abstract　In view of the continuous application of concrete-encased concrete-filled steel tube structures in super long-span bridge engineering, the fiber models of linear member and arch structure are established, respectively. The model considers the damage degradation law of concrete under compression and the plastic development law of steel. The established model considered the strength and ductility improvement by confinement effects for the steel tube con-

---

基金项目：国家优秀青年科学基金项目（52122803）。
作者简介：
钟锦祥（1998—），男，广西大学在读硕士生，主要从事大跨径拱桥在长期荷载作用后的抗震性能研究。
安永辉（1986—），男，博士，教授，博士生导师，主要从事土木工程新型与智能结构研究。
* 马丹阳（1990—），男，博士，助理教授，硕士生导师，主要从事钢管混凝土加劲混合结构研究。
李松林（1998—），男，大连理工大学在读硕士生，主要从事大跨径拱桥在长期荷载作用后的抗震性能研究。

fined concrete and stirrup confined concrete. Based on balancing calculation accuracy and efficiency, the verification was carried out based on the linear members. The fiber model of the super long-span arch bridge is further established. The vertical load-displacement curve, stress-strain curve, and bending moment distribution are analyzed to clarify the stress state and deformation development law of the super long-span arch bridge. Based on the analytical results, the stress state and deformation development law of the super large span arch bridge are clarified, as well as the critical section.

Keywords super long span arch bridge finite element analysis fiber model internal force analysis
E-mail madanyang@ buaa.edu.cn

0 引言

目前,我国对桥梁工程建设提出了越来越高的要求,具备了受力合理、耐久性好等特点的拱桥成为当今时代的优选之一。近二十年来,钢管混凝土及其混合结构拱桥结构与技术不断创新、发展[1],不断突破更大的跨度。其中,平南三桥是世界上已建成的最大跨径拱桥,主桥跨径575m;天峨龙滩特大桥为在建的世界最大跨径拱桥,主桥跨径600m。为反映工程实际,本文以天峨龙滩特大桥设计方案为依托,根据设计施工图,采用有限元计算软件ABAQUS,建立特大跨拱桥的纤维模型,进行数值计算分析,以明晰此类拱桥的受力性能。

1 纤维模型建模过程

特大跨拱桥结构以正截面受力为主,纤维模型主要用于正截面受力状态下的内力和变形计算,且具有简单、高效的优点,适用于大跨拱桥的计算分析,近年来得到了广泛应用[2]。本节基于ABAQUS有限元分析软件建立了直线型构件与拱形结构的纤维模型,用于开展内力和变形分析。

1.1 模型特点

由于结构构件的截面行为复杂,很多情况下需要将截面行为细分为很多的小区域,这些小区域一般被称之为纤维。所以纤维模型是将梁柱构件的构件截面视为纤维截面,将构件截面离散成很多纤维(包括钢纤维和混凝土纤维),对每一根纤维只考虑它的轴向本构关系,各个纤维可以定义不同的本构关系[3],它是钢筋混凝土框架结构非弹性分析中最为细化并接近实际受力性能的分析模型[4]。与一般的模型相比,纤维模型能够很好地反映结构的正截面承载力和变形,且能考虑弯矩和轴力的耦合作用,进而得到广泛应用,如用于特大跨桥梁中的拱肋和桥墩等计算分析。

1.2 建模过程

为明晰纤维模型对于构件数值计算的分析效果,本文对比单根直线型构件与拱形结构模型,分析结构在轴向压力、弯矩作用下的受力性能。

1.2.1 直线型构件

以有限元计算软件ABAQUS[5]为平台建立纤维模型,运用PQ-Fiber子程序[6]定义材料本构。首先,根据试件尺寸创建二维平面部件,对于直线型构件建立单根梁部件;随后分别创建混凝土和钢材材料,并创建梁的箱形截面赋予给梁单元,设定梁截面的1方向与2方向,示意图见图 1a)。设定材料之后,在 ABAQUS 的关键字功能里利用*rebar 关键词,将钢筋、钢管以及其余部分的混凝土插入箱形截面的梁单元中,随后进行装配、设定分析步、相互作用、荷载以及划分网格等步骤,建立一个直线型构件模型。

1.2.2 拱形结构

与建立直线型梁单元过程相似,拱形结构首先用二维平面的线特征建立跨径为 300m 的半跨模型,同时建立 6 根立柱,其作为传输桥面上荷载的部件。在材料属性板块上创建混凝土、钢管等材料属性,考虑到钢管内混凝土部分主要受压,因此调用 UConcrete01 本构模型,即忽略抗拉强度的混凝土模型,其拉应力始终为零,而钢管外的钢筋混凝土部分则是调用 UConcrete02 本构模型,即考虑抗拉强度的混凝土模型,防止主拱截面外侧部分受拉,钢管与钢筋则调用 USteel03 钢材本构模型,即拉压不等强的弹塑性随动硬化单轴本构模型。拱截面材性分布如图 2 所示。

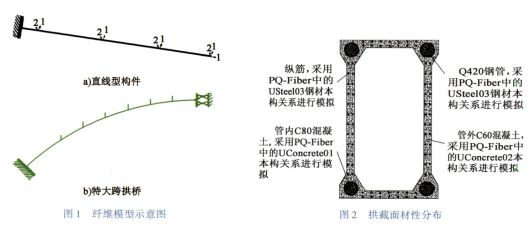

图 1　纤维模型示意图
Fig. 1　Schematic view of the fiber model

图 2　拱截面材性分布
Fig. 2　Material distribution of the arch section

调用材料的本构模型后,依据实际工程设计方案分段创建 12 个工程实际的混凝土箱形截面,将其赋予给拱形梁单元,设定截面的 1 和 2 方向,如图 1a)所示,随后再用*rebar 关键词命令在 12 个截面上依次插入钢筋、钢管、管内混凝土等共计 3312 根纤维。在完成构件的基本建立后,进行装配、设立分析步、相互作用、荷载以及划分网格等步骤,最后提交分析,分析结果见 2.2 节。

2　模拟结果分析

本节开展了直线型构件在轴压作用下的纤维模型验证,确定了模型的适用性。在此基础上,进一步分析拱形结构在竖向压力作用下的荷载-位移曲线、轴向应力-应变关系与弯矩分布情况。

2.1　直线型构件受力状态分析

为验证上述建模方法的准确性,直线型构件根据刘丽英[7]进行的钢管混凝土加劲混合轴压短柱试验进行验证,其中 R1-1 试件管内管外均采用强度等级为 C50 的混凝土,钢管和纵筋的屈服强度分别为 325MPa 与 380MPa,而 R2-2 试件在钢管内采用强度等级为 C70 的混凝土。

根据前文所建立的直线型构件纤维模型,将模拟的结果与试验数据进行对比分析,如图3所示。经分析可知,在轴压状态下,模拟所得的试件R1-1、R2-2极限承载力分别为1215.8kN、1192.6kN,与实测所得的极限承载力1281.5kN、1273.5kN误差约5.1%、6.4%,可以看出对承载力模拟结果较好。但是模型下降段刚度明显低于实测结果,下降段偏于平缓,主要是因为模型中没有考虑外包混凝土压碎的机制,在后续模型中考虑进一步改进。

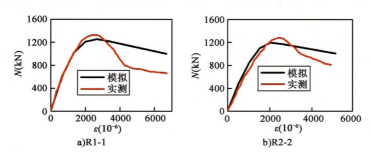

图3　直线型构件的荷载-位移曲线验证

Fig. 3　Verifications of the load versus displacement of the linear members

所建立的直线型构件纤维模型得到已有试验数据的验证,能较好地反映结构在现实状态下的受力与变形。

2.2　拱形结构加载过程分析

特大跨拱桥模拟过程中设立了三个分析步骤:第一阶段是对拱肋施加竖向均布荷载,根据截面的不同,竖向均布荷载从拱脚处893N/m递减至拱顶处的488N/m。第二阶段是施加立柱传递至拱轴上的竖向集中荷载,各立柱传输的荷载值在$5.47 \times 10^3 \sim 1.97 \times 10^4$kN范围内;第三阶段则是对前两个阶段的荷载继续等比例加载直至达到破坏。拱肋1/4跨轴向应力-应变关系曲线见图4[8]。在第二阶段竖向荷载作用下以及第三阶段荷载作用下,皆是拱脚处弯矩最大。第三阶段荷载下的弯矩达到了-9.96×10^5kN/m,拱脚和拱顶处为弯矩最大的截面。

3　结论

本文基于建立的直线型构件与拱形结构的纤维模型,开展了其在不同荷载作用下的受力状况与变形分析,主要结论如下:

(1)经直线型构件纤维模型计算结果与试验结果对比分析,显示极限承载力N_u的误差平均值为5.75%,验证了本文建模方法的适用性,

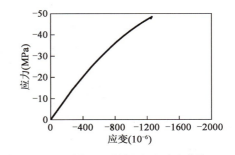

图4　拱肋1/4跨轴向应力-应变曲线

Fig. 4　Stress-strain curve of the 1/4 span of arch rib

为进一步研究特大跨拱桥在多种工况下的受力性能提供了方法。

(2)基于建立的拱形结构模型分析得出第三阶段荷载下的最大弯矩出现在拱脚和拱顶,说明拱脚和拱顶是控制拱形结构承载力的关键截面。

参 考 文 献

[1] 陈宝春,刘君平.世界拱桥建设与技术发展综述[J].交通运输工程学报,2020,20(1):27-41.
[2] 陶慕轩,丁然,潘文豪,等.传统纤维模型的一些新发展[J].工程力学,2018,35(03):1-21.
[3] 齐虎,孙景江,林淋.OPENSEES中纤维模型的研究[J].世界地震工程,2007(04):48-54.
[4] 张强,周德源,伍永飞,等.钢筋混凝土框架结构非线性分析纤维模型研究[J].结构工程师,2008(1):15-20,25.
[5] Simulia,ABAQUS Version 6.14-4:theory manual,users' manual,verification manual and example problems manual,2014.
[6] 刘丽英.新型钢管混凝土叠合柱轴压力学性能研究[D].福州:福州大学,2013.
[7] 汪勇刚,安竹石.基于有限元分析的大跨钢管拱桥主拱承压载荷计算研究[J].科技通报,2019,35(9):168-172.
[8] 张宗山.系杆拱桥结构受力分析[J].中国水运,2021,12:151-153.

采用单边螺栓连接的可拆装式钢管混凝土 K 形节点力学性能研究

虞振波 侯 超

(南方科技大学海洋科学与工程系 广东深圳 518000)

摘 要 加快发展建筑工业化,研发可拆装、可循环利用的结构构件,是建筑结构领域实现低碳减排的重要途径之一。本文提出了一种通过单边螺栓与曲面板连接件连接钢管混凝土弦杆与空钢管腹杆的新型可拆装式钢管混凝土 K 形节点,并研究了其在静力荷载下的力学性能。采用两腹杆铰接、弦杆一端自由一端轴拉的典型边界条件,对可拆装式钢管混凝土 K 形节点试件开展了系列力学性能试验,试验中的主要参数包括螺栓布置、螺栓直径和嵌入深度、曲面板连接件设计、弦杆径厚比、腹弦杆壁厚比、材料强度等。基于试验结果,深入分析了该类新型可拆装式节点的破坏形态、极限承载力、刚度和变形特性,明晰了各重要参数对节点力学行为的影响规律;并通过破坏部件拆除、杆件替换后的重复加载,研究了节点在循环服役期的力学性能并与初次加载阶段进行对比。结果表明,部分替换杆件的节点在多次服役期内的强度差整体均小于 5%,实现了钢管混凝土弦杆与单边螺栓等主要部件的有效重复利用。

关键词 钢管混凝土 K 形节点 单边螺栓 结构部件拆装替换 力学性能 试验研究

中图分类号 TU398[+].9 **文献标识码** A

Behaviour of blind-bolted CFST chord to CHS Brace Demountable K-joints

YU Zhenbo HOU Chao

(Department of Ocean Science and Engineering, Southern University of Science and Technology, Shenzhen, Guangdong, 518000, China)

Abstract Driven by the increasing demand of construction industrialization, the research and development on demountable and reusable structural components has become one of the key approaches to reduce carbon emission in the building industry. This paper presents a novel demountable K-joints formed by concrete-filled steel tubular (CFST)

作者简介:

虞振波(1989—),男,博士研究生,主要从事新型海洋工程结构方面的研究。

侯超(1988—),男,博士,副教授,主要从事高性能钢-混凝土组合结构、新型海洋工程结构方面的研究。

chords and circular hollow section (CHS) braces connecting through blind bolts and curved flush endplates (CFST K-joints for short). The behaviour of the proposed novel joints subjected to typical static loads is studied. A series of tests are conducted on demountable CFST K-joint specimens under a typical boundary condition where pined supports are applied at the ends of two braces whilst one end of the chord is under tension and the other is left free. The main parameters varied in the tests include the arrangement, diameter and embedment depth of the blind bolts, the design of curved flush endplate, the radius to thickness ratio of CFST chord, the brace to chord thickness ratio, the material strengths, and etc. Based on the test results, the failure mode, the ultimate bearing capacity, the stiffness and the deformation characteristics of the novel demountable joints are investigated, with the influence of those important parameters evaluated. Meanwhile, the behavior of the demountable joints in the repeated service periods are studied and compared with those in the initial loading stage after the disassembly of damaged components and the replacement of new ones. The results show that the differences in strength of the joints during multiple service periods are generally smaller than 5%, which testifies the effective reuse of the main structural components such as CFST chords and blind bolts.

Keywords concrete filled steel tubular K-joints blind bolts disassembly and replacement of structural components structural behaviour experimental investigation

E-mail houc@ sustech. edu. cn

0 引言

为加快建筑工业化,促进资源节约和循环利用。本文提出了一种采用单边螺栓与曲面板连接件连接的可拆装式钢管混凝土 K 形节点,研究了其在静力荷载下的力学性能。基于试验结果,深入分析了该类新型组合节点的破坏形态、极限承载力、刚度和变形特性,明晰了各重要参数对节点力学行为的影响规律;并通过破坏部件拆除、杆件替换后的重复加载,研究了节点在循环服役期的力学性能并与初次加载阶段进行对比。结果表明,部分替换杆件的节点在多次服役期内的强度差整体均小于 5%,可实现钢管混凝土弦杆与单边螺栓等主要部件的有效重复利用。

1 试验设计与结果

1.1 试验设计

为实现钢管混凝土 K 形节点的可拆装与主要结构部件的重复利用,在综合考虑节点区的抗拉与抗剪需求、螺栓连接及拆装的操作空间与施工可行性、缓解节点区应力集中等因素的基础上,提出采用单边螺栓与曲面板连接件连接的新型节点及其布置方案与施工工艺,实现节点连接的安全、可靠、经济、适用。如图 1 所示,该类新型节点试件由钢管混凝土弦杆、空钢管腹杆、曲面板连接件和单边螺栓组成。弦杆、腹杆和曲面板连接件均由热轧钢板卷制而成,腹弦杆夹角均为 45°,试件的离心率 e 为 0;弦杆由自密实混凝土填充;曲面板连接件对应的圆心角为 180°,其内弧面与弦管外壁紧密贴合。

开展了可拆装式钢管混凝土 K 形节点在两腹杆铰接、弦杆一端自由一端轴拉的典型边界条件作用下的力学性能试验研究。试验在 2000kN 自平衡反力架开展,如图 2 所示。试件的两个空钢管腹杆与固定在反力架上的铰支座连接,铰支座斜面通过定制螺杆与荷载传感器连接,在为腹杆提供铰接边界的同时,监测加载过程中的腹杆内力发展。钢管混凝土弦杆一端加载、一端自由,加载端由 1000kN 作动器施加水平轴拉荷载。在试验设计中,通过变化试件参数,探讨螺栓布置方式、螺栓直径和嵌入深度、曲面板连接件设计、弦杆径厚比、腹弦杆壁厚比、材料强度等重要参数对节点可拆装性能与力学性能的影响规律。

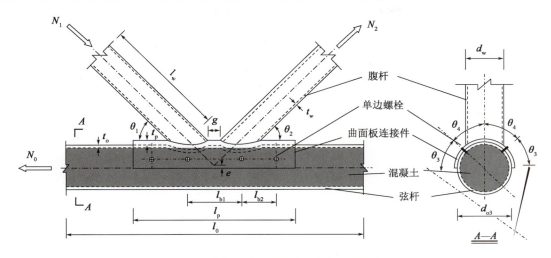

图1 可拆装式钢管混凝土K形节点示意图
Fig. 1 Schematic view of the demountable CFST K-joint

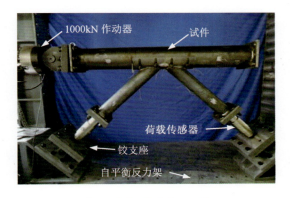

图2 节点试件加载示意图
Fig. 2 Testing setup for the demountable CFST K-joint

1.2 试验结果

在本试验参数范围内,大部分试件出现了受压腹杆局部屈曲破坏;当连接区域的曲面板连接件或弦杆强度与刚度相对较弱时,则出现曲面板连接件塑性失效或弦杆表面塑性失效;当单边螺栓布置不足或直径过小时,则可能出现螺栓破坏。因此,该类节点的破坏模态主要有四种,即受压腹杆局部屈曲、曲面板连接件塑性失效、弦杆表面塑性失效伴随曲面板连接件与弦杆的分离、螺栓破坏,如图3所示。

当试件采用锚固型单边螺栓时,螺栓嵌入管内并填充混凝土后可大幅提高节点的初始刚度,改善节点整体受力性能。在该节点试件出现受压腹杆屈曲破坏后,拆除已破坏的腹杆-曲面板连接件,并更换相应替换件,与仍处在弹性阶段的原钢管混凝土弦杆与单边螺栓等主要部件组成新的钢管混凝土 K 形节点试件，并进行第二阶段的重复加载试验；新试件再次出现受压腹杆屈曲破坏，其极限承载力与原试件相差 1.56%。对第二次受损的构件继续进行拆除替换，并进行第三阶段的重复加载试验；新试件同样出现受压腹杆屈曲破坏，其极限承载力与原试件相差 2.94%。试验结果表明，通过拆除替换部分受损构件后的节点，在循环服役期多次重复加载时的强度差整体均小于 5%，实现了钢管混凝土弦杆与单边螺栓等主要部件的有效重复利用。

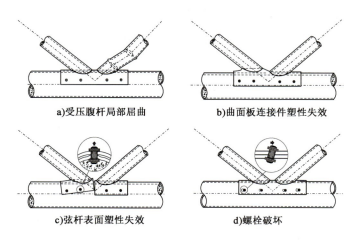

图3 节点试件典型破坏模态
Fig. 3 Typical failure modes of demountable CFST K-joint

在典型荷载边界下，可拆装式钢管混凝土 K 形节点表现出较好的延性与变形能力。在加载初期，荷载随变形的发展呈线性增长；随着节点变形的增加，荷载增速变缓；当试件进入塑性后，荷载维持不变的情况下，节点相对变形迅速增长，直至刚度相对较弱的构件发生塑性破坏，节点失去承载能力。分析得到的各节点试件对应典型破坏模态的荷载(N)-变形(δ)曲线，如图 4 所示：①模态 A-受压腹杆局部屈曲破坏，与其他破坏模态相比，表现出较好的刚度和强度。②模态 B-曲面板连接件塑性失效，与模态 A 相比，节点的强度和刚度都随着曲面板连接件厚度的降低而降低。③模态 C-弦杆表面塑性失效，在此类破坏模态下，受压腹杆的初始刚度与模态 A 相比有明显降低；同时，由于曲面板连接件分离设计，受拉侧弦杆壁无法提供足够的支撑力，随着荷载不断增大，最终导致弦杆表面塑性屈服，节点强度相比模态 A 亦显著降低。④模态 D-螺栓破坏，当单边螺栓布置的数量不足、直径偏小时，随着荷载的不断增加，螺栓所受的拉、剪应力不断增加，导致其纵向变形不断增大；而弦杆受力方向的改变进一步造成螺栓孔的应力集中，最终导致螺栓发生破坏并伴随螺栓孔的撕裂，节点刚度相比模态 A 同样显著降低。

由以上对四类典型破坏模态和 N-δ 曲线的分析可知，当发生受压腹杆局部屈曲破坏时，节点的强度与刚度相对最高，且可以较充分利用空钢管腹杆的材料强度；同时，钢管混凝土弦杆与单边螺栓等更有价值的主要部件可有效重复利用；通过拆除、替换部分受损构件后形成新的钢管混凝土 K 形节点仍可以继续有效服役。

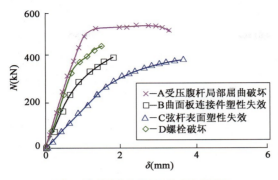

图 4　节点试件典型 N-δ 关系曲线对比
Fig. 4　Comparison of typical N-δ relations of joint specimens

2　结论

所设计的采用单边螺栓与曲面板连接件连接的可拆装式钢管混凝土 K 形节点,可通过破坏部件拆除、杆件替换后,实现钢管混凝土弦杆与单边螺栓等主要部件的有效重复利用。部分替换杆件的节点试件在循环服役期的力学性能并与初次加载阶段相比,其强度差整体均小于 5%。

参 考 文 献

[1]　韩林海. 钢管混凝土结构:理论与实践[M]. 3 版. 北京:科学出版社,2016.

[2]　HOU Chao, HAN Linhai, MU Tingmin. Behaviour of CFDST chord to CHS brace composite K-joints: Experiments[J]. Journal of Constructional Steel Research, 2017, 135.

[3]　Chao Hou, Lin-Hai Han. Analytical behaviour of CFDST chord to CHS brace composite K-joints[J]. Journal of Constructional Steel Research, 2017, 128.

[4]　Yusak Oktavianus, Huang Yao, Helen M. Goldsworthy, Emad F. Gad. Pull-out behaviour of blind bolts from concrete-filled tubes[J]. Proceedings of the Institution of Civil Engineers - Structures and Buildings, 2015, 168(10).

[5]　Wenjin Huang, Luigi Fenu, Baochun Chen, Bruno Briseghella. Experimental study on K-joints of concrete-filled steel tubular truss structures[J]. Journal of Constructional Steel Research, 2015, 107.

[6]　Dengyiding Jin, Chao Hou, Luming Shen, Lin-Hai Han. Numerical investigation of demountable CFST K-joints using blind bolts[J]. Journal of Constructional Steel Research, 2019, 160.

[7]　Brian Uy, Vipulkumar Patel, Dongxu Li, Farhad Aslani. Behaviour and Design of Connections for Demountable Steel and Composite Structures[J]. Structures, 2017, 9.

[8]　Fei Xu, Ju Chen, Wei-liang Jin. Experimental Investigation and Design of Concrete-Filled Steel Tubular CHS Connections[J]. Journal of Structural Engineering, 2014, 141(2).

分环浇筑的劲性骨架拱圈混凝土环间界面受力试验研究

林春姣 朱剑宇 肖周强 罗 转 卢章彦 秦昌宇 谭善晟

(广西大学土木建筑工程学院/工程防灾与结构安全教育部重点实验室/
广西防灾减灾与工程安全重点实验室 广西南宁 530004)

摘 要 为研究劲性骨架混凝土拱桥主拱圈的外包混凝土分环浇筑界面的受力特性,参照拱箱腹板浇筑方式,设计制作了两种板厚、两种浇筑方式(整体浇筑和分环浇筑)成型的4组试件,对分环成型的试件逐环施加预应力,进行全部试件的轴压破坏试验,测试了各试件受力过程中的应变、变形和极限承载力,获得了各试件的破坏形态和相关荷载-应变、箍筋荷载-应变、荷载-变形等变化曲线。试验结果显示:分环浇筑试件在受力过程中可能在分环界面处首先产生裂缝,界面两侧的混凝土之间产生一定的滑移,且环间初应力差可加大滑移程度,但其承载力与整体成型试件相比无明显降低。分析认为,分环浇筑成型混凝土的环间界面,对劲性骨架混凝土主拱圈的整体工作性有一定影响,但对其极限承载能力的影响不明显。

关键词 劲性骨架拱桥 主拱圈混凝土 分环浇筑 分环界面 试验
中图分类号 U448.22 **文献标识码** A

基金项目:国家自然科学基金项目(51878186)。
作者简介:
林春姣(1971—),女,副教授,主要从事桥梁工程研究。
朱剑宇(1996—),男,硕士研究生,主要从事拱桥方面的研究。
肖周强(1997—),男,硕士研究生,主要从事拱桥方面的研究。
罗转(1999—),男,硕士研究生,主要从事拱桥方面的研究。
卢章彦(1998—),男,硕士研究生,主要从事拱桥方面的研究。
秦昌宇(1998—),男,硕士研究生,主要从事拱桥方面的研究。
谭善晟(1996—),男,硕士研究生,主要从事拱桥方面的研究。

## Experimental Research on the Mechanical of the Concrete Interface Between Rings of Rigid Skeleton Arch Ring

LIN Chunjiao　ZHU Jianyu　XIAO Zhouqiang　LUO Zhuan　LU Zhangyan　QIN Changyu　TAN Shansheng

(School of Civil and Architectural Engineering of Guangxi University/Key Laboratory of Disaster Prevention and Structural Safety of the Ministry of Education/Guangxi Key Laboratory of Disaster Prevention and Structural Safety, Nanning, Guangxi, 530004, China)

Abstract　In order to study the mechanical characteristics of the concrete interface of the main arch ring of the rigid skeleton arch bridge, which were formed by ring pouring, the concrete pouring way of the box web of main arch, four groups of test members were made with two thicknesses in two casting ways: one is to pour concrete into a whole in onetime, another is to divide the concrete into three layers and pour them into a whole layer by layer. And initial stresses were applied to the different concrete layers of the later ones. All members were subjected to axial compression until failure. The strain, deformation and ultimate bearing capacity of each specimens during the loading process were tested, and the failure mode and related load-strain, stirrup load-strain, load-deformation and other curves of each specimens were obtained. The test results show that cracks may be caused at the concrete interface firstly during the loading process of the members formed by layers, and a certain slippage will occur on the concrete layers interface, and it will increase with the initial stress difference, but its bearing capacity is not significantly reduced compared with that of the onetime-pouring ones. According to the analysis, the interface between layers of the encased concrete of main arch ring has a certain effect on its integration, but is not obvious on its ultimate bearing capacity.

Keywords　rigid skeleton arch bridge　main arch ring concrete　pouring in layers　concrete interface of layers test

E-mail　llccwj@163.com

0　引言

随着国家大力建设高速铁路网，劲性骨架混凝土拱桥因其具有施工难度低、刚度大、经济性好、抗震性能好等特点而受到青睐[1-2]。劲性骨架混凝土拱桥的施工方法是先形成劲性拱骨架，然后在拱骨架上浇筑外包混凝土形成主拱圈。由于外包混凝土的浇筑量较大，劲性拱骨架无法承受一次性整体浇筑的重量，所以需要对外包混凝土进行分环浇筑，以保证施工过程中的结构安全[3-4]。

一般认为，分环浇筑的外包混凝土环间界面可能成为拱圈结构的薄弱部位，影响拱圈的整体承载，所以有必要对混凝土分环界面的受力机理及其对整体结构的影响进行深入研究。这种分环浇筑的混凝土界面，与新旧混凝土界面有相似之处，因此，目前分析其界面受力性能也参考新旧混凝土界面方面的研究成果[7-13]。由于劲性骨架拱的主拱圈混凝土分环界面主要在腹板或者腹板与顶底板衔接处，界面接缝较小，且往往在同一块腹板上出现1~3条接缝，因此，其受力性能对于拱箱的整体工作性能非常重要，值得进行深入研究。

为了掌握分环浇筑的劲性骨架拱桥主拱圈外包混凝土各环之间界面的工作性能，掌握环与环之间接缝的传力特性，本文模拟劲性骨架中分环浇筑的腹板，分别设计了2组分环浇筑和2组整体浇筑的试件，进行破坏试验。

1 试验设计

根据试验目的,设计两种尺寸试件进行试验,每种尺寸再分为整体浇筑和分环浇筑 2 种成型方式,每组 5 个试件,总共 4 组 20 个。试件设计参数如表 1 所示。

试 件 参 数 表 表1
Parameter of test members Tab. 1

组别	试件尺寸 (mm)	纵筋 (配筋率ρ)	箍筋 (配箍率ρ_{sv})	分环数量	第一环初应力 (MPa)	第二环初应力 (MPa)	数量
Z-250	250×450×1000	10Φ12 (1.0%)	φ8@50/100 (0.4%)	1	—	—	5
F-250	250×450×1000	10Φ12 (1.0%)	φ8@50/100 (0.4%)	3	4.02	8.04	5
Z-300	300×450×1000	10Φ12 (0.84%)	φ8@50/100 (0.33%)	1	—	—	5
F-300	300×450×1000	10Φ12 (0.84%)	φ8@50/100 (0.33%)	3	4.02	8.04	5

对分环浇筑的试件逐步施加初应力,预应力施加程序参照主拱圈施工过程进行。整体浇筑试件一次性浇筑成型,不施加初应力。

2 试件破坏形态

四组试件在加载过程中出现的现象和破坏形态大致如下:F-250 组的试件在加载初始阶段,分界面未出现裂缝;加载至 $0.5N_u$(试件峰值荷载)时,三个试件在分界面出现从端部向中部发展的长裂缝;加载至 N_u 时,两个分界面均开裂,已有裂缝增大,最终破坏时,侧面出现斜裂缝,分界面发生出现错位,有较大响声。Z-250 组的试件在加载初始阶段,主要在边角出现裂缝;加载至 $0.5N_u$ 时,试件上、下部出现纵向短裂缝;加载至 N_u 时,端部裂缝增多,两侧出现纵向长裂缝,最终破坏时,试件中部出现明显的密集水平裂缝,破坏过程较缓慢。F-300 组的试件在加载初始阶段,有两个试件第二分界面出现长裂缝;加载至 $0.5N_u$ 时,另两个试件在第一分界面出现长裂缝。加载至 N_u 时,全部试件分界面出现长裂缝。试件破坏时出现斜裂缝,有较大响声,破坏较突然。Z-300 组的试件在加载初始阶段,有少量边角部位细裂缝;加载至 $0.5N_u$ 时,各试件上、下部出现纵向短裂缝;加载至 N_u 时,端部裂缝增多,试件左右两侧开始出现纵向长裂缝;破坏时中部出现明显的密集水平裂缝,破坏过程较缓慢。

典型破坏形态见图 1。

图 1 典型破坏形态

Fig. 1 Failure Modes of test members

3 试验结果

3.1 混凝土荷载-应变曲线

图2为4组试件中间截面不同横向位置处在不同加载阶段的典型的混凝土应变分布曲线图,曲线图中部分加载阶段的数据点缺失表示应变片因混凝土开裂而损坏。分环浇筑试件容易在分界面开裂,且承受更大环间初应力差的第二分界面先开裂,开裂后两侧混凝土应变不一致。

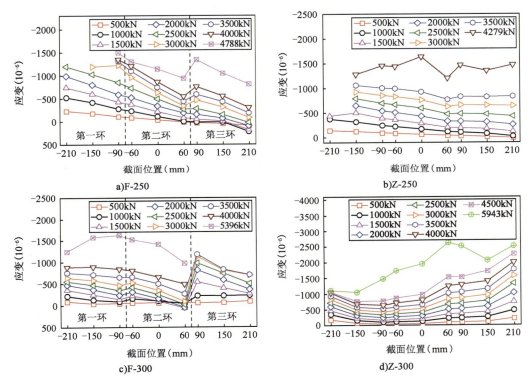

图2 试件混凝土荷载-应变曲线
Fig.2 Load-concrete strain curves of test members

3.2 分界面滑移分析

限于测试条件,采用试件左右两侧面的变形对比进行界面滑移分析,典型变化情况如图3所示。分界面出现裂缝后,两侧变形存在差值,各混凝土环在出现了滑移的现象,整体浇筑试件未出现滑移现象。

3.3 分界面箍筋荷载-应变曲线

图4为典型试件分界面箍筋应变随荷载变化图。混凝土分界面开裂后,混凝土无法传递应力,分界面处的应力传递更多由箍筋承担,分界面处的箍筋应变值明显增大;整体浇筑试件不存在分界面,相应部位的箍筋箍筋应变曲线增长趋势稳定,未发生应变突增现象。

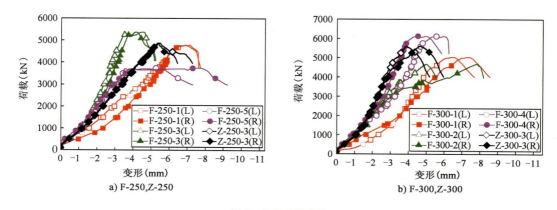

a) F-250, Z-250

b) F-300, Z-300

图 3 荷载-变形曲线

Fig. 3 Load-deformation curves of test members

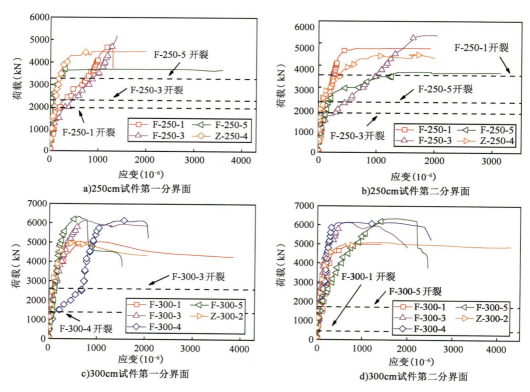

a) 250cm 试件第一分界面

b) 250cm 试件第二分界面

c) 300cm 试件第一分界面

d) 300cm 试件第二分界面

图 4 箍筋荷载-应变曲线

Fig. 4 Load-strain curves of transverse reinforcement bars of test members

3.4 试件承载力

20 个试件的受压试验结果和理论强度如表 2、表 3 所示。本文试验中各试件均单次浇筑成型,计算时按照实际强度取值。对比各试件的实测极限荷载和理论极限承载力看到,各尺寸的两组试件中,少数比值稍低(0.88、0.89、0.81),其余分环浇筑与整体浇筑试件的实测值和理论值之比差别不大。结合具体试验,实测值与理论值相差较大的试件主要是制作时端部有轻微质量问题,加载过程中产生更大损伤,导致承载力与计算值的比值有较大下降。总体而言,正常分环浇筑试件与整体浇筑试件相比,承载力没有明显下降,但是分环浇筑试件的分界面在加载过程中容易出现开裂和滑移,影响整体性。增大板厚和混凝土环初应力差,会加大影响。因此,控制混凝土浇筑质量和分界面的黏结能力是保证分环浇筑试件承载能力的关键。

250cm 厚试件的承载力 表2
Bearing capacity of test members with 250 cm thickness Tab. 2

试件编号	实测极限荷载(kN)	承载力计算值(kN)	试验值/计算值
F-250-1	4788	5320.69	0.90
F-250-2	5396	5016.83	1.08
F-250-3	5376	5146.33	1.04
F-250-4	4101.5	4675.50	0.88
F-250-5	3742.5	4105.84	0.91
Z-250-1	4279	4281.94	1.00
Z-250-2	4152.5	4398.53	0.94
Z-250-3	4871	4654.01	1.05
Z-250-4	4507.5	4654.01	0.97
Z-250-5	4088	4529.41	0.90

300cm 厚试件的承载力 表3
Bearing capacity of test members with 300 cm thickness Tab. 3

试件编号	实测极限荷载(kN)	承载力计算值(kN)	试验值/计算值
F-300-1	5036	5710.94	0.88
F-300-2	4679	5857.44	0.80
F-300-3	6121	5781.15	1.06
F-300-4	6143	6038.36	1.02
F-300-5	6339.5	6021.65	1.05
Z-300-1	5943	5770.58	1.03
Z-300-2	5096	5414.02	0.94
Z-300-3	5615	5414.02	1.04
Z-300-4	5721.5	6037.72	0.95
Z-300-5	4651.5	4519.04	1.03

4 结论

本文通过浇筑的混凝土试件受压破坏试验,初步得出以下结论:

(1)正常分环浇筑试件的承载力与整体浇筑试件相比无明显下降,但分环浇筑试件的分界面在加载过程中易出现裂缝,影响结构的整体性。

(2)分环浇筑试件的分界面出现裂缝后,两侧混凝土产生滑移,增大板厚和混凝土环的初应力差,将加大影响。

(3)分界面处箍筋能有效承担混凝土开裂后的应力传递,维持结构整体受力,可提高混凝土浇筑质量和分环界面的黏结能力。

上述研究成果可为分环浇筑的劲性骨架混凝土拱桥主拱圈提供参考依据,但本文试验中的试件较劲性骨架混凝土拱主拱圈的结构形式简单,且试件制作和分环界面的处理也较实际工程更为简化,对分环界面的传力机理、影响因素和处理措施等仍在进一步研究中。

参 考 文 献

[1] 郑皆连.我国大跨径混凝土拱桥的发展新趋势[J].重庆交通大学学报(自然科学版),2016,35(S1):8-11.

[2] 赵人达,张正阳.我国钢管混凝土劲性骨架拱桥发展综述[J].桥梁建设,2016,46(06):45-50.

[3] 林春姣,郑皆连,李翔,等.斜拉扣索调整南盘江特大桥拱圈的结构应力[J].广西大学学报(自然科学版),2017,42(01):274-283.

[4] 邓年春,李长胜,郭晓,等.钢管混凝土劲性骨架拱桥主拱圈施工方法进展[J].科学技术与工程,2021,21(15):6132-6139.

[5] 吴海军,王薿民,陆萍.劲性骨架混凝土拱桥外包混凝土分环浇筑方案对结构受力的影响[J].重庆交通大学学报(自然科学版),2017,36(11):1-6.

[6] 曾吉策.劲性骨架拱桥混凝土浇筑最优方案的分析和设计[D].重庆:重庆交通大学,2016.

[7] 赵志方,周厚贵,等.新旧混凝土黏结机理研究与工程应用[M].北京:中国水利水电出版社,2003.

[8] 郑山锁,裴培,张艺欣,等.钢筋混凝土黏结滑移研究综述[J].材料导报,2018,32(23):4182-4191.

[9] 黄璐,卓卫东,谷音,等.界面剂对新旧混凝土界面粘结性能影响的试验研究[J].福州大学学报(自然科学版),2018,46(03):396-402.

[10] Khuram Rashid, Madiha Ahmad, Tamon Ueda, et al. Experimental investigation of the bond strength between new to old concrete using different adhesive layers, Construction and Building Materials,2022, 249:118798.

[11] Yan He, Xiong Zhang, R. D. Hooton, Xiaowei Zhang. Effects of interface roughness and interface adhesion on new-to-old concrete bonding[J]. Construction and Building Materials,2017, 151:582-590.

[12] 赵勇,邹仁博.高强混凝土新旧结合面抗剪性能试验[J].同济大学学报(自然科学版),2017,45(07):962-969.

[13] 张阳,吴洁,邵旭东,等.超高性能混凝土-普通混凝土界面抗剪性能试验研究[J].土木工程学报,2021,54(07):81-89.

一种拱桥用外置法兰连接构造研究

罗小斌[1]　张晓宇[2]　陆滨[1]　马瑞艺[1]

（1. 广西路桥工程集团有限公司　广西南宁　530004；
2. 广西交通设计集团有限公司　广西南宁　530004）

摘　要　为解决钢管混凝土劲性骨架拱桥拱肋节段间主弦管连接难题，本文设计了一种拱桥用外置法兰连接构造，进行了1∶1足尺模型制造、连接工艺试验，模拟空中连接、焊接施工工序；监测了实桥节段环缝焊接过程连接构造的应力；利用ABAQUS有限元软件建立了连接构造模型，计算了结构在弯矩、轴力荷载下的应力、变形。研究结果表明：该外置法兰连接构造能实现空中快速准确定位，连接强度满足拱桥悬臂拼装施工需求。

关键词　外置法兰　连接　拱桥
中图分类号　TU398[+].9　　　　**文献标识码**　A

Research on a Kind of External Flange Connection Structure for Arch Bridge

LUO Xiaobin[1]　ZHANG Xiaoyu[2]　LU Bin[1]　MA Ruiyi[1]

（1. Guangxi Road and Bridge Engineering Group Co., Ltd, Nanning, Guangxi, 530004, China；
2. Guangxi Communications Design Group Co., Ltd, Nanning, Guangxi, 530004, China）

Abstract　In order to solve the problem of connecting the main chord between the arch rib segments of the concrete-filled steel tubular rigid skeleton arch bridge, an external flange connection structure for the arch bridge was designed, and the 1∶1 full-scale model manufacturing and connection process tests were carried out to simulate the air connection and welding construction processes; The stress of the connection structure during the welding process of the circumferential seam of the real bridge segment was monitored; The connection structure model is established by using ABAQUS finite element software, and the stress and deformation of the structure under bending moment and axial load are calculated. The results show that the external flange connection structure can achieve rapid and accurate positioning

---

作者简介：
罗小斌(1985—)，男，学士，高级工程师，主要从事大跨度拱桥施工技术研发及管理方面的研究。
张晓宇(1989—)，男，硕士，高级工程师，主要从事大型桥梁设计方面的研究。
陆滨(1999—)，男，学士，助理工程师，从事大跨度拱桥施工技术研发及管理方面的研究。
马瑞艺(1994—)，女，硕士，助理工程师，从事大跨度拱桥施工技术研发及管理方面的研究。

in the air, and the connection strength can meet the needs of cantilever assembly construction of arch bridge.

Keywords external flange connect arch bridge
E-mail 282250772@ qq. com

大跨度钢管混凝土拱桥温度参数取值研究

石 拓[1]　郭 晓[2*]　于孟生[3]

（1. 广西路建工程集团有限公司　广西南宁　530001；
2. 广西大学土木建筑工程学院　广西南宁　530004；
3. 广西交科集团有限公司　广西南宁　530007）

摘　要　为研究得到合理的大跨度钢管混凝土拱桥温度参数取值，依托西藏雅鲁藏布江藏木特大桥进行了长期温度观测试验。试验结果表明，钢管混凝土拱桥有效温度与日平均气温更接近，与极端气温相差较大。进一步对试验结果进行数理统计分析，研究发现钢管混凝土拱桥计算合龙温度应以有限元方法反算确定；最高有效温度建议取最高气温当天的日平均气温加2℃，最低有效温度建议取最低气温当天的日平均气温减2℃；研究发现桁式主拱上、下弦杆梯度温差可忽略，该温度效应同样可忽略不计；单管日温差影响范围建议取25cm，截面上、下缘最高温度分别取16℃和10℃，单管梯度温差效应较大不可忽视。研究成果能够补充和修正我国规范中钢管混凝土拱桥温度效应设计计算中的相关规定。

关键词　钢管混凝土　拱桥　计算合龙温度　有效温度　梯度温差

中图分类号　U441　　　**文献标识码**　A

Research on Temperature Parameters of Long-span Concrete-filled Steel Tube Arch Bridge

SHI Tuo[1]　GUO Xiao[2*]　YU Mengsheng[3]

(1. Technical Center Office, Guangxi Road Construction Engineering Group Co., Ltd., Nanning, Guangxi, 530001, China;
2. College of Civil Engineering and Architecture, Guangxi University, Nanning, Guangxi, 530004, China;
3. Bridge Research Institute, Guangxi Transportation Science and Technology Group Co., Ltd., Nanning, Guangxi, 530007, China)

Abstract　In order to obtain the reasonable temperature parameters of long-span concrete-filled steel tube arch

---

作者简介：
石拓（1990—），男，博士，工程师，主要从事桥梁施工、大体积混凝土控裂方面的研究。
*郭晓（1993—），男，硕士，副教授，主要从事桥梁施工控制、桥梁抗震方面的研究。
于孟生（1989—），男，博士，高级工程师，主要从事桥梁施工监控方面的研究。

bridge, long-term temperature observation tests were carried out based on Tibet Yarlung Zangbo River Zangmu Bridge. The test results showed that the effective temperature of concrete-filled steel tube arch bridge were closer to the daily average temperature and were quite large difference from the extreme temperature. Based on the statistical analysis of a large number of experimental data, it was considered that the closure temperature of concrete-filled steel tubular arch bridges was mainly calculated by software; the maximum effective temperature was suggested to take the daily average temperature plus 2℃ on the hottest day, the minimum effective temperature was suggested to take the daily average temperature minus 2℃ on the coldest day; gradient temperature difference between the upper and lower chords of truss main arch did not exist, and the temperature effect could be ignored; the influence range of daily temperature difference of single pipe was recommended to be 25cm, and the maximum temperature of upper and lower edge of section is 16℃ and 10℃ respectively. The gradient temperature difference effect of single pipe was large and cannot be ignored. The research results could supplement and amend the relevant provisions in the Chinese code for the design and calculation of temperature effects in concrete-filled steel tubular arch bridges.

Keywords concrete filled steel tube　Aarch Bridge　calculation of closure temperature　effective temperature　gradient temperature difference

E-mail guoxiao7868@163.com

0　引言

钢管混凝土(concrete-filled steel tube, CFST)是在钢管内加填混凝土形成的一种组合材料[1]。该类材料被大量应用于拱桥主拱拱肋,该类桥型被称为钢管混凝土拱桥。中国川藏铁路正在大力建设中,其中桥梁占比尤为突出。钢管混凝土拱桥在刚度、耐久性、经济方面的优势令其在该线路峡谷山区中具有广泛的应用前景[2-3]。

温度计算理论是钢管混凝土拱桥设计理论的重要组成部分,常用的桥梁温度荷载计算参数包括合龙温度、最高有效温度、最低有效温度、梯度温差等。CFST拱桥与普通桥梁存在差异,该桥型主拱由两种材料组成,二者的热学特性与力学特性不一致,且考虑到建造时先钢管合龙、再混凝土合龙的顺序,该桥型的温度参数取值较普通桥梁情况更为复杂。目前我国《钢管混凝土拱桥技术规范》(GB 50923—2013)[4]和《公路钢管混凝土拱桥设计规范》(JTG/T D65-06—2015)[5]两个规范对CFST拱桥温度参数取值做出相关规定,但某些温度参数取值规定不一致,且部分温度参数取值未明确规定。同时,国内外许多专家也对该桥型的温度荷载计算参数取值问题进行了研究[6-12],但是目前相关研究绝大多数采用数值模拟方法对平原地区钢管混凝土拱桥进行分析,所得结果存在未考虑西藏高原高寒地区气候特点影响,未考虑超大跨度时结论的适用性,缺乏足够试验数据验证等问题[13]。

因此,本文依托目前世界最大跨度铁路钢管混凝土拱桥——拉林铁路藏木特大桥,针对西藏地区独特气候下的典型温度场和温度效应问题展开较为深入的理论分析与试验研究。

1　项目概况

西藏雅鲁藏布江藏木特大桥位于西藏山南市加查县,横跨雅江,连通桑加峡谷。桥址位于新建山南至林芝省道(S306)边,距老省道约7km,距加查县约17km,距拉萨约325km,与外界道路通畅。

该桥采用一跨过江方案,主跨为430m的中承式CFST拱桥,全桥主梁为一联5跨的预应力混凝土连续梁,孔跨布置为(39.6+32)m 连续梁+430m 中承式 CFST 拱桥+(28+34.6)m 连续梁,桥梁总长 525.5m。主桥总体布置如图 1 所示。

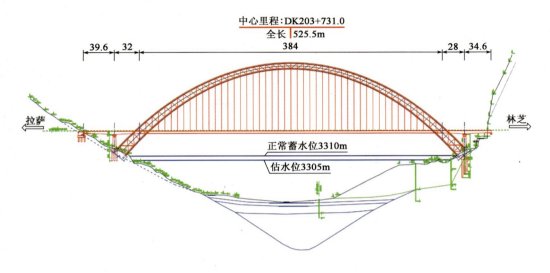

图 1 藏木特大桥总体布置图(尺寸单位:m)
Fig 1 General Layout of Zangmu Bridge(Unit:m)

藏木特大桥设计矢高为 112m,矢跨比达 1∶3.84;主拱线形选用悬链线形式,其中拱轴系数为 2.1;主拱内倾角为 4.59°,拱肋拱顶处中心距为 7m,拱脚中心距为 25m;桁式主拱采用桁高渐变形式,最大、最小桁高位置位于拱顶和拱脚,高度是 8.8m 和 15m;拱肋形式采用四肢桁式;主拱肋直径采用变截面形式,主拱肋拱脚部分位置直径 1.8m,其余钢管直径 1.6m;钢管壁厚同样根据跨径变化,为 24~52mm。

2 结论

基于西藏雅鲁藏布江藏木特大桥项目,进行了长期温度场观测试验,对大量试验数据进行了数理统计分析,分别对钢管混凝土拱桥计算合龙温度、有效温度、桁式截面温差、单圆管梯度温差等参数进行了研究。研究得到主要结论如下:

(1)主拱截面日照温度场分布及变化呈现非均匀分布、非线性变化特性。主拱截面内部温度随日气温变化较小,主拱截面平均温度与日平均气温更接近,与气温相差较大。

(2)钢管混凝土拱桥计算合龙温度应根据有限元方法反算确定,无条件实测水化热温度时《钢管混凝土拱桥技术规范》中计算公式依然适用。

(3)最高有效温度建议取最高气温当天的日平均气温加 2℃,最低有效温度建议取最低气温当天的日平均气温减 2℃。

(4)研究发现桁式主拱上、下弦杆梯度温差可忽略,该温度效应同样可忽略不计。

(5)单圆管日温差影响范围建议取 25cm,截面上、下缘最高温度分别取 16℃和 10℃,单管梯度温差效应较大需重视。

参 考 文 献

[1] 韩林海.钢管混凝土结构:理论与实践[M].3版.北京:科学出版社,2016.
[2] ZHENG Jjie-lian L,Wang Jian-jun. . Concrete-filled steel tube arch bridges in China[J]. Engineering,2018,4(1):143-155.
[3] 郑皆连.大跨径拱桥的发展及展望[J].中国公路,2017,13:40-42.
[4] 中华人民共和国国家标准.钢管混凝土拱桥技术规范:GB 50923—2013[S].北京:中国计划出版社,2013.
[5] 中华人民共和国行业标准.公路钢管混凝土拱桥设计规范:JTG/T D65-06—2015[S].北京:人民交通出版社股份有限公司,2015.
[6] SHI Tuo,ZHENG Jie-lian,DENG Nian-chun et al. Temperature Load Parameters and Thermal Effects of a Long-Span Concrete-Filled Steel Tube Arch Bridge in Tibet[J],Advances in Materials Science and Engineering,2020,9710613.
[7] SHI Tuo,Deng Nianchun,CHEN Zheng,et al. Vertical gradient temperature difference of the main arch with single pipe section in Tibet based on statistical analysis[J]. Advances in Materials Science and Engineering,2020,9767621.
[8] 林春娇,郑皆连,黄海东.圆截面钢管混凝土拱水化热温度场试验研究[J],混凝土,2009,10:13-15.
[9] 陈津凯,陈宝春,刘振宇.钢管混凝土拱均匀温差设计取值研究[J].土木工程管理学报,2013,30(4):1-7.
[10] 陈宝春,徐爱民,孙潮.CFST拱桥温度内力计算时温差取值分析[J].中国公路学报,2000,13(2):52-56.
[11] LIU Jiang,LIU Yongjian,ZHANG Chenyu,et al. Temperature action and effect of concrete-filled steel tubular bridges:A review[J]. Journal of traffic and transportation engineering(english edition). 2020,7(2):174-191.
[12] LIU Jiang,LIU Yongjian,ZHANG Guojing,et al. Prediction Formula for Temperature Gradient of Concrete-Filled Steel Tubular Member with an Arbitrary Inclination[J]. Journal of Bridge Engineering. 2020,25(10),04020076.
[13] 石拓.西藏地区大跨度钢管混凝土拱桥温度场及温度效应研究[D].南宁:广西大学,2020.

大跨度拱桥弯矩增大系数的计算分析及探讨

黄庆钧[1]　黄 君[1,2]　滕晓丹[1,3,4]*

（1. 广西大学土木建筑工程学院　广西南宁　530004；
2. 南宁学院土木与建筑工程学院　广西南宁　530200；
3. 广西防灾减灾与工程安全重点实验室　广西南宁　530004；
4. 工程防灾与结构安全教育部重点实验室　广西南宁　530004）

摘　要　大跨度拱桥的弯矩是拱桥结构设计的重要依据之一，而采用线弹性理论计算的拱桥截面弯矩往往比实际的拱桥截面弯矩小，需要将根据线弹性理论计算的拱桥截面弯矩乘以一个增大系数，进行拱桥截面承载力验算。基于弯矩增大系数的重要性，本文系统回顾了拱桥弯矩增大系数计算方法的现有研究成果，阐述各类方法的求解思路，总结各类方法的特点及局限性，并对国内外规范中的拱桥的弯矩增大系数计算方法进行了介绍。研究表明，现有文献和国内外规范中有关拱桥弯矩增大系数的计算方法存在较大差异，因此本文对拱桥弯矩增大系数的计算方法提出了改进建议。

关键词　大跨度拱桥　弯矩增大系数　承载力验算　桥梁工程
中图分类号　U441+.5　　　**文献标识码**　A

Calculation Analysis and Discussion on Moment Amplification Coefficient of Long-span Arch Bridge

HUANG Qingjun[1]　HUANG Jun[1,2]　TENG Xiaodan[1,3,4]*

(1. School of Civil Engineering and Architecture, Guangxi University, Nanning, Guangxi, 530004, China;
2. College of Architecture and Civil Engineering, Nanning University, Nanning, Guangxi, 541699, China;
3. Key Laboratory of Disaster Prevention and Engineering Safety of Guangxi, Nanning, Guangxi, 530004, China;
4. Key Laboratory of Disaster Prevention and Structural Safety of Ministry of Education, Nanning, Guangxi, 530004, China)

作者简介：
黄庆钧(1997—)，男，硕士研究生，主要从事工程结构与力学方面的研究。
黄君(1987—)，女，博士，讲师，主要从事工程结构与力学计算等方面的研究。
*滕晓丹(1984—)，女，博士，讲师，主要从事工程结构与力学、钢管混凝土结构的性能方面的研究。

Abstract The bending moment is one of the important basis for the structural design of long-span arch bridge. The bending moment of arch bridge section calculated by linear elastic theory is often smaller than the actual bending moment, therefore, it is necessary to multiply the linear bending moment by a moment amplification coefficient for resistance verification. Since the moment amplification coefficient is importance, the calculation methods for the moment amplification coefficient of arch bridge are systematically reviews in this paper. The solving ideas of various methods are expounded, the characteristics and limitations of various methods are summarized, and the calculation method for bending moment amplification coefficient of arch bridge in domestic and foreign are introduced. The presented research shows that there are great differences in the calculation results of various calculation methods for moment amplification coefficients. Some suggestions for improving the calculation method of the moment amplification coefficient of the arch bridge are put forward.

Keywords long-span arch bridge   moment amplification coefficient   resistance verification   bridge Engineering

E-mail   xdteng@ gxu.edu.cn

0　引言

钢管混凝土拱桥具有较强的跨越能力,目前世界最大跨径的钢管混凝土拱桥——平南三桥,主桥跨径达575m,正在修建的钢管混凝土拱桥——天峨龙滩特大桥,主桥跨径达600m。大跨径钢管混凝土拱桥截面弯矩的计算是一个十分重要的问题,一直以来都是桥梁领域学者关注的热点和焦点。采用线弹性理论计算的拱桥截面弯矩,由于几何和材料非线性的影响,往往比实际的拱桥截面弯矩小。因此需要把线弹性理论计算的拱桥弯矩乘上一个系数进行放大,进行拱桥截面承载力验算。

学者们对拱结构的弯矩增大系数进行了深入的研究。基于等截面直梁的小挠度理论,李国豪等[1]、卫星[2]建立了在荷载作用下拱的挠度与截面弯矩的微分方程,求解出拱变形后拱轴线挠度解析表达式,进一步得到了拱各截面的弯矩与截面位置的关系。通过比较考虑挠度后的截面弯矩与不考虑拱轴线变形的截面弯矩,得到拱桥的弯矩增大系数,但该理论仅仅考虑了截面的竖向位移。李俊[3]认为拱变形后,尚需研究拱轴线位移的解析表达式,目前只能通过有限元计算得到数值解。李俊以静力平衡理论为基础,截取拱段隔离体,对荷载作用下变形前后的拱段隔离体进行受力分析;对考虑截面水平位移和竖向位移的拱段截面弯矩与不考虑截面位移的拱段截面弯矩进行比较,得到计算拱桥弯矩增大系数的表达式;并揭示出拱桥非线性计算的弯矩比线弹性计算的弯矩增大的原因为水平推力与竖向位移作用、竖向力与水平位移作用、外荷载与位移作用引起了附加弯矩。在设计规范中,拱桥的弯矩增大系数用偏心受压构件的偏心距增大系数来代替,把拱桥视为偏心受压构件,按照拱桥受约束类型的不同,将拱轴线长度换算成不同的偏心受压构件的计算长度。在规范中,偏心受压构件的二阶增大弯矩计算,是将线弹性计算弯矩乘以《公路钢筋混凝土及预应力混凝土桥涵设计规范》(JTG D 620—2004)规范、《钢筋混凝土及预应力混凝土桥涵设计规》(JTG 3362—2018)等规范规定的偏心距增大系数 η,对线性计算弯矩进行放大,然后采用放大后的弯矩,对构件进行截面强度验算。拱桥由拱肋、吊杆、系杆等共同受力,针对这一受力特性,尼颖升等[4]、郭峰等[5]基于能量变分原理,推导出拱桥拱肋弯矩增大系数的计算公式。现有的设计规范中有关拱桥弯矩增大系数的计算公式应用对象是偏心受压直杆构件,该计算公式简单实用,考虑了一定的安全系数,偏保守。所以本文归纳并对比了现有国内外设计规范及文献中关于弯矩增大系数的计算方法,并提出了其存在的问题和未来的研究方向。

1 基本理论

1.1 考虑初应力的小挠度理论[1]

在拱的静力分析中,通常按照一阶理论进行,即不考虑拱变形。这对于刚度较大的粗短拱是可行的,但将导致柔拱的弯曲应力被显著低估。因此,有必要按照二阶理论对柔拱进行内力分析,即先按一阶理论计算出拱的变形,再考虑轴力在该变形上引起的附加弯矩。为了简化计算,通常参照压弯杆分析引用的增大系数,将按一阶理论得到的拱的弯矩和挠度增大,从而将求解拱的弯矩和挠度问题转变为求增大系数问题。

考虑初应力的小挠度理论,将拱视为具有初弯曲的压弯杆件,如图1所示,将具有初弯曲 v_0 的压弯杆 AB 视为拱,在水平外力 N 的作用下 AB 杆弯曲变形进一步增大到 v,其挠曲线的微分方程为:

$$EI(v'' - v_0'') + Nv = 0 \tag{1}$$

式中,EI 为拱截面的抗弯刚度;v'' 为拱挠曲线的两次导;v_0'' 为拱初始挠曲线的二次导。

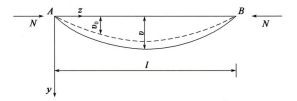

图1 具有初始挠曲的压弯杆件

Fig. 1 Bending member with initial deflection

令 $\alpha^2 = N/EI$,则式(1)可写成:

$$v'' + \alpha^2 v = v_0'' \tag{2}$$

设初弯曲为正弦曲线,表达式如下:

$$v_0 = v_{0m}\sin\frac{\pi z}{l} \tag{3}$$

式中,v_{0m} 为跨中最大初挠度。

根据边界条件:

$$\begin{cases} z = 0, v = 0 \\ z = l, v = 0 \end{cases} \tag{4}$$

得

$$v = \frac{v_{0m}}{1-\xi}\sin\frac{\pi z}{l} \tag{5}$$

$$M = \frac{Nv_{0m}}{1-\xi}\sin\frac{\pi z}{l} \tag{6}$$

式中,

$$\xi = \frac{Nl^2}{\pi^2 EI} \tag{7}$$

跨中最大弯矩为：

$$M_m = \mu N v_{0m} = \mu M_{0m} \tag{8}$$

式中，μ 为弯矩增大系数，由轴力的二阶效应引起，即：

$$\mu = \frac{1}{1-\xi} \tag{9}$$

参照上述压弯杆分析引用的增大系数，可推导出无铰拱最大弯矩处（$z = 3l/16$ 处）的增大系数为：

$$\eta = \frac{1+0.121}{1-\gamma} \tag{10}$$

式中，

$$\gamma = \frac{N}{N_{cr}} \tag{11}$$

$$N_{cr} = \frac{\pi^2 E I_x}{S_0} \tag{12}$$

式中，N 为按一阶理论计算的拱四分点处的轴力；S_0 为拱的计算长度，$S_0 = a \cdot S$；S 为拱轴长度之半；a 为拱的长度计算系数，无铰拱的 a 值根据拱轴线的类型取值，取值范围在 0.68 ~ 0.72 之间。

1.2 基于等截面直梁推导的小挠度理论[2]

在基于等截面直梁推导的小挠度理论，并进行了两个假设：①拱截面变形按平面变形考虑，截面法线方向与切线方向的夹角在变形前后保持不变，且拱圈截面变形符合胡克定律。②拱的弹性中心的位置在变形前后保持不变，即忽略拱轴变形引起弹性中心位置的改变。在不计轴力影响、不考虑剪切变形的情况下，建立无铰拱基本方程：

$$\frac{d^2 v}{dx^2} = -\frac{M(x)}{E I_x \cos\varphi} \tag{13}$$

式中，v 为拱截面的挠度；设 $I_x = I_d/\cos\varphi$，I_d 为截面惯性矩，φ 为拱截面切线与 x 轴的夹角。如图 2 所示，抛物线无铰拱的拱轴线方程为：

$$y = f - \frac{f x^2}{l^2} \tag{14}$$

式中，f 为拱肋计算矢高。

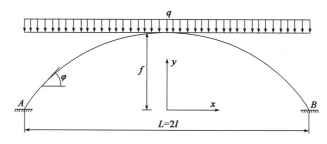

图 2 抛物线无铰拱受均布荷载

Fig. 2 Parabolic unhinged arch subjected to uniform load

任意截面弯矩 $M(x)$ 可表示为：

$$M(x) = Hv(x) + M_A - H\left(f - \frac{fx^2}{l^2}\right) + \frac{q(l^2 - x^2)}{2} \tag{15}$$

式中,H 是按挠度理论计算的拱脚处水平推力;q 为拱上的外均布荷载;EI_d 为拱截面的抗弯刚度;其他字母含义同上。

设拱脚 A 处的弯矩为 M_A,该无铰拱的拱截面挠度函数 $v(x)$ 可根据边界条件求解得到,拱顶和拱脚的边界条件为:

$$\begin{cases} x = 0, v'(x) = 0 \\ x = l, v'(x) = 0, v = 0 \\ x = -l, v = 0 \end{cases} \tag{16}$$

求解得:

$$v(x) = -c_2 - c_1[2l\cos kl/(k\sin kl) + x^2 - 2/k^2] \tag{17}$$

其中,

$$c_1 = \frac{f}{l^2} - \frac{q}{2H} \tag{18}$$

$$c_2 = \frac{M_A}{H} - f + \frac{ql^2}{2H} \tag{19}$$

$$k^2 = \frac{H}{EI_d} \tag{20}$$

由式(16)和式(17),整理得考虑拱圈挠度 v 后的拱脚弯矩:

$$M_A = -Hc_1[2l\cos kl/(k\sin kl) + l^2 - 2/k^2] + Hf - \frac{ql^2}{2} \tag{21}$$

不考虑拱圈挠度 v 对截面内力影响时,基于弹性理论计算的拱脚线性弯矩 $\overline{M}_A$ 为:

$$\overline{M}_A = -\frac{c_1 \overline{H} l^2}{3} + \overline{H} f - \frac{ql^2}{2} \tag{22}$$

其中,

$$c_1 = \frac{f}{l^2} - \frac{q}{2H} \tag{23}$$

按挠度理论计算的推力 H 与弹性理论计算 $\overline{H}$ 大致相同,故拱脚弯矩增大系数为:

$$\eta = \frac{M_A}{\overline{M}_A} = \frac{-c_1[2l\cos kl/(k\sin kl) + l^2 - 2/k^2] + c_1 l^2}{2c_1 l^2/3} = \frac{3[1 - kl/\tan kl]}{k^2 l^2} \tag{24}$$

令,

$$H_{cr} = \frac{\pi^2 EI_d}{(2l)^2} \tag{25}$$

$$k^2 l^2 = \frac{H l^2}{EI_d} = \frac{4\pi^2 H l^2}{4\pi^2 EI_d} = \frac{\pi^2}{4} \frac{H}{H_{cr}} \tag{26}$$

式(24)可化简为:

$$\eta = \frac{M_A}{\overline{M}_A} \approx \frac{1}{1 - 0.18(H/H_{cr})} = \frac{1}{1 - \dfrac{H}{\pi^2 EI_d (0.424L)^2}} \tag{27}$$

1.3 静力平衡理论[3]

如图3所示,在距左拱脚X_1处,将拱轴线截断,取无铰拱左拱脚和拱轴线1号截面之间的拱段作为隔离体,图中虚线是拱变形后的拱轴线。坐标原点在左拱脚,水平向左为X方向,竖直向上为Y方向,P为隔离段上的竖向外力。

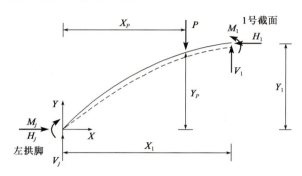

图3 无铰拱拱内截面内力分析

Fig. 3 Internal force analysis of the inner section of unhinged arch

当不考虑拱轴线变形时,图3隔离体对无铰拱1号截面取矩,得到1号截面线性计算的弯矩M_1:

$$M_1 = M_j + V_j X_1 - H_j Y_1 - P(X_1 - X_P) \tag{28}$$

式中,M_j为无铰拱左拱脚线性计算的弯矩,由计算确定;V_j为无铰拱左拱脚竖向反力,由实测或计算确定;H_j为无铰拱左拱脚水平推力,由实测或计算确定;P为无铰拱左拱脚与1号截面间的竖向外荷载(含拱段自重),由实测或计算确定;X_1、Y_1为变形前的拱轴线,1号截面到左拱脚的水平距离、垂直距离,由实测或计算确定;X_P、Y_P为变形前的外荷载P作用位置到拱脚的水平距离、垂直距离,实测或计算确定。

令1号截面竖向位移v_1、水平位移u_1,外荷载P作用位置的拱圈截面竖向位移v_p、水平位移u_p。竖向位移方向均向下,水平位移方向均向右。则计入拱轴线变形后,无铰拱1号截面考虑拱轴线变形后非线性计算的弯矩M_1'为:

$$M_1' = M_j' + V_j(X_1 + u_1) - H_j(Y_1 - v_1) - P[(X_1 + u_1) - (X_P + u_P)] \tag{29}$$

$$M_1' = M_1 + M_j' - M_j + V_j u_1 + H_j v_1 + P(u_P - u_1) \tag{30}$$

由式(24)可得,无铰拱1号截面非线性计算的弯矩比线性计算的弯矩多出四部分组成,分别为拱脚弯矩的非线性部分$(M_j' - M_j)$、V_j与u_1形成的附加弯矩$V_j u_1$、H_j与v_1形成的附加弯矩$H_j v_1$、以及P和水平位移差$(u_P - u_1)$引起的附加弯矩$P(u_P - u_1)$。由此可知,拱截面的水平位移同样会对拱桥非线性计算的弯矩产生影响,传统的拱桥挠度理论只考虑竖向位移对拱桥弯矩增大系数影响并不全面。因此,同时考虑拱截面竖向位移和水平位移的拱桥截面弯矩增大系数η_{M1}为:

$$\eta_{M1} = \frac{M_1'}{M_1} = 1 + \frac{M_j' - M_j}{M_1} + \frac{V_j u_1}{M_1} + \frac{H_j v_1}{M_1} + \frac{P(u_P - u_1)}{M_1} \tag{31}$$

1.4 国内外规范

国内外规范中,均无专门针对拱桥弯矩增大系数的计算公式。规范中通常将拱视为偏心受压构件,拱轴线长度按拱受约束情况换算成直杆计算长度,随后按照偏心受压杆件截面的承载能力极限状态偏心距增大系数放大弯矩值。规范中计算弯矩增大系数的常用方法主要有刚度法和曲率法,以下将分别介绍两种方法的计算公式以及我国《公路钢筋混凝土及预应力混凝土桥涵设计规范》(JTG 3362—2018)和美国规范的计算方法。

1.4.1 刚度法

刚度法,首先由弹性稳定理论引出临界力表达式,然后建立杆件变形后的微分方程,并推导出挠度的公式,进一步推导出偏心受压杆件的弯矩增大系数。随后考虑实际因素,对截面的极限承载力乘上一个小于1的刚度修正系数。偏心距增大系数 η 的基本表达式为:

$$\eta = \frac{1 + 0.234 N/N_{cr}}{1 - \frac{N}{N_{cr}}} \approx \frac{1}{1 - \frac{N}{N_{cr}}} = \frac{1}{1 - \frac{N l_0^2}{\pi^2 \alpha EI}} \tag{32}$$

式中,N 为截面计算轴力;N_{cr} 为临界轴力;EI 为截面抗弯刚度;l_0 为计算长度;α 为刚度折减系数。

对于匀质弹性材料拱,刚度法具有很好的计算精度,我国《公路钢筋混凝土及预应力混凝土桥涵设计规范》(JTJ 023—85)、澳大利亚 AS 3600 规范、美国 ACI 318-02 规范及桥梁设计规范(AASHTO-LRFD)等均采用该方法计算拱桥的弯矩增大系数。

1.4.2 曲率法

采用以截面曲率表示的偏心距增大系数的方法又称为曲率法。极限曲率 η 表达式考虑材料非弹性和变形与内力间的非线性关系,一般计算公式为:

$$\eta = 1 + \frac{f}{e_0} = 1 + \left(\frac{1}{\rho}\right)\frac{l_0^2}{e_0 \beta} \tag{33}$$

式中,ρ 为截面曲率;e_0 为初始偏心距;l_0 为计算长度;β 为与挠曲线形状有关的系数。

使用这类方法的主要设计规范有英国 CP110(72) 规范、欧洲 CEB-FIP(90) 规范以及我国《混凝土结构设计规范》(GB 50010—2010)、《公路钢筋混凝土及预应力混凝土桥涵》(JTG D62—2004)规范。我国《公路钢筋混凝土及预应力混凝土桥涵设计规范》(JTG 3362—2018)中,η 值计算公式也采用了曲率表达方法。

1.4.3 中国《公路钢筋混凝土及预应力混凝土桥涵设计规范》(JTG 3362—2018)[6]

我国《公路钢筋混凝土及预应力混凝土桥涵设计规范》(JTG 3362—2018)给出的拱桥弯矩增大系数 η 计算公式:

$$\eta = 1 + \frac{1}{1300 e_0/h_0} \left(\frac{l_0}{h}\right)^2 \zeta_1 \zeta_2 \tag{34}$$

$$\zeta_1 = 0.2 + 2.7 \frac{e_0}{h_0} \le 1.0 \tag{35}$$

$$\zeta_2 = 1.15 - 0.01 \frac{l_0}{h} \le 1.0 \tag{36}$$

式中,l_0 为拱圈的计算长度,按如下规定采用:三铰拱取 $0.58 L_a$;二铰拱取 $0.54 L_a$;无铰拱取 $0.36 L_a$,L_a 为拱轴线长度;e_0 为轴向力对截面重心轴的偏心距,取值不小于 20mm 且不小于偏压方向截面最大尺寸的 1/30;h_0 为截面有效高度,对圆形截面取 $h_0 = r + r_0$;h 为截面高度,对圆形截面取 $h=2r$；ζ_1 为荷载偏心率对截面曲率的影响系数；ζ_2 为构件长细比对截面曲率的影响系数。

1.4.4 美国桥梁设计规范[7]

美国桥梁设计规范中,弯矩放大系数 η：

$$\eta = \frac{C_m}{1 - \dfrac{P_u}{\varphi P_e}} \tag{37}$$

式中,P_u 为轴向荷载弹性设计值；φ 为轴向受压抗力系数；P_e 为欧拉压屈荷载,除了钢和混凝土的结合柱,P_e 可按下式计算：

$$P_e = \frac{\pi^2 EI}{(Kl_u)^2} \tag{38}$$

式中,l_u 为受压构件无支承长度；K 为有效长度系数；EI 为截面抗弯刚度。

2 结论

(1)在小挠度理论中,仅考虑了竖向挠度如何对拱桥的弯矩增大系数产生影响,其主要通过建立挠度与弯矩的微分方程,求解出拱变形后拱轴线挠度解析表达式,从而进一步得到拱各截面的弯矩与其位置的关系。通过比较考虑挠度的弯矩与不考虑挠度的弯矩,求解出拱的弯矩增大系数,但未考虑拱变形后的拱截面的水平位移。按照李俊[3]的试验可知,拱变形后,截面的水平位移和竖向位移在同一数量级上,故只考虑截面竖向位移求取拱桥弯矩增大系数的拱桥挠度理论,对拱桥的弯矩增大部分计得不全面。

(2)李俊[3]基于静力平衡理论,提出弯矩零点法,即在拱轴线弯矩零点处,将拱轴线截断,再对弯矩零点处取矩,可以求出在荷载作用下拱轴线变形前后的拱脚弯矩,随后对变形前和变形后的弯矩进行比值,求得拱脚弯矩增大系数。根据模型拱肋上缘钢筋应变符号的变化,内插计算出距左拱脚截面形心最近的弯矩零点位置,则认为该处为第一弯矩零点处。这种查找截面位置的方法是存在问题的,内插计算是一种线性的方法,拱肋上缘钢筋应变与弯矩的关系不是线性的。对于小型模型构件来说,真正的弯矩零点的位置和用上述方法得到的弯矩零点的位置可能相差不大,但随着拱桥尺寸的增大,两者的位置差距会越来越大。

(3)规范中,将钢筋混凝土拱等效为柱子的计算模式是存在问题的。

计算长度问题：以前和现有的各种规范均引用了无铰拱计算长度 $S_0 = 0.36S$ 的概念,其实 $0.36S$ 只是基于线弹性屈曲稳定分析的临界水平推力计算得出。到目前为止,拱桥弯矩增大系数可以采用 $0.36S$ 的计算长度尚没有试验证实。

力边界问题：拱桥在等效为柱的过程中,只考虑了轴力和弯矩,没有考虑剪力,这是不全面的。

位移边界问题：钢筋混凝土无铰拱拱圈,由于位移边界的不同,截面初始偏心距按变形后的位移计算的增大系数,与截面的弯矩增大系数并不一致。

荷载组合问题：按照钢筋混凝土偏心受压柱试验成果总结出的弯矩增大系数公式,其试验条件是直接荷载作用,并没有反映和包括温度变化、混凝土收缩徐变等间接作用,温度内力、混凝土收缩徐变内力是否需要进行非线性的放大,放大多少。

轴力、初始偏心距取值问题：由于钢筋混凝土拱圈各个截面线弹性计算的轴力和弯矩不同，等效柱只能选取一个轴力和初始偏心距，就出现了轴力和初始偏心距的取值问题。

（4）上述的理论方法中均未考虑拱脚水平推力对拱圈所产生的负弯矩对弯矩增大系数的影响。为了确定荷载作用下拱的实际弯矩，需考虑拱脚水平推力及拱截面水平位移对拱桥弯矩增大系数的影响，今后可在这两方面展开深入讨论。

参 考 文 献

[1] 李国豪,项海帆,沈祖炎,等.桥梁结构稳定与振动[M].北京:中国铁道出版社,1992.
[2] 卫星.钢筋混凝土肋拱二阶设计方法研究[D].成都:西南交通大学,2005.
[3] 李俊.钢筋混凝土拱桥的弯矩增大系数研究[D].成都:西南交通大学,2012.
[4] 尼颖升,徐栋.基于能量变分原理推导系杆拱拱肋弯矩增大系数[J].公路交通科技,2014,31(03):70-77.
[5] 郭峰,李鹏飞,毛佳艳,等.大跨度拱桥拱肋偏心距增大系数计算方法[J].吉林大学学报(工学版),2022,52(06):1404-1412.
[6] 交通运输部.公路钢筋混凝土及预应力混凝土桥涵设计规范:JTG 3362—2018[S].北京:人民交通出版社股份有限公司,2018.
[7] American Association of State Highway and Transportation Officials [S]. Washington, D. C: LRFD Bridge Design Specifications, 2nd Ed., AASHTO, 1998.

钢筋混凝土拱桥强劲骨架成拱法的主拱结构设计技术

肖 雨 牟廷敏 梁 健 康 玲

(四川省公路规划勘察设计研究院有限公司 四川成都 610041)

摘 要 大跨径强劲骨架钢筋混凝土拱桥具跨越能力强、刚度大、承载能力高,更加适应山区地形的特点,在山区桥梁建设中广泛应用。本文结合 G4216 屏山新市至金阳高速公路跨度 510m 的西宁河特大桥,对强劲骨架成拱法的钢筋混凝土拱圈结构选型及关键参数进行探讨,提出了矢跨比、拱轴系数、主拱截面高度等参数初选原则及取值范围,以西宁河特大桥为工程背景,验证了其合理性。

关键词 拱桥 强劲骨架 拱轴系数 矢跨比 承载能力

中图分类号 TU448.22 **文献标识码** A

Design Technology of Main Arch Structure of Reinforced Concrete Arch Bridge by Strong Skeleton Arch Forming Method

XIAO Yu   MOU Tingmin   LIANG Jian   KANG Ling

(Sichuan Highway Planning, Survey, Design and Research Institute CO., Ltd, Chengdu, Sichuan, 610041, China)

Abstract The long-span reinforced concrete arch bridge with strong frame is widely used in bridge construction in mountainous areas because of its strong crossing capacity, high stiffness and high earing capacity, which is more suitable for mountainous terrain. Combined with the Xining River Bridge of G4216 Pingshan Xinshi Jinyang Expressway with a span of 510m, this paper discusses the type election and key parameters of reinforced concrete arch ring structure using the strong frame arch forming method, and puts forward the principle and range of primary selection of parameters such as rise span ratio, arch axis coefficient and main arch section height. Taking Xining River Super Major Bridge as the engineering background, its rationality is verified.

作者简介:

肖雨(1973—),男,学士,正高级工程师,主要从事桥梁工程领域的设计和研究。

牟廷敏(1964—),男,学士,教授级工程师,主要从事桥梁工程和混凝土材料领域的设计和研究。

梁健(1978—),男,硕士,正高级工程师,主要从事桥梁工程领域的设计和研究。

康玲(1988—),女,硕士,工程师,主要从事桥梁工程领域的设计和研究。

Keywords arch Bridge strong frame arch axis coefficient rise span ratio carrying capacity
E-mail 327446150@qq.com

0 引言

当路线跨越山区深谷时,钢筋混凝土拱桥以其刚度大,承载能力高,对运输和场地要求低,受温度变化影响小及与地形协调,后期养护方便等诸多优点,成为山区修建大跨径桥梁的首选。

20世纪90年代后,国内外已经建成或在建的主跨超过200m的混凝土拱桥,其成拱技术一般为悬臂安装法和钢管混凝土劲性骨架法。其中,除悬臂安装法建成了主跨329m的美国胡佛大桥外,其余各大桥均采用钢管混凝土劲性骨架法建成,如已建成主跨420m的万县长江大桥、主跨312m的南宁邕江大桥。

从主跨365m的广元昭化嘉陵江大桥开始,大跨径钢筋混凝土拱桥强劲骨架法具有跨越能力强、刚度大、承载能力高,更加适应山区地形的特点,已在主跨416m南盘江和主跨445m的北盘江铁路混凝土拱桥等,山区桥梁建设中广泛应用。已成为现代300m以上混凝土拱桥的主要建造技术。

1 背景工程概述

西宁河特大桥为G4216宜宾新市至金阳高速公路的重点桥梁工程。处于向家坝电站库区,桥位跨越西宁河。河谷宽度约380m,河床呈U形河谷。桥梁宽度为整幅式30.5m,荷载等级为公路—Ⅰ级,地震基本烈度为Ⅶ度。

根据路线总体、地形、地质条件及使用功能要求,该桥最终选用了跨径510m的上承式钢筋混凝土拱桥跨越西宁河,其总体布置图如图1所示。

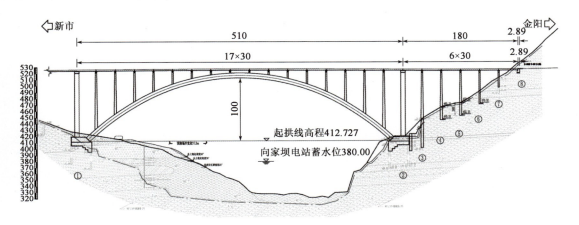

图1 西宁河特大桥布置图(尺寸单位:m;高程单位:m)
Fig.1 layout of Xining River Bridge(Unit:m)

2 主拱结构形式

2.1 拱圈形式的选择

钢筋混凝土拱桥拱圈的结构形式,总体可以分成肋拱及板拱。对国内2012年之后建成的

13座跨度大于200m的钢筋混凝土拱桥进行调研,其中采用板拱的拱桥共7座,占53.8%;采用分离式肋拱形式的拱桥共6座,占46.2%,其截面形式均采用箱形截面。可见,对于大跨或超大跨径的混凝土拱桥,主拱圈基本截面形式均采用箱形截面,单箱单室或单箱多室截面。

对于高速公路桥梁,一般来说桥面宽度宽,拱上立柱的横向间距较宽。如果采用整体式板拱结构,则拱圈宽度接近于桥面宽度,不经济。同时,根据对已建成的一系列钢筋混凝土拱桥的实桥调查表明:拱圈宽度大于15m时,采用整体式板拱结构,在主拱、拱座及拱上垫梁容易出现较多纵桥向裂缝,部分裂缝宽度超过了规范规定的限值。采用分离式双箱主拱结构则可以避免上述情况,分离式拱肋具有以下特点:①主拱横向受力更合理;②主拱受温度影响更小;③施工更加方便;④减少材料数量;⑤盖梁受力最佳。

西宁河特大桥主拱跨径510m,桥面宽度30.5m,拱圈如采用板拱形式,其拱圈宽度将达到22.5m。结合调研结果及同类型桥梁工程经验,西宁河特大桥采用分离式的肋拱形式,箱形截面。

箱形截面具有整体性好,抗扭刚度大,经济等优点。为了减轻自重,方便施工,本桥采用了钢管腹杆-混凝土的新型组合箱形结构。即在混凝土主拱圈的箱形截面中,以钢管腹杆代替混凝土腹板,形成由钢腹杆联结上、下混凝土顶底板的新型组合箱形截面,如图2所示。

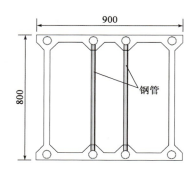

图2 拱圈断面示意图(尺寸单位:cm)
Fig. 2 Schematic diagram of arch ring section

2.2 劲性骨架的构造

采用钢管混凝土作为劲性骨架的钢筋混凝土拱桥,因骨架太弱,造成施工工序多、工期长,限制了这种桥型的发展。因此,要获得钢管混凝土骨架与外包混凝土的最佳匹配,充分发挥复合结构的高强性能,必须进一步提高骨架的强度。

骨架的承载能力能够满足拱圈底板、腹板、顶板三环独立加载的主拱骨架成为强劲骨架。其指标体现为:①截面含钢管混凝土率>8%;②钢管混凝土截面承载力与全截面承载力之比>20%。

为实现强劲骨架,可以通过加大弦杆数量和直径或者提高管内混凝土强度等级的途径。西宁河特大桥钢管混凝土骨架采用了8根ϕ540的钢管(壁厚22~26mm),内灌C100混凝土,作为强劲骨架。

空间桁架稳定性更强,但加工更复杂,外包混凝土更困难,在相同施工条件下,质量控制更难。而平面桁架,加强横隔刚度后,也能满足受力和稳定的需要。二者的选用决定于钢结构加工场地的大小和吊装的能力。西宁河特大桥桥位地形狭窄,节段加工受到水路及陆路运输的限制,骨架不能通过整节段运输的方式进场。因此采用"化整为零,集零为整"的方法,利用现有的国道、省道运输杆件至现场加工场,现场拼装为桁片再组装为小节段进行安装,如图 3 所示。

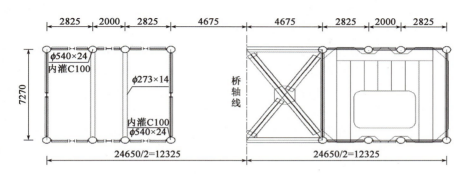

图3　骨架断面示意图(尺寸单位:mm)

Fig. 3　Schematic diagram of frame section(Unit:mm)

3　主拱结构设计与参数

3.1　桥面系

对于大跨径的钢筋混凝土拱桥,其恒载效应占到总效应的 80% 左右,桥面系的选择应符合自重轻、架设方便、易于维护、耐久性好、造价经济等原则。

西宁河特大桥通过对预制 T 梁、钢-混组合梁和钢梁进行了比较,通过比较(表1),桥面系(图4)采用预制 I 梁+现浇组合桥面板的形式,其自重和吊重比 T 梁减少了 30%,价格较钢梁大大降低,同时也没有大量的后期养护工作。

桥面系单位质量比较表　　　　　　　　　　　　表1

Comparison of unit weight of bridge deck system　　Tab. 1

构件	每平米质量(t/m²)	吊重(t)
T 梁	1.59	76
I 梁	1.10	57
钢梁	0.85	48

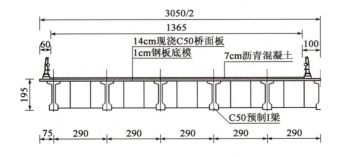

图4　预制 I 型梁断面(尺寸单位:cm)

Fig. 4　Prefabricated I-beam section(Unit:cm)

3.2 矢跨比

矢跨比是拱桥结构的一个重要参数,矢跨比的选取对拱圈的内力及稳定均有影响。钢筋混凝土拱桥的矢跨比,主要取决于桥位的地形、地质条件,同时结合主拱结构的受力及与周围环境的协调性进行选择。拱桥的恒载水平推力与竖向反力的比值,随矢跨比的减小而增加,矢跨比减小,拱的推力增大,主拱圈内的轴力也增大,对混凝土拱圈本身是有利的,但对拱座及基础的水平推力增加,对地基承载力要求也随之增加。

根据研究,钢筋混凝土拱桥合理的矢跨比在1/4~1/5.5之间,在此区间内,钢筋混凝土拱桥极限跨径最大。本文统计了国内36座已知的劲性骨架混凝土拱桥,矢跨比在1/3.7~1/9之间(图5)。通过以上调研及分析,确定劲性骨架混凝土拱桥的矢跨比一般为取值为1/4~1/6之间。对于西宁河特大桥矢跨比的选择,在结合地形、路线总体设计,地质条件的基础上,确定矢跨比为1/4.7。

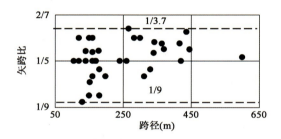

图5 已建劲性骨架混凝土拱桥矢跨比关系图

Fig. 5 Relationship diagram of rise span ratio of built rigid frame concrete arch bridge

3.3 拱轴系数

拱桥最显著的特点是在承受竖向荷载时,拱脚处会产生水平推力,当拱轴线与拱圈荷载压力线重合时,拱圈内只有轴力,而无弯矩和剪力,此时的拱轴线称为合理拱轴线。考虑到混凝土大跨度拱桥,其恒荷载在所有荷载中所占比重最大,因此一般可用恒载压力线作为合理拱轴线。拱轴线的优化过程中就是拱轴线不断地逼近恒载压力线的过程。在大跨径混凝土拱桥中,为使拱轴线尽量接近恒载压力线,也有采用高次抛物线(三次或四次)和样条函数作为拱轴线。采用高次抛物线和样条曲线拟合拱轴线时,曲线参数较多,优化较为复杂。且曲线参数与拱圈的内力分布关系规律不明显,根据曲线参数不容易判断出拱圈内力的分布规律。

根据本文统计的国内36座已知的劲性骨架混凝土拱桥中,采用悬链线的为26座,占72.2%;可见悬链线是劲性骨架混凝土拱桥采用的最主要的拱轴线。当拱轴线采用悬链线时,矢跨比确定后,主拱各点坐标就取决于拱轴系数m。

对于采用劲性骨架法施工的特大跨径混凝土拱桥,其主拱圈是逐步形成的,采用悬链线作为拱轴线时,拱轴系数m是根据全桥结构恒载确定的,在劲性骨架的裸拱状态时与拱轴线偏差较大(拱圈分阶段形成),为改善外包混凝土阶段的受力,其拱轴系数m应结合主拱施工阶段进行比较选定,根据经验一般在1.4~2.8之间选取。

西宁河特大桥净矢高100m,矢跨比1/4.7,拱轴线也采用悬链线,在此基础上对拱轴系数进行优化比选。选取拱轴系数分别为2.0、1.9、1.8、1.75、1.6进行比选,计算采用考虑施工阶段的成桥模型,计算在承载能力极限状态下,不同拱轴系数的承载能力,见表2。

不同拱轴系数下的承载力安全系数 表2
safety factors of bearing capacity under different arch axis coefficients Tab.2

部 位	承载力安全系数				
	$m=1.6$	$m=1.75$	$m=1.8$	$m=1.9$	$m=2.0$
拱脚	1.05	1.14	1.17	1.15	1.22
$1/4L$	1.24	1.17	1.20	1.16	1.13
拱顶	1.26	1.20	1.19	1.01	0.98

由表2可知,拱脚的承载力安全系数随着拱轴系数增大而减小;拱顶的承载力安全系数随着拱轴系数增大而增大,当拱轴系数为1.75、1.8时,拱顶与拱脚的承载力安全系数较为接近,兼顾拱圈承载力安全系数分布及有利于调整等因素,本桥拱轴系数最终选用1.8。

3.4 拱圈结构尺寸

3.4.1 拱肋高度及宽度

主拱圈高度主要取决于拱的跨度和主拱混凝土材料的强度,如采用高强混凝土,可减小截面尺寸,从而减轻主拱自重。拱圈的高度与主拱的跨度、材料强度、矢跨比、施工方法及主拱布置形状均有关系,设计时可以根据以往经验初拟一个高度,反复试算后综合各方面因素进行比较得到。

本文根据近年来我院设计的6座跨径大于260m的劲性骨架钢筋混凝土拱桥,绘制出跨径与拱圈高度关系见图6。根据统计数据,对于等高度的拱圈,其高度可以取跨径的1/40~1/65进行试算,变高度拱圈可以取平均值进行试算。综上,西宁河特大桥拱圈高度取为9m。

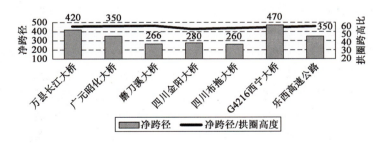

图6 跨径与拱圈高度(尺寸单位:m)
Fig.6 span and arch ring height(Unit:m)

拱圈的宽度对拱桥的横向稳定性影响很大,为保证横向稳定性,主拱圈以不小于1/20进行控制。但对于大跨径的混凝土拱桥,往往采用分离式的双肋布置,肋之间采用横向联系进行连接,其横向联系较整体的板拱弱。因此除了对拱肋全宽进行控制外,还应对单根拱肋宽度进行控制。本文根据近年来我院设计的6座跨径大于260m的劲性骨架钢筋混凝土拱桥,绘制出跨径与拱圈宽度关系见图7。对于分离式双肋拱圈,拱肋全宽以跨径的1/20进行控制;单肋宽度不大于跨径的1/45。对于整体式板拱,拱圈宽度以跨径的1/45控制。

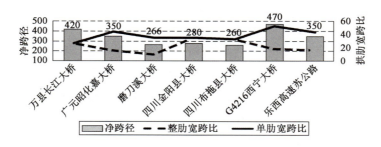

图7 跨径与拱圈宽度（尺寸单位：m）

Fig.7 span and arch ring width(Unit:m)

3.4.2 顶、底及腹板厚度

对于采用劲性骨架法施工的混凝土拱桥，其最小板厚与劲性骨架的结构尺寸有关，外包混凝土必须全部包裹劲性骨架，同时保证一定的保护层及钢筋等其他构造的尺寸。如采用钢管混凝土作为劲性骨架，则其最小板厚由钢管的直径和连接杆件的尺寸来确定。在满足最小板厚的基础上，箱形截面的各部分可根据受力的不同（拱圈采用分阶段成型，截面各部分施工的时间不同，其结构受力有所不同），选择不同的板厚。大跨径混凝土拱桥其主拱受力主要为承受自重及上部结构传来的恒载，活载所占比例小，增加板厚对结构的应力改善不明显，其板厚的选择在满足结构最小板厚的基础上，应更根据结构的受力合理的选择及优化。

大跨径钢筋混凝土拱桥，拱脚部位承受较大的弯矩，拱圈截面一般采用变高度。但变高度的拱圈会带来外包混凝土施工困难。为减小外包混凝土施工难度，同时简化外包混凝土施工，西宁河特大桥拱圈采用等截面。为适应拱脚处较大的弯矩，在拱脚至1号立柱范围内通过增设箱梁内侧腹板的方式提高拱脚段的承载能力，即拱脚段采用单箱三室的截面形式，拱顶段采用单箱单室的截面（图8）。拱圈顶、底板厚度根据计算及构造要求综合选用0.48m，同时拱脚至1号立柱范围为渐变段，顶、底板厚度由0.75m 线性变化至0.48m。

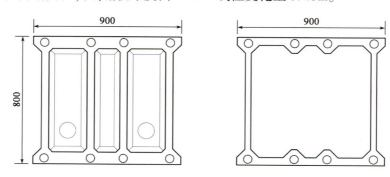

图8 拱脚及拱顶截面示意图（尺寸单位：cm）

Fig.8 cross section of arch foot and arch crown(Unit:cm)

对于拱圈这种偏心受压截面，顶底板截面厚度提供的承载力效率较腹板高，因此在构造允许和施工质量能够得到保障的情况下，尽量采用较薄的腹板厚度并保证稳定及施工需要，为确定腹板厚度,针对腹板厚度0.35m、0.4m、0.55m进行比选,见表3。从表中可以看出,随着腹板厚度增加,对拱脚段的承载力均有所提高,但对于拱顶截面来看,还略有下降。经综合比较,在满足构造要求的基础上,本桥腹板厚度选用0.35m。

不同腹板厚度对比结果 表3
comparison results of different web thicknesses Tab. 3

部位	承载力安全系数		
	0.35m	0.4m	0.55m
拱脚	1.17	1.23	1.25
1/4L	1.20	1.21	1.23
拱顶	1.19	1.15	1.17

4 结论

(1)对于特大跨径的混凝土拱桥,桥面系应尽量轻型化,减少恒载的效应;当拱圈宽度大于15m时,宜采用分离式的拱肋形式。

(2)当采用劲性骨架法成拱的钢筋混凝土拱桥,其骨架应采用强劲骨架,骨架可采用加强横隔的平面桁架,减轻吊装重量,简化施工工序,缩短施工时间。

(3)对于采用强劲骨架法成拱的混凝土拱桥,矢跨比可在1/4~1/6之间选取;拱轴线可采用悬链线,拱轴系数可在1.4~2.8之间选取。

(4)分离式拱肋高度可在跨径的1/40~1/65之间初选;拱肋总宽宜小于跨径的1/20,单根拱肋宽度宜小于跨径的1/45。

(5)钢筋混凝土拱桥强劲骨架成拱法的主拱结构设计技术在西宁河特大桥中得以应用并验证,可供同类桥梁在设计中予以参考。

参 考 文 献

[1] 谢邦珠,庄卫林,蒋劲松,等.钢管混凝土劲性骨架成拱技术的兴起和发展[C]//第二十一届全国桥梁学术会议论文集.北京:人民交通出版社股份有限公司,2014.

[2] 四川省交通厅.万县长江公路大桥技术总结[M].成都:电子科技大学出版社,2003.

[3] 韩林海,牟廷敏.钢管混凝土混合结构设计原理及其在桥梁工程中的应用[J].土木工程学报,2020,53(5).

[4] 陈宝春.钢管混凝土拱桥综述[J].桥梁建设,1997(2).

[5] 赵人达,张正阳.我国钢管混凝土劲性骨架拱桥发展综述[J].桥梁建设,2016,46(6).

[6] 韦建刚,陈宝春.国外大跨度混凝土拱桥的应用与研究进展[J].世界桥梁,2009(2).

[7] 谢海清,徐勇.沪昆高铁北盘江特大桥合理结构形式研究[J].高速铁路技术,2018,12.

[8] 陈宝春,林上顺.钢筋混凝土拱极限承载力研究综述[J].福州大学学报(自然科学版)2014,4.

[9] 陈宝春,叶琳.我国混凝土拱桥现状调查与发展方向分析[J].中外公路,2008,28(2):

89-96.
[10] 张建民,郑皆连.拱桥稳定性研究与发展[J].广西交通科技,2000,12.
[11] 邵长宇,现代拱桥[M].北京:人民交通出版社股份有限公司,2019.
[12] 李国豪.桥梁结构稳定与振动[M].北京:中国铁道出版社,2010.

施工与监测

连续拱桥施工方案优化方法

安永辉[1,2]　陈晓煌[1]　李连冉[1]　郑皆连[1*]　欧阳效勇[3]
（1. 广西大学土木建筑工程学院　广西南宁　530004；
2. 大连理工大学建设工程学部　辽宁大连　116023；
3. 中交第二公路工程局有限公司　陕西西安　710065）

摘　要　本文提出了采用智能控制索平衡连续拱桥中间墩及其上部施工塔架的不平衡力的单幅拱肋施工方法，对中间墩进行施工阶段模拟。结果表明：张拉智能控制索后，中墩扣塔塔顶最大水平位移可控制在2cm之内，且墩底不出现拉应力；单拱肋合拢状态稳定系数满足规范要求。以世界最大跨双跨连续拱桥为例，与传统施工方法相比，缆吊系统横向移动次数减少为1/9，施工难度降低，施工效率和安全度均提高。本方法中单幅拱肋施工的扣索可在另一幅拱肋安装时重复使用，且新安装的节段对之前节段的扣索力影响很小，故也能节约扣索量；合计节约扣索量超一半。

关键词　钢管混凝土拱桥　连续拱桥施工　智能控制索　单拱肋施工　智能监测

中图分类号　U445.4　　**文献标识码**　A

Construction Scheme Optimization Method for the Continuous Arch Bridge

AN Yonghui[1,2]　CHEN Xiaohuang[1]　LI Lianran[1]　ZHENG Jielian[1]　OUYANG Xiaoyong[3]
(1. College of Civil Engineering and Architecture, Guangxi University, Nanning, Guangxi 530004, China;
2. Faculty of Infrastructure Engineering, Dalian University of Technology, Dalian, Liaoning 116023, China;
3. CCCC Second Highway Engineering Co. Ltd., Xi'an 710065, China)

Abstract　A single arch rib construction method utilizing the intelligent control cable, to balance the unbalanced force of middle pier and its upper tower of continuous arch bridge, is proposed. Simulation of construction stage on the

---

基金项目：国家优秀青年科学基金项目（52122803）。
作者简介：
安永辉（1986—），男，博士，教授，博导。主要从事土木工程新型与智能结构研究。
陈晓煌（1993—），男，博士生。主要从事桥梁结构设计理论与分析方面的研究。
李连冉（1999—），男，硕士。主要从事超高性能混凝土拱桥设计理论与分析方面的研究。
＊郑皆连（1941—），男，中国工程院院士。主要从事桥梁设计、施工和管理方面的研究。
欧阳效勇（1962—），男，博士，正高级工程师。主要从事桥梁工程技术研发与管理工作。

middle pier shows that maximum horizontal displacement of the top of the buckle tower on middle pier can be controlled within 2 cm, and no tensile stress appears at the bottom of middle pier when the intelligent control cable is tensioned to the target force. The stability coefficient of single arch rib on closure state meets the code requirements. The largest double span continuous arch bridge was taken as an example to illustrate the superiority of the new construction scheme. Compared with the traditional method, the number of lateral movements of the cable hoisting system is reduced to 1/9, which has advantage on ease construction and improvements on construction efficiency and security. For the single arch rib construction method, the cable can be reused on the installation of another arch rib, and more cables can be saved because the newly installed segment has little impact on the cable force of the previous segment. In total, more than half of the amount of cables can be saved.

Keywords concrete-Filled steel tubular arch bridges continuous arch bridge construction intelligent control cable single arch rib construction intelligent monitoring

E-mail zhengjielian@163.com

0 引言

随着交通强国等国家战略的实施,越来越多的大跨钢管混凝土拱桥正在修建[1]。郑皆连院士提出的拱桥斜拉扣挂施工方法已成为当前大跨拱桥的常规施工方法[2]。缆索吊装系统可将拱肋节段吊运至安装位置,而斜拉扣挂是保证拱圈线型及拱肋合龙精度的关键施工工艺[3]。

单跨拱桥斜拉扣挂安装拱肋节段的工艺已较为成熟[4]。对于双堡特大桥等两跨连续拱桥的施工,中墩及其上的扣塔扣挂拱肋节段时,由于节段安装存在先后顺序,中墩左右两侧节段存在不对称、不平衡的工况,对中墩及其上的扣塔受力不利。目前,斜拉扣挂安装拱肋节段的工艺,在双跨或多跨连续拱桥中应用还不多,现阶段研究成果仍不成熟。

1 连续拱桥施工方案优化方法

1.1 双堡特大桥概况

以世界最大跨双跨连续拱桥——双堡特大桥为例,本部分介绍连续拱桥施工方案优化方法。双堡特大桥主桥(图1)采用两跨连续上承式钢管混凝土桁架拱桥,单拱计算跨径380m,矢高80m,矢跨比1/4.75;拱轴线采用悬链线,主拱圈高度(弦管中心距)从拱顶6.5m变化到拱脚11.0m,单侧拱圈宽7.5m(弦管中心距),两幅拱圈横向中心距17.5m。

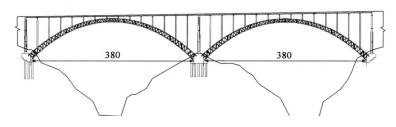

图1 双堡特大桥主桥布置(尺寸单位:m)

Fig.1 Arrangement of main bridge of Shuangbao super large bridge(Unit:m)

1.2 常规施工方案

常规施工方案(以③节段为例)示意如图2所示,2跨2幅4个拱肋同时对称施工,右跨③

节段与已安装的②节段采用法兰临时固定,左跨用常规拉索平衡中墩,待左跨以同样的方式固定第③节段后,放松常规拉索,最后张拉第 3 对扣索,完成③节段的斜拉扣挂。

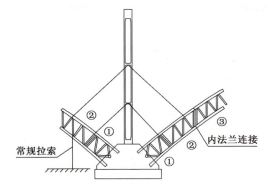

图 2　常规施工方案示意图

Fig. 2　Schematic diagram of conventional construction scheme

1.3　提出的新施工方案

新施工方案(以⑦节段为例)示意如图 3 所示,双堡特大桥单拱肋横向宽度为 7.5m,面外刚度较大,新施工方案采用左右两跨单幅施工,单幅斜拉扣挂拱肋直至合拢,拆卸扣索后再用相同方法扣挂另一幅拱肋直至合拢,随后安装横撑形成双拱肋整体受力状态,便可进行后续灌注混凝土等工序施工。同时,新施工方案安装新节段时即刻张拉扣索,采用智能控制索的方式保证桥墩与扣塔处于平衡状态。单幅拱肋施工可使缆吊系统横向移动次数减小为原来的1/9。智能控制索平衡中墩的施工方式,使新节段不再处于悬臂状态,法兰受力小,扣索索力变化也很小。

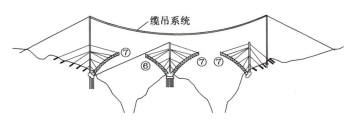

图 3　新施工方案示意图

Fig. 3　Schematic diagram of new construction scheme

中墩及其上的扣塔扣挂拱肋节段时,①~③节段安装时无需设置智能索,依靠桥墩自身刚度抵抗不平衡力;④~⑥拱肋节段施工时,智能控制索上锚点设置在墩顶处;⑦~⑨拱肋节段施工时,智能控制索上锚点分别设置在相应扣索扣点处。

1.4　新施工方案验算

新施工方案验算(以③节段为例)采用 Midas Civil 软件,拱肋、桥墩、扣塔采用梁单元,扣索采用桁架单元。不设置智能控制索时,当桥墩右侧安装③节段而不平衡时,桥墩上扣点位移为 12.3mm,墩底截面均未出现拉应力,可见①~③节段安装时可不设置智能控制索。

其余节段安装时,以扣塔顶位移不超过 20mm 为迭代计算目标,求得各节段所需施加智能控制索水平力。不平衡工况时,智能控制索所需最大水平力为 383.6t,施工难度不大,可采用常规钢绞线或光纤FRP复合智能拉索。不平衡工况时,张拉相应智能控制索后,④~⑨节段塔顶最大偏位仅为18.9mm,桥墩及扣塔处于竖直平衡状态,智能控制索平衡中墩不平衡力的施工方法可行。

①~⑨节段斜拉扣挂全过程施工模拟中,钢管最大初应力为92.8MPa,满足《公路钢管混凝土拱桥设计规范》(JTG/T D65-06—2015)第7.3.2条不大于0.65倍钢管强度设计值的要求(0.65×295=191.9MPa)。

新施工方案与原施工方案相比,1~9号扣索索力大幅度减小,扣索用量更少。假如使用单拱肋施工方案,安装另一幅拱肋时,其扣索可重复利用,经计算新方案与常规施工方案相比,中墩可节约63%的扣索用量。

对中墩斜拉扣挂拱肋节段施工全过程进行稳定分析,中墩斜拉扣挂最不利工况出现在最大悬臂不平衡阶段,此时稳定性系数为18.6,满足规范中弹性稳定系数不应小于4.0的要求。单拱肋合拢拆除扣索后,单拱肋合龙状态时稳定性系数为6.45>4.0,满足要求。

综上,新施工方案变形、强度、应力、稳定验算均能满足要求,本文提出的采用智能控制索平衡中墩不平衡力的施工方法与单幅拱肋施工方法是合理可行的,具有重要的工程应用价值与推广前景。

2　结论

(1)本文提出了采用智能控制索平衡中墩不平衡力的施工方法与单幅拱肋施工方法,并论证了提出施工方案的经济性与优越性。通过建立有限元模型对提出的施工方案全过程中的变形、强度、应力、稳定进行验算,结果为提出方案的可行性与合理性提供了可靠依据。

(2)本文提出的智能控制索平衡中墩不平衡力的施工方法,能用于跨江、跨海等连续拱桥的施工,单拱肋施工方法也能应用于单跨拱桥的施工,有较大的应用与推广价值,具有良好的经济效益和社会效益。

参 考 文 献

[1] 陈宝春,韦建刚,周俊,等.我国钢管混凝土拱桥应用现状与展望[J].土木工程学报,2017,50(06):50-61.

[2] 郑皆连,徐风云,唐柏石.广西邕宁邕江大桥千斤顶斜拉扣挂悬拼架设钢骨拱桁架施工仿真计算方法[C]//中国公路学会桥梁和结构工程学会1996年桥梁学术论文集,1996.

[3] 林春姣,郑皆连.南盘江特大桥拱圈混凝土斜拉扣挂法施工分析[J].桥梁建设,2016,46(05):116-121.

[4] 韩玉,秦大燕,郑健.CFST拱桥斜拉扣挂施工优化计算方法[J].公路,2018,63(01):100-104.

桁式组合拱桥拆除重建综合解决方案研究与应用

张胜林

(贵州省公路工程集团有限公司　贵州贵阳　550003)

摘　要　二十世纪八九十年代修建的桁式组合拱桥,已不能满足现状交通流和荷载的要求。通过对桁式组合拱桥技术状况现状以及运营需求分析,并结合此类桥型的结构体系特点和悬臂拼装工艺分析,拟定"拼装逆过程"的拆除总体思路,提出"在原桥位建新桥,老桥作为建新桥的通道,新桥作为拆老桥的支撑"的"拆建一体化"工程解决方案;厘清"拆建一体化"的技术路线和关键技术要点,在对旧桥病害和检测数据分析的基础上,拟定混凝土和预应力的物理力学参数,选定拆除过程中结构体系转换的合理时机,通过有限元分析拆除全过程,确保新、旧桥结构和施工安全。拆除过程中监测各阶段各节点的位移情况,与理论计算结果进行对比分析,验证理论计算模型、结构劣化参数取值的合理性和准确性。通过上述研究和实践,并改进创新工艺工法、质量安全控制的方法和手段,建立桁式组合拱桥拆除重建成套施工技术体系,构建桥梁拆除和重建的环保理念,为国内桥梁管养提供一种新的思路。

关键词　桁式组合拱　拆建一体化　体系转换　技术体系　环保

中图分类号　580.1020　　**文献标识码**　A

Research and Application of a Comprehensive Solution for the Demolition and Reconstruction of Trussed Combination Arch Bridge

ZHANG Shenglin

(Guizhou Highway Engineering Group Co., Ltd, Guizhou, Guiyang, 550003)

Abstract　The trussed combination arch bridge built in the 1980s and 1990s can no longer meet the current traffic flow and load bearing requirements. Based on the analysis of the current technology of trussed combination arch bridge and its future operational demand, in combination with the research on and the cantilever erection technology

---

作者简介:

张胜林(1971—),女,工程技术应用研究员。主要从事公路桥梁施工技术与管理。

and the general idea of "reverse assembly", a project solution called "integration of demolition and construction" has been developed. This solution means that the new bridge will be built at the location of the old bridge, using the old bridge as a pathway for building the new bridge and the new bridge as the support for the demolition of the old bridge. Based on the analysis of the defect and detection data of the old bridge, in order to select the physical and mechanical parameters of concrete and inherent stress and the timing of the structural system transformation in the demolition process, it is important to figure out the technical route and key technical points of "integration of demolition and construction". Through the finite element analysis of the whole process of demolition, the safety of the new and old bridge construction is effectively ensured. In order to verify the rationality and accuracy of the theoretical calculation model and the value of structural deterioration parameters, the displacement of each node at each stage monitored in the demolition process is compared with the theoretical calculation results. The research and practice mentioned above indicated a new way of thinking for bridge management in China, which not only focuses on the improvement and innovation of the technological method and quality safety control measures, but also the establishment of a complete set of construction technology system of trussed combination arch bridge demolition and reconstruction, while taking into consideration the environmental impact of bridge demolition and reconstruction.

Keywords　trussed combination arch bridge　integration of demolition and construction　system transformation　technology system　environmental protection

E-mail　331700583@qq.com

0　引言

桁式组合拱桥悬拼合拢后,在墩(台)顶至跨中之间的一个适当位置断开,使由桥墩(台)伸出的伸臂桁架和跨径中部的桁架拱串联起来,成为一种拱、梁式组合体系桥梁。在跨径、矢跨比确定的前提下,通过选择断缝位置,人为地调节各杆件内力,使全桥各杆件受力均匀,材料利用更充分、合理。但由于建设时期较早,原设计荷载标准低;在结构体系方面,双竖杆断缝处的刚度突变以及边中箱的内力分配对桥梁变形有影响;在施工工艺方面,接头处的浇筑方式不利于保证接头混凝土的密实性,对桥梁耐久性有影响;以及交通量、载重量急剧增加。上述因素造成后期运营病害严重,加固改造难度大,成本高,效果不明显。

国省干道等改造需求日益迫切,公路桥梁桥址资源日趋紧缺,解决节约资源的问题,需要综合考虑桥梁结构、施工方法和拆除技术,提出经济合理的工程解决方案。

1　桁式组合拱桥拆除重建技术路线

1.1　桥梁拆除技术

施工条件与拆除技术选择,受桥址附近建筑物或构筑物的制约。U形河谷的地形条件也不允许设备就地拆除,河流(湖泊)的环保要求更不允许就地废弃材料。

1.2　桁式组合拱桥拆除重建技术路线

1.2.1　总体思路

基于对桁式组合拱桥的结构特点及悬臂拼装工艺的分析,拆除方法为"拼装逆过程",从拱顶向两拱脚对称、倒退拆除。拆除过程结构体系转换——桁式组合拱体系转换为悬臂桁架体系,采取适宜的技术措施保证全过程各阶段的结构安全。

1.2.2 拆建一体化综合解决方案

以花鱼洞大桥为例,新建桥梁在原桥位布设,桥面高度保持不变;同时考虑原拱座地质状况不良,需要避让,拟定了中承式拱的方案——拆除重建桥型采用180m中承式钢管混凝土拱桥。将拆建过程充分整合,老桥拆除过程中结构处于悬臂状态,需要扣挂,而新建的中承式拱拱圈可以提供扣挂支点,拟定了综合解决方案:搭设缆索吊机,拼装新建拱拱肋,将老桥节段扣挂在钢拱肋上,拆除老桥,最后实施新桥桥面系。

1.2.3 结构和施工安全控制

对桁式组合拱桥拆除过程进行模拟分析,模拟拆除过程中剩余部分、新建钢管拱及扣索受力情况和位移的变化,通过拆除过程中调整扣索索力保证旧桥拆除过程中的稳定性,直至安全拆除。

2 原桥位拆除重建实施

2.1 工程概况

花鱼洞大桥位于G320清镇市境内,跨越红枫湖,全桥孔跨布置为5×15m+150m+4×15m,主跨为150m预应力混凝土桁式组合拱桥。大桥于1991年3月建成通车;2015年6月由国家道路及桥梁质量监督检验中心进行了专项检测,检测报告总体结论为花鱼洞大桥主要控制截面的承载能力和结构强度及刚度已不能满足原设计规范的要求。

在贵州省公路局批复同意花鱼洞拆除重建方案,项目新建桥梁为1-180m中承式钢管混凝土拱桥,新桥桥位无变化,桥梁设计荷载采用公路-Ⅰ级。

2.2 桁式组合拱拆除技术要点

2.2.1 扣挂系统设计

在桁式组合拱下弦各节点附近设置临时吊点,并用钢绞线作为临时吊索锚固于钢管拱对应的节点处,半跨各设6组吊索(全桥共12组)。临时吊索示意如图1所示。

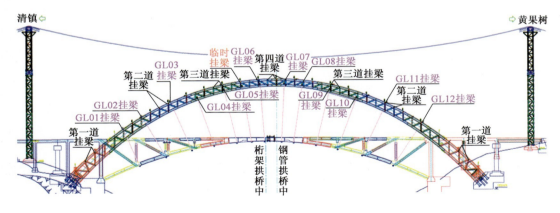

图1 临时吊索示意图

2.2.2 拟定拆除顺序

按"拼装逆过程"原则,划分了24个拆除步骤。

2.2.3 体系转换及索力调整原则

(1)吊索张拉后,在拱顶附近截面轴向力呈压力状态;

(2)吊索初张力为400kN,二次吊索调索主要针对3号、4号、5号和6号吊索,调整后的吊索索力值为460kN、470kN、410kN和220kN;

(3)开拱后拱桥体系转换,要能承载拱圈的部分重量。

2.2.4 结构计算及结果

采用 MIDAS/Civil 进行有限元建模,共划分为2870个单元。计算拆除过程中扣索索力值、旧桥在各施工阶段下的截面应力、旧桥在各施工阶段下的位移值、钢管拱结构各施工阶段应力情况以及旧桥拆除过程中屈曲分析。

2.2.5 计算结果分析

(1)总体情况

开拱前,通过张拉吊索,减小实腹段轴向压力值,开拱阶段截面轴向压力合计为40kN。开拱后,在拆除剩余构件过程中变形均匀,结构变形较小,吊索索力值基本稳定。

(2)双竖杆对拉杆受力情况

在双竖杆处设置工字钢分配梁和精轧螺纹对拉杆,并对对拉杆施加对拉力。对拉力随结构拆除不断变化,其中最大对拉力为682kN;开拱后,随着拆除推进,对拉力逐渐减小,最终为0,如图2所示。

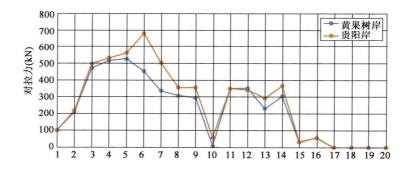

图2 双竖杆对拉杆受力情况

(3)开拱前后对比

比较开拱前后,桁式拱桥的轴力在开拱值后减小至零,且开拱前后的轴力都在控制范围内;桁式拱桥的实腹段,在开拱前后变形幅度小,且变形平缓;实腹段的应力也减小。桁式组合拱体系平稳转换为悬臂桁架结构。开拱前后各项参数对比见表1。

开拱前后各项参数对比表 表1

项 目	开 拱 前	开 拱 后
应力(MPa)	-1.6	-0.3
轴力(kN)	-19.5	0
弯矩(kN·m)	419.3	-78.1
变形(竖向/水平)(mm)	-21	-23/1

3 结构计算与监测结果对比分析

3.1 观测点布置

在上下弦各节点、断缝两侧以及实腹段节段分界点布置位移观测点(图3),在各施工阶段监测各节点挠度变化情况,分析理论计算与实际监测数据的差值。

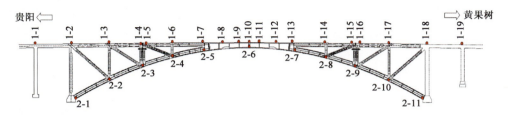

图3 位移观测点布置图

选取具有代表意义的吊索第一次张拉阶段、实腹段中箱2号底板对称拆除阶段、开拱切割阶段、开拱完全断开阶段、实腹段顶板及底板拆除完成阶段,共五个典型工况,进行实测挠度值与理论挠度值对比。

3.2 左侧上弦测点典型工况实测挠度值与理论挠度值对比

左侧上弦测点典型工况实测挠度值与理论挠度值对比如图4所示。

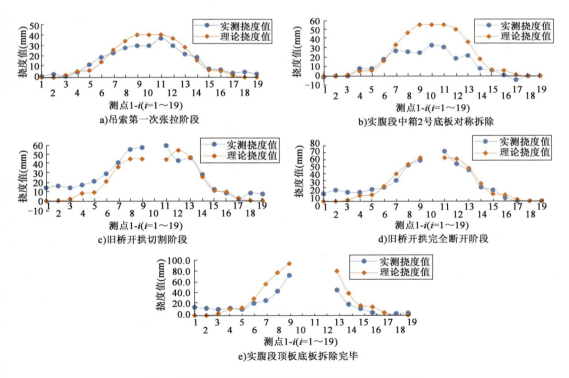

图4 左侧上弦测点典型工况实测挠度值与理论挠度值对比

249

3.3 对比分析

总体情况实测值比理论值偏小；理论值与实测值较吻合。拆除全过程结构变形平稳，幅度可控。

具体各工况：扣索张拉后，上弦跨中 1～10 左侧小 10mm，右侧小 7.2mm，下弦跨中 2～6 左侧大 0.8mm，右侧大 1.8mm，所有测点差值均在 10mm 以内，理论值与实测值吻合程度高。实腹段中箱 2 号底板对称拆除阶段，上弦跨中 1～10 左侧小 21.8mm，右侧小 20.7mm，下弦跨中 2～6 左侧小 12.8mm，右侧小 18.8mm，除左侧 1～9、1～12 两个点偏小，差值均在 20mm 以内，理论值与实测值较吻合。开拱过程及以后各阶段，除个别点偏小，其余理论值与实测值差值在 20mm 以内。

4 结论

拱桥是一种有推力的结构，拆除过程中风险大、技术难度高，国内外一般采取爆破拆除法。花鱼洞大桥结合新建钢管混凝土拱辅助拆除桁式组合拱桥，巧妙利用拱肋的刚度安装吊索倒装法拆除旧桥，满足景区和饮用水源的严苛环保要求；同时施工安全性显著提升，可同时实现一次进场完成老桥拆除和新桥建设，节省施工工期，具有较高的社会效益。

对于桁式组合拱桥拆除全过程的理论计算和实际监测结果，进行对比，分析造成偏差的影响因素，如混凝土的收缩徐变、预应力钢束松弛、节点刚度弱化等，可采取"控制变量法＋迭代法"，对实测挠度与理论挠度拟合定量分析，持续深入研究。

参 考 文 献

[1] 谢福君,张家生.基于实用效应的桥梁加固或拆除重建方案比选[J].铁道科学与工程学报,2019,16(07):1714-1718.

[2] 柏江源.公路桥梁维修加固的工作步骤和桥梁损害的维修方法[J].四川水泥,2020(02):56.

[3] 欧键灵,唐明裴,宁平华.广东清远北江四桥总体方案技术研究[J].城市道桥与防洪,2016(06):69-72,10.

[4] 杨梓.徐文平.旧桥拆除方法要览和案例简介[J].特种结构,2016(6):88-90.

[5] 石成.钢筋混凝土连拱上部结构拆除施工与控制[D].成都：西南交通大学,2008.

[6] 包立新.大跨度预应力混凝土桁式组合拱的拆除技术[C]//中国公路学会.全国斜拉桥关键技术论文集(2012).中国公路学会：《中国公路》杂志社,2012:271-276.

大跨劲性骨架拱桥制造关键技术研究

罗小斌 马瑞艺 侯凯文

(广西路桥工程集团有限公司 广西南宁 530004)

摘要 劲性骨架拱桥因钢筋混凝土提供的受力面积和截面惯性矩都远大于相比于钢管混凝土拱桥,因而比钢管混凝土拱桥具有承载力大、跨越能力更强的优势,因此,主拱圈加工面临着更高精度难题。为提高劲性骨架加工制作精度以及现场安装便利,以在建的世界最大跨径拱桥——天峨龙滩特大桥为工程依托,详细分析了劲性骨架加工在加工制作精度控制方面所采用的关键加工技术。得到如下结论:(1)筒节压头处理工艺,弥补三芯辊压制盲区,避免形成尖角和桃心形,提高筒节卷制后椭圆度一次验收合格率。(2)外置通过标准模具成套制作,唯一编号,配套钻孔、密贴面铣面,成套报检、安装工艺提高成拱加工精度。(3)原材料下料时割缝补偿量、主弦管装配时以拱脚端作为基准端,拱顶侧预留焊接收缩余量;片装单元件装配时弦管对接处预留焊接收缩余量等措施有益于提高精度。研究结果为同类工程提供参考。

关键词 劲性骨架 大跨拱桥 外置法兰 压头工艺

中图分类号 TU398$^+$.9 **文献标识码** A

Research on the Key Technology of Manufacturing Long-span Stiff Skeleton Arch Bridge

LUO Xiaobin MA Ruiyi HOU Kaiwen

(Guangxi Road and Bridge Engineering corporation, Guangxi University, Nanning, Guangxi, 530004, China)

Abstract Arch bridges play an increasingly important role in the transportation industry due to their advantages of good integrity, high bearing capacity and beautiful structure. There are even bigger technical difficulties in the installation. In order to improve the fabrication precision of stiff skeleton and the convenience of on-site installation, this paper takes the world's largest span arch bridge under construction—Tian'e Longtan Bridge as the project support, analyzes the stiffness in detail. Skeleton processing is the key processing technology used in processing and manufacturing precision control. The following conclusions are obtained: (1) A well-adhered flange is beneficial to

---

作者简介:

罗小斌(1985—),男,学士,高级工程师,主要从事大跨度拱桥施工技术研发及管理方面的研究。

马瑞艺(1994—),女,硕士,助理工程师,主要从事大跨度拱桥施工技术研发及管理方面的研究。

侯凯文(1989—),男,博士,工程师,主要从事大跨度拱桥施工技术研发及管理方面的研究。

fast and accurate positioning on site and to ensure the line shape. The standard unit parts of the flange are made in sets through standard molds, and unique numbers are made. The complete set of inspection and installation process improves the processing accuracy of the arch. (2) the indenter treatment process makes up for the blind area of the three-core roller, avoids the formation of sharp corners and peach hearts, and improves the first-time acceptance rate of the ovality after the tube section is rolled. (3) Reserve welding shrinkage compensation and cutting compensation. When the main chord is assembled, the arch foot end is used as the reference end, and the welding shrinkage margin is reserved on the dome side; the cutting compensation amount is added during the programming of the CNC blanking, and the cutting compensation amount is determined according to the cutting test. The research results provide reference for similar projects.

Keywords　stiff skeleton arch bridge　long span arch bridge　steel structure processing　key technology　external flange　indenter treatment process

E-mail　1220453527@ qq. com

0　引言

拱桥以整体性好、结构美观等优势,在交通线路中发挥着越来越重要的作用,与钢管混凝土拱桥相比,劲性骨架拱桥具有成桥后钢管不外露,钢管内填充混凝土的同时钢管外包混凝土,钢筋混凝土提供的受力面积和截面惯性矩都远大于钢管混土,故劲性骨架拱桥承载力大于钢管混凝土拱桥[1-2]。天峨龙滩特大桥是在建的最大跨径上承式劲性骨架拱桥,其由主弦管、腹杆、横隔、平联杆件组成的空间桁架结构,拱肋加工过程中节段端面尺寸、节段长度、腹杆位置、节段侧面平面度、节段扭曲控制是拱肋制造精度控制的重难点。目前国内针对劲性骨架拱桥加工虽开展了较多分析,但由于加工环境、跨径、结构形式、端面尺寸、材质等不同,可参考的工程案例相对较少,劲性骨架拱桥的关键加工技术方面还需进一步研究[3-5]。因而,课题详细分析了劲性骨架加工在控制高精度方面的关键技术,具体包括①筒节制作精度控制技术②片装单元件平联杆偏心处置方案③外置法兰精度控制技术④焊接质量控制技术。愿研究结果为类似工程提供参考与借鉴。

1　劲性骨架加工关键技术

劲性骨架全部构件在厂内加工成整节段,采用"$N+1$ 节段(至少 $2+1$)卧式耦合拼装工艺"保证线形,节段间采用外置法兰连接。为实现劲性骨架高精度合龙主要采取的过程控制措施有:

1.1　筒节制造精度控制技术

主弦管由筒节"以折代曲"焊接而成,装配精度要求高,焊接过程中变形复杂,为确保筒节质量主要采取:(1)筒节划分时尽可能筒节长度一致,使板材规格最少,便于筒节加工成型,使环缝避开节点,减少节点处焊接应力。(2)通过切割试验确定切割补偿量和切割参数,保证切割精度。钢管对接焊缝由于两根对接管有折线,确定折角角度,板材需要开制过渡的坡口。(3)控制下料误差,确保筒节周长,定期抽检复核,针对不同板厚调整参数。控制坡口切割量,增设辅助线。(4)压头处理。为了满足虾弯制作和总成节段接头钢管错边量,在卷制前先将板材两端由 1300t 压力机进行预压头,压制成设计弧度,弥补三芯辊压制盲区,同时提高筒节卷制后椭圆度一次验收合格率,避免形成尖角和桃心型,减少校圆对焊缝扰动。压头前标注长度方向中心线(筒节母线)、压头定位线,作为检查、定位基准,严格控制筒节长边方向与滚板机辊轴平行,压头间距不大于 5cm/道,压头质量不可过重。(5)滚圆前用石笔画出筒节母线,作为加工检查和后道工序定位和划线基准。(6)筒节装配:筒节在专用胎架上装配,纵缝装配时严格控制间隙,预留一定焊接收缩余量。(7)筒节焊接:埋弧自动焊时引、熄弧版应与母材同厚度、同坡口,引熄弧长度≥80mm。(8)筒节校圆:将筒节放回卷板机二次校圆,下压量不宜过大,多次压制成型,对圆弧线形用专用样板检测。局部校圆时对局部位置标记复校,同步检查筒节直径。(9)筒节完工:检验筒节长度、纵向弯曲、椭圆度、管端不平度。对筒节直径应分类登记,弦管制作时遵循"大对大、小对小"原则,控制对接错台量。

1.2 片装单元件偏心处置

对片装单元件各部位均采用全站仪进行地标放样,采用定位钢板,在定位钢板上施作样冲+墨线,保证基准准确,作出明显标记,长期留存。通过型钢制作成的钢墩加定位斜撑形成胎架,在胎架上用型材来调节。上弦管单元件上胎架定位,单元件上胎架时对准地样上的中心线,并采用工装将其定位。弦管单元件定位后,按地样线从拱顶端往拱脚端吊装平联单元件,值得注意的是弦管对接间隙预留焊接收缩余量 2~3mm,具体的焊接收缩余量由焊接形式、焊接量、工艺试验以及经验确定。平联杆为主拱肋上弦之间、下弦之间平面联系构件。劲性骨架平联与钢管偏心为 18cm < $D/4$ = 22.5cm。为充分考虑此偏心的影响,在构造上加强节点。平联杆通过水平节点板与弦管连接;且该水平节点板与腹杆的环向节点板连接形成整体,传力可靠,节点刚度大,节点受力及稳定性均满足要求。

1.3 外法兰盘制造与精度控制技术

法兰盘是重要的连接、导向、传力构件,传递轴向力同时还受弯矩作用,为解决天峨龙滩特大桥主弦管内部操作空间狭小以及吊装过程中环缝数量多的问题,天峨龙滩特大桥拱肋接头采用 3 套 U 型法兰和 1 套 I 型法兰的外置法兰形式。外置法兰盘与管外壁刚性固定,在一定程度上减小了焊接变形,且法兰盘采用标准模具制作成标准单元件,单元件唯一编号,成套端面铣面,配套安装,经铣面后的法兰盘变形被大大削弱。节段之间仅一条环缝,大大减小安装焊接工作量和焊接收缩应力[6]。相比于内法兰,益于现场安装、快速对接。法兰端面的密贴度影响着端头受力和成拱后的线型[7-8],存在安全隐患,控制法兰精度显得尤为重要。主要采取以下措施控制法兰精度:(1)通过标准磨具将法兰盘制作成标准单元件,对单元件唯一编号。(2)法兰盘成套制作,配套钻孔、密贴面铣面,成套报检;配套制作完成后,检验连接板之间的间隙是否满足≤1mm,采用 0.2mm 的塞尺检查盘面密贴情况,用标准冲钉检查全数检查通孔情况。(3)法兰预拼安装时,严格按照预先匹配成对的编号进行配套安装,在节段接头处按设计图纸尺寸精确定位,以地样为基准先定位拱脚侧法兰,控制垂直度及平面投影位置,再以拱脚侧法兰、拱顶侧地样为基准定位拱顶侧法兰,法兰根部通过点焊与弦管临时固定。调整接头钢管错边量,采用码板和接头连接螺栓等临时构造固定连接接头。(4)拱脚侧法兰焊接:用螺栓、冲钉和卡板固定卡紧,防止焊接变形;对拱脚侧法兰盘先分别打底焊接,对称施焊,后续填充盖面的措施进行密贴精度控制。(5)应力释放:拱脚侧法兰焊接完成后,通过碳刨机刨除拱顶侧法兰根部定位焊,将拱脚侧焊缝应力释放,检查拱顶侧法兰与弦管是否有间隙,管节对接口错边量、法兰连接板间的密贴情况,管口对接是否有间隙、法兰通孔情况。若不满足要求,则加码板、千斤顶、钢支撑需动火校正。法兰通孔错边 > 1mm 则需加螺栓、冲钉等。待各项指标满足要求后,焊接拱顶侧的法兰,焊接完成后再次检查管口对接错边量是否≤2mm。(6)法兰全部焊接完成后再次检查对接管口错边、间隙、法兰的通孔情况,若由于焊接收缩引起的变形过大,则通过校火作业校正。(7)将冲钉、螺栓、连接板拆除分类存放,连接板用石笔标记正反面,叠放整齐,现场安装时配套安装(图1)。

图1　外置法兰成套报检、配套安装

1.4　焊接质量控制技术

拱肋节段焊接工作量大、焊接种类多、露天焊接比例大,主拱圈材质为Q420D-Z25,可焊性较常规材料难度大,焊缝返修不宜超过两次,对焊接质量控制要求较高。通过以下措施控制焊接质量:(1)开展焊接工艺评定,确定焊接参数和方式,选择相匹配的焊接材料。(2)在满足规范要求的温度、湿度、风速环境下,采取对称、均衡、同步的原则焊接,不允许采用不对称焊接调整钢结构几何误差或错误,熔透焊必须采取焊前打磨、除湿、预热、过程中层间温度控制、焊后保温。(3)焊后变形超出允许偏差采用火工校正,温度控制在600℃~800℃,火工校正不能超过2次。(4)焊后为消除残余应力,减少应力集中,对相贯线焊缝焊后进行修磨,焊缝修平顺圆滑,且不伤母材。并由专业测量人员通过定时标定的高精度仪器,以合龙温度为依据,恒温测量,夏季选择早晚测量。采用吊垂线、尺量、经纬仪、全站仪等多种测量方法结合,多道把关。

2　结论

对劲性骨架拱桥加工关键技术进行分析总结,得出如下结论:

(1)压头处理将钢板端头压制成设计弧度,弥补三芯辊压制盲区,同时提高筒节卷制后椭圆度一次验收合格率,避免形成尖角和桃心型,减少校圆对焊缝扰动,是钢板卷制筒节前的关键工序。为弦管高质量制作创造有益条件,同时间接提高节段卧拼线型精度控制。

(2)单根片装主弦管装配时节段拱顶侧预留焊接收缩余量、原材料下料时割缝补偿量以及虾弯管制作时筒节中心预留焊接收缩余量都是拱肋制作时控制制作精度的重要措施。

(3)外置法兰通过标准模具成套制作成标准单元件,对单元件唯一编号,配套钻孔,密贴面铣面,成套报检,成套安装,焊后校正能提高成拱加工精度,相比于内置法兰,在作业空间狭小条件下外置法兰形式更有利于现场快速对接、精准安装与保证线型。

（4）考虑劲性骨架平联杆与主弦管偏心影响,平联杆通过水平节点板与弦管连接;水平节点板与腹杆的环向节点板连接形成整体,该构造有利于提高节点刚度,达到传力可靠、结构稳定的目的。

参 考 文 献

[1] 顾颖.大跨度劲性骨架混凝土拱桥稳定性分析[D].重庆:西南交通大学,2011.
[2] 杨默涵.劲性骨架钢筋混凝土拱桥的模型试验研究[D].重庆:西南交通大学.2014
[3] 邓年春,李长胜,郭晓,等.钢管混凝土劲性骨架拱桥主拱圈施工方法进展[J].科学技术与工程,2021,21(15):6132-6139.
[4] 王建江.大跨径上承式劲性骨架箱型拱桥施工技术[J].城市道桥与防洪,2020(06):138-142+20. DOI:10.16799/j.cnki.csdqyfh.2020.06.043.
[5] 胡伦.大跨度钢管混凝土劲性骨架拱桥施工控制及工序优化[D].重庆:西南交通大学,2014.
[6] 李彩霞,罗小斌,秦大燕.钢管混凝土拱桥法兰盘制作关键技术[J].公路,2017,62(3):2.
[7] 杨占峰.大跨径CFST拱桥拱肋安装线形影响因素分析与控制[J].公路,2020,65(8):5.

天峨龙滩特大桥斜拉扣挂系统关键技术研究

罗小斌　沈　耀　唐雁云　侯凯文

（广西路桥工程集团有限公司　广西南宁　530004）

摘　要　本文以天峨龙滩特大桥劲性骨架悬臂拼装分项工程为背景，对比了扣索前后分离、塔上张拉和扣索通长、地面张拉两种斜拉扣挂系统结构形式的可行性；利用拱桥斜拉扣挂优化计算程序、Midas Civil 有限元分析软件建立了劲性骨架施工阶段模型，对比了劲性骨架同时合拢、上下游先后合拢两种方案的扣索索力、拱肋线形、主弦管应力；利用 Midas GTS 建立了桩＋承台＋锚索的组合式扣索地锚，对比了锚索分级加载、分批加载两种加载方式的承台位移、锚索力变化、安全系数。研究结果表明：扣索前后分离、塔上张拉的斜拉扣挂形式更适宜，劲性骨架同时合拢方案的优于上下游先后合拢方案，组合式扣地锚锚索分批次张拉的安全储备充足，施工便利。2022 年 6 月 6 日，天峨龙滩劲性骨架历时 100 天，实现高精度合龙，验证了研究成果的可靠性。

关键词　斜拉扣挂　扣索　拱桥　地锚
中图分类号　TU398⁺.9　　　**文献标识码**　A

Research on Key Technologies of Cable-stayed Fastening System of Tian'e Longtan Super Major Bridge

LUO Xiaobin　SHEN Yao　TANG Yanyun　HOU Kaiwen

(Guangxi Road and Bridge Engineering Group Co., Ltd, Nanning,Guangxi,530004,China)

Abstract　Based on the sub project of cantilever assembly of rigid skeleton of Tian'e Longtan super major bridge, the feasibility of two structural forms of cable-stayed fastening system, i. e. front and rear separation of cable, tension on tower and full length of cable, and ground tension, is compared; The construction stage model of rigid skeleton is established by using the optimization calculation program of cable-stayed fastening of arch bridge and midas civil finite element analysis software. The cable force, arch rib line shape and main chord stress of the two schemes of

---

作者简介：
罗小斌（1985—），男，学士，高级工程师，主要从事大跨度拱桥施工技术研发及管理方面的研究。
沈耀（1978—），男，学士，高级工程师，主要从事大跨度拱桥施工技术研发及管理方面的研究。
唐雁云（1997—），男，学士，助理工程师，从事大跨度拱桥施工技术研发及管理方面的研究。
侯凯文（1989—），男，博士，工程师，从事大跨度拱桥施工技术研发及管理方面的研究。

simultaneous closure of rigid skeleton and closure of upstream and downstream successively are compared; Midas/gts is used to establish the combined cable anchor of "pile + cushion cap + anchor cable". The displacement of cushion cap, the change of anchor cable force and the safety factor of two loading methods of anchor cable grading loading and batch loading are compared. The results show that the cable-stayed form of cable separation and tower tension is more suitable. The scheme of simultaneous closure of rigid skeleton is better than the scheme of successive closure of upstream and downstream. The safety reserve of combined anchor cable tensioning in batches is sufficient and the construction is convenient. On June 6, 2022, the rigid skeleton of Tian'e Longtan lasted 100 days to achieve high-precision closure, which verified the reliability of the research results.

Keywords　diagonal buckle　buckle rope　arch bridge　ground anchor

E-mail　282250772@qq.com

组合式扣地锚施工关键技术及其应用研究

侯凯文 罗小斌 蒋 鹏 黄 酉

(广西路桥工程集团有限公司 广西南宁 530200)

摘 要 山区拱桥建设往往受坡陡壑深的地形地势影响，无法新设立重力式地锚，因此提出一种"桩基承台+超长锚索"的扣地锚组合型式。针对组合式扣地锚的设计、超长锚索的施工及其在斜拉扣挂系统中的应用技术，采用理论分析和现场试验的手段进行研究。主要成果如下：(1)组合式扣地锚利用桩基和承台主体结构作为锚碇，并施加预应力锚索以抵抗扣索力，从而实现其在斜拉扣挂系统中的应用。(2)提出采用顶驱双套管钻进的120m级超长锚索施工技术，通过现场试验验证其可行性。(3)优化扣索和锚索的张拉工序，提出组合式扣地锚在斜拉扣挂系统中的应用技术。该组合式扣地锚受力明确，为天峨龙滩特大桥的拱肋吊装合龙提供坚实基础，同时实现了"永临结合"，节约了成本，为后续山区桥梁建设提供参考依据。

关键词 拱桥 组合式扣地锚 超长锚索 施工工艺 现场试验 斜拉扣挂系统

中图分类号 TU398$^+$.9 **文献标识码** A

Research on the Technology and Application of Combined Fastening-anchoring Cable System

HOU Kaiwen LUO Xiaobin JIANG Peng HUANG You

(Guangxi Road and Bridge Engineering Group Co., Ltd., Nanning, Guangxi, 530200, China)

Abstract The construction of fastening-anchoring cable system of arch bridges in mountainous areas is limited by the terrain with steep slopes and deep gullies. Therefore, a combination of "pile cap + long anchor cable" was proposed. Specifically, three aspects of research content, including the design of combined fastening-anchoring cable system, the construction technology of long anchor cable, the application of combined fastening-anchoring cable system in cable-stayed fastening system were studied. The main results were as follows: (1) Pile foundation and pile cap were used as anchorages in combined fastening-anchoring cable system. Prestressed anchor cable was applied to resist the

---

作者简介：

侯凯文(1989—)，男，博士，工程师，主要从事桥梁工程、岩土工程的研究。

罗小斌(1985—)，男，学士，高级工程师，主要从事大跨度拱桥施工技术研发及管理方面的研究。

蒋鹏(1996—)，男，学士，助理工程师，主要从事大跨度拱桥施工技术研发及管理方面的研究。

黄酉(1998—)，男，学士，助理工程师，主要从事大跨度拱桥施工技术研发及管理方面的研究。

cable force, so as to realize the application in cable-stayed fastening system. (2) The construction technology of 120m long anchor cable with double casing drilling is proposed. Meanwhile, the working performance of anchor cable was verified by field tests. (3) The tensioning process of buckle cable and anchor cable was optimized. Then the application technology of combined fastening-anchoring cable system in cable-stayed fastening system was put forward. The stress of the combined fastening-anchoring cable system in application stage was explicitd, which provides a support for the construction of the Tian'e Longtan bridge. Besides, the "permanent and temporary combination" has been realized and the the cost has been saved. The case has been provided a reference for the construction of arch bridge in mountainous areas.

Keywords　arch bridge　combined fastening-anchoring cable system　extra long anchor cable　construction technology　field test　cable-stayed fastening system

　　E-mail　houkaiwen2008@ sina. com

天峨龙滩特大桥钢管混凝土灌注技术研究

沈 耀　侯凯文　罗小斌　匡志强

（广西路桥工程集团有限公司　广西南宁　530200）

摘　要　根据天峨龙滩特大桥主桥上承式劲性骨架混凝土拱桥的结构形式，管内混凝土采用真空辅助分级压注顶升进行施工。针对C80自密实混凝土制备和管内混凝土灌注技术两个方面开展研究，提出管内C80超高强自密实、无收缩混凝土制备与施工关键技术；提出管内混凝土真空辅助分级压注顶升的主要施工工艺和控制要点。再结合超声波对管内混凝土密实度进行检测，结果表明：C80超高强混凝土黏度、自密实性能以及流动性等性能良好，所提出的管内混凝土灌注工艺保证了灌注阶段的密实性，效果良好，为今后国内类似的大跨度拱桥钢管混凝土灌注施工积累了经验。

关键词　劲性骨架混凝土拱桥　钢管混凝土　真空辅助　C80高性能混凝土　灌注

中图分类号　TU398$^+$.9　　　**文献标识码**　A

Research on Casting Technology of Concrete-filled Steel Tube of Tian'e Longtan Bridge

SHEN Yao　HOU Kaiwen　LUO Xiaobin　KUANG Zhiqiang

(Guangxi Road and Bridge Engineering Group Co., Ltd., Nanning, Guangxi, 530200, China)

Abstract　According to the Tian'e Longtan bridge, which the structural form is rigid skeleton concrete arch bridge, the concrete in tube is graded casting by vacuum-aided. The preparation of C80 self compacting concrete and the casting technology are studied. The key technology of production of HPC (high performance concrete) of C80 is studied. The self compacting and non shrinkage characteristics of C80 concrete is put forward. The graded casting technology by vacuum-aided staged is put forward. Combined with ultrasonic to detect the compactness of concrete in the tube, the results show that high performance concrete of C80 has great viscosity, self compacting performance and fluidity. The proposed technology of concrete casting process in the tube ensures the compactness. Besides, the

---

作者简介：

沈耀（1978—），男，学士，高级工程师，主要从事大跨度拱桥施工技术研发及管理方面的研究。

侯凯文（1989—），男，博士，工程师，从事大跨度拱桥施工技术研发及管理方面的研究。

罗小斌（1985—），男，学士，高级工程师，主要从事大跨度拱桥施工技术研发及管理方面的研究。

匡志强（1991—），男，学士，工程师，主要从事大跨度拱桥施工技术研发及管理方面的研究。

project provide a reference for the concrete-filled steel tube construction of similar long-span arch bridges in China in the future.

Keywords rigid skeleton concrete arch bridge concrete-filled steel tube vacuum-aided high performance concrete of C80 casting

E-mail houkaiwen2008@ sina. com

超大跨钢管混凝土劲性骨架拱桥外包混凝土施工方案研究

赵玉峰 罗小斌 沈 耀 匡志强

(广西路桥工程集团有限公司 广西南宁 530011)

摘要 针对超大跨径钢管混凝土劲性骨架拱桥施工复杂、外包混凝土施工方案对劲性骨架受力影响较大的问题,以主跨为600m的天峨龙滩特大桥为背景,研究超大跨度劲性骨架混凝土拱桥外包混凝土的合理施工方法。采用Midas Civil 软件建立主拱圈模型,对不同分环分段方案进行施工过程分析,研究工作面数量对拱桥结构应力、挠度和稳定性的影响。研究结果表明:目前采用的3环6段8工作面的施工方案可有效控制劲性骨架及外包混凝土应力。劲性骨架外包混凝土最大拉、压应力分别为1.09MPa和10.9MPa,主弦管最大应力为327MPa,满足劲性骨架承载力及稳定要求。研究成果可为大跨度混凝土拱桥的修建提供技术支撑。

关键词 600m大跨拱桥 钢管混凝土劲性骨架 外包混凝土 分环分段施工

中图分类号 TU398$^+$.9 **文献标识码** A

Research on Construction Scheme of Externally Wrapped Concrete for Long Span Concrete Arch Bridge with CFST Stiff Skeleton

ZHAO Yufeng LUO Xiaobin SHEN Yao KUANG Zhiqiang

(Guangxi Road and Bridge Engineering Group Co., Ltd., Nanning, Guangxi, 530011, China)

Abstract In view of the complex construction of the long span concrete arch bridge with concrete-filled tubular stiff skeleton and the great influence of the construction scheme of wrapped concrete on the stiff skeleton, the Tian'e Longtan bridge with a main span of 600 metres was token as an example to study the reasonable construction scheme of wrapped concrete for long span concrete arch bridge with stiff skeleton. The arch model was established

---

作者简介:

赵玉峰(1989—),男,博士,工程师,主要从事大跨度拱桥施工技术研发及管理方面的研究。

罗小斌(1985—),男,学士,高级工程师,主要从事大跨度拱桥施工技术研发及管理方面的研究。

沈耀(1978—),男,学士,高级工程师,主要从事大跨度拱桥施工技术研发及管理方面的研究。

匡志强(1991—),男,学士,工程师,主要从事大跨度拱桥施工技术研发及管理方面的研究。

using Midas Civil, the construction process of different number of the dividing cross section rings and longitudinal section segments was analyzed and the influence of working platform on the stress, deflection and stability of arch bridge structure was studied. The research results show that dividing the arch ring into three rings, six segments in each ring and eight working platform is a reasonable construction scheme, which can effectively control the stress of the stiff skeleton and the concrete. The maximum tensile and compressive stress of the wrapped concrete are 1.09 MPa and 10.9 MPa respectively, and the stress of the main chord is 327 MPa, which are well controlled and meet the bearing capacity and stability requirements of the stiff skeleton. The research results can provide support for the construction of long-span concrete arch bridges.

Keywords 600 metres long-span arch bridge　concrete-filled steel tubular stiff skeleton　externally wrapped concrete　segmented construction

大跨度劲性骨架拱桥外包混凝土快速施工关键技术

叶增鑫 罗小斌 沈耀 匡志强

(广西路桥工程集团有限公司 广西南宁 530004)

摘要 结合主桥为600m上承式劲性骨架拱桥的天峨龙滩特大桥工程实例,研究大跨度劲性骨架拱桥外包混凝土快速施工关键技术。通过外包混凝土施工设备的布置与快速施工模架体系的设计,提出一套科学、合理、可行的外包混凝土快速施工关键技术。研究结果表明:(1)通过拱上布置塔吊及平台实现材料快速转运;(2)通过泵管布置,振捣布置,养护系统布置等施工布置实现外包混凝土快速施工;(3)以高空作业地面化为原则,底模在拱肋吊装节段同时安装,减少高空作业量;(4)设计吊架式施工外架,解决高空作业施工作业平台问题;(5)拱肋为变截面,以外包混凝土施工段为单元,设计易于安拆、调整的模板单元。研究成果可为大跨度混凝土拱桥的快速施工提供技术支撑。

关键词 劲性骨架拱桥 外包混凝土 施工布置 快速施工 模架

中图分类号 TU398+.9 **文献标识码** A

Key Technologies for Rapid Construction of Outer-Packed Concrete of Large-span Rigid Skeleton Arch Bridge

YE Zengxin LUO Xiaobin SHEN Yao KUANG Zhiqiang

(Guangxi Road and Bridge Engineering Group Co., Ltd, Nanning, Guangxi, 530004, China)

Abstract To investigate the key technologies for rapid construction of outer-packed concrete for long span concrete arch bridge with stiff skeleton, the Tian'e Longtan bridge with a main span of 600 meters deck rigid skeleton arch bridge was combined as the project case. Through the layout of outer-packed concrete construction equipment and

---

作者简介:
叶增鑫(1995—),男,硕士,助理工程师,主要从事大跨度拱桥施工技术研发及管理方面的研究。
罗小斌(1985—),男,学士,高级工程师,主要从事大跨度拱桥施工技术研发及管理方面的研究。
沈耀(1978—),男,学士,高级工程师,主要从事大跨度拱桥施工技术研发及管理方面的研究。
匡志强(1991—),男,学士,工程师,主要从事大跨度拱桥施工技术研发及管理方面的研究。

the design of rapid construction formwork system, a set of scientific, reasonable and feasible key technologies for rapid construction of outer-packed concrete are proposed. The research results show that: (1) To realize the rapid transfer of materials, the tower cranes and platforms are arranging on the arch; (2) Through the layout of pump pipes, concrete vibration and curing system, the rapid construction of outer-packed concrete can be realized; (3) based on the principle of working at heights is like working on the ground, the bottom formwork is installed at the arch rib hoisting section at the same time, so as to reduce work at heights; (4) Design hanger platform to solve the problem of working at heights; (5) The arch rib is of variable cross-section, and the outer-packed concrete construction section is taken as the unit, and the formwork unit that designed is easy to install, dismantle and adjust. The research results can provide technical support for the rapid construction of long-span concrete arch bridges.

Keywords　rigid skeleton arch bridge　outer-packed concrete　construction layout　rapid construction formwork and equipment

E-mail　18577760336@163.com

特大跨中承式钢箱拱桥主拱空间复合转体合龙成拱关键技术

李 畅 牟廷敏 梁 健 王 戈 范碧琨

(四川省公路规划勘察设计研究院有限公司 四川成都 610041)

摘 要 重庆城口至开州高速公路蓼子特大桥为单跨252m中承式双肋钢箱拱桥,桥梁跨越深切峡谷,两岸拱座均位于斜向山脊上,山体纵桥向坡度70°~80°,横桥向坡度近70°,受两岸地形地质条件限制和桥下吊装平台渡汛风险影响,缆索吊装-斜拉扣挂法难以实施,采用转体工艺合龙成拱。针对复杂陡峭斜坡地形条件、无边跨中承式拱桥转体配重难、山区峡谷口阵风效应突出等难题,为实现快速有效合龙成拱,首次提出基于单拱肋的三维空间复合转体工艺及其配套的可快速拆卸的无配重自适应平衡技术。研究实践表明:大桥双幅拱肋在8天内经竖转提升、平转和竖转下放等共计12次复合转体顺利合龙,实现了转体结构体系快速转换和主拱无合龙段快速施工,相比现有整幅桥梁转体技术减少山体开挖约25万 m^3,对各种复杂地形受限条件下的桥梁施工提供新选择。

关键词 中承式钢箱拱桥 转体施工 空间复合转体 单拱肋 无平衡重 无合龙段
中图分类号 U448.22;U445.4   **文献标识码** A

Key Technology of Long Span Half-through Steel Box Arch Bridge with Hybrid Three-dimensional Rotation Construction

LI Chang MOU Tingmin LIANG Jian WANG Ge FAN Bikun

(Sichuan Highway Planning,Survey,Design and Research Institute Co.,Ltd,Chengdu,Sichuan,610041,China)

作者简介:

李畅(1993—),男,硕士,工程师,主要从事桥梁工程领域的设计和研究。

牟廷敏(1964—),男,学士,教授级高级工程师,主要从事桥梁工程和混凝土材料领域的设计和研究。

梁健(1979—),男,硕士,教授级高级工程师,主要从事桥梁工程领域的设计和研究。

王戈(1985—),男,硕士,高级工程师,主要从事桥梁工程领域的设计和研究。

范碧琨(1970—),女,学士,教授级高级工程师,主要从事桥梁工程和混凝土材料领域的设计和研究。

Abstract Liaozi bridge of Chongqing Chengkou to Kaizhou expressway is a half-through steel box arch bridge with a 252m long span. The bridge spans deep valleys and arches are located on oblique ridges. The longitudinal slope of the mountain is 70 ° ~ 80 °, and the transverse slope is about 70 °. Due to the terrain and geological constraints and the risk of the river under the bridge, the cable-stayed fastening method is difficult to implement, and the rotation construction is adopted. In view of the complex terrain conditions, the difficulty of rotating counterweight of non-side span arch bridge, and the prominent gust effect at mountain valleys, a hybrid three-dimensional rotation based on a single arch and its supporting fast detachable self-adaptive balance technology without counterweight are proposed. The research practice shows that the arch ribs are successfully closed by 12 combined rotations such as vertical lifting, horizontal rotation and vertical lowering within 8 days, which realizes the rapid conversion of the rotation system and the rapid construction of the arch without closure. Compared with the existing whole bridge rotation technology, the excavation is reduced by about 250000m^3, providing a new choice for bridge construction under various complex terrain and restricted conditions.

Keywords half-through steel box arch bridge rotation construction hybrid three-dimensional rotation single arch rotation without counterweight no closure segment

E-mail 292563843@ qq. com

0 引言

重庆城口(陕渝界)至开州高速公路蓼子特大桥为计算跨径252m中承式钢箱拱桥,矢跨比1/4,拱轴系数 $m = 1.3$。桥梁采用双向四车道高速公路标准。全桥按整幅设计,桥宽30.4m。主拱共左右两道拱肋,拱肋中心间距28m,拱肋截面为变高度箱形截面,宽2.4m,高由拱脚的5.5m渐变到拱顶3.0m。全桥共设置两道肋间横梁和四道K撑。拱座设计为分离式拱座,拱座基础宽8m,拱座宽5.4m,拱座基础均埋置于中风化岩层。桥梁总体布置图见图1。

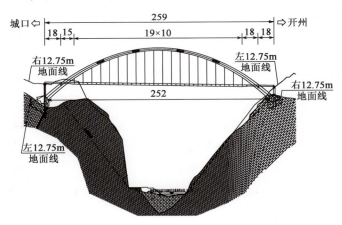

图1 蓼子特大桥总体立面布置(尺寸单位:m)
Fig.1 General elevation layout of Liaozi Bridge(Unit:m)

桥位山体陡峭、沟壑深切、岩体表层破碎。两岸拱座均位于斜向山脊上,山体纵桥向坡度70°~80°,横桥向坡度近70°(图2),导致左右拱肋地面高差近30m。桥梁位于山区峡谷口,阵风效应明显,施工期间抗风问题突出。桥下跨越为季节性河流,几乎年年发生山洪。常规的缆索吊装-斜拉扣挂法因两岸地形地质条件限制布设困难,同时桥下吊装平台位于河中存在渡汛风险,为减小施工难度和施工风险,选择转体工艺合龙成拱方案[1-6]。

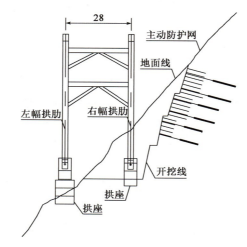

图 2　蓼子特大桥城口岸横断面布置(尺寸单位:m)
Fig. 2　Cross section layout of Liaozi Bridge at Chengkou(Unit:m)

1　总体施工方案

1.1　总体方案设计

常规的基于整幅桥梁采用平转+向上竖转相结合的转体工艺[2-3],因受陡峭斜坡地形条件限制,面临以下难题:

(1)左右拱肋地面高差接近30m,导致山外侧拱肋拼装支架高度高达38m,支架材料用量大。

(2)平转环道直径为26m,部分环道基础悬出地面,需要增设桩基和墩柱作为环道的支撑结构,实施难度大。

(3)上转盘尾部与山体冲突,需要大量开挖山体,生态环境破坏大。

根据桥位地形条件和桥梁结构特征,创造性的提出以单拱肋作为转体单元,采用向上竖转+平转+向下竖转的三维空间复合转体工艺进行合龙,单拱肋合龙后再进行横撑安装。每个拱肋均可独立地在拱座后方引桥或路基上适当高程位置进行拼装,仅需搭设少量低矮支架即可(图3)。其单肋分幅转体方案程序如表1所示。

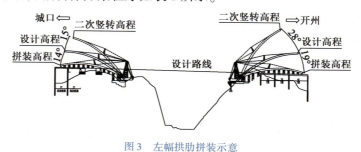

图 3　左幅拱肋拼装示意
Fig. 3　Assemble diagram of the left arch rib

基于单肋分幅的空间复合转体工艺程序　　　　表1
Hybrid three-dimensional rotation process based on single arch rib　　Tab. 1

拱　　肋	转 体 程 序
城口岸右 单半幅拱肋	拼装角度：−14° 竖转提升：由−14°～+28° 平转角度：182° 竖转下放：由+28°至设计高程0°
开州岸右 单半幅拱肋	拼装角度：−19° 竖转提升：由−19°～+15° 平转角度：182° 竖转下放：由+15°至设计高程0°
城口岸左 单半幅拱肋	拼装角度：−19° 竖转提升：由−19°～+15° 平转角度：182° 竖转下放：由+15°至设计高程0°
开州岸左 单半幅拱肋	拼装角度：−19° 竖转提升：由−19°～+28° 平转角度：180° 竖转下放：由+28°至设计高程0°

注：拼装角度和竖转角度均以设计高程为基准，低于设计高程的角度为负值，反之为正值。

1.2　施工重难点

本桥转体工艺的施工重难点如下：

（1）桥梁位于陡峭斜坡地形，全桥共转体12次，平转最大角度达182°，最大竖转提升角度达47°，最大竖转下放角度达28°，转体体系转换、转体次数、竖转角度、平转角度均为世界前列[7-11]。

（2）桥梁设计为单跨中承式拱桥，无边跨作为转体结构配重，若采用常规的配重方法则竖转过程中需要反复调整，且空间受限、调整时间长，导致配重措施难度大。

（3）桥址位于典型的山区峡谷口，阵风效应突出，转体窗口期时间短，对复合转体的体系转换和拱肋快速合龙要求高。

（4）桥梁转体为基于单拱肋的复合转体工艺，转体结构长细比较大，需要重点关注转体结构的抗倾覆性和稳定性。

2　转体结构体系设计

2.1　平转结构体系

桥梁拱座沿高度方向分为上下两部分，上半部分组成平转体系的上转盘，并与拱肋、索塔、扣索连接；下半部分组成平转体系的下转盘，作为转体体系的基础；上转盘和下转盘之间设置球铰、撑脚、环道和牵引反力座等。考虑单拱肋转体结构重心较高、环道半径较小等因素，采用球铰和撑脚共同支撑的平转承重体系，以提高平转过程中结构的稳定性。

(1) 下转盘。

下转盘设置 $\phi 6.78 \mathrm{m}$ 的环道,环道宽 $1.1 \mathrm{m}$。环道在工厂预制,现场分节段拼装。环道由镜面不锈钢板、钢板和环向型钢劲性骨架组成。镜面不锈钢板接头采用焊接方式。每块钢板用 6 幅螺栓连接,下端用双螺帽,在钢板底部加劲角钢处增设钢筋,与预留槽内预埋钢筋焊接,防止预留槽内混凝土灌注时中部上拱。

(2) 上转盘。

考虑转盘制作及主拱预埋段、索塔钢管、撑脚、球铰等预埋,转盘内设置劲性骨架,以保证埋设精度和加强上转盘整体性。为减小上转盘下缘在脱架后出现的较大拉应力,在上转盘下缘设置纵向预应力束,预应力束规格为 $\phi_s 15.2-18$。

(3) 球铰与撑脚。

球铰支承直径为 $2 \mathrm{m}$,球铰球面直径为 $8 \mathrm{m}$。球铰的下球面板上镶嵌填充聚四氟乙烯橡胶滑板,并涂抹四氟黄油粉润滑,与上球面板组成摩擦副。球铰中心设置中心定位轴,中心定位轴直径 $260 \mathrm{mm}$,伸入上下球铰分别为 $283.5 \mathrm{mm}$、$558.5 \mathrm{mm}$。

撑脚共两类,A 类撑脚为平转时非受力撑脚,仅起到稳定作用,其由两根 $\phi 700 \times 18$ 钢管混凝土组成,共 7 对;B 类撑脚为平转时的受力撑脚,其由三根 $\phi 700 \times 18$ 钢管混凝土组成,共 1 对。撑脚上端埋于上转盘内,下端支承在下转盘环道上。撑脚下端设置内嵌聚四氟乙烯复合滑板的千岛走板,走板厚 $50 \mathrm{mm}$,内嵌四氟乙烯复合滑板,四氟蘑菇头外漏 $6 \mathrm{mm}$。B 类撑脚与环道接触直接受力,A 类撑脚与环道预留间隙 $3 \mathrm{mm}$。

(4) 平转牵引系统。

平转牵引体系由钢绞线、连续张拉千斤顶和牵引反力座组成。牵引采用一组钢绞线形成转动力偶,钢绞线一端锚固于上转盘中,缠绕在上转盘上,另一端则与连续张拉千斤顶相连,牵引索采用一对 $\phi_s 15.2-18$。

2.2 竖转结构体系

竖转结构体系由竖转铰、扣索、平衡索、索塔、撑架和后锚系统等组成。竖转时,通过在上转盘尾部张拉扣索使拱肋以竖转铰为转动中心完成竖转提升和竖转下放,同时在上转盘尾部设置后锚系统确保竖转过程中上部结构的平衡。

(1) 索塔及撑架。

索塔为钢管或钢管混凝土组成的变截面桁架结构,索塔高 $34.335 \mathrm{m}$。每个索塔由四根主管组成,其中斜主管(倾斜 $15°$)和直主管管径为 $\phi 900 \times 20$,支管管径有 $\phi 600 \times 16$ 和 $\phi 480 \times 16$ 两种规格。纵桥向索塔为变截面,其塔顶钢管中心间距为 $2.6 \mathrm{m}$,塔底钢管中心间距为 $11.8 \mathrm{m}$;横桥向索塔为等宽,钢管中心间距为 $3.5 \mathrm{m}$。在直主管索塔顶端 $10 \mathrm{m}$ 范围和斜主管内灌注 C50 混凝土。

为降低索塔高度及调整主拱受力和变形,在 $1/4L$ 附近处设拱上撑架,撑架为空钢管桁架结构,主管直径为 $\phi 600 \times 20$,支管管径为 $\phi 480 \times 16$ 和 $\phi 300 \times 16$ 两种规格。

(2) 扣索与平衡索。

扣索为拱肋竖转提升和竖转下放设置,第一组扣索采用 4 束 $\phi_s 17.8-16$ 钢绞线,第二组扣索采用 4 束 $\phi_s 17.8-15$ 钢绞线;平衡索为减小索塔受力设置,共采用 4 根 $\phi_s 15.2-18$、6 根 $\phi_s 15.2-12$,竖向分两排锚固在索塔上。

第一组扣索前端锚于拱肋前端,第二组扣索前端锚固于拱肋 1/4L 附近,扣索后端锚固于上转盘尾部,并在此端张拉。平衡索上端锚固于索塔顶部,下端锚固于上转盘尾部,并在此端张拉。

(3)索鞍。

索鞍只起转向作用,由钢板焊成整体结构,扣索在索鞍上能自由滑动,因此与扣索接触面设置滑轮。索鞍和索塔通过设置在索塔顶端的混凝土传剪箱进行连接。由于扣索 1 和扣索 2 与索塔的角度不同,分别对应两种不同转向角度的 A 类索鞍和 B 类索鞍(图4)。

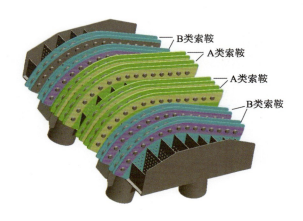

图 4 竖转索鞍结构三维示意

Fig. 4 Three-dimensional diagram of the vertical rotation cable saddle structure

(4)竖转铰。

拱脚段拱肋预留嵌补段设置竖转铰。根据受力需要,设计为三耳板竖转铰,铰心采用 ϕ420mm 的销轴,销轴材质采用 40Cr,为提高竖转铰的局部刚度,耳板横向间设置钢管作为加劲(图5)。为加强平转过程中竖转铰的局部刚度,设置了可快速安装和拆卸的竖转铰临时封铰设施。

2.3 竖转平衡结构体系

为平衡竖转过程中拱肋重心不断变化产生的不平衡力矩,在上转盘尾部设置后锚系统。后锚系统采用预应力岩锚(锚固端)+转换梁+自锚式预应力组合形式,即后锚下端设置预应力岩锚与岩体锚固,后锚上端设置自锚式预应力与上转盘连接,并在上转盘顶面张拉,自锚式预应力与预应力岩锚之间设置转换梁(图6)。

预应力岩锚采用 M15-6 环氧钢绞线,自锁式预应力锚固体系规格为 M15-9 环氧钢绞线,转换梁采用钢筋混凝土结构。该转体装置的设置,使竖转过程中通过锚固系统自动调节的索力所产生的抵抗力矩与不断变化的拱肋倾覆力矩保持平衡。对于单跨拱桥,可以在拱肋在向上竖转时有意识的竖转到比设计高程高的位置,在此位置进行平转,进而可以取消配重,施工简单方便,材料消耗低,不受现场空间限制,同时锚固系统承载力高,降低了施工风险。

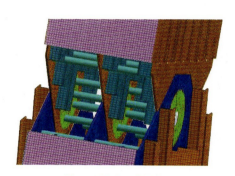

图 5 竖转铰三维示意
Fig. 5 Three-dimensional diagram of the vertical hinge

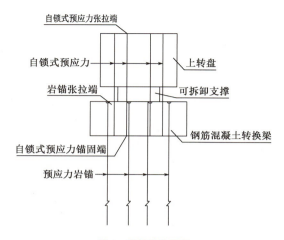

图 6 后锚系统示意
Fig. 6 Diagram of the rear anchor system

3 转体施工工艺

向上竖转＋平转＋向下竖转的三维空间复合转体工艺主要包括转体前施工准备、竖转提升、平转、竖转下放、拱肋合龙及横撑安装等工序，以右幅为例，其转体流程如图7所示。

3.1 平转结构体系

下转盘制作：预埋环道劲性骨架，在劲性骨架上，安装环道钢板，用螺栓精确调整环道钢板高程和球铰（包括中心定位轴）的位置，满足要求后浇筑槽口内混凝土，并按设计要求浇筑牵引索反力座和辅助千斤顶反力座。

球铰安装：下球铰安装后清理球面，将中心销轴插入套管中，调整好垂直度与周边间隙；用四氟黄油填满聚四氟乙烯滑板之间的间隙，使黄油面与四氟滑板面持平。然后将上球铰吊装到位，套进中心销轴内，微调上球铰位置，使之水平并与下球铰外圈间隙垂直。球铰安装完毕对周边进行保护，确保杂质不进入到摩擦面内。

上转盘制作：待上球铰安装完成后，即可进行上转盘施工，同时需预埋固定好牵引索、主拱预埋段、扣索和平衡索预埋管和索塔柱脚。混凝土到达龄期后，按程序分阶段张拉纵向预应力束。

后锚施工：预应力岩锚施工前，首先进行岩锚的锚固力破坏试验即拉拔试验。预应力岩锚和混凝土转换梁施工完成后，在转换梁和上转盘之间设置可拆卸支承。

3.2 拱肋竖转提升

扣索和平衡索的所有钢绞线应依次编号，确保每根钢绞线安装位置准确、避免相互打搅。张拉后锚系统的自锁式预应力，张拉完成后分别按照设计索力的20%、40%、60%、80%、100%共5级同步协调张拉扣索和平衡索进行拱肋脱架，脱架完成后，全面检查转动结构体系的可靠性。

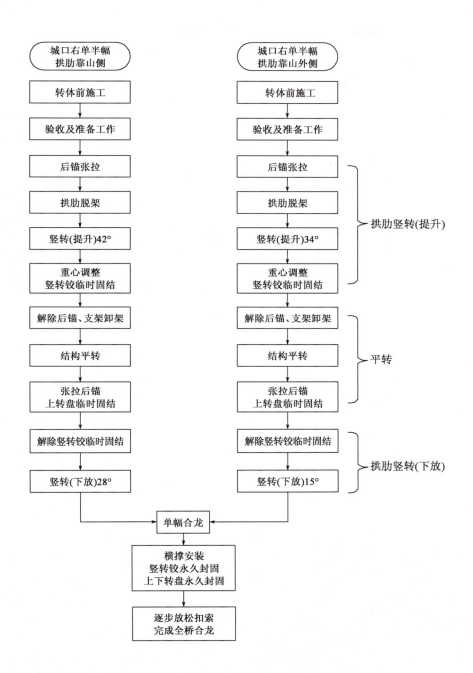

图 7 单幅拱肋转体流程示意
Fig. 7 Diagram of the single arch rib rotation process

监测脱架状态下拱肋的温度变形情况,进行拱肋的精确测量与配切工作。配切完成后,同步液压系统开始竖转提升,每级竖转过程中保持扣索1和扣索2的合理索力比例关系(图8),并实时监测拱肋悬臂端沿横桥向的两处顶点高程,做到拱肋高程和索力双控。同时监测扣塔水平位移,若位移超过预定值,则间断调整平衡索的索力,以改善扣塔的受力状态。竖转过程中应注意启动、止动匀速,竖转时应控制角速度不大于0.0025rad/min,加速度不大于0.005m/s²。拱肋竖转提升过程见图9。

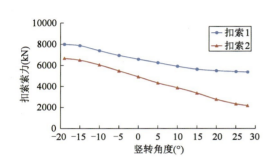

图8 竖转角度-扣索索力关系曲线

Fig. 8 Vertical rotation angle-cable force curve

图9 开州岸右幅拱肋(靠山外侧)竖转提升

Fig. 9 The right arch rib at Kaizhou (outside the mountain) is lifting by vertical rotation

3.3 拱肋平转

竖转完成后,拆除后锚系统的自锁式预应力,快速安装竖转铰临时封铰设施,由此完成竖转结构体系到平转结构体系的转换。全面检查和清除拱肋平转范围内的障碍物,并根据撑脚压力结果核实转体结构重心是否满足设计要求,满足要求后,同步张拉牵引索千斤顶,进行试平转,转动无误后正式平转。平转时应控制角速度不大于0.01rad/min,加速度不大于0.003m/s²。拱肋平转过程见图10和图11。

图10 城口岸右幅拱肋(靠山侧)平转

Fig. 10 The right arch rib at Chengkou (near the mountain) is rotating horizontally

图11 城口岸左幅拱肋(靠山外侧)平转

Fig. 11 The left arch rib at Chengkou (outside the mountain) is rotating horizontally

即将平转到设计轴线时,停止连续牵引,靠点动到位,当拱肋轴线满足设计要求后,通过快速楔紧所有撑脚与环道间隙、楔紧保险腿与下转盘间隙等方式进行上转盘与下转盘的临时固结。

3.4 拱肋竖转下放

平转完成后,再次张拉上转盘尾部的自锁式预应力,垫实前撑脚,解除临时封铰措施,以此从平转结构体系转换到竖转结构体系。同步液压系统开始竖转下放,每级竖转过程中保持扣索 1 和扣索 2 的合理索力比例关系,并实时监测拱肋悬臂端沿横桥向的两处顶点高程,做到拱肋高程和索力双控。同时监测扣塔水平位移,若位移超过预定值,则间断调整平衡索的索力,以改善扣塔的受力状态。竖转过程中应注意启动、止动匀速,竖转时应控制角速度不大于 $0.0025\mathrm{rad/min}$,加速度不大于 $0.005\mathrm{m/s^2}$。拱肋竖转下放过程见图 12。

即将下放到设计高程时,调整拱肋轴线和高程,按照设计轴线和高程调整,与已经下放到位的对岸侧拱肋进行合龙对接。

3.5 拱肋合龙

利用单拱肋竖转下放提供的有利条件,取消常规的合龙段,通过详细的监测、监控、BIM 模拟、脱架后拱肋姿态扫描等综合技术,精确计算出扣索索力和拱肋合龙口端面的余量配切数据,在拱肋竖转前进行精准配切(图 13),最大限度减少了横风、太阳侧照等因素对转体施工的影响,保证拱肋精确对接合龙,合龙后立即张拉缆风绳。本方法取消了合龙段吊装、减少高空焊接作业量约 50%,提高了施工工效,确保了在合龙窗口期实现快速合龙。

图 12　左幅拱肋竖转下放
Fig. 12　The left arch rib is lowering by vertical rotation

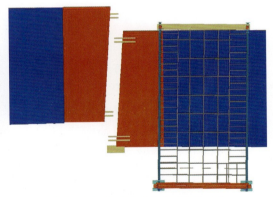

图 13　拱肋取消合龙段直接合龙示意
Fig. 13　Diagram of the direct closure without closure segment

3.6 拱肋横撑安装

利用提前安装在拱肋上的鹰嘴吊进行拱上临时横撑安装(图 14)。临时横撑安装完成后,逐步分级放松扣索和平衡索,将拱脚竖转铰封固,变为固定端,同时浇筑上下转盘间封固混凝土,至此完成拱肋转体施工。

图 14 拱肋临时横撑安装

Fig. 14 The temporary cross brace of arch rib is hoisting

4 结论

(1)蓼子特大桥采用以单拱肋作为转体单元,因地制宜利用拱座后方引桥或路基作为拼装平台,采用向上竖转+平转+向下竖转的三维空间复合转体工艺进行合龙,首次实现三维空间转体合龙成拱。

(2)针对无边跨拱桥结构配重难以实施的问题,提出自锁式预应力+转换梁+预应力岩锚形成的后锚系统来替代配重,竖转过程中自适应,且拆除和再次安装快速,避免了竖转过程中配重反复调整。

(3)针对山区峡谷口阵风效应突出,提出取消合龙段,利用拱肋下放直接合龙成桥,在较短的窗口期实现合龙快速化。

(4)针对单拱肋转体结构的高长细比,采用球铰和撑脚共同支承的平转受力模式,以及三耳板竖转铰及其配套的临时封铰设施,确保了结构转体过程中的抗倾覆性能和稳定性能。

(5)与现有的整幅桥梁平转与向上竖转相结合的转体技术,减少山体开挖方量约 25 万 m^3,极大地保护了自然生态环境。

(6)桥梁于 2022 年 8 月 23 日开始进行转体,转体次数共 12 次,历时 8 天完成左右幅拱肋转体合龙。实践表明:其创新的单拱肋三维空间复合转体技术,拓展了拱桥转体工艺边界,丰富了拱桥施工工艺,对各种复杂地形受限条件下的桥梁施工提供新选择。

参 考 文 献

[1] 张联燕,程懋方,谭邦明.桥梁转体施工[M].北京:人民交通出版社,2002.

[2] 庄卫林,黄道全,谢邦珠.丫髻沙大桥转体施工工艺设计[J].桥梁建设,2000(1):37-41.

[3] 牟廷敏,范碧琨,梁健.佛山市东平大桥的创新与实践[C]//2009 年桥梁与都市国际论坛

论文集. 2009:189-198.

[4] 许颖强,陈冬,聂振龙. 大跨度钢箱桁架拱桥拱肋架设施工技术[J]. 世界桥梁,2020,48(2):35-39.

[5] 祝良红,许鑫,余昆. 香溪长江公路大桥大跨度钢箱桁架推力拱合龙技术[J]. 世界桥梁,2019,47(2):17-21.

[6] 张春新. 西江特大桥钢箱提篮拱架设施工技术[J]. 桥梁建设,2015,45(5):7-12.

[7] 李德彪,何旭飞,夏焕文. 等. 大理至保山铁路澜沧江大桥施工测量技术[J]. 世界桥梁,2020,48(3):32-37.

[8] 高吉才. "提篮式"钢管混凝土拱桥竖向转体施工[J]. 世界桥梁,2002(3):32-34,44.

[9] 郭强,薛志武. 沪通长江大桥大跨多肋柔性拱竖转工艺研究[J]. 公路,2019(6):96-100.

[10] 韦有波. 西溪河特大跨度钢管混凝土拱桥转体施工控制[J]. 铁道建筑,2015(12):15-18.

[11] 唐学庆,郭子华. 盘锦内湖大桥主拱转体施工控制[J]. 中外公路,2018,38(1):200-204.

基于多源感知的大跨径钢管拱桥整体提升智能化施工控制关键技术研究

张坤球[1]　石　拓[1*]　谢开仲[2]　陈家海[1]

(1. 广西路建工程集团有限公司　广西南宁　530001；
2. 广西大学土木建筑工程学院　广西南宁　530004)

摘　要　为实现大跨径钢管混凝土拱桥整体提升精准化、智能化施工控制,本文依托平陆运河旧州特大桥项目进行了研究。平陆运河旧州特大桥为260m跨径下承式柔性系杆钢管混凝土拱桥,受现场地质、地形条件等因素影响,拱肋采用低位拼装及中段门式塔架整体提升施工工艺。借助有限元软件进行塔架、支架结构设计优化及拱肋施工过程仿真分析,基于高灵敏视觉技术智能感知施工全过程塔架、支架及拱肋变形和受力变化情况。建立智能实时监控体系,实现拱肋施工过程中结构内力、空间状态、索力和温度的实时监测,开展拱肋节段低位高精度立体智能化拼装及吊装过程精准控制技术研究,构建温度、风速、振动等因素影响数据库,提出多因素影响下塔架及拱肋结构状态评估理论及结构状态预测数学模型,最终基于机器学习方法形成整套大节段钢管混凝土拱桁整体提升施工智能控制技术。研究成果首次明确了大跨径钢管混凝土拱桥主拱整体提升施工工艺及关键技术参数,可为后续类似工程施工提供参考。

关键词　钢管混凝土拱肋　整体提升　多源感知测试　机器学习　智能控制

中图分类号　U441　　**文献标识码**　A

作者简介：

张坤球(1968—),男,学士,教授级高工,主要从事公路、桥梁工程施工控制方面的研究。

*石拓(1990—),男,博士,工程师,主要从事桥梁施工、大体积混凝土控裂方面的研究。

谢开仲(1974—),男,博士,教授,主要从事桥梁施工控制理论、施工监控等方面的研究。

陈家海(1991—),男,硕士,工程师,主要从事公路、桥梁施工控制方面的研究。

Research on Key Technologies of Intelligent Construction Control for Integral Lifting in Long Span Steel Tube Arch Bridge Based on Multi-source Perception

ZHANG Kunqiu[1]　　SHI Tuo[1*]　　XIE Kaizhong[2]　　CHEN Jiahai[1]

(1. Technical Center Office, Guangxi Road Construction Engineering Group Co., Ltd, Nanning, Guangxi, 530001, China;
2. College of Civil Engineering and Architecture, Guangxi University, Nanning, Guangxi, 530004, China)

Abstract　In order to realize the precise and intelligent construction control of the overall lifting in the long-span concrete-filled steel tubular arch bridge, the research was carried out based on the Jiuzhou super large bridge project of Pinglu canal. Jiuzhou super large bridge of Pinglu canal is a 260m span through flexible tied steel tube concrete arch bridge. Affected by site geological and topographical conditions, the middle arch rib adopted the construction technology of low-level assembly and integral lifting by portal tower. The design of tower and bracket were optimized, and the construction process of steel pipe arch rib was simulated and analyzed by finite element software. Based on high-definition image recognition technology, the deformation and stress changes of the tower, bracket and arch rib in the whole construction process were intelligently perceived. The intelligent real-time monitoring system was established to achieve real-time monitoring of structural internal force, space status, cable force and temperature during arch rib construction. Then the research on low position high-precision three-dimensional intelligent assembly of arch rib segments and precise control technology in hoisting process were carried out. The influence database of temperature, wind speed, vibration and other factors was built, and the state evaluation theory and mathematical model of structure state prediction in tower and arch rib under the multiple factors influence were proposed. Finally, a complete set of intelligent control technology for integral lifting construction of large section concrete filled steel tubular arch truss was formed based on the machine learning method. The research results clarified the construction technology and key technical parameters of the main arch integral lifting for the first time, which could provide strong support for the construction of subsequent similar projects.

Keywords　concrete filled steel tube arch rib　overall improvement　multi source perception test　machine learning　intelligent control

E-mail　1179848174@qq.com

0　引言

钢管混凝土(concrete-filled steel tube, CFST)是在钢管内加填混凝土形成的一种组合材料。它能充分发挥钢材和混凝土的优势，具有强度高、延性好、施工方便等诸多优点，在工程中得到了广泛的应用[1]。在桥梁工程中，CFST通常是用作拱桥主拱肋的材料，相应的拱桥称为CFST拱桥。由于CFST拱桥较好地解决了拱桥拱肋材料高强化与施工轻型化两大关键难题，在过去的近30年间在全世界范围内，特别是在我国得到了蓬勃发展，数量和跨径均迅速增大[2-5]。

CFST拱桥施工方法包括支架法、转体法、缆索吊装法、其他方法等。在施工方法上，中小跨径CFST拱桥可以根据经济与建设条件选择合适的施工方法，而大跨CFST拱桥的施工方法则比较单一，仅采用缆索吊装系统法[6-7]。但有部分CFST拱桥受地质、地形、周围环境等条件限制，无法采用缆索吊装法，且传统施工控制方法数据采集及分析方法较为单一[8-9]。

鉴于此，本文依托跨径260m的平陆运河旧州特大桥进行主拱整体提升关键技术研究，在完成塔架、支架优化设计分析的同时，基于高灵敏视觉技术及机器学习方法，建立CFST主拱智能施工全过程实时监控体系,提出多因素影响下塔架及拱肋结构状态评估理论及结构状态预测数学模型,实现 CFST 主拱整体提升智能化施工控制,可为类似工程施工提供支持。

1 项目概况

K52+760 平陆运河旧州特大桥,采用(3×40+34.49)m 先简支后连续预应力混凝土小箱梁+260m(计算跨径)下承式钢管混凝土系杆拱桥+(2×40)m 先简支后连续预应力混凝土小箱梁,桥梁全长 525.184m。

主拱拱脚与主墩采用固结体系,通过在拱脚间张拉柔性系杆平衡拱肋水平推力。主桥采用下承式钢管混凝土系杆拱桥,计算跨径 260m,主拱采用钢管混凝土桁式结构,整束挤压钢绞线吊索体系,桥面主梁采用格构式钢-混凝土组合梁,主墩采用纵向凯旋门式矩形空心墩,单肢桥墩尺寸为 4.5m(纵向)×8.5m(横桥向),壁厚 1.0m。主桥立面图如图 1 所示。

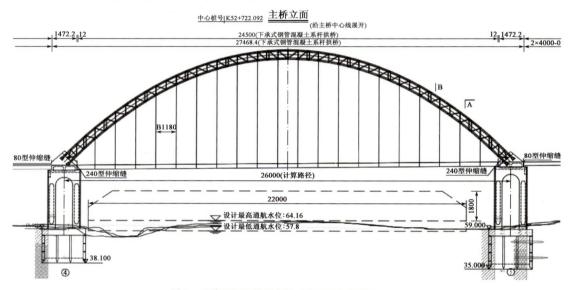

图 1 平陆运河旧州特大桥立面图(尺寸单位:mm)
Fig. 1 Elevation of Pinglu canal. Jiuzhou super large bridge(Unit:mm)

2 结论

基于平陆运河旧州特大桥主拱整体提升项目,进行了支架、塔架优化计算,建立了 CFST 拱桥主拱智能提升全过程监测系统,提出多因素影响下塔架及拱肋结构状态评估理论及结构状态预测数学模型,最终基于机器学习方法形成整套大节段钢管混凝土拱桁整体提升施工智能控制技术。研究得到主要结论如下:

(1)应用有限元软件进行支架、塔架结构优化计算分析,提出优化方案节省钢材 20%。

(2)基于高灵敏视觉技术等多种测试技术,实现施工全过程塔架、支架及拱肋变形和受力变化情况智能感知。

(3)建立智能实时监控体系,完成拱肋施工过程中结构内力、空间状态、索力和温度实时监测,最终实现拱肋节段低位高精度立体智能化拼装及吊装过程精准控制。

（4）构建温度、风速、振动等因素影响数据库，提出多因素影响下塔架及拱肋结构状态评估理论及结构状态预测数学模型。该模型预测结果与实际施工测试结果基本一致。

参 考 文 献

[1] 韩林海.钢管混凝土结构:理论与实践[M].3版.北京:科学出版社,2016.
[2] ZHENG Jielian,Wang Jianjun. Concrete-filled steel tube arch bridges in China[J]. Engineering,2018,4(1):143-155.
[3] 郑皆连.大跨径拱桥的发展及展望[J].中国公路,2017(13):40-42.
[4] 郑皆连,王建军,冯智,等.钢管混凝土拱段真空辅助灌注工艺试验[J].中国公路学报,2014,27(6):44-50.
[5] SHI Tuo,ZHENG Jielian,DENG Nianchun,et al. Temperature Load Parameters and Thermal Effects of a Long-Span Concrete-Filled Steel Tube Arch Bridge in Tibet[J]. Advances in Materials Science and Engineering,2020,9710613.
[6] 石拓.西藏地区大跨度钢管混凝土拱桥温度场及温度效应研究[D].南宁:广西大学,2020.
[7] 潘栋.超大跨钢管混凝土拱桥施工过程中的智能主动控制研究[D].南宁:广西大学,2020.
[8] 罗力军,尹光顺.连续刚构拱桥拱肋大节段整体提升过程计算分析[J].铁道建筑,2020,60(11):44-47.
[9] 蔡栋林,程琳刚,仵彦波.竹溪河大桥斜跨钢箱主拱安装施工方案研讨[J].公路交通技术,2021,37(3):84-90.

基于改进 PSO 优化算法的 CFST 拱桥斜拉扣挂索力计算

谢开仲　傅　灏*　姚宏欣　陈齐威

（广西大学土木建筑工程学院　广西南宁　530004）

摘　要　钢管混凝土（CFST）拱桁斜拉扣挂施工的线形精确程度，对于 CFST 拱桥全寿命服役性能具有重要意义，在众多影响拱桁线形的因素中，斜拉扣挂的索力对拱桁线形的影响最为直接。为了使合龙松索后的线形最大程度接近目标线形，本文通过影响矩阵原理，构建索力与线形的目标函数，通过将 PSO 算法进行相关改进，通过分析关键参数惯性权重和学习因子在算法运行中的特点和作用，将其由固定值改变为随算法迭代进行非线性赋值，提高算法的收敛能力。利用最优化理论中的罚函数思想，将约束优化问题转化为无约束优化问题，并利用改进之后的 PSO 算法作为求解目标函数的工具，通过 Python 软件编写程序，实现斜拉扣挂索力的自动求解。结果表明，改进之后的 PSO 算法收敛速度更快，在第 19 次迭代已经找到全局最优解，未改进的 PSO 算法为 27 次，迭代效率提高 29.6%。将计算得出的索力带入有限元分析模型中，控制点与目标线形最小差值仅为 1.74mm，最大值为 10.83mm，远小于规范要求，拆索线形更加精确。

关键词　钢管混凝土拱桥　斜拉扣挂悬拼　PSO 优化算法　一次张拉　罚函数

Calculation of Cable Force of CFST Arch Bridge with Diagonal Buckling based on Improved PSO Optimization Algorithm

XIE Kaizhong　FU Hao*　YAO Hongxin　CHEN Qiwei

（School of Civil and Architectural Engineering, Guangxi University, Nanning, Guangxi, 530004, China）

Abstract　Among the many factors that affect the alignment of CFST arch trusses, the most direct influence of the cable force on the alignment of the trusses is the cable force on the trusses. In order to make the alignment of the bridge after the cable loosening as close to the target alignment as possible, this paper constructs the objective function of cable

---

作者简介：

谢开仲（1974—），男，广东河源人，博士生导师，E-mail: xiekaizhong@163.com。

force and alignment by the principle of influence matrix, and improves the convergence ability of the PSO algorithm by analyzing the characteristics and roles of inertia weight and learning factor of key parameters in the operation of the algorithm, and changing them from fixed values to non-linear assignment with the iteration of the algorithm. Using the idea of penalty function in the optimization theory, the constrained optimization problem is transformed into an unconstrained optimization problem, and the improved PSO algorithm is used as a tool to solve the objective function, and the program is written by python software to realize the automatic solution of the slanting buckling cable force. The results show that the improved PSO algorithm converges faster and already finds the global optimal solution in the 19th iteration, compared with 27 iterations for the unimproved PSO algorithm, with 29.6% improvement in iteration efficiency. The minimum difference between the control point and the target line is only 1.74mm, and the maximum value is 10.83mm, which is much smaller than the requirement of the specification, and the dismantling line is more accurate.

Keywords concrete filled steel tubular arch bridge   cable-stayed fastening-hanging methods   PSO optimization algorithm   penalty function

0 引言

钢管混凝土拱桥是一种结合了钢和混凝土两种材料的新型结构体系桥梁，不仅造型优美，受力性能优越，便于施工，作为重要的桥梁类型得到了大量的应用。据不完全统计，目前已建有400余座钢管混凝土拱桥[1]。位于广西的平南三桥跨径已达575m，在建的天峨龙滩特大桥主跨也达到了600m。

CFST 拱桥的常用施工方法是斜拉扣挂悬拼法，随着跨径的不断突破，拱肋节段数和拼装重量也不断增加，对于拱肋节段的线形控制的要求也越来越高，因此，斜拉扣挂索力的精确计算尤为重要。扣索力的计算方法主要分为两类，分别是解析法和数值法。解析法主要有力矩平衡法和零弯矩法[2-4]。力矩平衡法基于结构力学原理，其计算思路简单明确，在斜拉悬拼的过程中，将两段节段之间的链接视为铰接，由此以铰接点弯矩为零的思路，建立起节点的平衡方程，由此计算出扣索的索力值。零弯矩法则是在力矩平衡法的基础上，以积分的方式，对节点力系建立起相应的平衡方程。解析法在钢管混凝土拱桥发展的早期应用较广，但随着跨径与节段数的倍增，这种方法的计算精度已经达不到要求。因此，结合有限元软件与数学优化思想的数值法可以弥补解析法的不足性。数值法主要包括了正装迭代法，倒拆分析法和定长扣索法[5]。正装迭代法是模拟实际的施工顺序，不断进行迭代得到最终的索力值，尽管过程简单直接，但是需要反复迭代与调索，效率低。倒拆分析法是逆转施工过程，分析倒退的每一步对结构的影响，相当于正装迭代法的逆过程，其结果能与正装迭代法进行互补，但是对于现在的大跨拱桥来说，施工步骤多，节段多，具体计算起来十分麻烦，也很难得到精确解。定长扣索法则是采用一次调索的方法，预先将节段张拉到控制位置，使合龙松索后的拱圈线形满足要求。随着有限元软件的发展，数值法结合最优化理论，得到不断改进。张治成等[6]将最优化理论引入大跨拱桥的线形调整中，将拱肋控制点的高程偏差最小为优化目标，采取一分析法对索力调整量这个设计变量进行迭代优化，应用效果非常好。张建民等[7]通过 ANSYS 软件，将一阶分析法与正装迭代法进行结合，令合龙时的节点坐标方程与设计拱轴线的差值作为目标函数，根据计算的结果来分析最优化计算的程度。朱连伟等[8]通过带修正常数的影响矩阵，以相邻节段之间的扣索力最大差值的限值为约束条件，对正装迭代算法进行优化，使扣索力更加均匀。周倩等[9]基于零阶优化法，提出了利用扣索内力法确定索力的初始迭代值，利用

ANSYS 程序,对每个迭代子步进行自动搜索和宏观调整,最优化理论在扣索力优化方面有了大量应用,是可行的。

粒子群算法简称 PSO 算法,是一种经典的启发式算法,仅有三个关键参数,因此在智能随机优化算法中优势明显,在土木工程领域得到广泛应用。PSO 优化算法是最早由 Eberhart 和 Kennedy[20]两位博士提出,这是一种基于迭代的优化策略,通过自然界中鸟类进行觅食活动而受到的启发。在一个鸟群中,每一只鸟都是一个主体,一开始每个主体的原始位置和飞行的方向都是随机的。对于每一个主体来说,它都能够与其他的主体和环境进行信息交流,根据得到的信息来改变自己的飞行方向和速度,在一次又一次的信息交互中,最终慢慢接近食物。淡丹辉等[10]为了实现斜拉桥索力自动调索,基于影响矩阵原理,结合 PSO 智能算法,实现高效调索。陈志军等[11]利用标准 PSO 优化算法寻找无约束目标函数的全局最优解,利用 Matlab 自带的工具箱,求解出独塔斜拉桥成桥索力的最优值。占玉林等[12]将 PSO 算法与响应面法相结合,简化了异形斜拉桥的索力优化过程,先利用响应面法构建优化目标函数与成桥索力的响应面方程,再利用 PSO 算法快速求解。为了克服 PSO 算法的缺点,许多的学者对该算法进行了改进。Ali Nadi Ünal 等[13]通过对粒子设置次数阈值,一旦某个粒子超过一定次数仍然没有改良,那么就会将该粒子初始化。Chao Zhang 等[14]将人工蜂群算法与 PSO 算法相结合,提出时变参数,将个体极值最优的学习因子随迭代减小,一定程度上提高了算法的收敛能力。王梦娇等[15]将极限学习机算法与 PSO 算法相结合,将灰色绝对关联度作为适应度函数,得到的 PSO 优化极限学习机法模型的预测精度更高,速度更快。

约束优化问题是最优化理论中的一个重要部分,在将最优化理论应用到具体算法中,通常将约束优化问题转化为无约束优化问题。一般采用罚函数法和拉格朗日乘子法进行转化,再与相关算法结合[16],对于不等式约束,一般选用罚函数法。王林军等[17]将外罚函数法与结构可靠性分析相结合,将可靠度优化问题转化为无约束优化问题。朱琴跃等[18]基于 PSO 算法,利用罚函数建立起牵引逆变器多目标优化模型,试验和仿真的结果相适应,证明罚函数下的无约束优化模型是可行的。贾彦等[19]同样利用罚函数法将非线性约束条件转化为系列无约束问题,解决了风光储系统的优化配置问题。由此可见罚函数结合算法在工程领域有着大量应用。本文利用最优化理论原理,针对斜拉扣挂索力难以精确求解的问题,通过约束最优化方法中的惩罚函数法,将约束优化问题转化为无约束优化问题,结合 PSO 算法,利用计算机语言 Python 进行程序设计,对斜拉扣挂索力进行自动优化。

1 基于改进的 PSO 算法的索力优化

1.1 标准 PSO 优化算法

PSO 优化理论基于群体智能的并行优化搜索技术,在实际的应用过程中,将鸟群抽象为用若干个粒子构成的原始种群,粒子个数为种群规模。每一个粒子都有它的属性(位置矢量和速度矢量),维数就是待解决问题的空间维度。现假设有一个 d 维的空间,那么可以用 $\boldsymbol{X}_i = [x_{i1}, x_{i2}, x_{i3}, \cdots, x_{id}]$ 来表示粒子的位置矢量,$\boldsymbol{V}_i = [v_{i1}, v_{i2}, v_{i3}, \cdots, v_{id}]$ 来表示粒子的速度矢量。每个粒子的适应度由目标函数确定,每个粒子都在不断调整自己的位置,更新适应度,方式是追踪个体极值和群体极值,分别记做 $\boldsymbol{P}_i = [p_{i1}, p_{i2}, p_{i3}, \cdots, p_{id}]$ 和 $\boldsymbol{P}_g = [p_{g1}, p_{g2}, p_{g3}, \cdots, p_{gd}]$。

由上述两个极值,粒子由下式更新自己的速度和位置:

$$v_{ij}(t+1) = \omega v_{ij}(t) + c_1 r_1 [(p_{ij})_j(t) - x_{ij}(t)] + c_2 r_2 [(p_{gj})_j(t) - x_{ij}(t)] \tag{1}$$

$$x_{ij}(t+1) = x_{ij}(t) + v_{ij}(t+1) \tag{2}$$

式中,c_1、c_2 为学习因子;r_1、r_2 为[0,1]之间的随机数。

根据上述更新公式可以看出,PSO 的迭代方式由三部分组成,第一部分是粒子本身的惯性表现,由 ω 惯性因子控制;第二部分是粒子的自我认知部分,使得粒子能够进行全局搜索,由 c_1 控制;第三部分是粒子之间信息的交互,反映了整个种群的"社会经验",是一种群体认知行为,可提高粒子全局搜索的能力,由 c_2 控制。

在实际的工程中,一般会在一个限定区间内取得最优解,所以种群粒子的位置同样需要限制住,所以 $x_{\min} \leq x \leq x_{\max}$。同时为了避免因粒子更新速度过于快速而导致算法局部不收敛、"早熟",同样需要对更新速度进行限制处理,所以 $v_{\min} \leq v \leq v_{\max}$。

1.2 PSO 算法的改进

PSO 算法的优点在于思路简单,编程难度不高,程序容易实现,仅有三个关键参数,因此在智能随机优化算法中优势明显;其缺点也很明显,就是容易早熟收敛到全局最优解,且在迭代的后期收敛速度慢。针对 PSO 的改进,一般分为三大方面:实现参数的自适应变化、引入一些其他的机制(随机的因素、速度位置的边界变化、后期压缩最大速度等)、结合其他智能优化算法(遗传算法、免疫算法、模拟退火算法等),前文进行过相关介绍。本文对 PSO 算法的改进,着重在于对 PSO 算法的参数改进。通关分析算法的本质,了解惯性权重,以及两类学习因子在算法整个迭代过程中的作用变化,引入非线性自适应惯性权重和自适应学习因子,来增强粒子的搜索能力,帮助粒子摆脱"早熟"和不收敛问题。

1.2.1 非线性自适应惯性权重 ω

对于标准 PSO 算法,惯性权重为一个固定的常数。在粒子迭代的前期,需要保证粒子的惯性权重大一些,这样才能保证每个粒子能独立搜索全局空间,保证自己的属性,但是随着迭代的进行,需要减少 ω 的取值,以此向其他粒子学习看齐。为了综合粒子的全局搜索能力和局部搜索能力,要求惯性权重能随着迭代的进行而动态调整。Shi 等[21]提出了随着迭代次数而线性递减的权重因子,$\omega(k) = \omega_{\min} + \frac{\omega_{\max} - \omega_{\min}}{N} \times (N-t)$,$N$ 为最大迭代次数。这种线性递减的惯性权重在一定程度上改善了算法的搜索能力和计算效率,但是仍然存在"早熟",局部最优和求解精度不够理想的等缺点。参照 Shi 教授对 ω 的线性递减思想,引入非线性自适应权重,按下式计算:

$$\omega(t) = \omega_{\min} + (\omega_{\max} - \omega_{\min}) \times \cos\left(\frac{\tau}{\tau_{\max}} \times \frac{\pi}{2}\right) \tag{3}$$

式中,$\omega_{\min}$ 为惯性权重初始设定的最小值;$\omega_{\max}$ 为惯性权重初始设定的最大值。

在算法迭代的前期,非线性自适应权重因子可以增强粒子的全局搜索能力,随着迭代的进行,递减的惯性权重可以避免粒子陷入局部最优解,提高计算精度。

1.2.2 自适应学习因子 c_1、c_2

学习因子 c_1 控制着粒子向个体极值的发展,学习因子 c_2 控制着粒子向全局极值的发展。在迭代的初期,为了粒子能尽可能搜索到整个空间,应当保证 c_1 大一点,c_2 小一点,提高粒子的搜索效率;在迭代的后期,应当保证 c_1 小一点,c_2 大一点,通过将固定常数的学习因子改为随着迭代次数更改的自适应学习因子 c_1、c_2,达到优化算法的目的,具体公式如下:

$$c_1 = c_{1\max} - (c_{1\max} - c_{1\min}) \times \cos\left[\frac{\pi}{2} \times \left(1 - \frac{t}{t_{\max}}\right)\right]^2 \tag{4}$$

$$c_2 = c_{2\min} + (c_{2\max} - c_{2\min}) \times \cos\left[\frac{\pi}{2} \times \left(1 - \frac{t}{t_{\max}}\right)\right]^2 \tag{5}$$

式中，$c_{1\max}$ 为自学因子初始最大值；$c_{2\max}$ 为群学因子初始最大值；$c_{1\min}$ 为自学因子初始最小值；$c_{2\min}$ 为群学因子初始最小值；t 为当前迭代次数；$t_{\max}$ 为总迭代次数。

1.3 罚函数法

罚函数法是解决约束优化问题的常用方法，其基本思想为通过构造辅助函数，将约束问题转化为无约束问题。通过构造惩罚项，对不满足约束条件的非可行解或者可行域内试图冲破边界的点进行惩罚，迫使其接近可行域。因此，对于有约束的优化问题，其形式一般为：

$$\min: f(x)$$
$$\text{s.t.} \begin{cases} g_i(x) \leq 0 & (i = 1,2,\cdots,m) \\ h_j(x) = 0 & (j = 1,2,\cdots,m) \end{cases}$$

式中，$g(x)$ 和 $h(x)$ 分别代表不等式约束和等式约束。

因此构造带着惩罚项的新目标函数为：

$$\min: F(x,\sigma) = f(x) + Ma(x) \tag{6}$$

$$a(x) = \sum_{i=1}^{p}[\max(0, g_i(x)]^2 + \sum_{j=1}^{q}[h_j(x)]^2 \tag{7}$$

惩罚项为 $Ma(x)$，根据罚函数的相关知识[22]，可以得到当罚因子 M 为确定值时，上述新目标函数的 $F(x,M)$ 的最优解与原目标函数 $f(x)$ 的最优解是一致的。

2 斜拉扣挂索力优化方法

2.1 索力优化模型的建立

通过采用的改进的PSO算法对斜拉扣挂索力进行优化，使得拱桁合龙之后的线形与目标线形尽可能接近，达到线形最优的目的。选取拱肋悬臂端相应的控制点，以合龙之后的拱桁线形与目标线形的差值最小作为目标函数，建立多个控制点位移差值的目标方程 $f(x) = \sqrt{s_1^2 + s_2^2 + s_3^2 \cdots + s_n^2}$，在斜拉扣挂索力和实现线形最优目的中，采用影响矩阵原理，通过得到单位扣索力作用下的控制点位移向量，与目标位移向量叠加，其结果作为目标方程 $f(x)$ 的具体表达。在实际工程中，规范允许的拱圈高程偏差为 $\pm L/3000$，因此，需要在满足规范的情况下达到线形最优的目的。

目标函数：

$$\min f(x) = \sqrt{s_1^2 + s_2^2 + s_3^2 \cdots + s_n^2} \tag{8}$$

$$s = \Delta_f f + \Delta_{空} \tag{9}$$

约束条件：

$$\begin{cases} -\sigma < \sigma_n < \sigma \\ 0 < f < \dfrac{nN_p}{k} \\ -L/3000 \leq s_n \leq L/3000 \end{cases} \tag{10}$$

式中，s 为控制点位移与目标线形差值；Δ_f 为扣索力影响矩阵；$\Delta_{空}$ 拱圈自重荷载影响矩阵；f 为扣索力；N_p 为单根扣索的屈服力；σ 为拱肋钢材的容许应力；K 为安全系数；n 为扣索根数;L 为主跨径长度。

采用罚函数将上述约束优化问题转化为无约束的目标优化问题,即通过增加惩罚项的方式,构造出新的目标函数:

$$\min: F(x,\sigma) = \sqrt{s_1^2 + s_2^2 + s_3^2 \cdots + s_n^2} + \text{Ma}(x) \tag{11}$$

2.2 基于改进的 PSO 算法优化模型求解

采用改进的 PSO 算法进行索力优化,达到线形最优的目的,具体算法流程如图 1 所示。

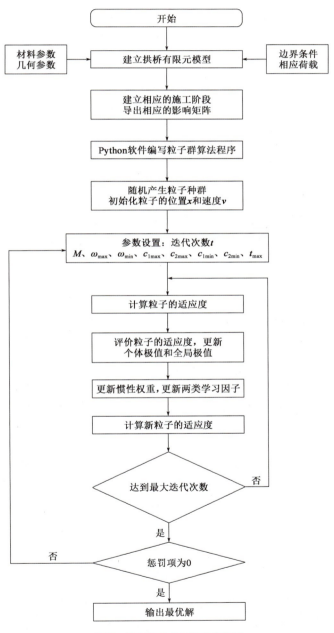

图 1　斜拉扣挂索力优化流程图

由图1可知,当流程启动之后,整个优化过程就开始了。初始化粒子之后,随即计算出相应的适应度,分析出其个体极值和全局极值,更新粒子的速度与位置,并按照之前改进的自适应惯性权重与学习因子计算更新之后的适应度,并且判断个体极值和全局极值是否更新。当迭代次数达到设定的最大迭代次数并且惩罚性小于预设精度时,按照流程输出最优解。如果不满足以上条件,则继续迭代计算或者参数重新初始化。

3 工程实例

3.1 工程概况

以广西某跨右江大桥为工程背景。该桥主桥为计算跨径187m中承式钢管混凝土拱桥,计算矢跨比1/4,拱轴系数$m=1.2$,计算矢高为47.569m。拱肋为钢管混凝土桁架式结构,共两片拱肋,横桥向中心间距为24.5m。拱肋采用等高度四管钢管桁式截面,高4.2m,宽2.4m。上、下弦管直径为900mm,壁厚16~20mm,管内灌C50微膨胀混凝土;腹杆钢管直径为406mm,壁厚14mm;横向缀管直径610m。单根拱肋分8个节段加工制作及安装,节段最大质量为75t。钢管拱肋采用斜拉扣挂悬臂拼装法施工,半跨拱肋分4段安装节段,全桥共划分为4个吊装节段。

广西某跨右江大桥主拱肋立面、横断面分别如图2、图3所示,主要材料特性见表1,有限元计算模型见图4。

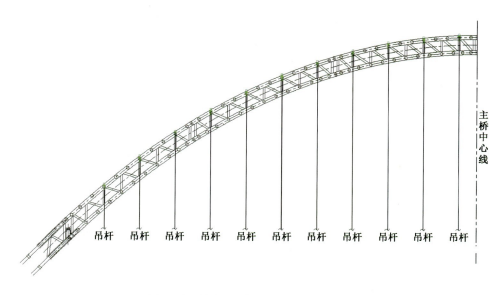

图2 广西某跨右江大桥主拱肋立面示意图

主 要 材 料 特 性 表1

材 料	弹性模量(MPa)	泊 松 比	线膨胀系数(1/℃)	重度(kN/m³)
Q345	2.06×10^4	0.3	12×10^{-6}	78.5
Strand1860	1.95×10^4	0.3	12×10^{-6}	78.5

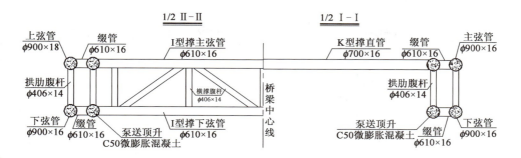

图 3　广西某跨右江大桥主拱肋横断面图

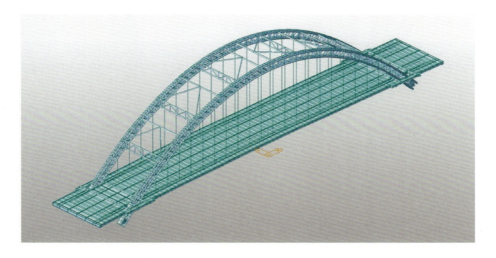

图 4　广西某跨右江大桥有限元计算模型

3.2　索力优化过程分析

按照前文所建的 PSO 优化模型,首先通过图纸以及相关参数,通过有限元软件 Midas Civil 建立起桥梁模型,划分好施工阶段,并提取相关的影响矩阵,其索力影响矩阵与自重影响矩阵为 4-1,4-2。通过 Python 软件,编写改进前的 PSO 算法程序和改进之后的 PSO 算法程序。两者的区别在于,前者的惯性权重和学习因子是固定常数,后者的惯性权重和学习因子是随着迭代次数而自适应的,其他参数取值相同。目前在 PSO 算法的应用中,ω 的经典取值,一般在 0.4~0.9 之间,这个范围内的 ω 能保证算法具有良好的局部收敛能力和全局收敛能力,所以,改进前的 PSO 算法的的惯性权重取固定值 0.9,改进后的惯性权重 ω_{max} 取 0.9,ω_{min} 取 0.4。改进前的学习因子 c_1 和 c_2 取固定值 0.5,改进之后的学习因子 $c_{1max}=2$、$c_{1min}=0.5$、$c_{2max}=2$、$c_{2min}=0.5$。迭代次数定为 100 次,种群规模 m 定为 50。在罚因子的初始值得选取上,取 $0.1 \times 2^{k-1}$ 进行试算,将罚因子的迭代过程一同编入基于 Python 语言编写的改进 PSO 优化算法,做到自动化迭代试算,惩罚项的精度 10^{-3}。该大桥共有四组索,选取对称的单组四个索力作为设计变量 $F=(x_1,x_2,x_3,x_4)^T$。为了体现该算法的优越性,将比规范允许值更小的数值作为优化目标,基于此,以线形高程偏差30mm为约束条件优化索力。

$$\begin{bmatrix} 0.0270 & 0.0700 & 0.0704 & 0.0740 \\ 0.0836 & 0.3266 & 0.3301 & 0.4792 \\ 0.0862 & 0.4008 & 0.4082 & 1.0280 \\ 0.0806 & 0.3991 & 0.4072 & 1.3483 \end{bmatrix} \quad (12)$$

$$\begin{bmatrix} -112.2561 & -526.0347 & -535.8472 & -1515.4345 \end{bmatrix}^T \quad (13)$$

粒子算法相关参数见表2。

粒子算法相关参数 表2

ω_{max}	ω_{min}	c_{1max}	c_{1min}	c_{2max}	c_{2min}
0.9	0.4	2	0.5	2	0.5
V_{max}	V_{min}	S_{min}	S_{max}	m	T
50	−50	50	1000	50	100

3.3 优化结果分析

算法的收敛速度是评判算法优越性的重要指标,因此,将改进前的PSO算法和改进后的PSO算法的收敛速度,结果如图5所示,由图中可以清晰看出改进前的PSO算法和改进后的PSO算法都有很不错的收敛精度,收敛速度也很快,但是改进后的PSO算法收敛速度更快,在整个迭代过程中算法收敛速度均大幅度快于普通PSO算法,并且在第19次迭代找到全局最优解,普通PSO算法在第27次迭代找到全局最优解,收敛速度提升了29.6%。

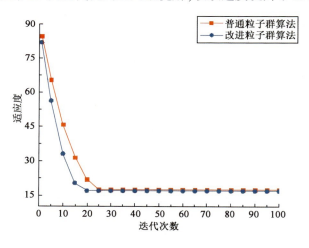

图5 算法改进前后效果对比图

优化结果体现在合龙松索后,选取的控制点位移与目标线形的位移接近程度。通过将改进之后的PSO算法的结果代入Midas Civil中进行计算,比较控制点与目标线形的差值(表3)。

施工阶段扣索力见表4。

施工与监测

施工阶段控制点与目标线形差值(mm) 表3

施工阶段	控制点1	控制点2	控制点3	控制点4
吊装拱1	28.96			
吊装一字撑	-4.99			
吊装拱2	6.89	61.32		
吊装1号I撑	-5.98	2.60		
吊装1号K撑	-8.60	-7.65		
吊装拱3	4.97	56.89	148.58	
吊装2号I撑	-2.06	22.98	83.03	
吊装2号K撑	-6.48	3.12	48.57	
吊装3号K撑	-13.07	-29.73	-19.97	
吊装拱4	0.95	16.50	16.62	16.65
合龙	1.08	17.80	16.40	15.86
吊装3号I撑	1.92	18.59	14.46	11.44
吊装4号K撑	2.77	20.55	12.85	5.96
封铰	2.77	20.55	12.85	5.96
拆索	1.74	10.23	8.90	10.83

施工阶段扣索力(kN) 表4

施工阶段	扣索1	扣索2	扣索3	扣索4
吊装拱1	70.40			
吊装一字撑	77.57			
吊装拱2	75.51	223.77		
吊装1号I撑	77.87	253.72		
吊装1号K撑	78.31	258.97		
吊装拱3	76.49	233.51	387.75	
吊装2号I撑	77.72	250.02	413.54	
吊装2号K撑	78.52	259.87	427.43	
吊装3号K撑	79.64	275.56	453.74	
吊装拱4	76.43	245.55	427.66	548.90
合龙	76.40	245.33	427.65	549.00
吊装3号I撑	76.19	243.96	427.73	549.50
吊装4号K撑	75.98	242.50	427.68	550.07
封铰	75.98	242.50	427.68	550.07

索力优化对比见图6。由图6可以看出,优化前后除f1两者比较接近,优后的扣索力较未优化的扣索力都有不同程度的减小,由表3中数据可知,合龙拆索后,经过优化后的各控制点位移与目标线形的差值最小值为1.74mm,最大值为10.83mm,远小于优化目标30mm,规范值

62.3mm,在减小扣索力的同时使成拱线形更加接近目标线形,且整个过程中各扣索索力变化均匀,证明该改进的 PSO 算法得出的结果是有效的,能应用到实际工程中。

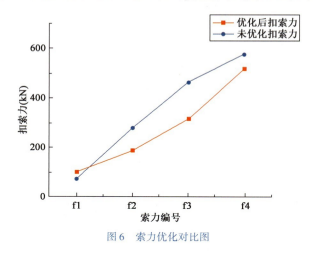

图 6 索力优化对比图

4 结论

本文的主要研究是在于改进 PSO 算法,通过对其主要三个参数的进行自适应变化,平衡该算法中粒子在局部搜索和全局搜索的能力,同时结合最优化理论中罚函数的思想,提出一种钢管混凝土拱桥斜拉扣挂索力的优化方法,并且以广西某跨右江大桥作为工程背景加以应用,得出的主要结论如下:

(1)基于 PSO 算法的斜拉扣挂索力优化方法,在利用 Python 语言编写程序和有限元软件模拟的情况下,实现斜拉扣挂索力的智能化、自动化的精准求解。

(2)基于自适应惯性权重和自适应学习因子的改进,算法在收敛速度有所改善。

(3)优化之后的索力更加均匀,拱圈拼装线形能满足规范要求。

(4)本文提出的研究方法不仅适用于斜拉扣挂索力的优化,同样适用于其他类型的索力优化,例如钢管混凝土拱桥的吊杆调索,斜拉桥的成桥索力优化等。

参 考 文 献

[1] 陈宝春,韦建刚,周俊,等.我国钢管混凝土拱桥应用现状与展望[J].土木工程学报,2017,50(06):50-61.

[2] 张玉平,李传习,董创文."零弯矩法"应用于斜拉扣挂索力确定的讨论[J].长沙交通学院学报,2004(01):15-18.

[3] 周水兴,江礼忠,曾忠,等.拱桥节段施工斜拉扣挂索力仿真计算研究[J].重庆交通学院学报,2000(03):8-12.

[4] 刘邵平.特大跨径钢桁拱吊装索力计算方法探讨[J].现代交通技术,2011,8(06):34-36,56.

[5] 韩玉,秦大燕,郑健.CFST 拱桥斜拉扣挂施工优化计算方法[J].公路,2018,63(01):100-104.

[6] 张治成,叶贵如,陈衡治.大跨度钢管砼拱桥拱肋吊装中的扣索索力计算[J].浙江大学学报(工学版),2004(05):90-94.

[7] 张建民,郑皆连,肖汝诚.钢管混凝土拱桥吊装过程的最优化计算分析[J].中国公路学报,2005(02):40-44.

[8] 朱连伟,邓年春,于孟生,等.600m级拱桥斜拉扣挂施工扣索索力的正装迭代优化算法[J].铁道建筑,2020,60(12):18-21.

[9] 周倩,周建庭,陈静雯,等.钢管混凝土拱桥扣索一次张拉索力优化改进算法[J].福州大学学报(自然科学版),2019,47(03):412-416.

[10] 淡丹辉,杨通.基于影响矩阵及粒子群算法的斜拉桥自动调索[J].同济大学学报(自然科学版),2013,41(03):355-360.

[11] 陈志军,刘洋,杨立飞,等.基于粒子群优化算法的独塔斜拉桥成桥索力优化[J].桥梁建设,2016,46(03):40-44.

[12] 占玉林,侯之瑶,邵俊虎,等.基于响应面法及粒子群算法的异形斜拉桥索力优化[J].桥梁建设,2022,52(03):16-23.

[13] Ali Nadi Ünal, Gülgün Kayakutlu. Multi-objective particle swarm optimization with random immigrants[J]. Complex & Intelligent Systems,2020,6(3):635-650.

[14] Chao Zhang, et al. An improved multi-objective particle swarm optimization and its application in raw ore dispatching[J]. Advances in Mechanical Engineering, 2018, 10(2): 168781401875737-168781401875737.

[15] 王梦娇,魏新劳.粒子群优化极限学习机的短路电流预测技术[J].电机与控制学报,2022,26(01):68-76.

[16] 陈宝林.最优化理论与算法[M].北京:清华大学出版社,2005.

[17] 王林军,王锬,杜义贤,等.一种基于外罚函数法的结构可靠性分析方法[J].三峡大学学报(自然科学版),2019,41(01):92-96.

[18] 朱琴跃,戴维,谭喜堂,等.基于粒子群算法的牵引逆变器多目标优化控制策略[J].同济大学学报(自然科学版),2020,48(02):287-295.

[19] 贾彦,李文雄,赵萌,等.罚函数改进粒子群算法的风光储系统优化配置[J].太阳能学报,2019,40(07):2071-2077.

[20] Kennedy J, Eberhart R. C. Particle Swarm Optimization. In: IEEE International Conference on Neural Networks,IV. Piscataway, NJ: IEEE Service Center,1995:1942-1948.

[21] Shi Y, Eberhart R. C. Comparing Inertia Weights and Constriction Factro in Particle Swarm Optizimation. In Proceedings of the IEEE International Congress on Evolutionary Computation, vol.1:84-88.

[22] RAY R N, CHATTERJEE D, GOSWAMI S K. A GN based optimal switching technique for voltage harmonic reduction of multilevel inverter[J]. Expert Systems with Applications, 2010,37(12):7796.

[23] 王燕军.最优化基础理论与方法[M].上海:复旦大学出版社,2011.

劲性骨架混凝土拱桥钢管拱肋外法兰连接构造优化研究

杨盼杰* 黎栋家 凌塑奇

（广西交通设计集团有限公司 广西南宁 530029）

摘 要 天峨龙滩特大桥为主跨600m劲性骨架混凝土拱桥，为了实现快速、高标准的建设目标，本文通过对劲性骨架节段连接处内法兰与外法兰的简要对比分析，并结合该桥劲性骨架结构自身特性，得出外法兰高水准设计的必要性；且本文提出了3种外法兰结构方案，利用ABAQUS建立法兰盘三维弹塑性模型，从受力性能和可施工性角度研究分析，综合比选出了"有端板带定位孔拼接板式外法兰"方案；并对该选用方案进行工程应用分析，得出该法兰盘在拱肋1~5号节段可以连续吊装4节段，6~8号节段可以连续吊装3节段，9~12号节段以及合龙段最多只能连续吊装2节段后再进行弦管环缝焊接的工程建设指导性结论。

关键词 混凝土拱桥 劲性骨架 外法兰 吊装节段数

中图分类号 U445.464 **文献标识码** A

Stiff Skeleton Concrete Arch Bridge Study on Optimization of External Flange Connection Structure

YANG Panjie* LI Dongjia LING Suqi

(Guangxi Communications Design Group Co., Lt. d, Nanning, Guangxi, 530029, China)

Abstract Tian'e Longtan Bridge is a 600m stiff skeleton concrete arch bridge with its main span. In order to achieve the goal of rapid and high standard construction, this paper briefly compares and analyzes the inner flange and the outer flange at the joints of stiff skeleton segments, and combines the characteristics of the stiff skeleton structure of the bridge, and concludes the necessity of high-level design of the outer flange. In this paper, three kinds of external flange structure schemes are put forward, and a three-dimensional elastoplastic model of the bridge was established by

---

作者简介：

*杨盼杰（1993—），男，硕士研究生，主要从事大跨径复杂桥梁研究。

黎栋家（1982—），男，硕士研究生，主要从事大跨径复杂型桥梁研究。

凌塑奇（1994—），男，硕士研究生，主要从事大跨径复杂型桥梁研究。

ABAQUS to analyze the dynamic characteristics of the flange, then the scheme of "splicing plate external flange with end plate and positioning hole" is selected from the perspective of mechanical performance and constructability. The engineering application of this selection scheme is analyzed, and the guiding conclusion of engineering construction is drawn that the flange can be continuously hoisted for 4 segments at the arch rib 1～5 segment, 3 segments at the arch rib 6～8 segment, and only 2 segments at most at the 9～12 segment and the closure segment before the circumferential seam welding of chord tube.

Keywords　Concrete arch bridge　stiff skeleton　outer flange　number of hoisting segments
E-mail　gxjt-ldt163ypj@163.com

0　引言

法兰盘连接从发展到应用已经有 200 多年历史，1809 年，法兰盘的首次铸造由英国人 Erchardt 提出[1]，直到 20 世纪初，法兰盘连接才逐步地被推广应用，并逐渐衍生出多种形式的法兰形式[2-4]，在大跨径钢管混凝土拱桥中法兰结构得到广泛的应用。钢管混凝土拱桥中常见的法兰结构大致可分为两种，分别是内置式法兰盘和外置式法兰盘[5-6]，内置式法兰盘设置于钢管内部，因此适用于大管径情况，现行规范推荐当主拱主管直径大于 600mm 时，宜采用内法兰作临时连接；当钢管管径较小或内置法兰不易施工时可采用外置式法兰。天峨龙滩特大桥为主跨 600m 的劲性骨架混凝土拱桥，劲性骨架主弦管管径为 900mm，管内混凝土采用 C80 高强度等级混凝土，由于管径相对较小，当采用内法兰结构时不仅不易操作，而且内法兰占用较大的管内面积，泵送高强度等级混凝土施工时将很大程度上影响其流动性和均质性，容易产生堵管现象，结合该桥整体结构的特殊性，决定采用外置式法兰结构。但外置式法兰结构形式能否满足结构安全、精准、快速的施工要求，成为亟须解决的问题。

基于以上问题，结合实际设计过程中法兰设计流程，本文详细介绍了多种外法兰设计方案，并从结构受力和可施工性方面详细阐述了各法兰方案的优缺点，最终比选出一种受力合理、满足精准快速施工的外法兰结构形式。

1　工程背景

天峨龙滩特大桥为广西壮族自治区南丹至天峨下老高速公路控制性工程。桥梁全长 2488.55m，其中主桥为计算跨径 600m 的上承式劲性骨架混凝土拱桥，劲性骨架主弦管管径为 900mm，采用 35mm 和 30mm 两种壁厚，全桥共有 48 个拱肋节段，其中最长节段为 30.5m，最重节段达 169t，采用"缆索吊装+斜拉扣挂"施工工艺进行安装，精度要求高，施工难度大。主桥立面如图 1 所示。

在具体的施工中，天峨龙滩特大桥劲性骨架节段为在预制场采用"3+1"节段卧式耦合工艺匹配制造，法兰结构与主拱肋整体预制卧拼能很好地验证法兰连接施工工艺，能满足各节段间的高精度拼装要求，即能有效避免拱肋节段间装配力较大，接头处骨架钢管外径线拼接后误差大的问题。劲性骨架现场如图 2 所示。

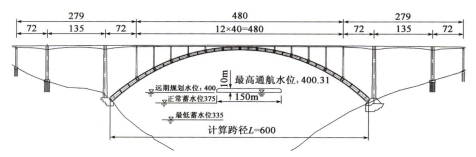

图 1 主桥立面示意图(尺寸单位:m;高程单位:m)
Fig. 1 Schematic diagram of main bridge(Unit:m)

图 2 劲性骨架现场图
Fig. 2 Site diagram of stiff skeleton

2 外法兰方案优化分析

2.1 外法兰方案介绍

该方案为标准圆形外法兰形式(图3),肋板通过焊接方式分别与法兰圆板和钢管外壁相连,两片法兰圆板通过高强螺栓连接,法兰底缘预留过焊孔便于主弦管连续施焊。

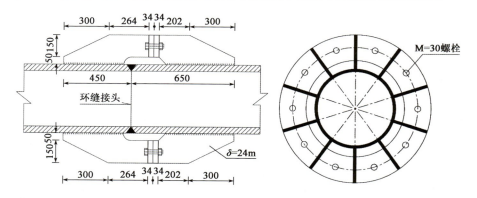

图 3 标准圆形外法兰示意图(尺寸单位:mm)
Fig. 3 Schematic diagram of standard outer flange(Unit:mm)

该法兰通过4片整体式单拼接板均匀布置于主弦上,每片拼板分短板和长板分别焊于相邻节段的主弦上,3号和4号单拼接板在上一节段主弦外壁处焊长板,下一节段主弦外壁处焊短板,1号和2号拼接板在上一节段主弦外壁处焊短板,下一节段主弦外壁处焊长板。

拼接板式法兰如图4所示。

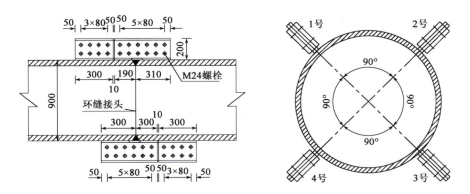

图4 拼接板式外法兰示意图(尺寸单位:mm)
Fig. 4 Schematic diagram of spliced plate outer flange (Unit:mm)

该方案结构形式分为三块整体式双拼接板和一片整体式单拼接板。每块整体式双拼接板含两片整体式单拼接板,每片单拼板分短板和长板分别焊于相邻节段的主弦上。一片整体式单拼接板由一块短板、一块长板及两块连接板组成,2号单拼板的长板焊接于上一节段主弦外壁处,短板焊接于下一节段主弦外壁处,当整个法兰拼接完成后,可保证对主拱拼接处连续施焊,从而形成一个整体。

2.2 外法兰方案比选

从受力和施工性能(图5、表1)进行方案比选,并优选出有端板带定位孔拼接板式法兰方案。有端板带定位孔拼接板式外法兰如图6所示。

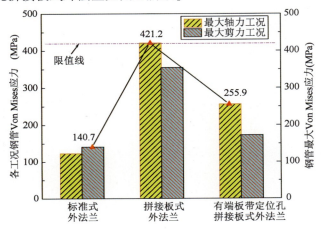

图5 各方案主弦钢管应力图
Fig. 5 Stress diagram of main chord steel pipe in each scheme

297

各法兰方案可实施工性能汇总表　　　　表1
Implementable workability of each flange scheme　　Tab. 1

关注点	标准式	拼接板式	有端板拼接板式
主弦连续施焊难易程度	较难	易	较易
法兰是否需要切除	是	否	否
法兰构造是否与其他永久构件相冲突	是	否	否
影响外包混凝土钢筋布置程度	—	很小	较小
影响外包混凝土浇筑密实性程度	—	很小	较小
定位精准程度	优	较差	优
施工效率	低	中	中

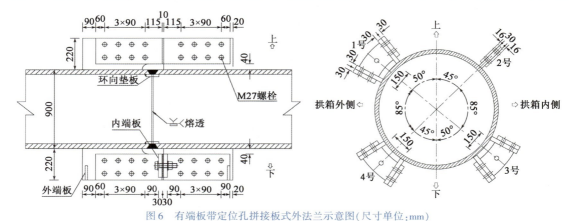

图6　有端板带定位孔拼接板式外法兰示意图(尺寸单位:mm)

Fig. 6　Schematic diagram of spliced plate outer flange with end plate and positioning hole

3　选用方案工程应用分析

依据斜拉扣挂施工工艺,采用 Madis Civil 模拟施工过程,提取各节段法兰接头分别在连续吊装2节段的接头内力、连续吊装3节段的接头内力及连续吊装4节段的接头内力,并分别对法兰盘进行结构计算分析。各工况法兰各构件应力见图7。

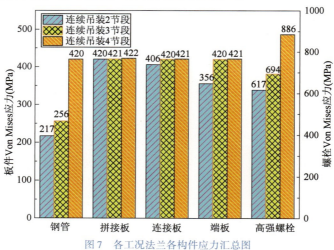

图7　各工况法兰各构件应力汇总图

Fig. 7　Stress summary diagram of each component of flange under various working conditions

按照各吊装焊接方案的包络控制,得出连续吊装 2 节段进行焊接最优,可作为法兰所承受的最大内力。由此可得:节段 1~5 可以连续吊装 4 节段进行焊接,节段 6~8 可以连续吊装 3 节段进行焊接,节段 9~12 以及合龙段最多只能连续吊装 2 节段进行焊接。

法兰接头内力见图 8。

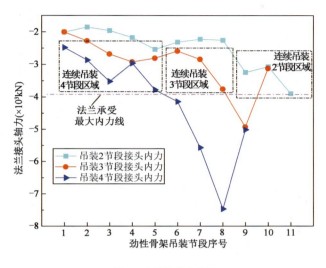

图 8　法兰接头内力图

Fig. 8　Internal diagram of flange joint

4　结论

本文依托天峨龙滩特大桥,提出了 3 种外法兰方案,并从受力性能和可施工性对外法兰方案进行综合比选,并对选用方案进行工程应用分析,得出各劲性骨架节段法兰结构适用于吊装的最大节段数,主要结论如下:

(1)通过对 3 种法兰方案进行多重非线性分析可得,标准外法兰方案、有端板带定位孔拼接板式外法兰方案钢管在受力上均较合理。

(2)通过对各法兰方案进行可施工性分析,得出有端板带定位孔拼接板式外法兰能实现高质量的精准定位,各构件位置布置合理,对外包混凝土影响程度低,其余法兰方案均不能完全满足可施工性的各项要求。

(3)综合分析可得,有端板带定位孔拼接板式外法兰可作为选用方案,并对该方案进行工程应用分析,得出:节段 1~5 可以连续吊装 4 节段后进行焊接,节段 6~8 可以连续吊装 3 节段后进行焊接,节段 9~12 以及合龙段最多只能连续吊装 2 节段后进行焊接。

参 考 文 献

[1] 季学凯. 装配式法兰连接钢管混凝土格构墩设计关键问题研究[D]. 合肥:合肥工业大学,2021.

[2] Kato B, Hirose R. Bolted tension flanges joining circular hollow section members[J]. Kato B; Hirose R, 1985, 5(2).

[3] Yu Luan, Guan Zhenqun, Cheng Gengdong, Song Liu. A simplified nonlinear dynamic modelfor the analysis of pipe structures with bolted flange joints[J]. Journal of Sound and Vibration, 2011, 331(2).

[4] 冯德奎. 大型法兰盘在输电塔中的应用研究[D]. 上海:同济大学,2007.

[5] 王元清,宗亮,石永久. 钢管结构法兰连接节点抗弯承载性能的试验研究[J]. 湖南大学学报(自然科学版),2011,38(07):13-19.

[6] 李彩霞,罗小斌,秦大燕. 钢管混凝土拱桥法兰盘制作关键技术[J]. 公路,2017,62(03):146-147.

缆扣塔合一的钢箱提篮拱桥施工技术研究

裴必达[1,2]　姚浩真[1]　李传习[1,2]　冯浩轩[3]　董创文[1,2]

（1. 长沙理工大学土木工程学院　湖南长沙　410114；
2. 长沙理工大学桥梁工程安全控制教育部重点实验室　湖南长沙　410114；
3. 广东省路桥建设发展有限公司　广东广州　510660）

摘　要　本文以龙琅高速公路车田江大桥为工程背景，为保证该桥的施工安全性与时效性，针对缆扣塔合一的钢箱提篮拱桥施工过程进行了细致研究。本文通过有限元软件 Midas Civil 建立了精细化施工全过程的全桥有限元分析模型，根据计算结果对临时横撑数量、扣背索拆索顺序以及主梁安装顺序进行了优化。优化结果表明，原设计的 18 道临时横撑过于保守，当临时横撑数量由 18 道减少到 8 道时，同样可以保证施工过程中的结构安全性，而施工工期则可缩减约一个月；对四种不同的拆索方案从缆扣塔的应力水平、稳定性和拱肋应力水平及线形变化等角度进行分析，发现四种拆索方案均能满足施工过程中的安全性要求，但自上而下的拆索顺序对桥梁施工状态的影响最小。三种不同的主梁安装顺序中，从跨中和边跨交替安装钢主梁的施工方案对拱肋线形的影响最小。该施工优化的分析结果已用于实桥建设中，并取得了较好的效果，同时可为同类桥梁的建设提供参考。

关键词　桥梁工程　钢箱提篮拱桥　有限元分析　缆扣塔合一　施工技术优化

中图分类号　TU398+.9　　**文献标识码**　A

作者简介：

裴必达(1988—)，男，博士，讲师，主要从事钢桥与钢混组合结构桥梁结构性能及大跨桥梁数值仿真方面的研究。

姚浩真(1997—)，女，硕士研究生，主要从事桥梁结构分析与施工控制方面的研究。

李传习(1963—)，男，博士，教授，主要从事桥梁结构分析与施工控制、UHPC 材料与结构、钢结构疲劳等方面的研究。

冯浩轩(1998—)，男，硕士研究生，主要从事桥梁结构分析与施工控制方面的研究。

董创文(1978—)，男，博士，讲师，主要从事桥梁结构分析与施工控制与大跨结构数值仿真方面的研究。

Research on Construction Technology of Steel Box Basket Arch Bridge with Cable-Stayed Tower and Cable Hoisting Tower Integrated

PEI Bida[1,2]   YAO Haozhen[1]   LI Chuanxi[1,2]   FENG Haoxuan[3]   DONG Chuangwen[1,2]

(1. School of Civil Engineering, Changsha University of Science and Technology, Changsha, Hunan, 410114;
2. Key Laboratory of Bridge Engineering Safety Control of Ministry of Education, Changsha, Hunan, University of Science and Technology, Hunan Province, Changsha, Hunan, 410114;
3. Guangdong province Luqiao construction development limited company, Co., Ltd, Guangzhou, Guangdong, 510660)

Abstract   Taking Chetianjiang Bridge of Longlang Expressway as the engineering background, in order to ensure the safety and timeliness of the bridge construction, this paper makes a detailed study on the construction process of steel box basket arch bridge with cable-buckle-tower integration. In this paper, the finite element analysis model of the whole bridge in the whole process of fine construction is established by the finite element software Midas Civil. According to the calculation results, the number of temporary cross braces, the sequence of cable removal and the installation sequence of main beams are optimized. The optimization results show that the original design of 18 temporary cross braces is too conservative. When the number of temporary cross braces is reduced from 18 to 8, the structural safety in the construction process can also be guaranteed, and the construction period can be shortened by about one month. Four different cable removal schemes are analyzed from the angles of stress level, stability, arch rib stress level and linear change of cable buckle tower. It is found that all four cable removal schemes can meet the safety requirements in the construction process, but the top-down cable removal sequence has the least influence on the bridge construction state. Among the three different installation sequences of main beams, the construction scheme of alternately installing steel main beams from mid-span and side-span has the least influence on arch rib alignment. The analysis result of the construction optimization has been used in the actual bridge construction, and achieved good results. At the same time, it can also provide reference for the construction of similar bridges.

Keywords   bridge engineering   steel box basket arch bridge   finite element analysis   cable and tower are integrated   construction technology optimization

E-mail   peibida@csust.edu.cn

0   引言

近年来,随着我国生产力的快速发展,国内桥梁建设取得了丰硕的成果。在钢箱提篮拱肋节段吊装过程中,为了便于拱轴线的控制,缆索吊装系统的索塔和扣塔往往以"索扣分离"的形式布置,但在某些情况下,由于场地地形的限制,难以布置索塔和后锚,因此必须采用索塔扣塔一体化结构体系[1]。钢拱桥中的钢箱提篮拱桥不仅具有重量轻、强度高、跨度大的特点,而且由于其拱肋向内倾斜,结构的侧向刚度大于平行拱肋,从而避免了拱桥结构的面外失稳[2-7]。钢拱桥的快速发展不仅离不开施工方法的进步,也离不开与施工方法相对应的施工控制技术[8]。然而,在缆索吊系统吊装节段施工时会影响缆扣塔的偏位,从而影响吊装拱肋节段时的线形控制,因此缆扣塔合一的斜拉扣挂缆索吊装施工方法对拱肋线形更加难以控制。因此,精细化的施工过程分析显得尤为重要。在实际施工中,需要综合考虑不同施工工艺对桥梁结构的影响、现场施工条件的限制、施工机械的约束等因素,综合选择最适合桥梁的施工方案。合理的施工方案能够在保证结构安全的前提下,使整个施工过程对结构最终成桥后的内力和线形影响尽量小,同时还能大大节约材料和工期,因此通常需要根据精细化施工过程分析结果对施工过程进行施工过程优化分析。

本文以车田江大桥为工程背景,采用有限元软件 Midas Civil 建立了缆扣塔合一的中承式钢箱提篮拱桥精细化施工全过程全桥有限元模型,并对该桥临时横撑数量、扣背索拆索工序、钢主梁安装顺序等施工过程的优化进行了细致研究。该分析成果可直接用于实际工程,同时也可以为同类桥型的建设提供参考。

1 工程概况

车田江大桥位于湖南省新化县温塘镇车田江村,为龙琅高速公路上跨越车田江水库的关键控制性工程,主桥为中承式组合梁钢箱提篮拱桥,主跨为280m,铅垂面投影矢高64m(斜平面内64.987m),矢跨比为1:4.375,拱肋向内侧倾斜10°角,拱轴线线形为二次抛物线,拱轴线两侧拱顶处横桥向距离为13.830m,拱脚处横桥向距离为36.400m。

主梁构造为纵横梁组合桥面,桥面板为预制混凝土结构,预制混凝土板采用C60混凝土,桥面板现浇部分混凝土采用C60自密实混凝土。主桥全桥共设76道中横梁,分为普通次横梁、吊杆横梁、立柱横梁以及拱肋横梁三种类型。主桥每侧拱肋各设置29根吊杆,全桥共58根。吊杆纵桥向间距为7.5m,倾斜布置。拱肋采用变截面矩形截面,顶底板宽度均为2.56m,拱箱横向宽度为2.5m(为拱肋的腹板的外轮廓尺寸);拱顶拱肋高度为2.5m,拱脚位置拱肋高度为5m,拱肋的高度按线性方程变化。在拱脚处设置钢混结合段,端横隔板至拱座混凝土表面,内部灌注C50微膨胀混凝土形成封闭空间,钢板内壁均开孔并设置剪力钉,以传递钢与混凝土之间的剪力,拱座外表面的承压板下设置钢板,钢筋穿过钢板孔洞,形成刚性剪力连接建PBL键,通过钢板孔洞中的混凝土和贯通钢筋的协同作用传递剪力,同时全截面合理设置15-12型号预应力钢束。主桥桥面为单向 −1.4%纵坡,车行道桥面横坡为双向2%,人行道为1%。全桥位于直线上。车田江大桥整体结构布置如图1所示,拱肋节段划分如图2所示。

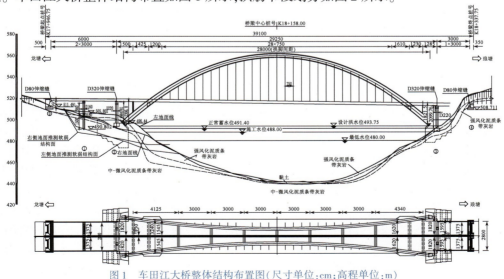

图1 车田江大桥整体结构布置图(尺寸单位:cm;高程单位:m)

Fig.1 Overall structural layout of Chetianjiang Bridge

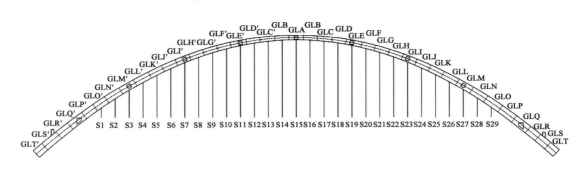

图 2 拱肋节段划分图
Fig. 2 Segment division diagram of arch rib

2 施工方法与技术

根据车田江大桥的结构设计特点及所处的地理环境,主桥上构安装施工采用斜拉扣挂式无支架缆索吊装方案,采取吊塔、扣塔合二为一的方案实施,缆索吊四个地锚采用承台和桩基相结合的桩台组合式锚碇。缆索吊设计单组缆索系统最大吊重控制荷载为 950kN,双组抬吊缆索系统最大吊重控制荷载为 1200kN。整个吊装过程中,吊装最大重量为 1156kN,因此最大重量拱肋节段采用双组抬吊,缆索吊索跨分布由龙塘岸至琅塘岸依次为:100m + 400m + 100m。缆索起重机系统主要由塔架支撑系统、锚固系统、绳索系统、跑车、机械部分和塔顶索鞍等组成。

车田江大桥主桥钢结构由专业钢结构厂家在加工厂加工制作、预拼完成后,根据运输条件分段、分块(上报设计院,征得设计院同意)运至施工现场,在现场拼装胎架上拼装成吊装节段,然后进行安装施工。车田江大桥主桥上部结构采用先拱后梁的施工顺序,拱肋节段悬拼采用无支架斜拉扣挂缆索吊装工艺进行安装施工。缆索吊采用两组独立的起吊系统。拱肋采用单侧起吊,左右两幅及两岸对称安装。拱肋合龙后拆除扣索系统,按照设计顺序安装拱上立柱、吊杆及桥面结构纵横梁及桥面板。由于受到合龙后拱肋横撑吊装空间的限制,安装钢梁时需先将钢梁运至浮船上,然后再进行吊装。钢梁安装时各个钢梁块段与部分桥面板同时安装,钢梁安装完毕同时形成桥面板安装通道。钢梁安装顺序由桥两岸吊杆区向跨中依次对称安装并合龙,然后安装两侧无吊杆区钢梁,直至钢梁安装完成。桥面板在预制场预制完成后,通过平板车运至安装区域采用汽车起重机从琅塘侧至龙塘侧对称安装桥梁中心线两侧的桥面板,形成运输通道后,从两岸向跨中对称安装剩余的桥面板。

3 有限元模型

3.1 有限元模型建立

采用 Midas Civil 软件建立精细化施工全过程全桥有限元模型,如图 3 所示,全桥共有 3484 个单元,2147 个节点,其中板单元 324 个,索单元 140 个。拱肋和横撑均用梁单元模拟,缆索及背扣索用索单元模拟,桥面板采用板单元模拟。拱肋采用 Q420qD 钢材,横撑采用 Q345qD 钢材,主缆、扣背索采用 Strand1960 钢绞线。最终桥梁构件的主要材料特性见表 1。

图3 有限元模型

Fig. 3 Finite element model

桥梁构件的主要材料特性表 表1
Main material characteristics table Tab. 1

结构名称	材料类型	泊松比	弹性模量(MPa)	重度(kN/m³)
拱肋钢材	Q420	0.31	2.06×10^5	78.5
拱肋横撑、立柱	Q345	0.31	2.06×10^5	78.5
吊杆	Wire1670	0.30	2.05×10^5	78.5
扣塔	Q345	0.31	1.95×10^5	78.5
扣索、背索	Strand1960	0.30	1.95×10^5	78.5
钢主梁	Q345	0.31	2.06×10^5	78.5
预制混凝土桥面板	C60	0.20	3.60×10^4	28.0

3.2 施工工序

缆索吊装法钢箱拱桥施工一般流程如下：①缆索吊装系统施工（扣塔、索塔、主缆等）；②分段架设主拱、临时横撑和永久横撑；③拆除背索和临时横撑；④安装主梁和吊杆；⑤桥面铺装、附属结构等。

3.3 扣背索索力确定的方法

扣背索分两次张拉，其扣索初张力计算采用力矩平衡法。下面以2号扣背索初拉力计算为例，叙述本桥扣索初张力计算流程。如图4所示，铰接点 O 为两个节段的连接处，此时将2号扣索对应拱肋节段单独受力分析，已知节段自重及其尺寸，对 O 点求矩为零，便可得到 $F_{扣}$ 即2号扣索的初张力。再根据扣塔受扣背索的水平分力互相抵消为原则，且扣背索角度已知的情况下，便可求出2号背索初张力。剩下的扣背索初张力可依照此方法逐段依次求解得出。而二次调索则是以拱顶底受力均匀，且应力尽量小为原则进行索力调整，二次调索结果如表2所示。

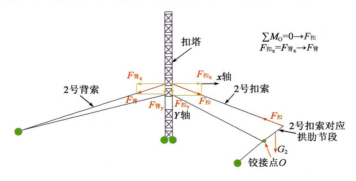

图4 2号扣索初张力计算图示

Fig. 4 Figure for calculation of initial tension of 2# buckle

扣背索二张力计算结果(kN)　　　　　表 2

Calculation result of the second tension of the back cable (kN)　　　Tab. 2

索 号	小桩号侧		大桩号侧	
	扣索	背索	扣索	背索
1 号	621.2	559.1	650.4	636.7/644.6
2 号	686.5	661.3	759.3	793.3/803.5
3 号	736.1	750.3	825.1	906.7/919.7
4 号	796.4	848.6	840.2	962.1/977.2
5 号	869.2	959.3	911.3	1081.8/1099.4
6 号	854.3	977.5	891.5	1099.1/1117.5
7 号	943.2	1118.6	911.2	1263.5/1284.8
8 号	1061.7	1303.5	891.7	1517.4/1514.3
9 号	1183.5	1492.9	988.2	1737.1/1767.2

3.4　有限元计算结果

由于篇幅有限,本文仅给出合理成桥状态下拱肋顶底缘的应力图,如图 5、图 6 所示。理论合理成桥状态阶段拱肋顶部均为压应力,最大压应力为 -130.7MPa,成桥状态阶段拱肋底部均为压应力,最大压应力为 -156.9MPa(备注:图中出现的拉应力均为拱肋横撑顶底的应力)。最大索力出现在小里程侧吊杆 J29,其值为 1884.7kN;最小索力出现在大里程侧吊杆 J20,其值为 953.5kN。桥面钢梁最大拉应力为 138.2MPa,最大压应力为 -137.7MPa。

图 5　合理成桥状态拱肋顶部应力图(单位:MPa)

Fig. 5　Stress diagram at the top of arch rib top in reasonable completed state (Unit:MPa)

图 6　合理成桥状态拱肋底部应力图(单位:MPa)

Fig. 6　Stress diagram at the bottom of arch rib in reasonable completed state (Unit:MPa)

4 施工工序优化

4.1 临时横撑施工优化

在拱肋施工阶段,利用临时横撑和永久横撑作为拱架之间的连接构件,以加强拱架的整体性,提高拱架的侧向刚度。鉴于不同施工阶段临时横撑结构可能受拉或受压,临时横撑布置方案对施工安全和桥塔应力合理分布起着关键作用[9]。原设计方案临时横撑共有18根,其布置如图7所示(图中红色竖线代表临时横撑)。在拱肋的实际施工过程中,由于工期紧张,施工方希望通过适当的优化节约工期。最终井盖优化计算后确定将18道临时横撑减少至8道临时横撑,其布置位置分别在GLN′节段、GLJ′节段、GLF′节段、GLB′节段、GLB节段、GLF节段、GLJ节段、GLN节段,其布置如图8所示。当临时横撑数量减少时,拱肋应力变形、索塔顶部水平偏移和施工稳定性都会受到影响。采用Midas分析临时横撑数量减少前后上述因素的差异,以此来检验临时横撑数量减少的可靠性。两种临时横撑布置方案除临时横撑数量不同外,施工顺序完全相同。

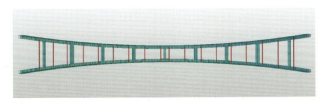

图7 原方案临时横撑布置图

Fig. 7 Temporary cross brace layout of the original scheme

图8 方案更改后临时横撑布置图

Fig. 8 Temporary cross brace layout after scheme change

拱肋线形是拱肋施工过程中施工控制的重点之一。因此,有必要分析临时横撑布置方案改变前后拱肋施工过程中其位移的变化,以确保上述方案改变后拱肋线形仍在理论控制范围内。原拱肋施工过程中的缆扣塔最大水平位移为:小桩侧扣缆塔-96.2mm,大桩侧扣缆塔125.5mm;但方案变更后,拱肋施工过程中缆扣塔最大水平位移为:小桩侧扣缆塔-108.3mm,大桩侧扣缆塔135.7mm;两种方案扣索塔顶最大水平位移为拱肋最大悬臂状态,即安装GLB/GLC和GLB′/GLC′段。有限元计算原临时横撑布置方案下各拱肋段临时横撑安装引起的位移,结果如表3、表4所示。从表中可以看出,临时横撑安装对拱肋的横桥向位移影响不大,但对纵桥向位移和竖向位移影响稍大,且随着拱肋的吊装,斜拉桥塔顶水平位移增大。临时横撑布置方案改变后的斜拉桥塔顶水平位移比方案改变前大,但位移增量均在1mm以内,在施工误差控制范围内。GLB/GLC和GLB′/GLC′拱肋段临时横撑对安装后拱肋位移影响最大,最大位移为:桥梁纵向位移$\delta_x = -10.2$mm,竖向位移$\delta_z = -34.7$mm。综上所述,理论上临时横撑布置方案的变化对拱肋线形影响最大,对应的施工阶段为拱肋最大悬臂状态。实际拱肋施工时,位移增量可以通过调整背索力和拱肋预拱度来抵消,以减少扣缆塔变形对拱肋线形的影响。此外,由于拱肋施工过程中受到横向风荷载等因素的影响,因此临时横撑优化过程中还需重点关注施工过程中的结构稳定性。临时横撑布置方案变更前后拱肋、顶部位移差异分别见表3、表4。

临时横撑布置方案变更前后拱肋位移差异(mm) 表3

Difference of arch rib displacement and top displacement of buckle tower before and after the change of temporary cross brace layout scheme (mm) Tab. 3

施工阶段	变更前位移			变更前位移		
	δ_x	δ_y	δ_z	δ_x	δ_y	δ_z
GLR/GLR′节段	0.0	0.0	0.0	0.1	0.1	−0.1
GLP/GLQ、GLP′/GLQ′节段	0.6	0.1	0.0	−0.6	−0.1	−0.8
GLN/GLO、GLN′/GLO′节段	1.8	0.0	0.0	−1.7	0.0	−2.8
GLL/GLM、GLL′/GLM′节段	3.4	0.1	0.0	−3.5	−0.1	−5.6
GLJ/GLK、GLJ′/GLK′节段	4.5	0.0	0.0	−4.8	0.0	−8.2
GLH/GLI、GLH′/GLI′节段	6.0	0.1	0.0	−6.8	−0.1	−13.1
GLF/GLG、GLF′/GLG′节段	7.0	0.0	0.0	−8.1	0.0	−18.4
GLD/GLE、GLD′/GLE′节段	7.9	0.1	0.0	−9.1	−1.8	−24.7
GLB/GLC、GLB′/GLC′节段	8.5	0.0	0.0	−10.1	−5.3	−34.9

临时横撑布置方案变更前后塔顶部位移差异(mm) 表4

Displacement difference of the top of the buckle tower before and after the change of the temporary cross brace layout scheme (mm) Tab. 4

施工阶段	揽塔顶部水平位移			
	原小桩号	原大桩号	新小桩号	新大桩号
GLR/GLR′节段	−0.8	0.6	−1.1	0.6
GLP/GLQ、GLP′/GLQ′节段	2.1	1.1	1.2	1.6
GLN/GLO、GLN′/GLO′节段	−1.2	7.2	−1.7	7.2
GLL/GLM、GLL′/GLM′节段	17.8	−4.5	14.8	−2.6
GLJ/GLK、GLJ′/GLK′节段	8.8	6.3	5.6	8.2
GLH/GLI、GLH′/GLI′节段	24.8	−8.3	17.8	−2.5
GLF/GLG、GLF′/GLG′节段	−11.2	26.9	−18.2	32.5
GLD/GLE、GLD′/GLE′节段	−27.5	46.5	−38.4	57.6
GLB/GLC、GLB′/GLC′节段	−96.4	125.4	−108.3	135.4

拱肋合龙前的所有施工阶段屈曲分析特征值均满足规范要求,说明优化后的临时横撑布置方案拱肋施工过程中仍然具有足够的稳定性。

4.2 扣背索拆索施工优化

4.2.1 拆索顺序划分

为了研究拆索顺序对主拱内力、线形和索力增长的影响,并考虑实际拆索的施工便利性和经济效益,需要尽量减少跨多根索的索数,避免现场施工人员在拆背扣索时多次往返不同的拆索点,减少工作量。本文选取了既方便又满足工程需要的四种扣背索拆除方案进行比较,具体方案如表 5 所示。此外,以一次性拆索方案为对照组,验证四种不同的拆索顺序对拆索后拱肋状态是否有影响。根据表 5 中的几种拆索方案,在施工阶段对本工程背景桥梁的有限元模型进行修正,得到四种拆索方案模型和一次拆索模型。除了电缆拆除顺序,其他几个型号的施工顺序完全相同。本文选取拱肋跨度 8 个等分点的应力和位移作为分析对象。从模型的计算结果可以得出,四种拆索方案和对照组拆索前后拱肋的应力和位移变化基本一致,说明拆索顺序的不同对拆索后的桥梁状态没有明显影响,所以只分析拆缆过程中的差异。从拱肋应力、拱肋竖向位移、索力及其增量的角度分析了几种拆索方案的差异。

表 5 拆索方案
Tab. 5 Cable removal scheme

	拆索顺序
方案一	1 号索→2 号索→3 号索→4 号索→5 号索→6 号索→7 号索→8 号索→9 号索
方案二	9 号索→8 号索→7 号索→6 号索→5 号索→4 号索→3 号索→2 号索→1 号索
方案三	1 号索→3 号索→5 号索→7 号索→9 号索→2 号索→4 号索→6 号索→8 号索
方案四	9 号索→7 号索→5 号索→3 号索→1 号索→8 号索→6 号索→4 号索→2 号索
对照组	一次拆索完成

4.2.2 不同拆索顺序的拱肋应力差异

该模型中用于分析应力差的荷载均为施工阶段的荷载。根据上述有限元模型的计算结果,在左、右拱顶连线中点处,各阶段拆索拱肋应力基本处于中心对称状态。因此,选取如图 9 所示的五个参考截面作为分析对象,提取三种方案中参考截面拆索前后和拆索过程中上下边缘的最大应力值以及整个拱肋的最大应力值。模型的计算结果如图 10 ~ 图 13 所示。从图中可以看出,每个参考段处于不同的电缆拆除状态。其中,方案 1 拆索过程中拱肋 1/4 跨和跨中截面产生的最大应力大于其他方案,方案 1 拆索过程中的最大应力大于拆索后拱肋的最大应力。除了拱肋 8 个等跨处的参考截面应力外,还比较了每一步拆索时拱肋的极限应力。从图 13 中可以看出,方案 3 在拆索过程中拱肋的应力水平低于其他三个方案,方案 4 次之;在拆索的前四步中,方案二的拱肋应力极值大于方案一,而在后五步中正好相反。方案一拱肋应力极值(- 84.1 MPa)超过了撤索结束时拱肋应力极值(- 73.0 MPa),这也是四个方案中唯一一个拱肋应力超过撤索结束时的应力。综上所述,四种拆索方案的拱肋应力水平排序为:方案 1 大于方案 2,方案 4 大于方案 3。

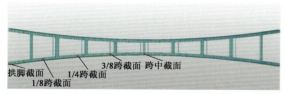

图9 参考单元具体位置图

Fig. 9 Refer to the specific location diagram of the unit

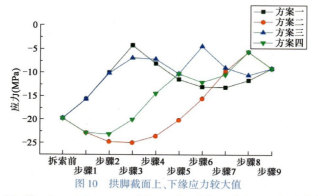

图10 拱脚截面上、下缘应力较大值

Fig. 10 The stress at the upper and lower edges of the arch foot section is larger

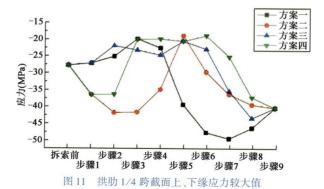

图11 拱肋1/4跨截面上、下缘应力较大值

Fig. 11 Stress at the upper and lower edges of 1/4 cross section of arch rib is larger

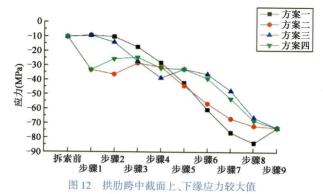

图12 拱肋跨中截面上、下缘应力较大值

Fig. 12 Stress at the upper and lower edges of the mid-span section of arch rib is larger

施工与监测

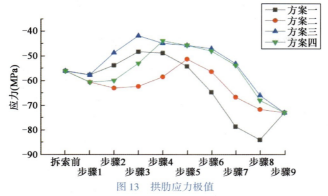

图 13 拱肋应力极值

Fig. 13 Extreme stress value of arch rib

4.2.3 不同拆索顺序的拱肋竖向位移差异

为了分析四种拆索方案下拱肋竖向位移的差异,分别提取了四种方案拆索过程中拱肋 1/8、2/8、3/8 和 4/8 截面处接头的竖向位移。具体位置见图 9(拆索前拱肋垂直位移定义为 0mm),有限元模型计算结果见图 14 ~ 图 17。从图中可以看出,四种方案在拆索过程中的竖向位移变化不同,但四种方案拆索后拱肋不同位置的竖向位移与拆索前相同。一般情况下,拱肋的竖向位移变化如下:在边跨附近,拱肋的竖向位移为负,在中跨附近,拱肋的竖向位移为正。

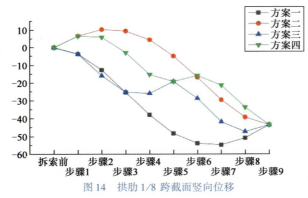

图 14 拱肋 1/8 跨截面竖向位移

Fig. 14 Vertical displacement of 1/8 span section of arch rib

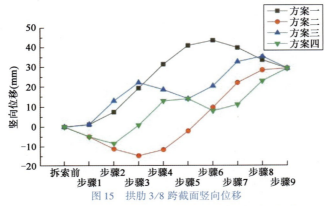

图 15 拱肋 3/8 跨截面竖向位移

Fig. 15 Vertical displacement of 3/8 cross section of arch rib

311

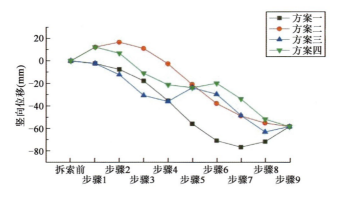

图 16 拱肋 2/8 跨截面竖向位移
Fig. 16 Vertical displacement of 2/8 cross section of arch rib

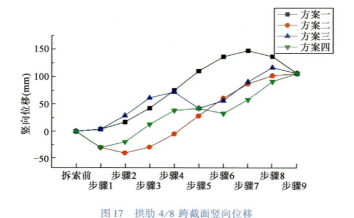

图 17 拱肋 4/8 跨截面竖向位移
Fig. 17 Vertical displacement of 4/8 cross section of arch rib

此外,方案 1 和方案 3 中电缆拆除过程中的垂直位移大于方案 2 和方案 4,且超过电缆拆除完成时的垂直位移。在方案二和方案四中,位移发生在拆索前的第三和第四步,与拆索完成时的竖向位移相反。而且方案二中的反向位移更为突出,最大值为 -41.2mm,对应于施工阶段方案二中拱肋跨中截面的位移(该截面最终理论竖向位移为 105.7mm)。计算不同缆索拆除方案下拱肋的竖向位移,使施工人员心里有数,便于识别桥梁的异常情况。此外,从上到下拆除电缆的顺序更加方便,施工时间更少,更适合实际施工需要。

4.3 钢主梁安装顺序施工优化

4.3.1 钢主梁吊装段划分

根据钢梁的结构和重量,根据现场和吊装条件的要求,对钢梁进行合理分段。本文以该桥为工程背景,该桥钢梁分 25 个吊装节段进行吊装。大多数钢梁吊装段由三根横梁及其相连的纵梁组成,一些特殊的吊装段由四根横梁及其相连的纵梁组成。钢主梁吊装段划分如图 18 所示。其中 1 号、2 号和 23 号吊装段包含 4 根横梁,其余吊装段均由 3 根横梁以及它们之间的纵梁组成。钢梁采用高强度螺栓连接,螺栓螺母等级为 10.9S。

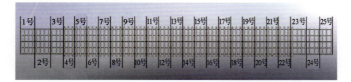

图 18　钢主梁吊装段划分图

Fig. 18　Division diagram of hoisting section of steel girder

本文工程背景,桥梁初始安装顺序可分为三种:①从 1/4 跨、3/4 跨向跨中安装钢梁,然后对称安装两侧钢梁,直至边跨;②从跨中位置向两侧对称安装钢梁;③钢梁依次安装在跨中位置和 1/4 跨位置。

4.3.2　钢主梁安装顺序对拱肋应力的影响

分别提取钢主梁安装过程中各阶段拱肋的最小和最大压应力(计算荷载为施工阶段荷载),结果如图 19 和图 20 所示。从结果可以看出,采用方案一安装钢主梁时,拱肋的最大和最小压应力分别为 -157.0MPa 和 -7.3MPa。采用方案二和方案三时,拱肋应力范围分别为 -113.0 ~ -5.5MPa 和 -108.0 ~ -5.5MPa。方案一前 15 个钢梁吊装段的拱肋最大压应力大于方案二和方案三,从第 16 个钢梁吊装段到钢梁安装完成,三个方案的拱肋最大压应力比较接近,方案三略大。方案一和方案三的最小压应力水平基本接近。综上所述,从对拱肋应力的影响来看,方案 1 拱肋的应力水平较高。

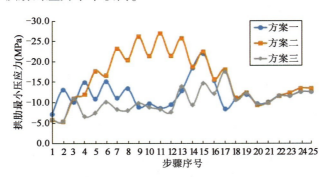

图 19　钢主梁安装过程拱肋最小压应力

Fig. 19　Minimum compressive stress of arch rib in steel girder installation process

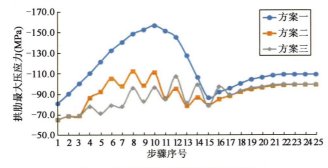

图 20　钢主梁安装过程拱肋最大压应力

Fig. 20　Maximum compressive stress of arch rib in steel girder installation process

4.3.3 钢主梁安装顺序对拱肋位移最值的影响

为了分析三种钢梁安装方案对拱肋位移的影响,分别提取了三种方案下钢梁安装过程中拱肋的最大位移、桥梁纵向位移的最大绝对值和竖向位移的最大最小值。结果如图21~图24所示。由于三种方案在主梁施工过程中拱肋的桥梁横向位移很小,差别不大,故不再对桥梁横向位移进行分析。从分析结果可以看出,不同主梁安装顺序下拱肋最大位移相差不大,三种方案下主梁施工时拱肋最大位移分别为89.4mm、88.2mm和88.5mm,但三种方案下拱肋位移峰值出现的阶段不同,方案一出现的最早,方案二和方案三出现的最晚。另外,三种方案最后7个主梁吊装节段施工时拱肋最大位移基本相同。从图22可以看出,拱肋的桥梁纵向位移最大绝对值曲线与拱肋位移最大值基本一致,三个方案的桥梁纵向位移最大值都在25mm左右。从图22和图24可以看出,三种方案拱肋最大和最小竖向位移峰值相差很小,三种方案拱肋最大位移峰值分别为60.8mm、60.3mm和60.3mm,最小值分别为-77.4mm、-76.3mm和-76.5mm,三种方案的竖向位移峰值顺序与组合位移一致。总的来说,主梁吊装段施工顺序对拱肋位移的影响没有对拱肋应力的影响大。从模型计算结果来看,三种方案下拱肋位移的峰值基本相同,平均值非常接近。

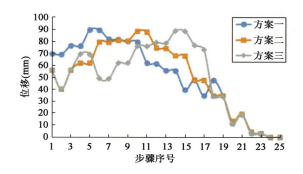

图21 不同吊装顺序拱肋最大位移
Fig.21 Maximum displacement of arch rib in different hoisting sequence

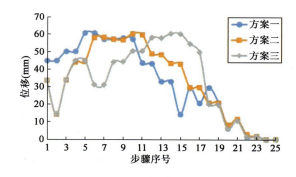

图22 不同吊装顺序拱肋竖向位移最大值
Fig.22 Maximum vertical displacement of arch ribs in different hoisting sequences

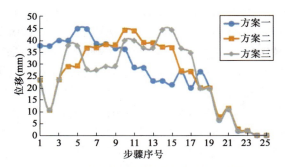

图 23 不同吊装顺序拱肋纵桥向位移最大值

Fig. 23 Maximum longitudinal displacement of arch ribs in different hoisting sequences

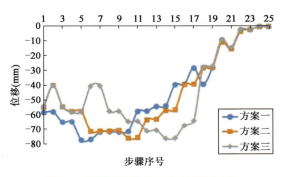

图 24 不同吊装顺序拱肋竖向位移最小值

Fig. 24 Minimum vertical displacement of arch ribs in different hoisting sequences

5 结论

本文以龙琅高速公路车田江大桥为工程对象,采用 Madis Civil 软件进行有限元计算分析,对该桥施工过程中遇到的一些问题,提出了合理的施工方案。本文主要结论如下:

(1)临时横撑由 18 根减少到 8 根后,拱肋施工稳定性仍满足规范要求,对拱肋受力影响较小;为类似桥梁的临时横撑数量提供了参考值。

(2)综合分析几种扣背索拆除方案对拱肋应力和位移的影响,自上而下拆除退扣索的施工顺序综合影响最小,最符合实际施工需要。

(3)设置了三种不同的钢梁安装方案,分析了三种方案对拱肋应力和位移的影响。从 1/4 跨和 3/4 跨向跨中安装钢梁,然后在两侧对称安装钢梁,直到边跨应力小于其他两种方案,而从跨中和 1/4 跨交替安装钢梁的方案对拱肋位移的影响最小。

参 考 文 献

[1] 王德明,张杰,刘夏.钢箱提篮拱桥缆塔扣塔一体化设计研究[J].施工技术(中英文),2022,51(12):55-58,67.

[2] 骆中林.斜拉扣挂钢箱拱桥施工控制及吊装精度影响因素分析[D].长沙:长沙理工大学,2008.

[3] 张石波,裴若娟.浅谈尼尔森体系的钢管混凝土提篮拱在铁路桥梁中的运营前景[J].桥梁建设,2001(04):56-58.

[4] 乔健,辛学忠.世纪之交铁路桥梁发展体会[J].铁道标准设计,2004(07):106-110.

[5] 杨兴旺,赵雷,李乔.提篮式系杆拱桥施工全过程承载力分析[J].四川建筑科学研究,2004(03):120-1220.

[6] 李乔,田学民,张清华.铁路大跨度提篮式系杆拱桥全桥模型试验[J].中国铁道科学,2003(01):90-95.

[7] 冯楚桥.铁路下承尼尔森体系钢管混凝土提篮式系杆拱桥研究与应用[J].工程与建设,2007(04):539-541.

[8] 向伟.特大跨钢箱提篮拱施工过程分析及控制[D].重庆:重庆交通大学,2012.

[9] 贺玖龙.斜拉桥异形索塔施工中临时水平横撑的应用研究[D].西安:长安大学,2015.

连续拱桥拉扣挂施工新型扣锚梁设计与分析

申伟[1] 田曦[1] 李鹏[1] 安永辉[1,2]* 欧阳效勇[3]

(1. 广西大学土木建筑工程学院 广西南宁 530004；
2. 大连理工大学建设工程学部 辽宁大连 116023；
3. 中交第二公路工程局有限公司 陕西西安 710065)

摘 要 大跨度钢管混凝土拱桥一般采用缆索吊装斜拉扣挂悬拼法施工。本文重点介绍斜拉扣挂体系中的一种新型扣锚梁装置,以双堡特大桥为背景,该装置根据连续拱桥左右两跨单幅施工的优化方案需求进行设计。为研究新型扣锚梁结构在拱肋施工中最不利荷载工况下是否满足强度验算,模拟施工中新型扣锚梁的实际受力状态,建立了等比例三维实体模型,使用 ANSYS 有限元分析软件计算新型扣锚梁模型在最不利荷载工况下的内力。计算结果表明,新型扣锚梁在现有规范下满足强度验算标准,符合该工程施工的使用需求。新型扣锚梁增加了控制索锚固区,在优化的施工方案中可减小临时固定法兰、已安装节段索力的应力,保证桥墩与扣塔处于平衡状态,对降低施工风险有积极意义。

关键词 连续拱桥 扣锚梁 施工 强度验算

中图分类号 U445.464 **文献标识码** A

Design and Analysis of a New Buckle-anchor-beam for Cable-stay Construction of Continuous Arch Bridge

SHEN Wei[1] TIAN Xi[1] LI Peng[1] AN Yonghui[1,2]* OUYANG Xiaoyong[3]

(1. College of Civil Engineering and Architecture, Guangxi University, Nanning, Guangxi, 530004, China;
2. Faculty of Infrastructure Engineering, Dalian University of Technology, DaLian, Liaoning, 116023, China;
3. CCCC Second Highway Engineering Co. Ltd., Xi'an, 710065, China)

基金项目：广西科技基地和人才专项（AD21220050）；国家优秀青年科学基金（52122803）；广西重点研发计划（AB22036007）。
作者简介：
申伟(1988—),男,博士,助理教授,主要从事结构智能监测与评估、特大跨桥梁结构设计理论与计算方面的研究。
田曦(1999—),男,硕士研究生,主要从事结构健康监测方面的研究。
李鹏(1997—),男,硕士研究生,主要从事工程结构腐蚀与防护方面的研究。
*安永辉(1986—),男,博士,博士后,教授,主要从事新型与智能土木工程结构研究。
欧阳效勇(1962—),男,博士,正高级工程师,主要从事桥梁工程技术研发与管理工作。

Abstract The long-span concrete-filled steel tube arch bridge is generally constructed by cable hoisting, cable-stay and suspension. This paper focuses on the introduction of a new buckle-anchor-beam device in the cable-stayed suspension system. Taking Shuangbao Bridge as the background, the device is designed according to the requirements of the optimization scheme of the left and right span single frame construction of the continuous arch bridge. In order to study whether the new buckle-anchor-beam structure meets the strength checking calculation under the most unfavorable load condition in the arch rib construction, the actual stress state of the new buckle-anchor-beam in the construction is simulated, and the equal proportion three-dimensional solid model is established. The internal forces of the new buckle-anchor-beam model under the most unfavorable load condition are calculated by ANSYS finite element analysis software. The calculation results show that the new type buckle anchor beam meets the strength checking standard under the existing specification, and meets the use demand of the project construction. The new buckle-anchor-beam increases the anchorage area of control cable, reduces the stress of temporary fixed flanges and installed segment cable forces in the optimized construction scheme, ensures the balance between pier and anchor tower, and has positive significance for reducing construction risks.

Keywords　continuous arch bridge　buckle-anchor-beam　construct　strength examination

E-mail　anyh@ dlut. edu. cn

0　引言

钢管混凝土拱桥以其造型优美、造价经济和结构独特等优势在世界各地被持续建造[1],拱桥的设计越来越成熟,但其施工方法各异,难度也较大,成为拱桥建设的关键难点[2]。斜拉扣挂作为大跨度连续拱桥最常用的施工方法,常与缆索吊运系统结合进行拱肋节段安装,安装过程中悬臂长度和扣索力合力越来越大,施工安全风险也逐渐加大,钢管拱肋安装关系到大桥建设的成败。扣锚索系统作为斜拉扣挂体系的重要组成部分,在缆索吊装系统吊装时用法兰临时固定拱肋新节段并张拉扣索,逐段固定拱肋保持平衡直至拱桥合龙[3]。斜拉扣挂悬拼法首次在1996年应用于主跨为312m的广西邕宁邕江大桥钢管混凝土劲性骨架拱桥上[4]。传统的扣锚梁设计有4个钢索锚固支座,为满足不同施工方法,设计出多锚固支座扣锚梁,新型扣锚梁结构复杂、受力较大,需验算结构的安全性并找出其薄弱点,保证施工的安全[5]。

1　工程背景

1.1　桥梁概况

双堡特大桥主桥为两跨连续上承式钢管混凝土变截面桁架拱桥,单拱计算跨径380m,矢高80m,矢跨比1/4.75;拱轴线采用悬链线,拱轴系数1.55。主拱圈采用钢管混凝土变高度空间桁架,四肢格构结构,断面高度从拱顶6.5m(弦管中心距)变化到拱脚11.0m(弦管中心距),单侧拱圈宽7.5m(弦管中心距),两幅拱圈横向中心距17.5m。

1.2　大桥拱肋安装施工方案

双堡特大桥采用斜拉扣挂法施工,且左右两跨单幅对称施工,单幅共划分9个节段(图1)。安装拱肋新节段时即刻张拉智能拉索保证桥墩与扣塔处于平衡状态(图2)。以扣点、墩顶和扣塔顶位移不超过10mm为迭代计算目标,经计算得出节段1、节段2、节段3施工时无需智能拉索;节段4、节段5、节段6拱肋施工时,智能拉索上锚点设置在墩顶处;节段7、节段8、节段9拱肋施工时,智能拉索锚点分别设置在扣塔的扣锚梁上。

在拱肋新节段安装施工中,右跨拱肋新节段安装时,扣锚梁系统扣索一端锚固在新拱肋节段前端吊点,另一端则锚固在沿扣塔顺桥向布置的扣锚梁上[6],当新节段安装好后即刻张拉智能拉索,锚索一端锚固在扣锚梁上,另一端锚固在地面调力设备锚点处,通过张拉智能拉索来平衡左跨,待左跨新节段也安装好后张拉扣索于扣锚梁上形成对称结构保证扣塔平衡,松开智能拉索继续下一拱肋节段的安装。

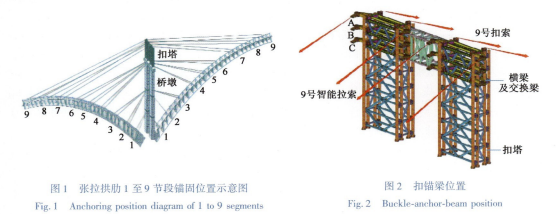

图 1　张拉拱肋 1 至 9 节段锚固位置示意图

Fig. 1　Anchoring position diagram of 1 to 9 segments of tensioned arch ribs

图 2　扣锚梁位置

Fig. 2　Buckle-anchor-beam position

2　新型扣锚梁设计与验算

2.1　新型扣锚梁主要构造

该斜拉扣挂体系中设计的新型扣锚梁大致可以划分为 5 个部分,即交换梁、横梁、牛腿、扣索锚固区、智能索锚固区,如图 3 所示。包括平行设置的两组交换梁、两组智能索牛腿及其中间的联梁,每组交换梁上均设有锚固支座,锚固支座上安装有倾斜设置的锚具;每组智能索牛腿上均设有智能索锚固支座,智能索锚固支座安装有可旋转的智能索吊具,智能索锚固支座与牛腿横梁构件固定连接;交换梁、横梁、智能索牛腿三者固定连接,安装在扣塔上。该设计在传统扣锚梁的基础上引入了智能索牛腿及其安装的智能索锚固装置,在不平衡拱肋节段安装过程中张拉智能拉索,使桥墩与扣塔处于平衡状态,保证施工过程的位移控制。

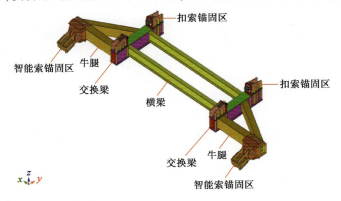

图 3　新型扣锚梁三维模型

Fig. 3　3D model of the new buckle-anchor-beam

2.2 新型扣锚梁强度验算

在拱肋新节段安装时,现有施工方案需在智能锚固区张拉智能索,扣锚梁的扣索锚固区及智能索锚固区都承受着很大索力,需要对扣锚梁进行施工过程中的强度验算,保证结构强度安全。安装过程中以扣点、墩顶和扣塔顶位移不超过20mm为计算目标,求得第九节段拱肋安装时所需施加智能拉索索力最大,以此工况作为扣锚梁荷载的最不利工况进行验算。查找《铁路桥梁钢结构设计规范》(TB 10091—2017)中Q345钢材的基本容许应力可得,Q345的弯曲容许应力为210MPa,对于施工临时结构,可扩大30%的安全余量,因此新型扣锚梁采用的容许应力为273MPa。

采用ANSYS、ABAQUS、MIDAS FEA有限元软件同时进行扣锚梁三维实体模型并进行验算,3个软件计算结果基本一致,并以ANSYS模型计算结果作为验算依据。新型扣锚梁采用Q355B结构钢,实体模型中材料密度为7850kg/m³;杨氏模量为200 MPa;泊松比为0.3。在ANSYS有限元软件中建立了新型扣锚梁及扣锚梁牛腿子结构的三维实体模型,对于规则构件采用了六面体单元划分网格,复杂构件采用四面体单元划分网格,为保证计算精度所有单元均采用二阶单元。使用MIDAS CIVIL建立了扣锚梁的梁杆模型进行辅助验算。计算时保留主体受力构件进行新型扣锚梁主体结构强度验算,施加最不利工况荷载,并施加相应约束进行受力计算。

2.3 计算结果分析

最不利荷载工况下,扣锚梁ANSYS实体模型计算得到最大变形值为11.99mm,最大变形发生在牛腿结构的智能索锚点附近。新型扣锚梁整体ANSYS实体模型的等效应力(Von-Mises)计算结果如图4所示。红色区域的等效应力大于273MPa,其中扣锚梁整体中牛腿根部及部分加劲肋应力超限。对扣锚梁牛腿子结构进行局部计算后发现,相同位置下牛腿子结构的受力明显减小,结合Midas杆系模型分析结构的计算结果,可判断这些超限区域是由于压力奇异导致的局部应力超限,认为在实际工作中结构受力并未超过许用应力。

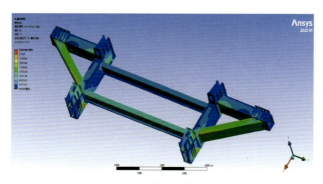

图4 扣锚梁的等效应力图
Fig. 4 Von-Mises of the buckle-anchor-beam

3 结论

以双堡特大桥斜拉扣挂吊装拱肋施工为实例,使用ANSYS等有限元分析软件进行索力最不利荷载工况下新型扣锚梁的内力计算并进行分析,得出了以下结论:

（1）该桥拱肋节段施工过程中新型扣锚梁结构等效应力不超过容许应力（273MPa），扣锚梁结构在增加牛腿构件后满足智能拉索的锚固需求，保证施工过程中新型扣锚梁的强度满足规范要求。

（2）该新型扣锚梁受力最大区域位于扣索锚固支座及牛腿子结构根部，可加强局部构造及调整板件尺寸来满足不同工程项目的施工需求。

参 考 文 献

[1] 陈宝春,刘君平.世界拱桥建设与技术发展综述[J].交通运输工程学报,2020,20(01)：27-41.

[2] 王瑀,储彤.大跨度钢箱拱桥拱肋安装控制技术[J].公路,2013(05):24-27.

[3] 郑皆连.大跨径拱桥的发展及展望[J].中国公路,2017(13):40-42.

[4] 郑皆连,等.500米级钢管混凝土拱桥建造创新技术[M].上海:上海科学技术出版社,2020.

[5] 段力,李元松,高学文.斜拉扣挂施工索梁锚固区的力学性能分析[J].中外公路,2020,40(06):174-178.

[6] 吴进明.缆索吊装斜拉扣挂法在钢管混凝土拱桥施工中的应用[J].宁夏工程技术,2007(01):57-60.

深山峡谷区隧间桥梁快速建造技术

许 诺[1]　牟廷敏[2]　李 畅[2]　康 玲[2]

（1.四川交通职业技术学院　四川成都　611130；
2.四川省公路规划勘察设计研究院有限公司　四川成都　610041）

摘　要　近年来，中国桥梁建设不断向深山峡谷等地域发展，以四川省为代表的山区公路建设桥隧比例高，沿线深山峡谷众多，两岸地势险峻陡峭，面临难以修建施工便道、材料和机械设备无法运输到桥址、场地狭窄、建设空间极其局促等诸多建设难题。尤其是需要隧道贯通后才能开展预制梁运输架设的隧间桥梁，由于隧道施工周期长，隧间桥梁经常成为影响全线竣工通车的控制性工程。本文依托典型的隧间桥梁工程——净跨140m 的五彝湾大桥，提出了一种便于快速施工的钢管混凝土桥梁及施工方法。通过本文提出的隧间拱桥设计方法，以及全装配化的预制件安装工艺和无须额外模板的施工方法，可加快隧道贯通后的桥梁施工进程。工程应用结果表明：依托工程采用本设计方案和施工工艺，节约建设成本1700万元，减少工期至6个月，即能克服可供隧间桥梁施工时间短的技术难题，又能保证大桥建造质量。

关键词　深山峡谷　隧间桥梁　快速建造　钢管混凝土　设计方法　施工方法
中图分类号　U443.35；U445.46　　**文献标识码**　A

Accelerated Construction Technology of Intertunnel Bridges in Deep Mountains and Valley Regions

XU Nuo[1]　MOU Tingmin[2]　LI Chang[2]　KANG Ling[2]

（1. Sichuan Communication Vocational and Technical College, Chengdu, Sichuan, 611130, China;
2. Sichuan Highway Planning, Survey, Design and Research Institute Co., Ltd, Chengdu, Sichuan, 610041, China）

Abstract　In recent years, China's bridge construction unceasingly develops into deep mountains and valley regions. Represented by Sichuan province, highways in mountainous areas have a high bridge-tunnel ratio. Along the

---

作者简介：
许诺（1994—），女，硕士，实习研究员，主要从事桥梁工程领域的教学和研究。
牟廷敏（1964—），男，学士，教授级工程师，主要从事桥梁工程和混凝土材料领域的设计和研究。
李畅（1993—），男，硕士，工程师，主要从事桥梁工程领域的设计和研究。
康玲（1988—），女，硕士，工程师，主要从事桥梁工程领域的设计和研究。

deep mountains and valley regions, with the steep terrain on both sides, which makes it extremely hard to build construction access, transport materials and mechanical equipment to the bridge site, highways in mountainous areas face difficulties in narrow sites, constrained construction space and many other construction problems. In particular, prefabricated beam transportation and erection of the tunnel bridge can only be carried out after the tunnel is completed. Because of the long tunnel construction period, the bridges between tunnels often become a controlling project that affects the completion and opening of the whole line. Based on a typical bridge between tunnels project, Wuyi Wan Bridge with a clear span of 140m, this paper proposes a concrete filled steel tube(CFST) bridge and its construction method which is convenient for accelerated construction. Through the design method of arch bridge between tunnels, the installation technology of prefabricated parts with full assembly and the construction method without extra template proposed in this paper, the construction process of bridge after tunnel penetration can be accelerated. The engineering application results show that the construction cost can be saved by 17 million yuan and the construction period can be reduced to 6 months, which can not only overcome the technical difficulties of short construction time for the tunnel bridge, but also ensure the construction quality of the bridge.

Keywords deep mountain and valley regions bridge between tunnels accelerated construction Concrete filled steel tube bridge Design method Construction method

E-mail 1339920909@qq.com

0 引言

山区公路建设地形起伏大,沿线巨型滑坡多,设计时多采用桥梁、隧道方式解决不良地质带来的基础建设难题,桥隧比例高,常出现桥隧相连的情况。当桥梁两端顺接隧道时,桥位处地形条件通常也面临 T 梁、小箱梁等常规桥梁的预制场地狭窄的困境。并且,桥梁两端隧道施工工作面小,建设空间局促,建设难度高,施工工期长,往往是整条线路工期的控制性工程。此外,若隧间桥梁采用常规预制桥梁,必须等两岸隧道施工完成后,才能进行预制梁的运输架设,这将进一步延长施工周期[1-2]。目前,对于深切峡谷中修建的中小跨径隧间桥梁,跨径在 60m 以下的桥梁,可采用单跨钢箱简支梁,通过贯通的隧道将钢箱梁运输到洞口采取顶推方式进行梁体架设,但当桥梁宽度大于隧道宽度时,钢箱梁可采用分幅制作、分幅顶推方式进行施工,顶推施工难度大,施工风险高,无法确保施工工期。跨径在 60m 以上的桥梁,若仍采用钢箱梁需要增大梁高或板件壁厚,若采用钢桁架梁桥,梁高较高,安装时需要在高度方向上分层顶推,施工难度将进一步增大[3-5]。在深切峡谷中修建跨径 60~150m 的隧间桥梁,为保证结构跨越能力,也可采用常规的拱桥结构。但常规拱桥结构单元尺寸大,利用隧道运输困难,工期压力大;并且在地形条件差的深切峡谷地区修建施工便道,施工难度骤增,建设成本高。因此,对于 60~150m 的隧间桥梁,当无法修建施工便道时,如何根据隧道的建设条件,提出一种合理的桥型和建造技术,满足施工速度快、难度低、经济性好等指标,对山区隧间桥梁的建造具有重要意义。

1 工程概况

五彝湾大桥全桥左右幅采用单跨 1~140m 的下承式哑铃型钢管混凝土拱桥,桥梁横梁为工字形,桥面板为波折钢-混凝土组合桥面板,两岸拱脚采用不等高布置方式以适应线路单向纵坡,其总体布置如图 1 所示。

图 1　五彝湾大桥总体布置图
Fig. 1　Overall layout of Wuyi Wan Bridge

2　关键技术

五彝湾大桥两岸接隧道，隧道长度超3800m，两岸地形陡峭，洞口间跨度大、地质灾害较多、桥位上跨五彝湾泥石流沟清水区，是典型的深山峡谷区隧间桥梁。桥梁孔跨布置需要考虑洪水和泥石流等地质灾害作用下的抗风险能力。若选择最为经济的简支梁桥，桥墩高度大，主梁与桥墩结构体系抗震能力差，跨径也不满足抗地质灾害要求[3]。因此，选择跨越能力大、承载能力高、经济性较好的下承式钢管混凝土拱桥方案。结合桥位处高陡边坡无法开设施工便道、无法搭设施工平台、依赖于两侧隧道贯通提供施工便道，开展桥梁施工的建设现状，又为避免隧间桥梁成为控制性工程而影响全线竣工通车时间，创新性地提出了一种适合隧间桥梁快速建造的设计与安装方法。

2.1　主拱结构构造

2.1.1　主拱设计

拱肋为单腹板哑铃型钢管混凝土结构，主拱净跨度为140m，净矢跨比为1/4.0，拱轴系数1.5。主拱径向高2.9m，主管直径1.2m，管内灌注C60混凝土，腹板采用带加劲肋的单腹板，腹板高0.5m。除靠近拱脚处的第一个节间距为5.5m，其余吊杆间距5m，在拱脚第一个吊杆节间范围内外包20cm厚的C40混凝土。拱肋中心间距15.75m，全桥共设置4道一字形横撑，每道横撑由四根主管及其支管形成的空间桁架组成，吊索采用15.2mm环氧喷涂钢绞线挤压成型为吊杆索体具体布置如图2、图3所示。

2.1.2　桥面系设计

桥面梁由工字钢横梁及其上的波折钢-混凝土组合桥面板组成，波折底钢板通过封板焊接在横梁上翼缘，波折底钢板厚8mm，波高17cm，波宽16cm，桥面板总厚度（含混凝土板和钢底板）为35cm，桥面铺装为8cm厚的改性沥青混凝土，钢-混凝土组合桥面板采用C40钢纤维混凝土。

2.1.3　拱座设计

拱桥拱座采用分离式拱座，分别设在隧道两侧洞口位置，桥台与隧道宽度一致。一方面，是由于桥梁路线净宽度（11.4m）宽于隧道净宽度（9.25m），另一方面，拱座直接设置在隧道洞口，可减少开挖、降低风险。

根据地形地质条件,两岸拱座采用重力式拱座和锚塞体拱座,拱座基础置于中风化基岩上。

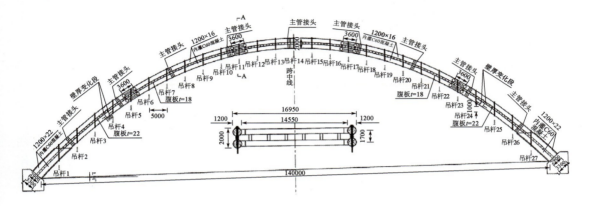

图 2　拱肋立面布置图(尺寸单位:mm)
Fig. 2　Elevation layout of arch rib

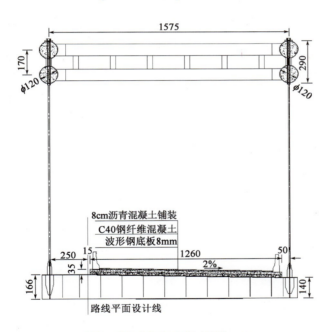

图 3　吊杆及桥面梁(尺寸单位:cm)
Fig. 3　Suspender and bridge deck beam

2.2　主拱内力计算

采用空间有限元软件 Midas Civi 建立该桥的整体模型进行内力计算。主桥一阶自振频率为 0.32HZ(主拱横向弯曲),主拱弹性稳定安全系数为 5.72(主拱横向失稳),主拱关键截面承载能力安全系数大于 1.2,如表 1 所示。可以看出,该钢管混凝土拱桥是一种受力合理,安全可靠的结构。

主拱承载能力验算结果 表1
Calculation results of bearing capacity of main arch Tab. 1

部 位	轴力(kN)	弯矩(kN·m)	结构抗力(kN)	安全系数
拱脚	-2.1×10^4	-2.06×10^4	2.76×10^4	1.20
$L/4$ 截面	-1.71×10^4	1.45×10^4	2.75×10^4	1.46
拱顶	1.57×10	1.78×10^4	2.03×10^4	1.33

2.3 关键施工技术

结合桥位地形特点和运输条件，主拱和桥面梁采用缆索吊装斜拉扣挂法进行安装，直接在山体上设置岩锚锚固吊装系统和扣挂系统。隧道贯通前，完成两岸岩锚施工，隧道贯通后在两岸岩锚上安装缆索和扣索形成缆索吊装系统。并且全桥钢结构加工制造、岩锚施工以及拱座开挖工作都可与隧道同步进行，隧道贯通6个月后即可完成大桥施工。

2.3.1 主拱加工及运输

受运输条件限制，全桥拆解成独立的、结构规则的、尺寸小的结构单元，隧道贯通前，在工厂内完成全桥结构单元的加工制造，包括主拱钢管、横撑、吊杆、钢横梁、波折桥面板等结构。加工完成的主拱单元在工厂进行预拼装，进行全面自检及复测，验收合格后方可运输至现场[6]。待隧道贯通后，全桥结构单元通过隧道运输到两岸的隧道洞口。

2.3.2 主拱安装

主拱钢管安装采用两岸对称悬臂安装(图4)。因隧道洞口场地狭窄，无法满足大尺寸构件安装空间需求，为控制节段尺寸，五彝湾大桥单片拱肋共分为10个节段，节段长度控制在13m内，径向高度小于3.3m，最大质量不超过20t。利用缆索吊装系统将主拱钢管从两岸的隧道洞口对称起吊至安装位置；利用主拱节段间的导向板进行快速定位，通过张拉扣索调整拱肋高程，使拱肋轴线位于设计高程，然后及时张拉缆风索，确保横向稳定，当安装误差满足规定要求后，连接节段接头，完成该节段主拱安装。

吊装顺序为每个节段内的上、下游拱肋及相应横撑同步进行，即每节段上游拱肋(或下游拱肋)→每节段下游拱肋(或上游拱肋)→每节段内横撑，以上步骤为一个循环，安装就位后再进行下节段的循环吊装，直至主拱合龙[7-8]。

图4 主拱安装
Fig. 4 Installation of main arch

2.3.3 管内混凝土灌注

主拱弦管内灌注C60高性能自密实混凝土，以泵压法、抽真空辅助法自拱脚向拱顶灌注[3]。C60混凝土中应掺入适量多功能高效减水和膨胀剂，且压注前应进行工地材料试验并测定各项性能指标是否满足要求；要求 C60 混凝土具有低泡、大流动性、收缩补偿、延后初凝（初凝时间应满足管内连续泵送要求）、不泌水、不分层、黏聚性能好和具有早强的工作性能[9-10]。

2.3.4 吊杆和桥面系施工

利用缆索吊装系统从两岸对称安装吊杆、钢横梁与波折钢板（图5）。首先将吊杆吊到拱肋下方，通过吊杆上端的锚具将吊杆锚固在拱肋上；然后将钢横梁从两岸隧道洞口对称起吊至安装位置与吊杆下端连接，最后将带端封板的波折钢板吊运至钢横梁顶面，通过焊接端封板将波折钢板固定在钢横梁上翼缘板。波折钢板安装完成后绑扎桥面钢筋，直接利用波折钢板和端封板作为模板浇筑桥面混凝土，无须额外安装模板，简化了工序，提高了施工效率，同时还减少了高空作业，降低施工风险。

图 5 吊杆和桥面梁安装
Fig. 5 Installation of suspenders and bridge deck beams

3 技术经济指标

通过对不同桥型的适用跨径、技术特点、工程造价进行比较，结果如表 2 所示。可以看出，在难以修建施工便道的深山峡谷区建造单跨超 100m 的隧间桥梁，本文提出的钢管混凝土拱桥，跨越能力强，施工简单，工期短，能实现隧间桥梁的快速建造，同时具有较好的经济优势，与钢箱梁相比，五彝湾大桥采用该方案可节约建设成本约 1700 万元。

技术经济指标 表 2
Technical and economic indicators Tab. 2

桥 型	适用跨径(m)	技术特点	工程造价(万元/m²)
简支梁	≤20	无施工便道时，桩基墩柱无法施工；有施工便道时，技术成熟，造价低	0.4
钢箱梁	≤60	施工工序较多	1.2
钢桁梁	70～100	桁高较高，利用隧道运输安装困难	1.4～1.6
钢管混凝拱桥	80～140	施工简单、工期短，全桥无模板化	0.75～0.95

4 结论

五彝湾大桥是一座便于快速施工的隧间拱桥，全桥可拆解成独立的、结构规则的预制构件，在施工便道无法到达桥址时，便于从高度、宽度均受限制的隧道中运输至洞口进行吊装。拱肋采用钢管混凝土结构、桥面板为波折钢-混组合桥面板兼做纵梁，解决了无法在局促空间运输、起吊体型庞大的格子梁问题,又节省钢纵梁材料用量。同时,在浇筑混凝土时无须额外搭设模板,提高施工效率,降低高空作业施工风险。隧道施工期间可同步开展桥梁结构工厂预制、两岸拱座开挖等工作,避免隧间桥梁成为全线控制性工程,隧道贯通6个月后可完成桥梁施工,该桥提出的快速建造技术可为深山峡谷区隧间桥梁的设计和施工提供技术参考。

参 考 文 献

[1] 陈军刚,陈孔令.西南山区常规桥梁设计典型问题分析[J].交通科技,2020(6):4.

[2] 卢昌明.山区高速公路常规桥梁设计要点分析[J].山东交通科技,2011,000(002):42-43,52.

[3] 汪红武,林梦果,代浩,等.山区装配式钢箱梁安装方案比选及施工关键技术[C]//2021年全国土木工程施工技术交流会论文集(上册).北京:人民交通出版社,2021.

[4] 张昱,程宏,边洪坡,等.窄箱型主梁钢-混组合结构桥梁在山区公路建设中应用研究[J].水电站设计,2020,36(2):5.

[5] 牟廷敏,梁健,李畅,等.一种便于快速施工的隧间拱桥及其施工方法:,CN110820519A[P].2020.

[6] 杨晓勇,胡伟.钢管混凝土拱桥拱肋制作工艺[J].中国公路,2014(11):2.

[7] 周水兴,向中富.桥梁工程(下册)[M].重庆:重庆大学出版社,2001.

[8] 张恒荣,姜海,程振国.大跨径钢管混凝土拱桥缆索吊装技术[J].公路交通科技:应用技术版,2012(6):4.

[9] 罗业凤,王建军,陈光辉.合江长江一桥拱肋钢管混凝土灌注施工[J].中外公路,2013,33(3):3.

[10] 刘斌.混凝土灌注顺序对哑铃型钢管混凝土拱的影响[J].现代交通技术,2008,5(2):4.

施工与监测

特大跨中承式钢筋混凝土肋拱桥成拱技术

康 玲　牟廷敏　范碧琨　王 戈

（四川省公路规划勘察设计研究院有限公司　四川成都　610041）

摘 要 钢筋混凝土拱桥主桥长度小、受力合理、全寿命周期维护成本低，成为深沟峡谷、地震多发等地区最具竞争力的桥型。特别是劲性骨架成拱的钢筋混凝土拱桥，无须支架、施工安全、截面参与施工受力，已经成为大跨钢筋混凝土拱桥建造的最优技术。原有劲性骨架法成拱技术，因为主拱结构构造差、骨架强度低、刚度小、外包混凝土施工环节多等原因，国内建设数量较少，尤其是特大跨径的中承式钢筋混凝土肋拱桥。为攻克技术难题，依托 320m 官盛渠江特大桥，对中承式劲性骨架钢筋混凝土拱桥再创新，提出了强劲骨架成拱法的特大跨中承式钢筋混凝土肋拱桥的建造技术，该技术提出的新结构、新材料、新工艺和新装备等科技成果，可简化特大跨钢筋混凝土拱桥施工流程、降低施工风险、节约施工工期，结构设计合理、材料利用率高、节约工程造价，社会经济效益十分显著。

关键词 特大跨拱桥　钢筋混凝土肋拱桥　中承式肋拱桥　强劲骨架技术　超高强钢管混凝土

中图分类号 TU398$^+$.9　　**文献标识码** A

Arch Formation Technology for Mega-Span Reinforced-Concrete-Ribbed Half-through Arch Bridges

KANG Ling　MOU Tingmin　FAN Bikun　WANG Ge

(Sichuan Highway Planning, Survey, Design and Research Institute Ltd., Chengdu, Sichuan, 610041, China)

Abstract The reinforced concrete arch bridge (RCAB) has become the most competitive bridge type in the deep valleys and earthquake-prone areas because of short main bridge, reasonable stress distribution and low cost for life-cycle maintenance. In particular, the RCAB with stiffened skeleton has become the optimal technology for the

---

作者简介：
康玲(1988—)，女，硕士，工程师，主要从事桥梁工程领域的设计和研究。
牟廷敏(1964—)，男，学士，教授级工程师，主要从事桥梁工程和混凝土材料领域的设计和研究。
范碧琨(1970—)，女，学士，教授级工程师，主要从事桥梁工程和混凝土材料领域的设计和研究。
王戈(1985—)，男，硕士，高级工程师，主要从事桥梁工程领域的设计和研究。

construction of mega-span RCAB. With higher safety, the RCAB with stiffened skeleton does not need extra support during construction, and its cross-section participates in resisting construction load. Due to the poor structure of main arch, low strength and stiffness of the skeleton, and excessive construction procedure of externally wrapped concrete, the original stiffened skeleton arch forming technology is rarely used in domestic construction, especially extra-large reinforced-concrete-ribbed half-through arch bridge. To overcome the technical problems, based on the 320m Guansheng Qujiang bridge, the RCAB with stiffened skeleton is innovated again, and the construction technology of mega-span reinforced-concrete-ribbed arch bridge with stiffened skeleton is proposed. The new structure, new material, new process and new equipment and other technological achievements proposed by this technology can simplify the construction process of the mega-span RCAB, reduce the construction risk and accelerate the construction period. Meanwhile, the proposed technology has obvious advantages of reasonable structural design, high utilization rate of material, low project cost, and remarkable social and economic benefits.

Keywords extra-large span arch bridges reinforced-concrete-ribbed arch bridge half-through ribbed arch bridge stiffened skeleton technology ultra-high-strength concrete-filled steel tube

E-mail 370236291@qq.com

0 引言

随着高速公路建设深入西部山区,高山峡谷地形居多,大跨桥梁建设增多,某高速公路20km长范围,300m左右的桥位规划多达20余处,但却面临区域地灾频发且经济欠发达的建设困境。通常,特大跨桥梁可选择桥型有悬索桥、斜拉桥和拱桥等,在相同桥位下,钢筋混凝土拱桥因主桥长度小、受力合理、建造成本低、后期维护成本少、抗灾性能好,而具有较强综合竞争力,因此300m左右钢筋混凝土拱桥市场建设需求巨大。

现代高速公路建设技术标准要求高,由路线高程决定的300m左右中承式特大跨钢筋混凝土拱桥,因跨径长、横向宽度大,建造面临几个技术难题:①综合考虑不影响车道布置、通行视线及行车舒适度几点因素,拱圈只能选择宽度较窄的肋式结构,且拱肋必须置于行车道宽度以外;与板式拱相比,减小宽度的肋拱承载力及刚度受到影响。②减小宽度的双肋拱桥受行车道宽度控制,肋间间距进一步加大,导致横撑长度大,其力学行为相当于受弯梁,分层浇筑过程,跨中混凝土弯矩大易开裂,施工极其困难。③施工常用的劲性骨架法外包钢筋混凝土分环次数过多,施工周期长,质量控制困难,且因跨径增大,劲性骨架腹杆稳定问题特别突出,缺乏先进的施工工艺和配套的施工设备。以320m官盛渠江特大桥为依托工程,从设计、材料、施工三方面取得技术成果,为同类桥梁建设提供技术支撑。

1 总体设计

官盛渠江特大桥为主跨320m的钢筋混凝土变截面双肋无铰中承式拱桥,矢跨比为1/4,拱轴系数为1.5。每片拱肋拱顶截面径向高3.5m,拱脚截面径向高6m,由超高强钢管混凝土主弦管和钢管腹杆连接形成全管结构强劲骨架,再外包C50混凝土形成宽3m的单箱单室梯形截面;两片拱肋间设置8道一字形箱形横撑形成全宽26m的主拱结构;钢格子梁上设置总厚度12.8cm的钢-混凝土组合桥面板形成超静定桥面梁结构;桥面梁与主拱之间采用整束挤压成型的钢绞线成品索体连接,形成拱梁结构体系;拱梁结构体系支撑于南北两岸重力式抗推力拱座基础上。结合地形、水文和通航特点,主拱强劲骨架安装采用缆索吊装、斜拉扣挂法,基于强劲骨架分2环外包钢筋混凝土形成主拱肋。

2 设计技术

2.1 拱肋等宽变高梯形截面构造技术

针对钢筋混凝土中承式肋拱桥,拱肋宽度窄、高度高的特点,提出了基于强劲骨架外包钢筋混凝土,形成梯形截面的强劲组合结构拱肋。主拱肋宽度仅3m,拱顶到拱底截面高由3.5m变化至6.0m,标准段顶、底、腹板厚0.65m,在拱脚段附近顶、底板厚度由0.65m线性变化至2.5m,腹板厚度由0.65m线性变化至1.0m(图1)。肋间通过数量少、刚度强劲的横撑支撑拱肋,形成强劲的主拱结构,既保证主拱承载力和刚度要求,又兼顾了主拱轻盈、美观的景观效果(图2)。

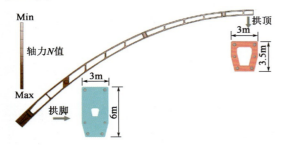 

图1 拱肋设计与内力变化关系　　　　图2 320m钢筋混凝土肋拱桥

Fig.1 The relationship between arch rib design and internal force　　Fig.2 320m reinforced-concrete-ribbed arch bridge

主拱以承受恒载为主,拱肋截面设计与其内力由拱顶至拱脚渐次递增规律匹配。计算得出拱顶截面安全系数1.48,拱脚1.38,满足受力要求;且全拱截面安全储备基本一致,材料利用率高。此设计构造,一阶自振频率0.205,动力特性满足要求。

2.2 拱肋强劲骨架构造技术

针对原有劲性骨架成拱技术主拱结构构造差、骨架强度低、刚度小,外包混凝土施工环节多的特点,首次提出了基于C100超高强钢管混凝土强劲主管、强劲腹管和强劲横撑,形成的拱肋强劲骨架构造(图3)。

图3 主拱强劲骨架构造

Fig.3 Stiffened skeleton structure of main arch

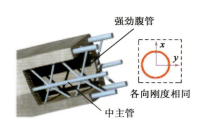

图 4 强劲骨架腹杆系构造
Fig. 4 The web member of stiffened skeleton

主拱主管采用 C100 超高强钢管混凝土构件,与 C60 钢管混凝土比较,承载能力提高约1.2倍、工程造价降低约40%、材料用量减少约28%。主拱腹杆采用各向刚度相同的强劲腹管代替传统型钢杆件、截面较高段落采用设置中主管的结构构造(图 4),保证了各项刚度均衡、腹杆长细比更小、刚度更大的强劲骨架腹杆的目标要求,腹杆稳定安全系数提高约 1.5 倍。腹管与主管在厂内通过相贯焊缝连接,简化连接节点构造,节省节点板材料用量 5% 及主拱骨架加工制造时间。

2.3 强劲骨架箱形横撑构造技术

针对钢筋混凝土中承式肋拱桥拱肋宽度窄、横向刚度弱的特点,提出了采用强劲的箱形截面形钢结构骨架,再外包钢筋混凝土成为箱形结构横撑。

由多肢角钢主弦杆、腹杆和横联杆连接形成的箱形截面强劲骨架满足一次外包钢筋混凝土的要求,避免逐层多次外包引起混凝土开裂等质量问题,达到成型质量高、耐久性好的目的;形成的箱形横撑构造简洁,抗弯、抗扭刚度大,与拱肋刚度匹配、造型风格一致。设计计算主拱 1 阶弹性稳定模态为纵向失稳,稳定系数 6.56,超出规范要求 1.64 倍。利用强劲骨架一次外包混凝土(图 5),无须额外临时施工设施、简化高空作业工序、降低施工难度,骨架兼作受力结构,可节省钢筋用量50%。

a)原有K形横撑

b)箱形结构横撑

图 5 构造简洁的箱形横撑
Fig. 5 Simple lateral box struts

3 材料技术

3.1 管内混凝土多功能外加剂与矿物掺合料降黏技术

针对超高强钢管混凝土 C100 胶材用量多,黏度大,泵送顶推难度大的问题,研制了多功能外加剂与矿物掺合料降黏技术:采用现代分子裁剪技术,在主链上引入阳离子酰胺吸附、分散基团(图 6),形成两性粒子改善吸附特性,增加对胶材粉体的强分散作用;侧链采用聚乙二醇醚等长聚醚基团提供强空间位阻效应,同时增设缓释基团,其水解释放小分子,强化颗粒之间的空间阻隔作用(图 7)。通过分散作用和空间位阻作用双重效应,实现超分散降黏、超长保坍能力,提高浆体流动性。采用具有极佳"滚珠效应"的粉煤灰微珠,降低水泥浆的剪切应力和塑性黏度(图 8),有效改善了混凝的工作性能。

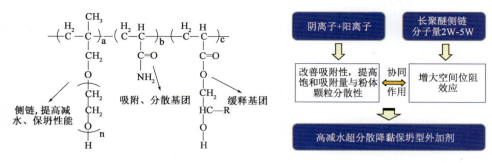

图6 分子链与官能基团设计
Fig. 6 Design of molecular chain and functional group

图7 减水剂作用机理
Fig. 7 Mechanism of water reducingagent

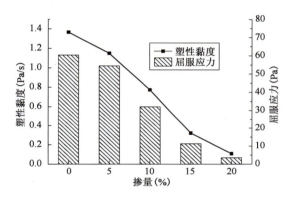

图8 微珠对浆体流变性影响
Fig. 8 Effect of microsphere on rheological properties of slurry

3.2 管内混凝土多膨胀源复合补偿收缩技术

针对超高强钢管混凝土C100胶材高,混凝土自收缩大,普通膨胀剂中后期膨胀效果差的问题,通过不同膨胀源材料匹配设计,利用EA型和HCSA型膨胀剂提升早期膨胀效应,采用氧化镁型膨胀剂保持后续膨胀(图9),实现混凝土全周期微膨胀控制。

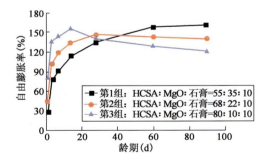

图9 不同膨胀剂复配比例下混凝土的膨胀性能
Fig. 9 Expansion performance of concrete with different proportions of expansive agent

3.3 管内混凝土内养护减缩技术

针对超高强钢管混凝土C100水胶比低,且与外界无水分交换的问题,基于"高吸水-稳定储水-可控释水"的设计思路,以高亲水性淀粉为骨架,以带-$CONH_2$等亲水基团的不饱和烃为支链(图10),开发内养护聚合物,其亲水基团提供聚合物吸液动力与储水稳定性,当混凝土内部湿度降低时,内养护聚合物释放水分,促进水泥、膨胀剂等持续水化,起到内养护作用,减小收缩(图11、图12)。

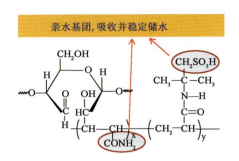

图10 内养护材料分子结构

Fig. 10 Molecular structure of internal maintenance materials

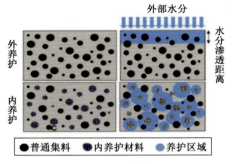

图11 释水内养护示意

Fig. 11 Schematic diagram of water release and internal maintenance

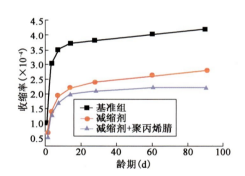

图12 减缩剂对收缩的影响

Fig. 12 Effect of shrinkage-reducing agent on shrinkage

采用发明的额定粉体材料用量的密实骨架计算集料组成设计的计算方法,进行集料组成与胶材设计,配合开发的多功能外加剂与矿物掺合料降黏技术、多膨胀源复合补偿收缩与内养护减缩技术,制备出的C100自密实补偿收缩机制砂高性能混凝土,扩展度超过650mm、初凝时间长达10h、28d自由膨胀率万分之1.41、胶凝材料总用量560kg/m³、28d抗压强度达119.4MPa、材料造价980元/m³。

3.4 强劲骨架力学性能研究及承载力计算方法

根据单肢、哑铃形、箱形等30组超高强钢管混凝土试件(图13),进行轴压、偏压、受弯试验,得出超高强钢管混凝土与普通钢管混凝土力学行为一样,具有较好的延性性能(图14),其力学行为符合钢管混凝土"统一理论",奠定超高强钢管混凝土构件计算的理论基础。根据是否受管内混凝土强度等级影响,对超高强钢管混凝土轴压、偏压、抗弯、抗剪承载力,提出理论计算公式,或延用普通钢管混凝土构件承载力计算公式增加修正系数(图15)。

图13 超高强钢管混凝土试验

Fig. 13 Ultra-high-strength concrete-filled steel tube test

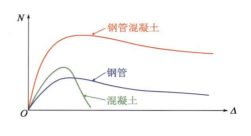

图14 荷载-位移曲线

Fig. 14 Load-displacement curve

受力类型	普通钢管混凝土	超高强钢管混凝土
轴压承载力	$\gamma N \leq \varphi_1 K_p K_d f_{sc} A_{sc}$ $f_{sc}=(1.14+1.02\xi_0)f_{cd}$	$\gamma N \leq \varphi_1 K_p K_d f_{sc} A_{sc}$ $f_{sc}=(1.490+0.689\xi_0)f_{cd}$
偏压承载力	$\gamma N \leq \varphi_1 \varphi_e K_p K_d f_{sc} A_{sc}$	$\gamma N \leq \varphi_1 \varphi_e K_p K_d f_{sc} A_{sc}$
抗弯承载力	$\gamma M \leq \gamma_m W_{sc} f_{sc}$	$\gamma M \leq \gamma_m W_{sc} f_{sc}$
抗剪承载力	$\lambda V \leq \gamma_v A_{sc} \tau_{sc}$ $\xi \geq 0.85,\ \gamma_v=0.85$ $\xi<0.85,\gamma_v=1.0$	$\lambda V \leq \gamma_v A_{sc} \tau_{sc}$ $\gamma_v=-0.2953+1.2981\sqrt{\xi_0}$

图15 普通钢管混凝土与超高强钢管混凝土承载力计算公式对比

Fig. 15 Comparison of calculation formulas for bearing capacity of ordinary concrete-filled steel tube and ultra-high strength concrete-filled steel tube

并通过3组主拱缩尺模型(图16)试验研究表明,超高强钢管混凝土主拱骨架与外包钢筋混凝土的组合截面,承载力提高约35%、刚度提高约10%。结合数学物理模型和力学原理,建立了超高强钢管混凝土强劲骨架形成的组合截面主拱的承载力计算方法(图17)。该方法计算值与试验值比值平均为0.948,标准偏差0.078,满足可靠度计算要求。

图16 缩尺模型试验

Fig. 16 Scale model test

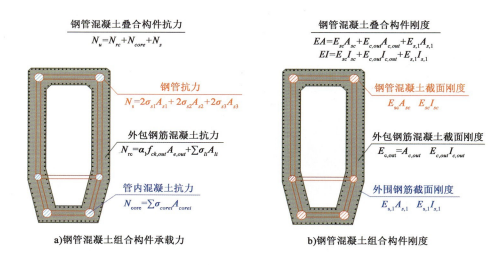

图 17 钢管混凝土组合构件承载力及刚度计算图示

Fig. 17 Calculation for bearing capacity and stiffness of composite concrete-filled steel tube members

4 施工技术

4.1 多功能轻型化施工平台技术

针对主拱外包混凝土高空作业难度大、风险高的问题,发明了由平台悬吊系统、型钢分配梁、缆索吊装系统组成的多功能轻型化施工平台装备(图18),攻克了操作平台、模板安装、材料堆放等高空作业难题,与常规施工平台比较,减轻重量约50%、节约临时材料52%。

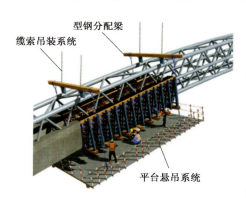

图 18 多功能轻型化施工平台

Fig. 18 Multifunctional light construction platform

4.2 拱圈2环外包混凝土施工工艺技术

普通主拱骨架,刚度小、强度低,外包钢筋混凝土一般分为8环合龙成拱,施工周期长达13个月,外包混凝土施工缝多、结构整体性差,模板反复在高空搬运、安全风险高。基于本项目提出的强劲骨架法、多功能轻型化施工平台装备,首次提出了底板和一部分腹板+剩余部分腹板与顶板,共计2环外包钢筋混凝土合龙成拱技术(图19)。外包钢筋混凝土分环次数由8次减少到2次,节约工期8月,且施工缝少、主拱整体性高。

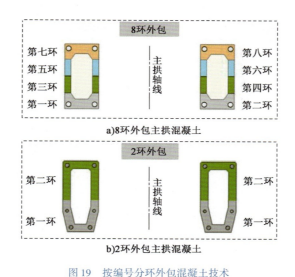

图 19 按编号分环外包混凝土技术
Fig. 19 Technology of external concrete wrapped in order

5 结论

项目提出的新结构、新材料、新工艺和新装备等科技成果支撑了世界最大跨度钢筋混凝土肋式拱桥主跨 320m 四川广安渠江大桥的顺利修建,该桥于 2018 年建成通车,主拱主管采用 C100 超高强钢管混凝土构件形成强劲骨架,主拱分 2 环外包混凝土,建安费 1.36 亿元,通车至今未出现任何质量问题。与斜拉桥比较,节省钢材 5084t,混凝土用量 2.3 万 m^3,缩短工期 6 个月,节约造价 4150 万元,社会经济效益显著。

参 考 文 献

[1] 梁健,肖雨,郑旭峰.凉山州金阳县金沙江溜索改桥设计技术进步[J].四川建筑,2018(01):173-176.

[2] 陈锦阳,韩林海,牟廷敏,等.拱形钢管混凝土加劲混合结构力学性能试验研究[J].西南公路,2018(03):85-91.

[3] 杨永清,文亚男,刘振宇.钢管混凝土劲性骨架对拱桥性能影响分析[J].西南公路,2013,(4):2-4.

[4] 丁庆军,徐意,牟廷敏.高石粉机制砂制备 C100 钢管混凝土的研究与应用[J].混凝土,2017(11):1-4.

[5] 丁庆军,刘凯,张高展,等.$MgSO_4$ 侵蚀条件下水泥浆体相组成及 Al 相转变[J].武汉理工大学学报,2016,38(5):1-7.

[6] 龚进.钢筋混凝土拱桥拱肋内灌 C100 混凝土施工工艺[J].江西建材,2018(03):62-63.

[7] 黄兴胜.磨刀溪特大桥索塔区小箱梁架设关键技术[J].西南公路,2017(02)-017.

天峨龙滩特大桥缆索吊机设计与试验研究

匡志强　罗小斌　侯凯文　唐雁云　叶增鑫

（广西路桥工程集团有限公司　广西南宁　530200）

摘　要　山区大跨径拱桥的缆索吊机设计与施工受地形地势影响，实施难度大。本文依托于主桥为600m上承式劲性骨架混凝土拱桥的天峨龙滩特大桥项目，采用理论分析，试吊试验等研究手段，对缆索吊机的布置与结构设计开展研究，再结合吊装试验对其进行验证，研究内容如下：(1) 通过方案对比，采用"吊扣分离"的缆索吊机总体设计；(2) 结合山区地形，因地制宜地提出主索、地锚、吊塔等缆索系统主要构筑物的设计形式；(3) 综合试吊配置、试吊方法、试吊流程等方面，制定出详细的缆索吊机试吊方案，再对比监测数据和数值模拟结果验证其可行性。结果表明，天峨龙滩特大桥缆索吊机结构安全，机具设备运行良好，满足设计和施工要求，为今后类似山区拱桥建设提供参考依据。

关键词　劲性骨架混凝土拱桥　缆索吊装系统　试吊　总体设计　数据分析

中图分类号　TU398$^+$.9　　**文献标识码**　A

Design and Experimental Study of Cable Crane for Tian'e Longtan Bridge

KUANG Zhiqiang　LUO Xiaobin　HOU Kaiwen　TANG Yanyun　YE Zengxin

(Guangxi Road and Bridge Engineering Group Co., Ltd., Nanning, Guangxi, 530200, China)

Abstract　The design and construction of cable crane for long-span arch bridge in mountainous areas are influenced by terrain. The structural form of Tian'e Longtan bridge is rigid skeleton concrete arch bridge. Relying on the project, the layout and structural design of the cable crane were studied by means of theoretical analysis and trial hoisting test. Further, the feasibility verification was combined with the hoisting test. The research contents were as follows：(1) The overall design of the cable crane was adopted through scheme comparison, which the lifting tower and buckle tower were separated. (2) Combined with the mountainous terrain, the design types of the main structures of the cable system such as the cable, ground anchor and lifting tower were proposed. (3) Based on the configuration, method and process of trial hoisting, a detailed trial hoisting scheme of cable crane was formulated. Meanwhile, the feasibility was verified by comparing the monitoring data and numerical simulation results. The results show that the cable crane structure of Tian'e Longtan bridge was secure, which meets the design and construction requirements. The case provides a reference basis for the construction of arch bridges in mountainous areas in the future.

Keywords　rigid skeleton concrete arch bridge　cable hoisting system　trial hoisting　overall design　data analysis

E-mail　429659917@qq.com.

600m级劲性骨架混凝土拱桥外包混凝土模板体系设计与施工

唐雁云　罗小斌　沈　耀　匡志强

(广西路桥工程集团有限公司　广西南宁　530011)

摘　要　劲性骨架混凝土拱桥的外包混凝土施工难度大,其模板体系的设计与施工则决定了拱桥的建设成败。依托于主桥为600m上承式劲性骨架混凝土拱桥的天峨龙滩特大桥项目,结合其底板环、腹板环、顶板环三环浇筑的划分原则,采用理论分析、数值模拟和模型试验等研究手段,分别开展模板体系的设计与施工技术研究。主要内容如下:(1)通过提前挂设底模,形成上下弦施工通道,解决作业人员拱上通行问题;(2)将腹板设计为标准大块模板和梯形大块模板,解决外包混凝土线型和外观质量问题;(3)设计施工吊架以及悬吊式平台,解决三环模板的施工问题,保障作业人员安全;(4)利用Midas civil软件,验证模板体系的强度和刚度,调整模板尺寸,保证模板的可靠性。通过对模板体系的设计,在保障外包混凝土施工质量和安全的前提下,提高了施工效率,为后续大跨径劲性骨架拱桥外包混凝土施工提供可靠参考价值。

关键词　拱桥　劲性骨架　外包混凝土　模板设计　施工平台

中图分类号　TU398$^+$.9　　**文献标识码**　A

Design and Construction of Outsourcing Concrete Formwork System for 600m Grade Stiff Frame Concrete Arch Bridge

TANG Yanyun　LUO Xiaobin　SHEN Yao　KUANG Zhiqiang

(Guangxi Road and Bridge Engineering Group Co., Ltd., Nanning, Guangxi, 530011, China)

Abstract　The construction of outsourcing concrete of the rigid skeleton concrete arch bridge is complicated. The design and construction of its formwork system determines the success or failure of the arch bridge construction.

作者简介:

唐雁云(1997—),男,学士,助理工程师,主要从事大跨度拱桥施工技术研发及管理方面的研究。

罗小斌(1985—),男,学士,高级工程师,主要从事大跨度拱桥施工技术研发及管理方面的研究。

沈耀(1978—),男,学士,高级工程师,主要从事大跨度拱桥施工技术研发及管理方面的研究。

匡志强(1991—),男,学士,工程师,主要从事大跨度拱桥施工技术研发及管理方面的研究。

Relying on the Tian'e Longtan Bridge Project whose main bridge is a 600m top-loaded stiff skeleton concrete arch bridge, combined with the three-ring pouring principle of bottom ring, abdomen ring and roof ring, the design and construction technology of formwork system were studied. Theoretical analysis, numerical simulation, model test and other research methods were adopted. The main contents are as follows: (1) The upper and lower chord construction channels were formed by pre-hanging the bottom formwork to solve the problem of workers passing through the arch; (2) The abdomen ring were designed as standard combination formwork and trapezoidal combination formwork combined to solve the outsourcing concrete line type; (3) The construction hangers and suspended platforms were designed to solve the construction problems of three-ring formwork and ensure the safety of operators; (4) The strength and stiffness of the formwork system were calculated by Midas civil software. Meanwhile, the size of the formwork were adjusted to ensure the reliability of the template. Through the design of the formwork system, not only the quality and safety of the outsourced concrete construction were ensured, but also the construction efficiency was improved. A reliable reference value was provided for the subsequent outsourced concrete construction of the large-span stiff skeleton arch bridge.

KEYWORDS　arch bridge　rigid skeleton　outsourced concrete　template design　construction platform
E-mail　1940291429@qq.com

0　引言

混凝土拱桥具有刚度大、承载潜力大、经济性好、对温度敏感度感性低等特点,近年来在山区高速铁路和高等级公路建设中受到青睐[1-2]。随着社会的发展,劲性骨架混凝土拱桥越来越受欢迎,其跨径更大,且劲性骨架可直接作为混凝土悬浇模板的支撑,减少了施工过程中的安全风险。在劲性骨架拱桥中,主拱圈外包混凝土的施工通常采用分环分段的浇筑方法,其施工质量是劲性骨架混凝土拱桥整个施工工作的重点,直接影响到大桥的使用年限,因此混凝土模板的设计和施工至关重要。

1　工程背景

1.1　工程概况

天峨龙滩特大桥是南丹至天峨下老高速公路的控制性工程,大桥位于河池市天峨县龙滩水电站上游6km处。全长2488.55m,其中主桥长624m,采用上承式劲性骨架混凝土拱桥方案,计算跨径600m,为世界上拱桥首次突破600m级跨径。大桥矢高为125m,矢跨比$f=1/4.8$,拱轴系数$m=1.9$,拱箱单肋采用单箱单室变高度截面,拱顶截面高8m,拱脚截面高12m,宽6.5m。劲性骨架采用钢管混凝土结构,管内填充C80自密实微膨胀混凝土,拱上采用空心或实心矩形混凝土立柱,桥面主梁为10×40m预制T梁,主桥两侧连接72m+135m+72m预应力混凝土连续刚构(图1)。

拱圈采用钢管混凝土劲性骨架法施工,先施工钢管混凝土劲性骨架,再以劲性骨架为支撑,施工外包混凝土。钢管混凝土劲性骨架采用缆索吊运斜拉扣挂工艺悬臂拼装,再进行管内混凝土灌注;外包混凝土采用3环7段8工作面施工工艺,共需浇筑C60混凝土约28000m³。大桥最大倾角43°,高空施工条件受限制,模板、钢筋安装困难,施工难度大(图2)。

图 1　天峨龙滩特大桥效果图
Fig. 1　The bridge Effect Diagram

图 2　外包混凝土拱肋断面图
Fig. 2　Cross section of wrapped concrete arch rib

2　外包混凝土模板体系设计

2.1　底板模板设计

底板环模板组成分为底模+外侧模+内模+压模+端模五部分，通过以折代曲控制外包混凝土线性，底板模板除外侧为为钢膜外，其余部分均为木模。底板底模在拱肋翻身后，拱肋吊装前，在钢结构加工厂安装拱肋，随同节段一起吊装。解决空中底板安装难题，同时底板环施工时，利用底模两端伸出的横梁作为平台骨架，铺设钢跳板及三角木，安装护栏，形成作业人员上下拱肋的施工通道，解决拱上通行和施工平台的问题。外包混凝土底板模板布置如图 3 所示。

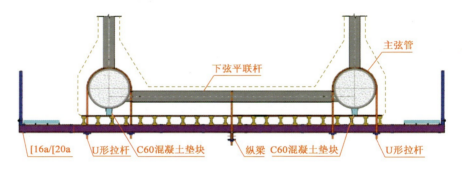
图 3　外包混凝土底板模板布置图
Fig. 3　Layout of Formwork for Outsourced Concrete Bottom Slab

2.2　腹板模板设计

腹板环模板分为外侧模+内侧模+压模+端模四部分，主拱最外侧侧模不受杆件的干扰，采用大块模板施工，解决外包混凝土线型和外观质量问题；内侧外侧模受横联、X 撑的干扰，内侧模受上弦平联杆件及横隔的影响，均采用小块散拼形式。

大桥腹板模板均由竹胶板+木工梁+背楞组合而成，模板的高度虽拱肋高度的变化而变化，腹板与底板一样，采取以折代曲方式匹配拱肋线形。腹板施工时，外侧设置吊架平台，作为腹板钢筋、模板安装的施工平台，吊架高度随着拱肋变化设计不同高度，满足腹板全高度施工需求，腹板内侧则搭设扣件式脚手架作为施工平台，脚手架底部设置通道，满足模板搬运需求（图 4）。

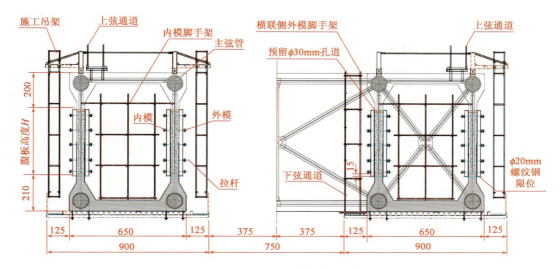

图 4　外包混凝土腹板模板布置图(尺寸单位:cm)

Fig. 4　Outsource concrete web formwork layout(Unit:cm)

2.3　顶板模板设计

顶板环模板分为外侧模+内侧模+压模+端模四部分,除外侧模采用钢模以外,其余均采用木模,顶板结构与底板结构相似,只需将底板环的外侧模、内模翻转180°,即可用于顶板环,其中顶板环内模设计为拼装单元,在箱内拼装成整体,再吊运至安装位置,减小空中模板的安装难度。顶板施工时,外侧模、外侧钢筋安装同样采用吊架平台和脚手架作为施工平台,箱内设悬吊式平台(图5)。

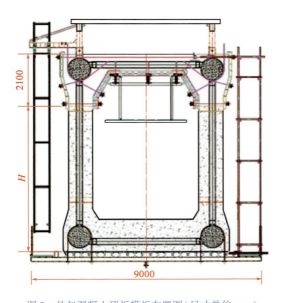

图 5　外包混凝土顶板模板布置图(尺寸单位:mm)

Fig. 5　Layout of formwork for outsourced concrete top(Unit:mm)

3 结论

以天峨龙滩特大桥外包混凝土施工为基础,进行模板体系的设计,结论如下:

(1)该桥跨径大,矢跨比高,混凝土用量多,外包混凝土的施工具有巨大的安全风险和质量风险,施工设计应尽量利用劲性骨架作为模板体系的支撑点,进行模板专项设计,才能保证混凝土的施工质量。

(2)外包混凝土的施工应仔细考虑相应的施工平台的设计,提供作业人员有安全保障的平台,才能实现混凝土的顺利施工,降低施工安全风险。

(3)劲性骨架混凝土拱桥的外包混凝土施工技术,是一项难度巨大的控制性工程,外包混凝土模板体系的研能有效降低施工难度和风险,提高混凝土的施工质量,保证桥梁的使用寿命,经济效益十分明显。

参 考 文 献

[1] 郑皆连.我国大跨径混凝土拱桥的发展新趋势[J].重庆交通大学学报(自然科学版),2016,35(增1):8-11.

[2] 陈宝春,刘君平.世界拱桥建设与技术发展综述[J].交通运输工程学报,2020,20(01):27-41.

施工与监测

基于叩击声信号和决策树的钢管混凝土结构近壁脱空深度检测

陈冬冬[1]* 沈周辉[1] 汪 莹[2]

(1. 南京林业大学土木工程学院 江苏南京 210037;
2. 中国建筑第五工程局有限公司 湖南长沙 410007)

摘 要 对钢管混凝土结构来说,表面下脱粘等近壁脱空的检测是一项繁重而费力的工作。为解决这一问题,本研究提出了一种新颖而简单的方法,将叩击声信号与机器学习方法相融合,将决策树模型用于训练中来检测不同深度的近壁脱空,并铸造了一个 CFST 试件,其中有三个深度分别为 3cm、5cm 和 8cm 的人工脱空,利用功率谱密度(PSD)对录制的声音信号进行分析。根据 PSD,提取 1~10kHz、间隔为 1000Hz 的 PSD 值总和作为决策树的属性。为了证明所提出的方法的可行性,随机选择了所有收集的信号中的 85% 来训练决策树,并使用剩下的 15% 记录的声音信号来验证决策树的有效性。这个过程重复了 100 次,以检验所提出的机器学习模型的鲁棒性。试验结果表明,100 次重复验证的平均精度高达 96.33%。因此,该方法在钢管混凝土结构的近壁脱空检测和评估中具有很大的潜力。

关键词 钢管混凝土结构(CFST) 决策树 机器学习 叩击声信号 功率谱密度(PSD)

中图分类号 TU375 **文献标识码** A

Depth Detection of Subsurface Voids in Concrete-filled Steel Tubular (CFST) Structure Using Percussion and Decision Tree

CHEN Dongdong[1]* SHEN Zhouhui[1] WANG Ying[2]

(1. College of Civil Engineering, Nanjing Forestry University, Nanjing, Jiangsu, 210037, China;
2. China Construction Fifth Engineering Co., Ltd., Changsha, Hunan, 410007, China)

Abstract The detection of interface debonding, such as subsurface voids, is a burdensome and laborious task

---

作者简介:
* 陈冬冬(1992—),男,博士,副教授,主要从事基于智能材料与算法的结构健康监测的研究。
沈周辉(1999—),男,硕士研究生,主要从事基于机器学习算法的界面脱空检测的研究。
汪莹(1989—),男,硕士,高级工程师,主要从事土木工程施工技术的研究。

for concrete filled steel tubular (CFST) structures. This study presents a novel but simple method by combing the percussion with machine learning method to solve the problem. A decision tree model was trained for detecting different depths of subsurface voids. A CFST specimen, which has three artificial voids with the depths of 3cm, 5cm and 8cm, was casted for the test. The power spectrum density (PSD) was applied to analyze the recorded sound signals. According to the PSD, the summation of PSD value from 1 kHz to 10 kHz with the interval of 1000 Hz were extracted for the attributes of decision trees. In order to demonstrate the feasibility of the proposed method, we randomly selected 85% of all collected signals to train the decision tree, and used the remaining 15% recorded sound signals to validate the decision tree. The process was repeated 100 times to examine the robustness of the proposed machine learning model. Experimental results demonstrated that the average correction rate of the 100 repeated validations is up to 96.33%. Therefore, the proposed approach has great potential in subsurface void inspection and evaluation for CFST structures.

Keywords　concrete-filled steel tubular structures (CFST)　decision tree　machine learning　percussion　Power Spectrum Density (PSD)

E-mail　chendongjt@163.com

0　引言

随着 CFST 结构截面的增大,大体积混凝土和近壁脱空的收缩会导致混凝土核心和钢管之间的脱粘和空隙脱空。脱空的检测仍然是一个难题,因为损坏隐藏在结构内部,无法直接检测。

脱空检测的现场检测方法包括破坏性和非破坏性方法。由于钻孔取样法具有简单直接的优点,在混凝土试验中被广泛使用[1]。然而,作为一种传统的破坏性方法,它并不适合于钢筋混凝土结构。超声波方法,如声发射[2]、超声波检测[3]和冲击回波方法[4]为检测隐藏在 CFST 结构中的脱空提供了不同的解决方案,但需要将大量的传感器嵌入或粘结在被检测结构上[5]。此外,基于超声波的方法通常要求检测人员具有几十年的专业经验,以从成千上万的正常测试信号中区分出脱空信号。因此,费力而复杂的检测过程限制了上述所有脱空检测方法的应用。

受传统疾病诊断方法中以叩击声作为判断人体健康状态标准的启发,本文利用叩击法检测 CFST 结构现场检测中的脱空位置和深度。试验结果表明,对于识别不同深度的脱空,所提出的方法可以获得较高的精度。这是一种检测 CFST 结构中脱空的有效方法。

1　CFST 脱空检测模型

1.1　决策树原理

决策树可以为机器学习建立有效且高效的模型[6]。决策树的分类可以被认为是一个"if-then"的策略,它包含三个部分:特征选择、决策树构建、决策树剪枝。其中有很多算法:ID3(交互式二分法版本 3)[7]、C4.5[8]、分类和回归树(CART)[9]、分类树快速算法(FACT)[10],通用无偏交互检测和估计(GUIDE)[11],快速无偏高效统计树(QUEST)[12]等。其中,CART 算法具有易于理解和解释的优点,对数据准备的要求不高,并且能够处理数字和分类数据。因此,本文应用 CART 算法对叩击信号数据进行分类。对于 CART 算法来说,关键是 Gini 系数的计算。

假设一组属性 p 有 Γ 类，$i\in\{1,2,3,\cdots,k\}$，k 是分类标签的数量。Gini 系数见式（1）：

$$GI(p) = \sum_{i=1}^{k} p_i(1-p_i) \tag{1}$$

除了 Gini 系数，还有其他因素影响 CART 算法的预测准确性，如剪枝。由于篇幅有限，这里不做讨论。关于停止规则、剪枝、树序列和树选择的更多详细信息可以在文献[13]中找到。

1.2 叩击声信号获取

1.2.1 试件准备及实验设置

CFST 试样包括两部分：钢管和核心混凝土。如图 1 所示，在浇筑核心混凝土之前，在钢管中间做了三个不同深度的人工脱空，分别为 30mm、50mm 和 80mm。钢管的厚度、高度和内径分别为 5mm、400mm 和 340mm。任何两个脱空之间的角度为 120°。核心混凝土的强度为 40MPa，每个脱空的宽度和长度分别为 100mm 和 100mm。

因为叩击时间很短（<0.1s），所以叩击声信号的采样率为 500kHz。声音记录设备[CCP 自由场 QC 麦克风（系列号为 238064）和麦克风处理器]被用来记录叩击声信号。此外，数据采集设备还包括一个数据采集卡（NI USB-6366）和一台带有数据采集系统的笔记本电脑。

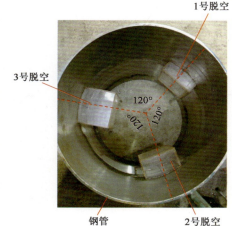

图 1 浇筑混凝土前的钢管柱

Fig. 1 The steel tubular column before casting concrete

1.2.2 数据采集和特征提取

与脱空区域相比，叩击点非常小。不同的叩击点会产生不同的声音。对脱空区域的所有点进行采样是非常重要的。因此，所有三个脱空区被分为 36 个小的子区，每个小子区被敲击五次。因此，每个脱空都记录了 180 个叩击声信号，并收集了 720 个信号用于训练决策树数据库。图 2a）、b）、c）显示了三个脱空的划分的子区。

a）1号脱空区　　b）2号脱空区　　c）3号脱空区

图 2 三个被分割的子区

Fig. 2 Three divided subzones

由于是随机敲击，记录信号的振幅是不同的。为了提取叩击信号的属性，采用了功率谱密度（PSD）。对于脱空和非脱空的信号，敲击信号的频率范围主要在 0～10kHz。然而，试验表

347

明,脱空和非脱空的 PSD 信号的频率是不同的。因此,应该从 PSD 处理的信号中提取适当的属性。PSD 信号被归一化为式(2):

$$N_i = \frac{y_i}{\max(y_j)} \tag{2}$$

式中,$i=j=1,2,3,\cdots,n$,n 为序号;y_i 为 PSD 信号;$\max(y_i)$ 为 PSD 信号的最大振幅;N_i 为归一化的 PSD 信号。

1.3 机器学习模型识别流程

数据选择对于训练和测试决策树非常重要。在本文的模型中,四个类别中 85% 的数据是随机和平均选择的。因此,612 个信号被用作训练数据,其他 108 个信号被用作测试数据。这个过程重复了 100 次,以测试提出的决策树模型的鲁棒性。

通过计算四个类中所有九个属性的 GI 值,可以得到最大的 GI 值为 0.75;然后,根据根节点,在 PSD 总和小于或等于 0.263 的条件下,将训练数据分为两个子集。其余数据的 GI 值将在同一迭代中计算。当所有子集的 GI 值为零时,迭代将停止。

为了评估所提出的决策树算法的鲁棒性,我们实施了 100 次重复测试结果。图 3 给出了 100 次测试的准确性的详细信息。总的来说,100 次测试的平均精度为 96.33%。该结果表明,这是一种可行的、有效的不同深度脱空检测方法,具有较高的准确性。

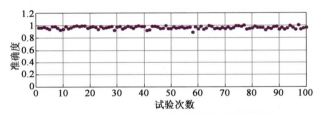

图 3　100 次重复试验的四个深度脱空的总体精度

Fig.3　The overall precision of four depths void for 100 repetition test

2 结论

本文提出了一种基于机器学习的 CFST 结构中的近壁脱空检测方法。敲击法被应用于"诊断"脱空的深度。本试验用功率谱密度(PSD)来分析记录的声音信号。根据 PSD 信号,从 1kHz 到 10 kHz,间隔为 1kHz 的功率谱密度和被提取出来用于决策树的属性。随机选择 612 个叩击信号进行训练,并选择 108 个叩击信号进行测试,这个过程重复了 100 次。四个深度的脱空总体准确度为 96.33%,这表明所提出的方法可以对不同深度的脱空进行高精度的分类。此外,还得到了对每个脱空深度的预测结果。可以得出的结论是,尽管每个深度的脱空的测试量不足,但预测精度很高,可以识别不同程度的脱空。

参 考 文 献

[1] Liu Jiahai, Yu Dingyong, Wang Guofu, et al. Size effect of core samples on bridge concrete strength with drilled core method[C].//2015 International Conference on Intelligent Transportation, Big Data and Smart City, IEEE, 2015:725-728.

[2] Xue Junqing, Briseghella B, Chen Baochun. Effects of debonding on circular CFST stub columns[J]. Journal of Constructional Steel Research, 2012, 69(1): 64-76.

[3] Iyer S, Sinha S K, Tittmann B R, et al. Ultrasonic signal processing methods for detection of defects in concrete pipes[J]. Automation in Construction, 2012, 22: 135-148.

[4] Sansalone M. Impact-echo: The complete story[J]. Structural Journal, 1997, 94(6): 777-786.

[5] Xu Bin, Chen Hongbing, Xia Song. Numerical study on the mechanism of active interfacial debonding detection for rectangular CFSTs based on wavelet packet analysis with piezoceramics[J]. Mechanical Systems and Signal Processing, 2017, 86: 108-121.

[6] Begenova S B, Avdeenko T V. Building of fuzzy decision trees using ID3 algorithm[C].// Journal of Physics: Conference Series. IOP Publishing, 2018, 1015(2): 022002.

[7] Quinlan J R. Induction of decision trees[J]. Machine learning, 1986, 1(1): 81-106.

[8] Quinlan J R. C4. 5: programs for machine learning[M]. Elsevier, 2014.

[9] Leo B, Friedman J H, Olshen R A, et al. Classification And Regression Trees. Chapman et [M]. 1984.

[10] Loh W Y, Vanichsetakul N. Tree-structured classification via generalized discriminant analysis[J]. Journal of the American Statistical Association, 1988, 83(403): 715-725.

[11] Loh W Y. Improving the precision of classification trees[J]. The Annals of Applied Statistics, 2009: 1710-1737.

[12] Loh W Y, Shih Y S. Split selection methods for classification trees[J]. Statistica sinica, 1997: 815-840.

[13] Steinberg D. CART: classification and regression trees[M]. The top ten algorithms in data mining. Chapman and Hall/CRC, 2009: 193-216.

FRP-钢管约束混凝土桥墩损伤声发射监测研究

都方竹[1,2]*　杨　栋[1,2]

(1. 山东建筑大学土木工程学院　山东济南　250101;
2. 建筑结构加固改造与地下空间工程教育部重点实验室(山东建筑大学)　山东济南　250101)

摘　要　基于GFRP-钢管约束混凝土桥墩轴压试验过程中监测得到的声发射损伤信号,利用声发射特征参数分析法,研究了FRP-钢管约束混凝土柱循环轴压荷载作用下的损伤演化全过程。运用b值分析法定量评价结构损伤程度,为结构临界失效预警提供参考;基于RA-AF关联分析法,有效识别出FRP-钢管约束混凝土柱不同损伤阶段的损伤及失效模式,提出了FRP-钢管约束混凝土桥墩损伤识别的新方法。

关键词　复合结构　钢管混凝土桥墩　声发射　结构健康监测　损伤识别

中图分类号　U441　　　**文献标识码**　A

Monitoring and Evaluating the Damage Behavior of FRP-Confined Circular Concrete-Filled Steel Tubular pier Using the AE technique

DU Fangzhu[1,2]*　YANG Dong[1,2]

(1. School of Civil Engineering, Shandong Jianzhu University, Jinan, Shandong, 250101, China;
2. Key Laboratory of Building Structural Retrofitting and Underground Space Engineering (Shandong Jianzhu University), Ministry of Education, Jinan, Shandong, 250101, China)

Abstract　According to AE signals gathered during the failure process of GFRP-CCFTs pier in compressive loading tests, characteristic AE feature analysis was used to elucidate the damage evolution process of GFRP-CCFT columns. The b-value analysis which provide quantitative information about the damage severity and structural instability, better characterize the critical material failure; Failure modes of GFRP-CCFT columns were differentiated through the correlogram with RA-AF analysis The proposed novel methods were capable of elucidating the damage growth, damage severity and failure modes for FRP-CCFTs structures.

作者简介:
* 都方竹(1991—),男,博士,讲师,主要从事结构健康监测、智能建造方面的研究。
杨栋(1998—),男,硕士生,主要从事结构健康监测、智能建造方面的研究。

Keywords composite structures concrete-Filled Steel pier acoustic emission structural health monitoring damage identification

E-mail dufangzhu20@sdjzu.edu.cn

0 引言

FRP-钢管约束混凝土结构是在钢管约束混凝土和FRP筒体混凝土结构的基础上新发展起来的一种工程结构形式[1],通过在钢管内放置钢筋笼并浇筑混凝土,钢管外粘贴FRP复合材料。这样既弥补了钢筋混凝土结构承载力不足的缺点,又可以将钢管与腐蚀环境分离开来,提高了钢管约束混凝土结构的承载能力和耐腐蚀能力,充分发挥混凝土、钢管和FRP三种材料的性能优势[2-3]。目前,国内外关于FRP-钢管约束混凝土结构的研究主要集中在承载力、本构关系和抗震性能等方面[4-6]。

实际工程应用中,FRP-钢管约束混凝土结构多应用于重大工程结构领域。该类结构一旦发生破坏,将会造成极大的人员伤亡和经济损失。因此,为保证FRP-钢管约束混凝土结构寿命周期内的安全性,有必要应用合理的监测方法,对FRP-钢管约束混凝土结构全寿命周期内的安全性和稳定性进行监测和评估。本文利用声发射技术对GFRP-钢管约束混凝土柱循环轴压荷载作用下的损伤演化全过程进行监测,并对其不同损伤程度和失效模式进行分类识别,实时掌握FRP-钢管约束混凝土结构的安全性和稳定性,为服役期内的FRP-钢管约束混凝土结构提供安全保障,具有重大科研意义和工程实用价值。

1 试验方案

本试验中试件尺寸参考我国《普通混凝土力学性能试验方法标准》(GB/T 50081—2002)并结合实际情况确定:圆柱直径250mm,高度580mm。混凝土为C45商品混凝土,钢管Q235,所有试件均包裹4层GFRP复合材料。试件制作时,以钢管作为模具,在钢管放置钢筋笼并分层振捣浇筑混凝土,具体制作过程参见我国《混凝土强度检验评定标准》(GB 50107—2010),FRP粘贴方式参考住建部《粘贴碳纤维增强复合材料加固混凝土工程施工与验收暂行规定》。本试验试件示意图和加工完成后的试件如图1所示,试件编号分组见表1,具体声发射参数设置见表2。

a)试件示意图   b)试件实物图   c)试验装置图

图1 试件加工图

Fig. 1 Construction schematic diagram of specimens

试件分组　　　　　　　　　　　表1
Specimen group details　　　　Tab. 1

试件组别	试件编号	钢管厚度	加载方式	试件数量	纵向钢筋	混凝土
CB	CB01	2mm	循环加载	2	4φ14	C45
	CB02	3mm	循环加载	2	4φ14	C45
CC	CC01	2mm	多次循环	2	4φ14	C45
	CC02	3mm	多次循环	2	4φ14	C45

声发射采集参数设置　　　　　　表2
DAQ salient features for AE system　　Tab. 2

门槛值	采样率	采样点数	增益 Gain	峰值定义时间 PDT	触发定义时间 HDT	触发闭锁时间 HLT
40dB	2MSPS	2048	40 dB	300μs	800μs	1000μs

2　结论

本文以 FRP-钢管约束混凝土桥墩作为工程研究对象，以声发射监测技术为主要技术手段，详细研究了 FRP-钢管约束混凝土桥墩循环荷载作用下的损伤演化过程、损伤程度、损伤机理及损伤失效模式，为 FRP-钢管约束混凝土组合结构的损伤监测及损伤识别提供了一种新思路、新方法，结论如下：

（1）FRP-钢管约束混凝土桥墩轴压荷载作用下损伤破坏过程可以划分为 3 个基本阶段，即弹性变形阶段、强化阶段和断裂失效阶段。循环轴压荷载作用下，声发射特征参数可以较好地表征 FRP-钢管约束混凝土桥墩的损伤演化过程。

（2）将 b 值分析法和 RA-AF 关联分析法引入 FRP-钢管约束混凝土桥墩循环荷载作用下的损伤程度及失效模式分析中，认为弹性变形阶段 b 值较大且波动范围小，拉伸裂纹的发展占据主导地位；强化阶段 b 值整体呈现震荡下降趋势，微损伤发展缓慢；断裂失效阶段试件发生较严重损伤，b 值出现迅速降低，剪切裂纹数量显著增加，FRP 与钢管的约束作用显著抑制内部钢筋混凝土桥墩剪切损伤的发展。

（3）结构临界破坏时，声发射累积能量与累积撞击数迅速增加，伴随着大量具有幅值大持续时间长的声发射信号，b 值迅速降低至 0.5 甚至更低，可以为 FRP-钢管约束混凝土结构的损伤诊断和养护维修提供保障，并为其临界破坏预警提供理论参考。

（4）FRP-钢管约束混凝土结构中同时包含 FRP、钢材、混凝土等多种材料，其外荷载作用下的损伤过程和损伤类型复杂，损伤类型较多，仅凭单一声发射参数很难准确识别 FRP-钢管约束混凝土桥墩的所有损伤类型，因此有必要同时参考多个声发射特征参数，根据各声发射特征参数的特点或利用一定的算法，对 FRP-钢管约束混凝土结构的损伤类型进行分类识别。

参 考 文 献

[1] Fam A Z, Rizkalla S H. Confinement model for axially loaded concrete confined by circular fiber-reinforced polymer tubes[J]. ACI Structural Journal. 2001, 98(4): 451-461.

[2] Meier U. Strengthening of structures using carbon fibre epoxy composites[J]. Construction and building materials. 1995, 9(6): 341-351.

[3] 谭壮, 叶列平. 纤维复合材料布加固混凝土梁受剪性能的试验研究[J]. 土木工程学报. 2003(11):12-18.

[4] Feng P, Cheng S, Bai Y, et al. Mechanical behavior of concrete-filled square steel tube with FRP-confined concrete core subjected to axial compression[J]. Composite Structures. 2015, 123: 312-324.

[5] Cai Z, Wang D, Smith S T, et al. Experimental investigation on the seismic performance of GFRP-wrapped thin-walled steel tube confined RC columns[J]. Engineering Structures. 2016, 110: 269-280.

[6] Teng J G, Hu Y M, Yu T. Stress-strain model for concrete in FRP-confined steel tubular columns[J]. Engineering structures. 2013, 49: 156-167.

基于光纤传感技术的钢结构腐蚀监测

樊 亮[1,2]* 郭川睿[3] 申 伟[4]

(1. 中国科学院海洋研究所 山东青岛 266071;
2. 广西科学院海洋腐蚀防护研究院 广西南宁 530007;
3. 深圳大学土木与交通工程学院 广东深圳 518060;
4. 广西大学土木建筑工程学院 广西南宁 530004)

摘 要 钢结构腐蚀会影响其使用性能,严重的腐蚀甚至会导致钢结构的破坏,造成巨大的经济损失,因此,需要对钢结构的腐蚀进行监测。传统腐蚀监检测方法,比如表观检查、挂片法、电阻法等准确度不高,且费时费力。本研究将利用两种光纤传感技术来开发腐蚀传感器,并对钢管的内、外表面进行腐蚀监测。镀有双层薄膜的长周期光纤光栅传感器以导电石墨烯掺杂银纳米线作为第一层薄膜,使光纤表面导电,利用电镀方法制作第二层厚度为 30 μm 的铁碳薄膜,用于模拟钢铁主要成分,并通过铁碳薄膜腐蚀引起波长漂移来监测钢结构外表面腐蚀。磁辅助非本征型法布里珀罗干涉传感器借助钢铁腐蚀引起磁力的变化,通过测量其内部腔长的改变,来对钢管道内表面腐蚀进行监测。以上传感器具有精度高、稳定性好、重复性好、抗腐蚀、抗电磁干扰、抗噪声等优点,适用于钢管道腐蚀的实时原位在线监测。

关键词 钢结构 光纤传感器 腐蚀 监测 灵敏度
中图分类号 U441 **文献标识码** A

Corrosion Monitoring of Steel Structures Based on Optical Fiber Sensing Technology

FAN Liang[1,2]* GUO Chuanrui[3] SHEN Wei[4]

(1. Institute of Oceanology, Chinese Academy of Sciences, Qingdao, Shandong, 266071, China;
2. Institute of Marine Corrosion Protection, Guangxi Academy of Sciences, Nanning, Guangxi, 530007, China;
3. College of Civil and Transportation Engineering, Institute of Urban Smart Transportation & Safety Maintenance, Shenzhen University, Shenzhen, Guangdong, 518060, China;
4. College of Civil Engineering and Architecture, Guangxi University, Nanning, Guangxi, 530004, China)

作者简介:
*樊亮(1989—),男,博士,研究员,主要从事结构健康监测与传感器研发。
郭川睿(1989—),男,博士,助理教授,主要从事结构健康监测与传感器研发。
申伟(1988—),男,博士,助理教授,主要从事桥梁智能监测与性能评估。

Abstract Corrosion affects the performance of steel structure during its active service, and serious corrosion may even lead to its destruction, causing huge economic losses. Therefore, it is necessary to monitor corrosion of steel structure. Traditional corrosion monitoring and detection methods, such as appearance inspection, corrosion coupon method, and electrical resistance method do not have high measurement accuracy, and it is time-consuming and laborious. In this study, two optical fiber sensing technologies will be used to develop corrosion sensors and monitor corrosion of the inner and outer surfaces of steel pipes. The long-period fiber grating sensor coated with double-layer film utilizes conductive graphene doped with silver nanowires as the first layer of film to make the fiber surface conductive. The second layer of iron carbon film with a thickness of 30μm is fabricated by electroplating, which is used to simulate the main components of steel. The external surface corrosion of steel structure is monitored by wavelength drift caused by iron carbon film corrosion. The magnetic assisted extrinsic Fabry Perot interference sensor monitors the internal surface corrosion of steel pipe by measuring the change of its cavity length, which is induced by the change of magnetic force between magnet and corroded steel. The above sensors have the advantages of high accuracy, good stability, good repeatability, corrosion resistance, electromagnetic interference resistance, noise resistance, and are suitable for real-time in-situ online monitoring of steel corrosion.

Keywords steel structure optical fiber sensor corrosion in-situ monitoring sensitivity

E-mail fanl@ qdio. ac. cn

0 引言

据统计,全世界每90s就有一吨钢铁变成铁锈。腐蚀悄无声息地对钢结构进行着破坏,不仅会缩短其使用寿命,还会增加维修和维护成本,甚至会引起建筑物坍塌等重大事故。腐蚀同时会引起巨大经济损失,对人力、物力和自然资源都会造成不必要的浪费。因此有必要对钢结构设施的腐蚀进行监测。

现阶段最常用的腐蚀监测技术为电化学传感技术。该技术能够直接测量金属的腐蚀速率,然而浪花飞溅区干湿交替、海工环境温度的变化等会严重影响腐蚀速率测量的准确性[1-2]。基于超声波法的传感技术利用压电换能传感器产生的高频声波穿过桩壁后,分析反射回波的传播时间或测量声波的振幅来监测钢铁腐蚀[3]。该技术只能粗略地确定局部腐蚀的发生位置,测量分辨率不高[4],测量中的环境噪声和电磁干扰也会影响该技术对腐蚀的判定。基于电磁方法的传感技术即漏磁(MFL)方法使用霍尔效应传感器磁化钢并检测磁通量[5],当磁力线遇到腐蚀部位和缺陷时,会观察到磁力线泄漏或弯曲[6]。然而,这种方法几乎无法对小缺陷或局部腐蚀进行定性分析[6],而且水、温度等参数以及周围磁场的干扰会严重影响测量的准确性[5]。以上传感器体积较大,而且测量准确性受到环境因素影响很大。因此,本研究将利用两种光纤传感技术来开发腐蚀传感器,并对钢结构设施的内、外表面进行腐蚀监测。

1 传感器设计以及监测原理

镀有双层薄膜的长周期光纤光栅(LPFG)传感器(直径125μm)结构构造如图1a)所示。以导电石墨烯掺杂银纳米线作为第一层薄膜,使光纤表面导电,利用电镀方法制作第二层厚度为30μm的铁碳薄膜,用于模拟钢筋主要成分。LPFG对周围介质或环境的折射率很敏感,铁碳薄膜腐蚀引起LPFG有效折射率的变化以及波长的漂移。将LPFG传感器布置于被监测钢结构表面,通过建立传感器监测数据与钢结构腐蚀速率的关系,来监测钢结构腐蚀。

内部腐蚀会降低钢管厚度,因此是钢管承载力下降的最主要原因之一。本研究设计了一种高灵敏度的磁辅助非本征法布里-珀罗干涉仪(EFPI)混合传感器,并应用于测量管道厚度损失。如图1b)所示,该传感器是一个由弹簧支撑的圆柱形磁铁、一个固定在管道上的反射镜(用于 EFPI 设置)和一个用于温度测量的光纤布拉格光栅组成。磁铁和钢管之间的磁力是管壁厚度的函数,可以通过 EFPI 腔长的变化来反映出来(磁铁和反射镜之间的距离)。

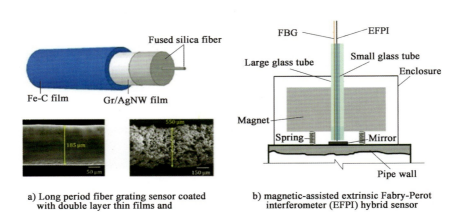

图1 镀有双层薄膜的长周期光纤光栅传感器以及磁辅助非本征法布里-珀罗干涉仪(EFPI)混合传感器构造

2 结论

基于光纤传感原理,设计镀有双层薄膜的长周期光纤光栅(LPFG)传感器以及磁辅助非本征法布里-珀罗干涉仪(EFPI)混合传感器,并对钢结构如钢管的内、外表面进行腐蚀监测,研究主要结论如下:

(1)该研究创新性的在光纤曲面上制作石墨烯层,使 LPFG 传感器导电的同时,提高了传感器的灵敏度和使用寿命。

(2)带有 30μm 厚 Fe-C 涂层的 LPFG 传感器可用于腐蚀监测,对应于 3.5 wt.%氯化钠溶液中 de 使用寿命为 46h。

(3)通过测量磁场强度证明,由于钢板与磁体之间的磁力增加,随着钢板厚度的逐渐减小,空腔长度减小。

(4)磁辅助非本征法布里-珀罗干涉仪(EFPI)混合传感器的管道厚度测量灵敏度为 3.5μm,可直接安装在现有钢管表面进行腐蚀监测。

参 考 文 献

[1] J. Ruppert, F. Frimmel, R. Baier, G. Binder, Comparison of corrosion rates obtained from laboratory and field data, Materials and Corrosion, 2016, 67(6).

[2] Sang-Bom Choe, Seung-Jun Lee, Effect of flow rate on electrochemical characteristics of marine material under seawater environment, Ocean Engineering, 2017, 141.

[3] R. F. Wright, P. Lu, J. Devkota, F. Lu, M. Ziomek-Moroz, P. R. Ohodnicki Jr, Corrosion Sensors for Structural Health Monitoring of Oil and Natural Gas Infrastructure: A Review, Sensors (Basel). 2019 Sep 13;19(18):3964.

[4] Noé Amir Rodríguez-Olivares, José Vicente Cruz-Cruz, Alejandro Gómez-Hernández, Rodrigo Hernández-Alvarado, Luciano Nava-Balanzar, Tomás Salgado-Jiménez, Jorge Alberto Soto-Cajiga, Improvement of Ultrasonic Pulse Generator for Automatic Pipeline Inspection, Sensors, 2018,18(9).

[5] Y. Shi, C. Zhang, R. Li, M. Cai, G. Jia, Theory and Application of Magnetic Flux Leakage Pipeline Detection, Sensors, 2015, 15(12).

[6] Bhagi, Purna Chandra. (2012). Magnetic Flux Leakage Testing: Basics. Journal of Non-Destructive Testing & Evaluation. 13. 7-19. ZHENG Jjie-lian L, Wang Jian-jun. Concrete-filled steel tube arch bridges in China[J]. Engineering, 2018, 4(1): 143-155.

CE-CFST 柱推出试验声发射特征分析

申 伟 温宇嘉 王 非 李 聪*

(广西大学土木建筑工程学院 广西南宁 530004)

摘 要 为研究钢管混凝土加劲混合结构(CE-CFST)界面黏结-滑移破坏过程,采用声发射(AE)监测系统对不同尺寸的 CE-CFST 柱试件推出实验进行了声发射测试,获得了撞击计数、幅值、能量等 AE 特征参数。试验结果表明:CE-CFST 柱的黏结-滑移过程可分为胶结段、非线性滑移段和滑移段三个阶段,AE 特征参数变化与荷载-滑移曲线的变化过程表现出较好的对应关系。胶结段声发射信号较少,幅值较低;非线性滑移阶段,由于外包混凝土与钢管界面之间开裂并扩展,AE 信号不断增多,开始出现高幅值信号,为试件出现界面黏结破坏提供了预警;滑移段,声发射信号较多,但幅值不高,主要由界面滑移摩擦产生;在试件加载的全过程中,AE 撞击计数率随荷载的增加而增大,在非线性滑移段明显增大。因此,AE 信号特征可以有效地反映 CE-CFST 界面黏结-滑移破坏过程,并为界面粘结破坏提供预警。

关键词 钢管混凝土加劲混合结构 声发射 推出实验 特征参数 黏结破坏

中图分类号 TU398 + .9 **文献标识码** A

Acoustic Emission Characteristics Analysis of Push-out Test on CE-CFST Column

SHEN Wei WEN Yujia WANG Fei LI Cong*

(College of Civil Engineering and Architecture, Guangxi University, Nanning, Guangxi, 530004, China)

Abstract To study the failure process of interface bond-slip of CE-CFST column, the Acoustic emission (AE) monitoring system was used to collect AE signals during the whole process of push-out test on CE-CFST column with different parameters. AE characteristic parameters such as impact count, amplitude and energy were obtained. The

---

基金项目:广西科技基地和人才专项(桂科 AD21220050);广西重点研发计划(桂科 AB22036007)。

作者简介:

申伟(1988—),男,博士,助理教授。主要从事结构智能监测与评估、特大跨桥梁结构设计理论与计算方面的研究。

温宇嘉(2000—),女,硕士研究生。主要从事基于声发射的结构健康监测方面的研究。

王非(1994—),男,硕士研究生。主要从事基于声发射的结构健康监测方面的研究。

* 李聪(1990—),男,博士,助理教授。主要从事大跨径钢管混凝土拱桥方面的研究。

results show that bond-slip process of the specimen can be divided into three stages: non-slip stage, nonlinear slip stage and slip stage. The changes of AE characteristic parameters show a good correspondence with the failure process of the specimen. In the non-slip stage, the AE signal is few and the its amplitude is lower. During the stage of nonlinear slip, the AE events increase continuously and high amplitude signals begin to appear, resulting from the propagation of interface crack. There are many AE signals in slip stage, but the amplitude is not high, which is mainly generated by interface slip friction. In the whole process of loading, AE impact count rate and energy release rate increase with the increase of load, especially which increases obviously in the nonlinear slip stage. Therefore, AE characteristics can effectively reflect the bond-slip process of CE-CFST, and provide early warning for interface bond failure.

Keywords concrete-encased concrete filled steel tubular acoustic emission push out test characteristic parameters bond failure

E-mail congli@ gxu.edu.cn

0 引言

钢管混凝土加劲混合结构（CE-CFST）是由内置的圆形钢管混凝土部分与钢管外包钢筋泥凝土部分混合而成的结构。作为一种新型结构体系，CE-CFST 柱具有承载力高、施工方便、抗震性能好等优点，广泛运用于我国西南地区的拱桥工程。桥梁工程领域是重大工程领域，对 CE-CFST 柱中钢管和混凝土的界面黏结性能有较高要求。黏结强度是使两种不同构件能够共同工作，以抵抗外界不同的拉、扭、剪、弯矩等荷载的重要性能。所以，这种黏结强度对 CE-CFST 柱的结构很重要。由于混凝土与钢管黏结界面隐蔽在内部，不能直接观察到其破坏过程。声发射技术作为一种无损检测技术，具有高灵敏性、适应性好等优点，被广泛应用于构件内部的损伤监测、诊断和识别。

目前，国内外对钢管混凝土加劲混合结构的研究还很不够充分，但对钢管混凝土的界面黏结破坏过程和声发射特征已经做了大量研究。钢管与混凝土的界面黏结力主要由化学胶结力、机械咬合力和摩阻力三部分构成，但各组成部分在黏结滑移各阶段的侧重有所不同。刘永健等通过方钢管混凝土和圆钢管混凝土试件的推出试验，对黏结应力的分布规律及影响黏结应力的主要因素进行了研究。赵卫平等采用声发射监测系统对9个钢管混凝土试件的推出试验进行了声发射信号特征分析。以上研究对象皆为钢管混凝土，而声发射技术对 CE-CFST 结构的界面黏结破坏还有待于进一步研究。本文通过对不同尺寸的 CE-CFST 柱试件的推出试验进行了声发射测试，分析了撞击计数、幅值、能量等声发射特征参数，获得了 CE-CFST 柱界面黏结破坏的声发射特征与黏结滑移的关系。

1 试验概况

本试验共制作了3组不同尺寸的 CE-CFST 柱，每组试件分别3根。试件外包混凝土材料均采用 C60，内部的钢管混凝土（CFST）芯上部突出外包混凝土 40mm，下部突出外包混凝土 10mm，以保证混凝土由上至下顺利推出。按照标准试验方法制作钢管混凝土试件并养护28d。

试验采用150t 级 MTS 施加荷载，采集系统使用东华 DH5921 采集仪，可与 MTS 数据同步，以便后期处理数据。试验荷载施加在试件顶部突出的 CFST 芯上，底部仅由外包混凝土抵住垫板，底部垫板中部开孔。声发射监测系统为美国物理声学公司（Physics Acoustic Corporation,PAC)生产的16通道声发射系统,为保证采集信号的多样性,采用R3α、R6α、R15α三种传感器共16个,前置放大器型号为PKxxl,放大增益为26db。

传感器布置在试件的3个侧面,2个相对的侧面布置6个,剩下1个面布置4个。布置6个传感器的面上,传感器竖向间距为250mm,横向间距为200mm,距边缘均为50mm。布置4个传感器的面上,传感器竖向间距为300mm,距竖向边缘150mm,横向间距为200mm,距横向边缘50mm。用耦合剂以及胶带固定传感器,具体布置图如图1所示。

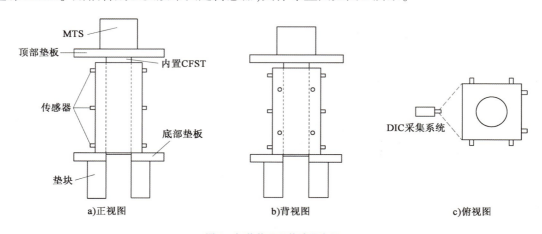

图1 加载装置和传感器布置

Fig. 1 Test setup and sensor arrangement

2 结论

(1)钢管混凝土加劲混合结构界面的黏结—滑移过程均可分为胶结段、非线性初滑移段和滑移段。外包混凝土的存在能增强CE-CFST柱的强度。

(2)声发射的撞击计数率、幅值、能量释放率较好地反应了试件的黏结—滑移破坏过程。胶结段的声发射信号较少,三种特征参数均较低;非线性滑移段的声发射信号不断增多,撞击计数率和能量释放率剧增,幅值随荷载增加的变化特征为试件出现界面黏结破坏提供了预警;滑移段的声发射信号较多,但增长稳定,主要由界面滑移摩擦产生。

参 考 文 献

[1] 韩林海,牟廷敏,王法承,等.钢管混凝土混合结构设计原理及其在桥梁工程中的应用[J].土木工程学报,2020(05):1-24.

[2] 康希良.钢管混凝土组合力学性能及黏结滑移性能研究[D].西安:西安建筑科技大学,2008:89-88.

[3] 刘永健,刘君平,池建军.钢管混凝土界面抗剪黏结滑移力学性能试验[J].广西大学学报(自然科学版),2010(01):17-23+29.

[4] 赵卫平,雷永旺,尹鹏,等.钢管混凝土界面黏结破坏的声发射特征及时空演化机制[J].建筑结构学报,2021(12):200-209.

[5] 赵兴东,唐春安,李元辉,等.花岗岩破裂全过程的声发射特性研究[J].岩石力学与工程学报,2006(S2):3673-3678.
[6] YAN Jiabao,XIE Wenjun,ZHANG Lingxin,et al. Bond behaviour of concrete-filled steel tubes at the Arctic low temperatures[J]. Construction and Building Materials,2019,210(210).
[7] Burud Nitin B., Kishen J. M. Chandra. Response based damage assessment using acoustic emission energy for plain concrete[J]. Construction and Building Materials,2020.

基于声发射的轴压荷载下 CE-CFST 柱损伤分析

李 聪　白 皓　王 非　申 伟*

(广西大学土木建筑工程学院　广西南宁　530004)

摘　要　钢管混凝土加劲混合结构(CE-CFST)凭借其良好的受力性能,在混凝土拱桥的拱肋、立柱等构件中具有广泛的应用前景。为研究 CE-CFST 受压损伤机制,开展不同钢管直径和配筋率的 CE-CFST 柱单轴压缩实验,利用声发射(AE)系统采集并分析其破坏全过程的 AE 信号。试验结果表明:在整个加载过程中,钢管混凝土加劲混合结构的破坏大致可以分为弹性、弹塑性、强化以及失效四个阶段;累计能量与累计计数均能较好反映加载过程中 AE 事件发生的数量及速率,在峰值荷载前急剧增多;通过分析整个加载过程中 RA(上升的时间与幅值的比值)和 AF(振铃计数与持续时间的比值)的密度可知,CE-CFST 柱试件轴压过程中同时发生拉伸破坏与剪切破坏,大致以峰值荷载为界,荷载越大,拉伸破坏与剪切破坏所占比例逐步减小。因此,利用声发射技术能够在一定程度上识别和预测轴压荷载下钢管混凝土加劲混合结构的损伤特征。

关键词　钢管混凝土加劲混合结构　声发射　单轴压缩试验　失效模式　损伤特征
中图分类号　TU398+.9　　**文献标识码**　A

Acoustic Emission-based Damage Analysis of CE-CFST Columns under Axial Compression Loading

LI Cong　BAI Hao　WANG Fei　SHEN Wei*

(College of Civil Engineering and Architecture, Guangxi University, Nanning, Guangxi, 530004, China)

Abstract　With its good force performance, the concrete-encased concrete filled steel tubular (CE-CFST) has a

---

基金项目:广西科技基地和人才专项(桂科 AD21220050);广西重点研发计划(桂科 AB22036007)。
作者简介:
李聪(1990—),男,博士,助理教授。主要从事大跨径钢管混凝土拱桥方面的研究。
白皓(1999—),男,硕士研究生。主要从事基于声发射的结构健康监测方面的研究。
王非(1994—),男,硕士研究生。主要从事基于声发射的结构健康监测方面的研究。
*申伟(1988—),男,博士,助理教授。主要从事结构智能监测与评估、特大跨桥梁结构设计理论与计算方面的研究。

wide range of application prospects in concrete arch bridges, such as arch ribs and arch columns. To study the damage mechanism of CE-CFST under compression, uniaxial compression tests of CE-CFST columns, with different steel pipe diameters and reinforcement ratios were carried out, and the AE signals of the whole damage process were collected and analyzed. The results show that the damage of the CE-CFST can be roughly divided into four stages: elastic, elasto-plastic, strengthening and failure. The cumulative energy and cumulative counts can well reflect the number and rate of AE events during loading, which increases sharply before the peak load. Analyzing the density of RA and AF during the whole loading process, tensile failure and shear failure occur simultaneously in the process of axial compression of CE-CFST column specimen. With the increase of load, the proportion of shear failure and the proportion of tensile failure decreases gradually, where the peak load is roughly taken as the boundary load. Therefore, the acoustic emission technology can be used to identify and predict the damage characteristics of the CE-CFST under axial compression load to a certain extent.

Keywords　concrete-encased concrete filled steel tubular　acoustic emission　uniaxial compression test　failure pattern　damage characteristics

E-mail　shenwei431@gxu.edu.cn

0　引言

钢管混凝土加劲混合结构(concrete-encased concrete filled steel tubular, CE-CFST)是钢管混凝土混合结构的基本形式。该类结构与空钢管结构相比,承载力高、刚度大、抗疲劳性能和耐久性能好;与钢筋混凝土结构相比,自重轻、抗震性能好;适用于桥梁、房屋建筑、公路、铁路等各类工程。但由于其结构的复杂性,对于内部损伤演化机制及裂纹特点不易观测,结构健康监测较为困难。本文利用声发射无损检测技术,凭借其适应性、时效性、敏感性等特点,在轴压试验下对 CE-CFST 柱试件进行实时的动态监测,实现对其损伤演化机制的认识及材料性能的评价。

目前针对 CE-CFST 结构已有的研究还较少,多是对钢管混凝土结构的研究。康玉梅等[1]借助单轴压缩试验,利用声发射对钢管混凝土结构的损伤过程及特征作研究分析,指出声发射撞击率、累计能量及累计撞击能很好地反映试件的破坏阶段与过程,同时也利用了陈智[2]所提出的在轴压试验下对钢管混凝土柱的 AE 特征参数组合值 RA(上升时间与幅值的比值)与 AF(振铃计数与持续时间的比值)进行分析,有效地说明不同的破坏阶段其裂纹具有不同的特点。欧佳灵等[3]同样在轴压试验下对圆形的钢管混凝土柱的承载能力进行了研究,分析了钢管的强化效应对试件内部核心混凝土约束的影响。

上述所提到的对于钢管混凝土结构的分析,涉及单一 AE 特征参数以及组合 AE 特征参数,参考上述方法对 CE-CFST 试件在轴向压缩作用下破坏全过程进行分析,即参照钢管混凝土结构的损伤演化过程对试验所采集的累计能量、累计计数、RA、AF 等 AE 特征参数随时间的变化规律进行研究,分析不同时段的相应特点,从而实现对 CE-CFST 柱的损伤过程以及不同破坏阶段的裂纹特点进行相应的识别。

1　试验概况

1.1　试件及实验设备

本试验设计制作多组不同尺寸规格的 CE-CFST 柱试件。试件混凝土采用广西桂威商品混凝土公司的 C60 商品混凝土，混凝土特性见表1。试件钢筋采用 HRB400，钢管采用 Q460 高强钢材，钢筋有两种规格，其特性见表2。本次分析仅取具有代表性的 3 种规格的试件，分别为钢管直径 89mm、127mm、159mm 外包方形混凝土均为 300mm×300mm×600mm；加载设备采用 12000kN 的压力设备。

混凝土材料表　　　　　　　　　　　　　　表1
Concrete material table　　　　　　　　Tab. 1

类　　型	强度等级	弹性模量 E_c (MPa)	轴心抗压强度 f_{cu} (MPa)	立方体抗压强度 $f_{cu,k}$ (MPa)
核心混凝土	C60	41.5	50.2	59.8
外包混凝土	C60	45.1	50.0	60.2

钢筋材料表　　　　　　　　　　　　　　表2
Rebar material table　　　　　　　　Tab. 2

类　　型	屈服强度 f_y (MPa)	极限强度 f_u (MPa)	弹性模量 E_s (MPa)
钢管 Q460	497.4	687.8	212.4
钢筋 φ8 箍筋	414.1	593.2	210.7
钢筋 φ12 纵筋	416.5	577.4	208.4

声发射采集系统采用美国 PAC 公司生产的 16 通道声发射系统，该系统可以对声发射特征参数进行实时、快速处理；前置放大器型号为 PKxxl，固定门槛值 40dB，采用 R3α、R6α、R15α 三种型号的型传感器共 12 个交替布置，采集 AE 信号，采样长度为 1024 个点，采样频率设为 1 MHz，带通滤波范围为 20～100kHz，具体的传感器型号选择与布置位置如图1所示。

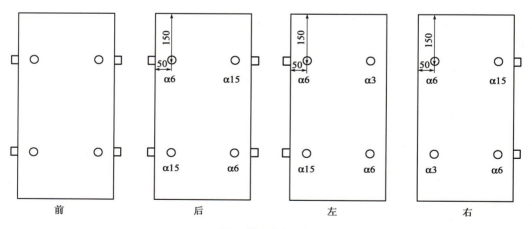

图1　传感器布置图
Fig. 1　Sensor arrangement diagram

1.2　试验过程

试验前根据现场情况合理设置好声发射采集参数，检查各传感器通道是否连接畅通，然后在试件待测点涂抹适量耦合剂，用定制支座将探头固定于试件表面指定位置，确保在加载过程中传感器不会掉落，再进行断铅试验以检测探头与试件是否贴合紧密并排除环境噪声对声发射采集的影响。试验采用单调分级加载，正式加载前进行多次的预加载试验，荷载加至 100～

200kN不等,确保试件平稳放置,同时位移计可以有效采集到作动器下降位移,预压次数与预压荷载根据实际情况选择。正式加载开始速度为5kN/s,当荷载加至预估极限荷载的70%左右且还未发生破坏,加载速度降至3kN/s,随后继续加载,达到荷载峰值,试件发生破坏,卸去荷载。试验过程中,保证轴向加载与声发射采集基本一致,并观察记录试件的变形及损伤状况。

2 结论

本文利用声发射系统采集单轴压缩作用下CE-CFST柱破坏全过程的AE信号,对单一特征参数以及组合特征参数进行相应的分析,可以得到以下结论:

(1)钢管混凝土加劲混合结构在单轴压缩下,损伤演化全程大致可分为4个阶段:弹性阶段、弹塑性阶段、强化阶段与失效阶段。试件的变形破坏特征与AE事件活动紧密相关,AE事件的累计能量和累计计数较直观地反映了CE-CFST柱的损伤及破坏过程。弹性阶段受预压影响发生极其轻微的裂纹,AE事件响应较低;弹塑性阶段随荷载增大有规律的稳步增加;强化阶段AE事件活动陡增,数量与强度都突然增大,预示着受压试件即将发生破坏;失效阶段基本上无新的AE事件发生,相应信号为零,试件失去承载能力。

(2)轴压作用下CE-CFST柱损伤全过程中的裂纹是由拉伸裂纹占主导并伴随有剪切裂纹,RA、AF均在受压破坏前有着较大的密度,峰值荷载后密度发生明显降低,相比较于CFST柱,有了外包混凝土的作用使得整个过程中的剪切裂纹在一定程度上被抑制,使得二者不呈现出以峰值荷载为界、交替占据主导位置的情况。

参 考 文 献

[1] 康玉梅,张乃源,任超,等.单轴压缩作用下CFST柱的声发射特征[J],东北大学学报(自然科学版),2021,42(05):720-725+740.
[2] 陈智.FRP-钢管约束混凝土损伤声发射监测及健康诊断[D].大连:大连理工大学,2015.
[3] 欧佳灵,邵永波.轴压作用下CFRP加固圆钢管混凝土短柱的承载力分析[J].工程力学,2019,36(10):180-188.
[4] 赵卫平,雷永旺,尹鹏,等.钢管混凝土界面黏结破坏的声发射特征及时空演化机制[J].建筑结构学报,2021,42(12):200-209.
[5] 陈胜军,吴成,张天舒,等.声发射技术在桥梁健康监测中的应用综述[J].工程与建设,2021,35(06):1216-1219.

考虑多因素耦合的拱桥吊杆服役寿命预测

喻志刚[1,2]　李启轩[1]　邓年春[1]　周筱航[1]

(1. 广西大学土木建筑工程学院　广西南宁　530004;
2. 中国铁建投资集团有限公司　北京　100855)

摘　要　吊杆是拱桥中的易损构件,其使用寿命通常远低于预期。为了避免坍塌事故发生,准确估计吊杆使用寿命至关重要。由于中承式拱桥的特殊结构形式,温度会导致吊杆产生额外的侧向弯曲,缩短其使用寿命。忽略温度的影响会使吊杆的使用寿命预测不准确。本文研究了温度对中承式拱桥吊杆的影响,并基于时变可靠度理论估算了吊杆的使用寿命。以一座大跨度中承式拱桥为例,对其短吊杆的使用寿命进行了预测,并对比了考虑和不考虑温度影响的结果。结果表明,考虑温度引起侧向弯曲的影响,最短吊杆的使用寿命缩短了7%左右,温度效应不应被忽略。

关键词　拱桥　吊杆　温度　疲劳　腐蚀

中图分类号　U445.464　　　　**文献标识码**　A

Service Life Prediction of Suspenders in Arch Bridge Considering the Coupling of Multiple Factors

YU Zhigang[1,2]　LI Qixuan[1]　DENG Nianchun[1]　ZHOU Xiaohang[1]

(1. School of Civil Engineering and Architecture, Guangxi University, Nanning, Guangxi, 530004, China;
2. China Railway Construction Investment Group Corporation Limited, Beijing, 100855, China)

Abstract　Suspenders are vulnerable components in arch bridges and their service lives are usually far below the expectation. In order to avoid collapse accidents, it is critical to estimate their service lives accurately. Due to the special structural form of half-through arch bridges, temperature can cause an additional lateral bending on the suspenders and shorten their service lives. Neglecting the effect of temperature will make the prediction of suspenders' service lives inaccurate. In this paper, the effect of temperature on the suspenders of half-through arch bridges is

---

作者简介:

喻志刚(1978—),男,博士生,高级工程师。主要从事桥梁结构设计理论与分析方法研究。

李启轩(1999—),男,硕士生。主要从事桥梁振动测试与分析研究。

邓年春(1975—),男,博士,教授级高级工程师。主要从事桥梁健康监测研究。

周筱航(1989—),男,博士,助理教授。主要从事桥梁健康监测研究。

investigated, and the service live of the suspenders is estimated based on the time-dependent reliability theory. A large span half-through arch bridge is taken as a case study. The service lives of its short suspenders are estimated, and theresults with and without considering the temperature effect are compared. The results indicate that the service life of the shortest suspender is shortened around 7% considering the effect of lateral bending caused by temperature, and the temperature effect should not be neglected.

Keywords　arch bridge　suspender　temperature　fatigue　corrosion
E-mail　zhou@ gxu. edu. cn

0　引言

拱桥造型美观、跨越能力大,其中的中、下承式拱桥对地形适应能力强,是桥梁工程中常采用的桥型之一。在中、下承式拱桥中,吊杆是重要的传力构件,关系到整个桥梁的安全。由于长期处于复杂的运营环境中,承受着动态荷载和环境侵蚀,吊杆是桥梁中较为薄弱的构件。然而,吊杆的损伤隐蔽性较强,不易进行检测,吊杆安全状态的评估一直是桥梁工程界关心的重点问题[1]。此外,中、下承式拱桥的吊杆可靠性往往远低于拱肋和桥面系等构件的可靠性,吊杆的可靠性在很大程度上决定了拱桥整体的可靠性水平。对吊杆安全状态评估不准可能造成维修养护的延误,进而导致吊杆断裂事故的发生,影响桥梁行车安全。因此,应准确对吊杆的使用状态和剩余寿命进行评估,并利用这些信息指导维护,以避免安全事故的发生。

1　工程实例

1.1　桥梁概况

本文以平南三桥为背景工程,对拱桥吊杆安全状态评估展开研究。该桥为中承式钢管混凝土拱桥,计算跨径560m,矢跨比为1/4,拱轴线为悬链线,拱轴线系数为1.5。拱肋采用四肢桁式结构,单肢钢管直径为φ1400mm,管内灌注C70混凝土,桥面板采用钢-混凝土组合桥面板,全桥共有64根吊杆,间距为15.5m,吊杆配置有环氧树脂涂层和HDPE套筒。建立其有限元模型如图1所示。

图1　桥梁有限元模型
Fig. 1　Finite element model of the main bridge

1.2　吊杆 S-N 曲线

吊杆在服役过程中,损伤的最主要来源为疲劳荷载。S-N 曲线常用于描述材料处于线性应变范围内的应力 S 与循环次数 N 的关系,反映了材料在交变应力下抵抗疲劳的能力。

Paulson[2]通过实验得出等级相当于我国1860级钢绞线在1050MPa平均应力下的S-N曲线表达式如下：

$$\lg N = 13.93 - 3.5\lg S_a \tag{1}$$

然而，在实际桥梁工程中，吊杆中的拉应力通常不会达到1050MPa。因此，考虑吊杆中的实际平均应力，本文使用Morrow公式修正平均应力的影响。另外，由于钢绞线和吊杆之间的差异，应使用1.6的折减系数计算吊杆中的应力幅[3]，综合上述因素可得到吊杆的S-N曲线：

$$\lg N = 15.01 - 3.5\lg \frac{\sigma_f}{\sigma_f - \sigma_m} - 3.5\lg(1.6S'_a) \tag{2}$$

1.3 修正的吊杆S-N曲线

吊杆的抗疲劳能力还与环境中的其他作用有关，其中主要作用为腐蚀和温度。吊杆的腐蚀过程受到许多因素的影响，如保护材料的老化、腐蚀离子的浓度、温度、湿度、外部载荷等。Li[4]研究了应力水平σ、pH值和Cl⁻浓度对钢丝腐蚀速率的影响，在Sloane[5]的研究中，跟踪了在温度和相对湿度循环变换下的钢丝腐蚀速率，并讨论了这两个环境变量对腐蚀速率的影响。由钢丝的腐蚀速率（深度）可以得出吊杆保护失效后的腐蚀率（面积损失），吊杆横截面如图2所示，每根吊杆由37根1860MPa钢绞线组成。

根据Luo[6]的研究，可认为钢绞线的极限抗拉强度与腐蚀率呈线性关系。在系统温度的影响下，吊杆将出现侧向弯曲角度θ以及额外的弯曲应力，如图3所示，这将进一步降低吊杆的极限抗拉强度[7]，结合两者可得修正后的吊杆S-N曲线：

$$\lg N = 15.01 - 3.5\lg \frac{2065 - 62.96\eta - 15.6\theta}{2065 - 62.96\eta - 15.6\theta - S_m} - 3.5\lg(1.6S'_a) \tag{3}$$

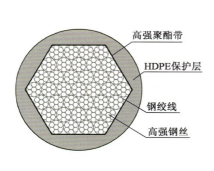

图2 吊杆横截面
Fig. 2 Schematic diagram of the suspender

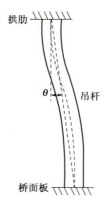

图3 吊杆侧弯
Fig. 3 Bending of the suspender

2 时变可靠度计算

2.1 吊杆功能函数

目前使用最广泛的累积损伤法则是Miner线性疲劳损伤累积理论，该方法认为在循环载荷作用下，疲劳损伤是可以线性地累加的，各个应力之间相互独立而互不相关，即各个应力循环是独立的，但这种方法没有考虑应力幅变化的影响，故可通过损伤度相当的原则将变幅应力

循环转化为常幅值应力循环,结合 S-N 曲线方程和等效应力幅,可推导出吊杆的功能函数:

$$g(x) = D_c - D(x) = D_c - \frac{N}{C}S_{eq}^m \qquad (4)$$

吊杆在服役期间承受的荷载为高周循环荷载,高周循环的随机荷载作用下,D_c 偏离 1 并不大,因此其均值取 1,变异系数取 0.3。

2.2 参数 C 的更新

由吊杆的 S-N 曲线可知,参数 C 耦合了腐蚀和温度的影响,先对 C 进行分析。

$$\lg C = 15.01 - 3.5 \lg \frac{2065 - 62.96\eta - 15.6\theta}{2065 - 62.96\eta - 15.6\theta - S_m} \qquad (5)$$

桥梁的恒载在服役期间变化很小,拱桥吊杆的疲劳损伤主要源自车辆活载所带来的应力幅变化,故取恒载的标准值作为恒载的大小用于后续吊杆平均应力的计算。将标准车辆荷载应用于桥梁有限元模型,可以获得吊杆的等效应力幅值。为了获取车辆荷载下吊杆的应力分布规律,将其模型理想化,即忽略多个车辆之间的耦合作用,只计算单个标准车辆荷载经过拱桥时所引起的应力幅。

由图 4 可知,当一辆多轴车经过桥梁时,仅引起吊杆一次较大应力幅变化,然后将日均车流量作为吊杆的日均应力幅循环次数可得到车辆荷载对吊杆的影响。本文采用《AASHTO LRFD》中定义的日均通行量 20000 辆作为车流量平均值,日均通行量可以认为呈正态分布,取日均应力幅循环次数的变异系数为 0.1262。

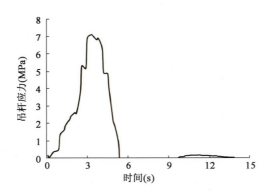

图 4 吊杆应力时程

Fig. 4 Stress time history diagram of suspender

根据桥址处气象数据统计,平南三桥的相对湿度约为 80%,年平均气温为 21.5℃,环境 pH 值和 Cl⁻浓度约为 5 和 0.1%,将以上数据代入腐蚀模型可得到吊杆每年的腐蚀速率:

$$R = 0.023 + 4.12\sigma^{0.47} \times 10^{-5} + 8Cl^- \times 10^{-2} - (Cl^-)^2 \times 10^{-2} + 3.66pH^{-2.77} +$$
$$(RH + 15) \times 10^{-3} + 1.8(T - 25) \times 10^{-3} \qquad (6)$$

已知拱桥合拢温度为 33℃,以温差 45℃为例展示吊杆变形情况,如图 5 所示。

图 5 系统温度作用下桥梁变形

Fig. 5 Deformation map of the bridge under the effect of system temperature

综合等效应力幅和弯曲角度等数值，确定最危险吊杆为短吊杆和次短吊杆，计算参数见表1，后续仅分析最危险吊杆，并给出两根吊杆偏转角度计算公式。

短吊杆和次短吊杆计算参数　　　　　　　　　　表1

吊　杆	短　吊　杆	次　短　吊　杆
长度 H_n(m)	5.294	19.001
距中线距离 ΔL_n(m)	240.25	224.75
弯曲角度计算公式(mrad)	$\theta_1 = 5.45\Delta_t \times 10^{-1}$	$\theta_2 = 1.42\Delta_t \times 10^{-1}$
平均应力(MPa)	428.89	486.01
等效应力幅(MPa)	22.37	21.66
等效应力幅标准差(MPa)	3.95	3.82

2.3 可靠度计算结果分析

在理想条件下，HDPE 护套的寿命可达 25 年。然而，桥梁的实际运行环境非常恶劣，HDPE 护套的寿命比预期的短得多。在本文中，将防腐涂层和 HDPE 护套的寿命共取为 10 年，即在前 10 年中，吊杆不会受到腐蚀。

本文使用一次二阶矩法计算时变可靠度，并用可靠性指数 β 量化吊杆的可靠性，并对短吊杆有温度影响和无温度影响的估计结果进行了比较，如图6和图7所示。作为桥梁的可更换构件，吊杆的临界值 β 通常取为 2.33。

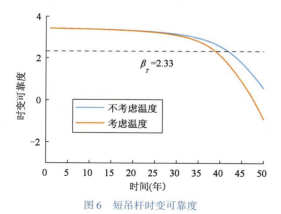

图6　短吊杆时变可靠度

Fig. 6　The time-dependent reliability of the shortest suspender

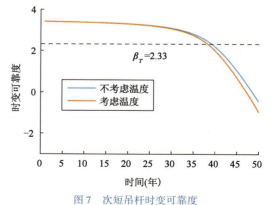

图7　次短吊杆时变可靠度

Fig. 7　The time-dependent reliability of the second shortest suspender

从结果可以看出,考虑温度引起的侧向弯曲将导致吊杆可靠性指标出现差异,并且随着服役时间的增加,差异逐渐明显。对于短吊杆,考虑温度的影响后其使用寿命从 42 年下降到 39 年,使用寿命下降 7.1%,而次短吊杆,其使用寿命分别是 39 年和 38 年,使用寿命下降 2.6%。结果表明,温度引起的侧向弯曲对短吊杆的使用寿命有显著影响,但对次短吊杆使用寿命的影响不显著,可以推断,对其他长吊杆的影响将进一步减弱。

3　结论

本文研究了中承式拱桥短吊杆的时变可靠度。除了疲劳和腐蚀的影响外,还进一步研究了温度引起的侧向弯曲对吊杆服役寿命的影响。通过本文研究得到如下主要结论:

(1) 对于中承式拱桥,温度效应会引起吊杆的侧弯,可通过修改吊杆的极限抗拉强度来考虑侧弯的影响,侧弯和腐蚀具有很强的耦合关系。

(2) 温度引起的侧弯对短吊杆的时变可靠度有显著影响,会导致其服役寿命估计结果的不同,因此不应忽略温度效应对吊杆寿命的影响。

参 考 文 献

[1] 高欣,欧进萍. 钢管混凝土拱桥索类构件的常见病害与检测方法[J]. 公路,2012,3:10-16.
[2] Paulson C, Frank K H, Breen J E. A fatigue study of prestressing strand[R]. University of Texas at Austin, 1983, 1-124.
[3] Birkenmaier M. Fatigue resistant tendons for cable-stayed construction[C]. IABSE, 1980: 1-16.
[4] Li R, Miao C, Wei T. Experimental study on corrosion behavior of galvanized steel wires under stress[J]. Corrosion Engineering, Science and Technology, 2020, 55(8): 622-633.
[5] Sloane M J D, Betti R, Marconi G, et al. Experimental analysis of a nondestructive corrosion monitoring system for main cables of suspension bridges[J]. Journal of Bridge Engineering, 2012, 18(7): 653-662.
[6] Luo X, Li Z. Study on mechanical properties of unbonded prestressed steel strand after corrosion [J]. Journal of the China Railway Society, 2008(02):108-112.
[7] Zhou Y, Deng N, Yang T. A study on the strength and fatigue properties of seven-wire strands in hangers under lateral bending[J]. Applied Sciences, 2020,10(6): 5-14.

基于实测数据的高铁大跨混凝土拱桥桥面线形分析与控制技术

杨国静 陈克坚 颜永逸

(中铁二院工程集团有限责任公司 四川成都 61003)

摘 要 大跨度混凝土拱桥受其结构特点、温度作用和混凝土收缩徐变等影响,不可避免地会在运营过程中出现竖向变形,直接影响到轨道线形。为了避免大跨拱桥在运营过程中出现较大的变形,影响运营行车安全和舒适,同时指导后期运营维护,减小养护工作量。本文依托一已建大跨混凝土拱桥,分析了该桥设置线形实时监测的必要性,提出了面向运营期间的桥面线形监测预警系统的设计方案。通过实测数据分析了桥面线形的变化趋势,研究了温度作用对桥面线形的影响规律,提出了实测数据中残余变形和温度变形的分离方法,得到了残余变形估计值。通过对不同特点变形值的评估,提出不同情况下的桥面线形调整量。研究结果表明:(1)桥面线形受温度变化影响较为敏感,沉降变形与温度作用有明显的相关性。(2)尽管桥址区昼夜温差较大,但大桥采用混凝土结构,温度导热性较差,结构整体由于日温差变化或骤然降温引起挠度的效应并不明显。(3)建立了一种大跨度拱桥残余变形估算方法。截至2020年6月29日,该桥的计算相对徐变变形约为20mm。(4)提出了一种基于健康监测系统的大跨拱桥桥面运营线形实时控制方法,既保证了运营行车安全,又充分考虑了不同荷载的变形特征。研究成果可用于指导运营期间的养护维修,也可为后续该类型桥梁的设计提供参考依据。

关键词 混凝土拱桥 线形调整 轨道不平顺 残余变形 运营维护

中图分类号 U24 **文献标识码** A

Bridge Deck Alignment Analysis and Control Technology of High-speed Railway Long-span Concrete Arch Bridge Based on Monitoring Data

YANG Guojing　CHEN Kejian　YAN Yongyi

(China Railway Eryuan Engineering Group Co., Ltd., Chengdu,Sichuan 610031)

Abstract Due to its structural characteristics, temperature, shrinkage and creep of concrete, it is unavoidable for the long-span concrete arch bridge to have the vertical deformation in the operation period, which directly affects the track alignment, thereby affecting traffic safety and comfort. In order to avoid the large deformation of railway bridges and maintenance and reduce the maintenance workload during the operation period, it is important to carry out the research on the bridge deck alignment analysis and control technology of long-span arch bridges. Based on a long-span concrete arch bridge, this paper analyzes the necessity of real-time monitoring of bridge alignment, and puts forward the design scheme of bridge deck alignment monitoring and warning system for operation period. The variation trend of bridge deck alignment is analyzed by measured data, and the variation regularity between bridge deck deformation and temperature is studied. The separation method of residual deformation and temperature deformation in measured data is proposed, and the estimated value of residual deformation is obtained. The bridge deck alignment adjustments for different conditions are proposed. The research results can be used to guide the maintenance during the operation period, and can also provide reference for the design of similar bridges.

Keywords　　concrete arch bridge　　bridge alignment　　track irregularity　　residual deformation　　operational maintenance

轨道平顺性是高速铁路行车安全性和舒适性的重要保证,而在列车荷载、温度和地基变形等影响因素下,桥梁不可避免地发生不均匀沉降,不仅使线路维修成本增加,而且有可能带来更大的安全隐患。

大跨度混凝土拱桥由于其结构特点、温度作用和混凝土收缩徐变等影响,不可避免地会在运营过程中出现竖向变形,直接影响到轨道线形,进而影响到行车安全性和舒适性。有别于常规简支梁桥竖向静态变形受单一沉降因素控制外,大跨混凝土拱桥实测竖向静态变形往往是温度作用和混凝土收缩徐变的耦合结果,使得大桥的线形评估和调整多采用直接组合值。

为了探明大跨混凝土拱桥徐变机理以及桥面变形与温度作用间的关系,国内外的学者对其展开了深入的研究。张正阳等基于北盘江大桥的模型实验,结合贝叶斯方法对拱桥的长期变形和收缩徐变建立了模型并开展了预测[1]。王永宝等建立了自然条件下徐变的预测模型[2]。还有众多学者开展了模型实验与理论分析,都获得了一定的研究效果[3-5]。但桥梁结构在运营过程中,施工过程、荷载和环境等等多方面因素不断变化,对模型实验和理论计算得到的结构变形影响较大。吴海军等利用重庆江津长江大桥的挠度监测系统的数据,分析得到了结构挠度与温度变化之间的滞后效应[6]。陈国良等利用挠度分量在时间尺度上不耦合的性质,提出了基于时间序列分析的挠度-温度效应分离方法[7]。刘刚等在推导了温度和挠度的理论关系后,得到了位移与整体升降温的线性关系,并基于粒子群算法提取到了温度对变形的影响效应,提出了一种消除长期健康监测中的温度效应的方法[8]。但上述方法较为复杂,或需要结合复杂的数学模型,或对关键参数的设置较为敏感,实用性不强。

此外,目前铁路大型桥梁缺乏相应的管养标准或养护规范,对于具有众多构件的运营期大跨拱桥桥面线形评估和调整控制方法也尚属空白。因此,为避免铁路桥梁在运营过程中出现较大的变形影响运营行车安全和舒适,同时指导后期运营维护,减小养护工作量,开展高铁大跨拱桥桥面线形监测、分析和控制技术的研究具有重要意义。

本文以云桂铁路南盘江特大桥为背景,分析了该桥设置线形实时监测的必要性,提出了面向运营期间的桥面线形监测系统设计方案。通过实测数据分析了桥面线形的变化趋势,研究了桥面变形与温度间的变化规律,提出了实测数据中残余变形和温度变形的分离方法,得到了残余变形估计值。并从运营安全角度,提出了基于一种健康监测系统的大跨拱桥桥面运营线形的实时控制方法,通过对不同特点变形值的评估,给出了桥面线形调整量。研究成果可用于指导运营期间的养护维修,也可为后续该类型桥梁的设计提供参考依据。

1 工程概况

云桂铁路南盘江特大桥为云桂铁路云南段重要工程之一,桥梁全长852.430m,设计时速250km/h。由于桥址位于典型的V字形峡谷,山高坡陡、地形复杂,主桥采用416m上承式钢筋混凝土拱桥,矢高99.0m,矢跨比99/416=1/4.2。拱轴线采用拱轴系数为1.6的悬链线。拱圈采用单箱三室的变宽等高箱型截面。拱圈高度为9.0m,在拱顶中央315m水平范围段为18m等宽,拱脚65m段为28m至18m变宽。引桥及拱上梁孔跨布置为:3×42m连续梁+(60+104+60)m连续刚构+8×39.5m预应力混凝土连续梁+2×60m T构+1×42m简支箱梁。桥梁总体布置如图1所示。拱圈横截面如图2所示。引桥和拱上墩柱采用双柱矩形刚架墩,其中交界墩高度102 m,拱上最高墩高58.9 m。拱座为明挖嵌岩基础,其余均为桩基础。主拱圈采用斜拉扣挂与劲性骨架相结合的施工方法。

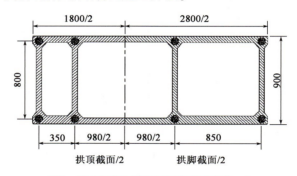

图1 南盘江特大桥总布置图(尺寸单位:m)

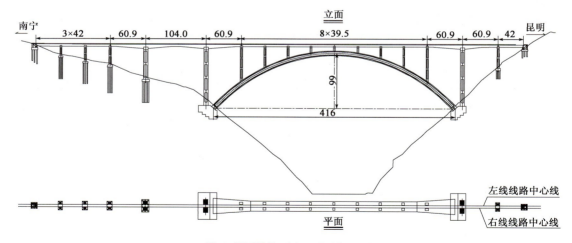

图2 拱圈横截面图(尺寸单位:cm)

2 大桥线形实时监测必要性

目前已建成的云桂铁路南盘江特大桥为采用劲性骨架施工法的第二大跨度的钢筋混凝土拱桥,其技术复杂和施工难度大。主要技术难点体现在以下两个方面:(1)拱圈采用斜拉扣挂与分环分段浇筑相结合的施工方法,其施工特点为结构体系转换次数多,结构刚度与强度逐步形成。同一截面的拱圈箱体,边箱先于中箱施工完,且时间间隔较长,这将导致同一截面混凝土各部分龄期有较大差异,给准确计算结构后期的收缩变形变形带来了很大的困难。(2)已有资料表明,对于大跨度拱桥,日照造成的局部温度应力会对结构产生巨大影响。由于该桥位于V形峡谷区,受地形条件的影响,可能导致桥梁的某一侧或局部位置受到强烈的日晒,而其余结构由于受山体的遮挡而结构温度较低。另外,桥面的遮挡作用也可导致主拱圈沿纵向温度分布不均匀,使得理论计算的温度变形与真实变形存在一定的差距。这些都给准确计算结构温度变形和内力造成了很大的困难。

查阅相关资料,发现对于采用此种施工方法的拱桥长期时变行为的研究并不多见,而用于大跨铁路桥梁也尚属于首例。上述的这些不确定变形会直接影响到桥面轨道线形,进而影响到列车行车安全性和舒适性。因此,有必要对南盘江特大桥桥面变形进行长期监测,通过实时监测,一方面确保运营行车安全,为日后养护管理决策(如确定线形调整的最佳时机及轨道的调整量)提供科学依据;另一个方面,掌握这种特殊桥型的收缩与徐变的变形特征及变化规律,为以后该类桥梁的设计和研究提供强有利的技术支撑。

3 大桥线形监测技术方案

为了准确测量拱圈收缩徐变、温度作用引起的梁部下挠,选取了拱上墩处共14个测点,采用静力水准仪对竖向变形进行观测,它能直接反映出梁部在运营期间由于拱圈收缩徐变和温度变化引起的上下起伏情况。监测基准点设置于大里程侧桥台处。考虑到传感器设备安装、更换方便且不影响后期运营维护、检查,将观测点设置在拱上墩对应的箱梁内部。同时,由于桥址处年温差及日温差较大,需考虑温度作用对结构的影响,通过在静力水准仪内集成温度传感器,实现了全桥温度的监测。鉴于桥址处日照充足,现场所有设备均采用太阳能板的供电方式。现场设备数据传输采用有线加无线的方式。测点布设如图3所示。中铁二院工程集团有限责任公司于2016年9月在云桂铁路南盘江特大桥顺利完成了桥面线形自动化监测系统的安装和调试。

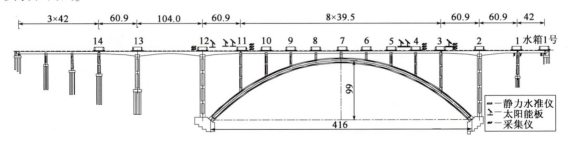

图3 南盘江特大桥测点纵向布置图(尺寸单位:m)

4 监测数据分析

4.1 桥面线形变化趋势分析

图4给出了系统运营从2017年1月1日到2020年6月29日的不同时间点,桥面各测点的沉降变形图。图5给出了系统运营从2017年1月1日到2020年6月29日的各测点平均温度随时间的变化图。

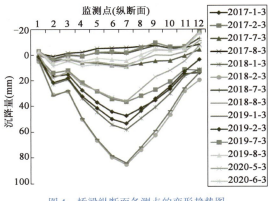
图4 桥梁纵断面各测点的变形趋势图

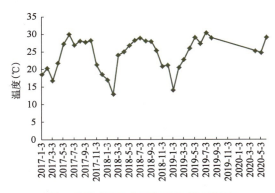
图5 桥梁各测点的平均温度变化趋势图

从图4和图5可知，(1)从2017年1月1日到2020年6月29日，温度曲线呈现了了明显的周期性变化。每年1、2月温度最低，约15℃左右；8、9月温度达到最高，约30℃左右。查阅丘北当地多年历史天气记录，月平均最高气温为27℃，发生在8月，月平均最低气温为7℃，发生在1月，实测的温度变化规律与大气温度变化规律基本一致。但由于温度测点设置于梁内，空气密闭，不透气，实测温度数值比实际的大气温度高。(2)桥面线形与温度变化有着直接的关系。当温度较高时，桥面线形较为平顺，如温度为30℃时(2017年8月1日)，拱顶相对桥台处沉降达到了5.6mm，线路最为平顺。温度低时，桥面线形较为不平顺，如2019年1月1日时的温度最低(14℃)，不均匀沉降差值最大，沉降量达到了84mm。主要原因分析为轨道精调完成时间为2016年9月，天气最为炎热时。因此，降温对结构变形影响较大。

4.2 昼夜沉降变形分析

由前述分析可知该桥变形受温度作用影响较为明显，本节针对南盘江大桥桥址处昼夜温差大的特点，开展昼夜沉降变化数据分析。选取了2020年度近三个月中温度变化较大的一天(2020年11月20日)开展分析，分别绘制这一天内不同时间段的桥面各测点的沉降变化和温度变化，如图6和图7所示。

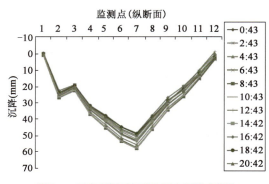
图6 一日内不同时间段各测点沉降变化量

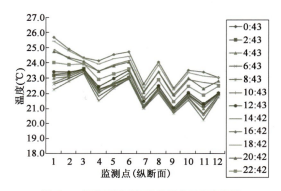
图7 一日内不同时间段各测点温度变化量

由图6和图7可知，(1)从短期的温度监测数据来看，相对于大气温度，梁内温度更为稳定。具体表现在一天之内，各测点实测的最高和最低温差基本在2℃之内，而大气日温差远高于该数值，表明温度监测数值不能完全等同于大气温度。(2)从短期的沉降监测数据来看，日沉降变化量基本在 5mm 以内。表明尽管桥址区昼夜温差较大,但大桥采用混凝土结构,温度导热性较差,结构整体由于日温差变化或骤然降温引起挠度的效应并不明显,远小于结构长期沉降变形值,可以忽略短期效应影响。

4.3 拱顶单点变形趋势分析

图 8 以拱顶测点为例,给出了从 2017 年 1 月 1 日到 2020 年 6 月 29 日变形和温度随时间变化的曲线。

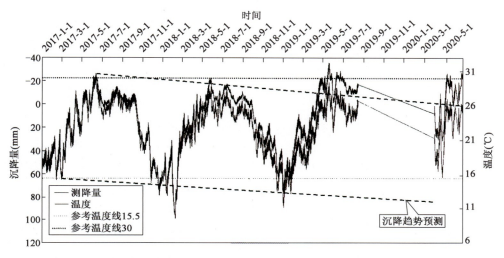

图 8　拱顶测点的挠度-温度曲线变化图

注：2019年9月～2020年4月,现场断电导致数据缺失。

由图 8 可知,(1)该测点变形受温度变化影响较为明显。具体表现为温度曲线与沉降变形曲线基本一致,当温度降低时,沉降变形值增大；温度升高时,沉降变形值减小。说明该测点的沉降变形与温度作用具有较明显的相关性。(2)从 2017 年 1 月 1 日到 2020 年 6 月 29 日,该测点的沉降曲线出现了明显的周期性变化。每年的 1、2 月沉降量达到最大,然后随着温度的逐渐升高,7、8 月时沉降量到达一年中最小值,之后随着温度的逐渐降低,沉降量再次增大。整条曲线出现了周而复始的规律性变化。(3)随着时间的延长,两条曲线的相对位置关系出现了明显的变化,具体表现为从初期的几乎完全重合,到后期的差距越来越大。其中,温度曲线基本保持在一定的范围内进行周期变化,而沉降量曲线出现了明显的下移,表明该测点已经出现了明显的收缩徐变下挠。通过扣除年温差对挠度的影响,绘制出该测点的最大和最小沉降量变化趋势曲线。粗略估计,截至到目前,该测点的徐变下挠变形量已经达到 20～25mm。

5　残余变形估计

5.1　残余变形估计方法

众所周知,桥梁长期监测的变形数据中,不仅有温度效应,还有残余收缩徐变变形和荷载效应。由于南盘江大桥为新建桥梁,且属于重大工程,施工质量控制要求高,可认为在运营早期阶段结构基本无损伤。对于荷载效应,可通过选取天窗不行车时间段的变形进行相应剔除。因此,本阶段大桥的主要变形成分为温度效应和收缩徐变效应,如何有效剔除温度效应成分变成了问题的关键。为快速分离出徐变和温度效应,本文提出了二次拟合回归分析算法。其过程如下:

(1)选取挠度变形和温度数据的日特征数据(通常可取凌晨时刻的数据,此时温度稳定,无列车荷载),假定日特征数据的总量为 N。

(2)计算温度效应影响周期。选取第一时间间隔天数为 i,计算日特征数据中的第 t 个数据和第 $t+i$ 个数据之间的挠度变形差 S_t^i 和温差 T_t^i,建立一个样本 (S_t^i, T_t^i),$t = 1, 2, 3, \cdots$,且满足 $t+i < N$,计算所有的 t,得到时间间隔 i 下的挠度变形差和温差形成的 1 个第一样本集 U_i^1,即 $U_i^1 = [(S_1^i, T_1^i), (S_2^i, T_2^i), (S_3^i, T_3^i), \cdots]$,对 U_i^1 以温差 T 为自变量得到拟合一次项系数,并取其绝对值为 k_i。依次计算 $i = 1, 2, 3, \cdots$,得到 $U_1^1, U_2^1, U_3^1, \cdots$,分别拟合计算 $k_1, k_2, k_3 \cdots$ 得到关于 i-k 的曲线,根据 i-k 曲线的拐点确定 i';i' 即为温度的最大影响天数,即影响周期。

(3)在温度影响周期下,建立线性的温度与变形影响关系系数。选取第二时间间隔天数为 p,得到 p 对应的 1 个第一样本集 $U_p^1 = [(S_1^p, T_1^p), (S_2^p, T_2^p), (S_3^p, T_3^p), \cdots]$。依次计算 $1p, 2p, 3p \cdots, np$,且 $np \leq i'$,得到 $U_p^1, U_{2p}^1, U_{3p}^1 \cdots$,将 $U_p^1, U_{2p}^1, U_{3p}^1 \cdots$ 集合形成第二样本集 $U^2 = [U_p^1, U_{2p}^1, U_{3p}^1, \cdots]$,对 U^2 以温差 T 为自变量得到拟合一次项系数,取该系数的绝对值为变形差和温差的线性关系系数为 K,此即在温度周期下的温度与变形影响系数,通常要求 K 的 R-square 指标 >0.85。

(4)以日特征数据的第一个数据为基准,用相邻两温度的温差 T 乘以系数 K,依次累计求和得到温度效应的变形曲线。

(5)用变形曲线减去温度效应曲线得到残余变形曲线。通过最小二乘拟合,进一步得到残余变形随时间的拟合公式,用以估计残余变形值。

5.2 分析结果

采用上述方法,如图 9 所示,拟合出挠度变形差和温差的线性关系系数 K 为 5.566(R-square 为 0.946)。图 10 为分离温度效应后的残余变形及拟合曲线。由图 10 可知,南盘江大桥自 2017 年 1 月 1 日至 2020 年 6 月 29 日发生的残余变形约为 20mm。

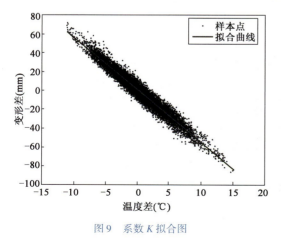

图 9 系数 K 拟合图

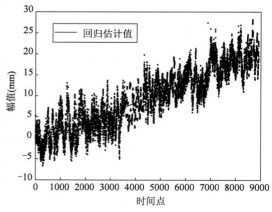

图 10 残余变形拟合曲线

6 桥面线形评估与控制技术

前述分析可知,温度作用(周期性荷载)和收缩徐变作用(非周期性荷载)性质不一致。周期荷载下的桥梁变形会随着一年内时间的变化进行自动调整,为了减小运营养护工作量,桥梁的合理线形控制目标应该是以成桥线形为中心的周期变形。本文研究提出了基于健康监测系统的大跨拱桥桥面运营线形的实时控制方法,其流程如图11所示,包含步骤如下:

(1)桥面线形评估,判断调高时机:通过桥面变形监测系统获得桥面各测点处的沉降变形量,对各测点处的沉降变形量进行高次拟合,获得变形后的桥面整体线形。沿纵桥向按照预设的基线长度计算基线中点与变形后的桥面整体线形的矢距。评估矢距值是否超限。如超限,进行调高。

(2)分离温度变形和残余变形并评估:采用前述方法获得残余变形估计值和温度变形最大和最小值,分别判断是否超过设计限值。

(3)根据不同情况,确定调整量:若残余变形超限,温度变形不超限,仅按残余变形值调整线形;若残余变形和温度变形均超限,按温度变形均值和残余变形之和进行调整。

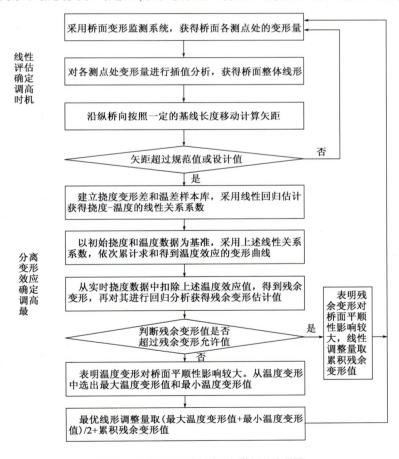

图11 大跨混凝土拱桥线形评估调整流程图

该方法的优势在于：通过采用组合评估+分类评估的方式，既保证了铁路要求的高平顺性以满足运营行车安全，又充分考虑了不同荷载的变形特征，如温度荷载引起的周期变形、收缩徐变荷载变形为递增变形对桥梁线形的影响，通过分类与设计假设的对比，提出了不同情况下的桥面线形调整值，解决了现有的采用单一组合变形值进行桥面线形调整量较大的问题。同时，考虑结合桥梁运营合理线形目标，通过对最大、最小温度变形值的评判，获得了温度变化区间，提出了基于运营合理线形的温度变形调整值，避免了由于忽略温度变形周期性造成的桥面线形调整频次增加的问题，显著降低了运营维护工作量和运营成本，对我国铁路运营管理具有重大意义。

采用上述方法，选取2019年1月（温度最低点时）的测点变形开展线形评估分析。对于大跨拱桥，目前规范还未明确规定长波基线长度及矢距限值。根据相关研究[9]，本次评估采用基线长为60m，矢距限值为10mm，计算正矢差如图12所示。由图可知，60m弦正矢差最大值为9mm，满足长波不平顺限值要求，行车安全性和乘坐舒适度良好。

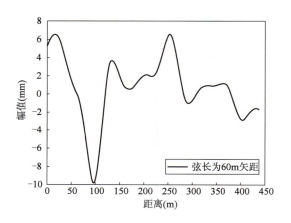

图12　南盘江特大桥60m弦正矢差分析图

7　结论

云桂铁路南盘江特大桥为世界级的特大型高速铁路桥梁，其结构复杂，该桥面线形监测系统的成功设计及应用具有代表性，可以为其他类似工程提供参考。通过对实测数据的分析得到如下结论：

（1）桥面线形受温度变化影响较为敏感。当温度降低时，不均匀沉降变形增加，桥面线形相对不平顺。随着温度的逐渐上升，沉降变形值逐渐减小，沉降变形与温度作用有明显的相关性。

（2）尽管桥址区昼夜温差较大，但大桥采用混凝土结构，温度导热性较差，结构整体由于日温差变化或骤然降温引起挠度的效应并不明显，远小于结构长期沉降变形值，可以忽略短期效应影响。

（3）提出了一种大跨度拱桥残余变形估算方法，通过确定温度和变形的影响系数，采用拟合分析的方法提取实测数据中残余变形和温度效应。截至 2020 年 6 月 29 日，该桥的残余变形约为 20mm。

（4）提出了一种基于健康监测系统的大跨拱桥桥面运营线形的实时控制方法，通过采用组合评估＋分类评估的方式，既保证了运营行车安全，又充分考虑了不同荷载的变形特征，避免了由于忽略温度变形周期性造成的桥面线形调整频次增加的问题。

参 考 文 献

[1] 张正阳，赵人达. 高速铁路混凝土拱桥长期变形贝叶斯预测[J]. 铁道科学与工程学报，2019，16(8)：1875-1881.
ZHANG Z Y, ZHAO R D. Bayesian prediction of long-term deflection of high-speed railway concrete arch bridges [J]. Journal of Railway Science and Engineering, 2019, 16(8): 1875-1881. (in Chinese)

[2] 王永宝，贾毅，廖平，等. 自然环境条件下混凝土徐变预测模型[J]. 铁道学报，2018，40(7)：100-108.
WANG Y B, JIA Y, LIAO P, et al. Prediction model of concrete creep in natural environment [J]. Journal of the China Railway Society, 2018, 40(7): 100-108. (in Chinese)

[3] 陈克坚，杨国静，胡玉珠. 铁路大跨度混凝土拱桥徐变变形控制因素研究[J]. 铁道工程学报，2019，247(4)：48-53.
CHEN K J, YANG G J, HU Y Z. Research on the creep control factors of railway long-span concrete arch bridge [J]. Journal of Railway Engineering Society, 2019, 247(4): 48-53.

[4] RAPHAEL W, ZGHEIB E, CHATEAUNEUF A. Experimental investigations and sensitivity analysis to explain the large creep of concrete deformations in the bridge of Cheviré [J]. Case Studies in Construction Materials, 2018, 9: 1-8.

[5] KOLÍNSKY V, VÍTEK J L. Verification of numerical creep and shrinkage models in an arch bridge analysis [J]. Structural Concrete, 2019, 20: 2030-2041.

[6] 吴海军，王旭燚，韦跃，等. 混凝土桥梁健康监测中的温度滞后效应[J]. 科学技术与工程，2018，18(27)：241-247.
WU H J, WANG X Y, WEI Y, et al. Temperature hysteresis effect in health monitoring of concrete bridges [J]. Science Technology and Engineering, 2018, 18(27): 241-247.

[7] 陈国良，林训根，岳青，等. 基于时间序列分析的桥梁长期挠度分离与预测[J]. 同济大学学报(自然科学版)，2016，44(6)：962-968.

[8] 刘刚，邵毅敏，黄宗明，等. 长期监测中结构温度效应分离的一种新方法[J]. 工程力学，2010，27(3)：55-61,100.
LIU G, SHAO Y M, HUANG Z M, et al. A new method to separate temperature effect from long-term structural health monitoring data [J]. Engineering Mechanics, 2010, 27(3): 55-61,100.

[9] 徐昕宇,郑晓龙,陈克坚,等. 基于弦测技术的铁路上承式拱桥桥面变形限制研究[J]. 铁道标准设计,2019,63(8):74-78.
XU X Y, ZHENG X L, CHEN K J, et al. Investigation on the limit value of deck deformation of railway deck arch bridge by chord measurement method [J]. Railway Standard Design,2019,63(8):74-78.

天峨龙滩特大桥外包混凝土设计及施工控制

陈 正[1] 陈 犇[1] 吴昌杰[1] 郑皆连[1*] 罗小斌[2] 徐 文[3] 杨 阳[1] 赵国欣[1]

(1. 广西大学土木建筑工程学院/省部共建特色金属材料与组合结构
全寿命安全国家重点实验室 广西南宁 530004；
2. 广西路桥工程集团有限公司 广西南宁 530200；
3. 江苏苏博特新材料股份有限公司/高性能土木工程材料国家重点实验室 江苏南京 211103)

摘 要 天峨龙滩特大桥为在建的世界最大跨度拱桥(跨径600m)，主拱圈外包混凝土浇筑方量大、泵送距离长、持续时间长，施工阶段工作性能持续保障难、浇筑均匀性控制难；在硬化阶段，持续水化作用下外包混凝土内外温差大、局部水化失水干燥收缩应力大，易导致裂缝和微缺陷的形成。为保证天峨龙滩特大桥外包混凝土质量，开展了足尺模型试验，揭示了工程大尺度条件下外包混凝土温度场时变规律和体积非均匀变化规律，提出了适用于天峨龙滩特大桥主拱圈外包混凝土的施工工艺精细化控制方案；揭示了不同原材料和配合比条件下外包C60高性能混凝土早期水化过程局部体积变化规律，提出了基于早期收缩补偿体积变形控制的高抗裂外包混凝土设计方法；建立了基于配合比及外加剂调整技术的长时段浇筑施工全过程工作性能控制方法，延长了混凝土最佳施工性能的保持时间，提高了泵送、浇筑施工的效率，有效保障了浇筑均匀性；揭示了外包混凝土入模及养护施工全过程中外界温湿度对开裂过程的影响机理，明确了混凝土入模温度控制要求，提出了基于混凝土水化环境温湿度调控的外包混凝土抗裂性能保障策略。

关键词 外包混凝土 工作性能 体积变形 施工控制 配合比设计

作者简介：
陈正(1982—)，男，博士，教授。主要从事混凝土性能设计与调控研究。
陈犇(1997—)，男，博士研究生。主要从事高性能混凝土研究。
吴昌杰(1996—)，男，博士研究生。主要从事混凝土体积稳定性研究。
*郑皆连(1941—)，男，学士，教授。主要从事大跨桥梁工程研究。
杨阳(1997—)，男，硕士研究生。主要从事混凝土体积变形研究。
赵国欣(1999—)，男，硕士研究生。主要从事混凝土流变性能研究。
罗小斌(1985—)，男，工程师。主要从事大跨度桥梁的施工管理与技术研究工作。
徐文(1985—)，男，博士研究生，高级工程师。主要从事高性能混凝土研究。

Construction Design and Control of Encased Concrete of the Tian'e Longtan Bridge

CHEN Zheng[1] CHEN Ben[1] WU Changjie[1] ZHENG Jielian[1]*

LUO Xiaobin[2] XU Wen[3] YANG Yang[1] ZHAO Guoxin[1]

(1. School of Civil Engineering and Architecture/State Key Laboratory of Featured Metal Materials and Life-cycle Safety for Composite Structures, Guangxi University, Nanning, Guangxi, 530004, China;

2. Guangxi Road and Bridge Engineering Group Co. Ltd, Nanning, Guangxi, 530011, China;

3. Jiangsu Sobute New Materials Co., Ltd, State Key Laboratory of High-Performance Civil Engineering Materials, Nanjing, Jiangxi, 211103, China)

Abstract The Tian'e Longtan Bridge, with a span of 600 meters, is the longest arch bridge under construction in the world. The construction of its main concrete-encased arch ring needs a large casting volume, long pumping distance and duration. At the casting stage, it is difficult to maintain the stability of concrete workability and control its uniformity. At the hardening stage, the encased concrete would produce internal temperature differences under continuous hydration, and local hydration would lead to moisture loss and dryness, thus increasing the shrinkage stress, which could cause its cracks or microdefects. To ensure the construction quality of encased concrete on the Tian'e Longtan Bridge, some full-scale model tests were conducted to test time-varying processes of temperature and non-uniformly volumetric variations inside the concrete, thus proposing a refined control scheme which is applicable to the casting of encased concrete on the main arch ring of the Tian'e Longtan Bridge. Tests were also carried out to observe the local volumetric variations of the C60 high-strength concrete with different raw materials and mix proportions, and a design scheme for encased concrete with high cracking resistance was put forward based on the early shrinkage compensation and volumetric deformation control. By adjusting the mix proportions and admixtures, a method was established to control the workability of encased concrete in the long time casting process, which helps to prolong the time when the concrete has the optimum workability, raise the pumping and casting efficiency, and effectively control the uniformity. A mechanism was revealed that the external temperature and humidity would have an influence on the cracking of encased concrete during the whole construction process from its casting to maintenance. Some requirements were also presented to control the casting temperature of the concrete. On these grounds, a method was proposed to ensure the cracking resistance of encased concrete by adjusting the temperature and humidity of the hydration environment of the concrete.

Keywords Encased concrete Workability Volumetric deformation Construction control Mix design

E-mail zhengjielian@163.com